MW01137797

The Reaper's Garden

THE REAPER'S GARDEN

*Death and Power in the World
of Atlantic Slavery*

❧

VINCENT BROWN

HARVARD UNIVERSITY PRESS

CAMBRIDGE, MASSACHUSETTS

LONDON, ENGLAND

First Harvard University Press paperback edition, 2010

Library of Congress Cataloging-in-Publication Data

Brown, Vincent, 1967–
The reaper's garden : death and power in the
world of Atlantic slavery / Vincent Brown.
p. cm.
Includes bibliographical references and index.
ISBN 978-0-674-02422-9 (cloth: alk. paper)
ISBN 978-0-674-05712-8 (pbk.)
1. Death—Social aspects—Jamaica.
2. Slavery—Jamaica. I. Title.
HQ1073.5.J26B76 2007
306.9086'912097292—dc22   2007025907

For the dead,
alive in so many more ways
than I can tell

Acknowledgments

OF ALL creative writers, historians should be the most skeptical of claims to originality. Our works depend upon so many sources that never appear in our footnotes—conversations with kin, friends, and casual acquaintances, the lyrics, rhythms, and melodies of our favorite music, the mood of our times. Yet at the same time, no announcement could possibly encapsulate the number of my contemporaries who are embedded in the story I have told, or all of the events of the recent past that have found their way into my turns of phrase and points of emphasis. This unforgivably partial list reflects just a few of the influences that have shaped this book.

Surely, the story I tell has been indelibly marked by the following happenings: the civil rights and Black Power movements; the crack wars of the 1980s and 1990s; the mushrooming of the U.S. prison industry; hip-hop's conquest of popular culture; the global AIDS pandemic; the collapse of the Soviet Empire and the triumphalism of global corporations; the U.S.-Soviet proxy wars in Asia, Africa, and Latin America and the terror wars that followed the events of September 11, 2001; the death of my beloved grandfather, Charles Samuel Greene (1905–2002), and the birth of my beloved daughter, Zareen Subramanian Brown in 2004.

I owe much of my perspective on the legacies of the past to masters of the art, philosophy, and spirit of the African diaspora, especially Khalid Saleem, Ava Vinesett, Pastel, Caxias, Ramos, and Chuvisco. *Axé!*

Several valued friends and counselors helped me nurture this project from its inception. Steven Hahn, whose lectures at the University of California, San Diego, first attracted me to the discipline of history, was my first adviser in the profession, and he has continued to have a profound impact on the choices I make. David Barry Gaspar's guidance in the early stages of this project was invaluable. He believed in me and my ideas enough to give me the greatest gift a reader can offer: patience. My early development as a scholar was shaped immeasurably by John D. French, Jane Gaines, Raymond Gavins, Lawrence Goodwyn, Nancy Hewitt, Julius S. Scott, and Peter H. Wood. Among the people who kept me going when I thought the coffin might close on my career as a scholar were Françoise Bordarier, Derek Chang, Katy Fenn, Paul Husbands, Nadine Le Meur, Paul Ortiz, Jody Pavilack, Sidarta Ribeiro, David Sartorious, Subir Sinha, Matthew Specter, Ajantha Subramanian, Rashmi Varma, and Richard Vinesett.

At conferences and at the invitation of colleagues at other universities, I have presented many of the themes and arguments that appear in *The Reaper's Garden*. I have learned immensely from the comments and criticisms of colleagues at Brandeis University, Florida International University, the University of Southern California–Huntington Library Early Modern Studies Institute workshop, New York University, Northwestern University, Princeton University, the University of Toronto, and Washington University. I also benefited from discussions of my work at the Slavery and Religion in the Modern Era conference in Essaouira, Morocco, in 2001, the Political Histories of Death in the Black Diaspora panel, held during the 2002 annual meeting of the Organization of American Historians (OAH), the Oceans Connect conference at Duke University in 2002, the New Directions in the Study of the Atlantic: Slavery, Continuing Conversations conference at Rutgers University in 2003, the Black Atlantic workshop of the Atlantic History Seminar at Harvard University in 2003, the Atlantic History Workshop on the Age of Revolution in the Atlantic World, held at Michigan State University in 2005, and Violence, Dissent, and the Shaping of New World Slavery, a panel held during the 2006 annual meeting of the OAH.

At Harvard University, I have benefited greatly from the advice and support of Emmanuel Akyeampong, David Armitage, Sven Beckert, Joyce E. Chaplin, Henry Louis Gates, Jr., Andrew Gordon, Evelyn Brooks

Higginbotham, Walter Johnson, Jill Lepore, Susan E. O'Donovan, and Laurel Thatcher Ulrich, as well as from the careful critiques of the participants in Harvard's Early American History workshop. A little writer's group in Cambridge kept me facing deadlines when I most needed them. For this I thank Robin Bernstein, Cheryl Finley, Barbara Rodriguez, and especially Glenda Carpio, whose close readings of several chapters compelled me to clarify my thoughts.

No historian could achieve anything without the help of library curators and archivists. I am especially indebted to the helpful people at the Public Record Office of the United Kingdom, the British Library, Cambridge University Library, the Bodleian Library, the Lambeth Palace Library, the Methodist Missionary Society Archives at the School of Oriental and African Studies, the House of Lords Record Office, the Institute of Jamaica, the Jamaica Archives, the National Library of Jamaica, the Rare Books, Manuscripts and Special Collections Library at Duke University, and Harvard College Library.

I am also grateful to Edward E. Baptist, Ian Baucom, Herman L. Bennett, Ira Berlin, Marie Burks, Alexander Byrd, Stephanie Camp, Vincent Carretta, Michelle Craig, Colin Dayan, Vasanthi Devi, Maria Grahn-Farley, Anthony Farley, Kim Hall, Jerome S. Handler, Engseng Ho, Sharon Ann Holt, Walter Johnson, Rebecca Ladbury, Michael McCormick, Roderick McDonald, Joseph C. Miller, C. Benjamin Nutley, Andrew Jackson O'Shaughnessy, Geeta Patel, Cory Paulsen, Charles Piot, Richard Price, Ellen Quigley, Louise Reid, Daniel Richter, Julie Saville, Philip Schwartzberg, Stephanie Smallwood, Werner Sollors, Orin Starn, K. S. Subramanian, Mark L. Thompson, David Wells, Kath Weston, Caron Yee, Kevin Yelvington, and Michael Zuckerman, all of whom, in various important ways, helped to make the completion of this book possible. Generous financial support has come from the Duke Endowment, Duke University's Center for International Studies, and fellowships from the University of Pennsylvania's McNeil Center for Early American Studies and Harvard University's Charles Warren Center, as well as the Lillian Gollay Knafel fellowship at the Radcliffe Institute for Advanced Study.

Special thanks go to my editor at Harvard University Press, Joyce Seltzer, for her enthusiastic encouragement. At the press I also thank Jennifer Banks and Susan Abel. The reports of two anonymous reviewers for Harvard Press, who have since become known to me as Laurent Dubois and James Sidbury, made a vital contribution to this work by pushing me to revise, clarify, or, in a few cases, reconsider aspects of my analysis. I am similarly indebted to an anonymous reviewer for questions, comments, and suggestions regarding an earlier draft of Chapter 4, which first appeared as "Spiritual Terror and Sacred Authority in Jamaican Slave Society" in *Slavery & Abolition* 24, no. 1 (April 2003), parts of which are reproduced herein with the permission of Taylor & Francis Group, Ltd.

Lessons learned from family members are often the deepest and most difficult to fathom. Nothing I could ever say or do would be enough to acknowledge the importance of the love and support I have received from my mother and father, Willie and Manuelita Brown, who taught me to cherish that most valuable thing: curiosity. Finally, I give thanks for Ajantha Subramanian, my best friend and most persuasive teacher, who has taught me to revel in life even as I meditate on death.

Contents

Illustrations

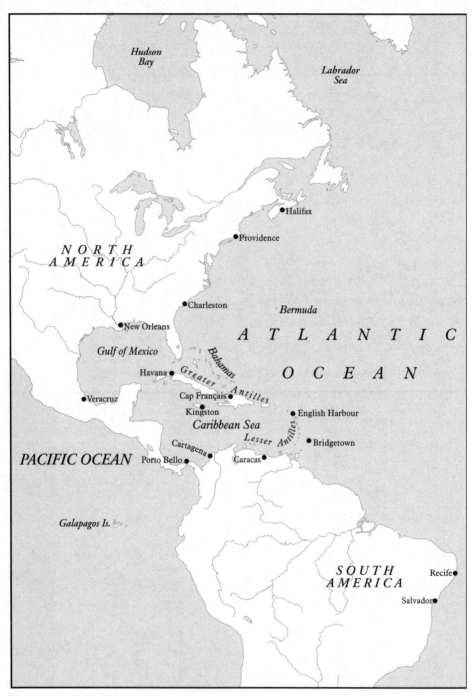

Map 1. The Atlantic Basin, drawn by Philip Schwartzberg

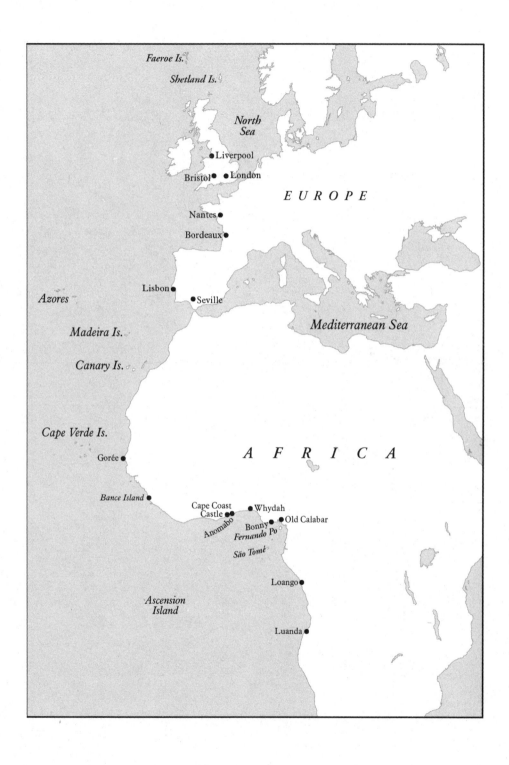

Faeroe Is.

Shetland Is.

North
Sea

● Liverpool

Bristol ● ● London

EUROPE

Nantes ●

Bordeaux ●

Lisbon ●

Azores

● Seville

Madeira Is.

Mediterranean Sea

Canary Is.

Cape Verde Is.

AFRICA

Gorée ●

Bance Island ●

Cape Coast
Castle ● ● Whydah

Anomabo ● ● Old Calabar

Bonny ●
Fernando Po

São Tomé

Loango ●

*Ascension
Island*

Luanda ●

Map 2. The Caribbean, drawn by Philip Schwartzberg

The Reaper's Garden

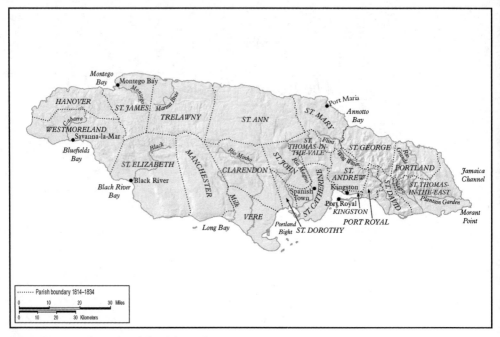

Map 3. Jamaica, drawn by Philip Schwartzberg

❦

Death, Power, and Atlantic Slavery

Only that historian will have the gift of fanning the spark of hope in the past
who is firmly convinced that even the dead will not be safe
from the enemy if he wins.

Walter Benjamin, "Theses on the Philosophy of History," 1940

AROUND 1800, a ship carrying the British traveler Robert Renny put into
Port Royal, Jamaica (Figure P.1). As it arrived, three or four black women
approached the side of the ship in a small canoe, bringing oranges and
other fresh fruits to sell to the sea-weary passengers. Sailors hoisted the
welcome produce aboard and cast down some coins to complete the
exchange. Their business done, the women prepared to depart. They gazed
at the white passengers crowded on deck, and it seemed to Renny that the
women were surprised at their number. Then, just as the canoe pushed
off, the women began to sing. One of them took the lead, calling verses,
while the others clapped their hands in time and responded with the
chorus. Writing in 1807, Renny remembered the song this way:

> New-come buckra,
> He get sick,
> He tak fever,
> He be die;
> He be die.

As far as the passengers could tell, the song contained no other words, but
the women continued to sing the ominous lyrics as long as they were
within hearing distance.[1]

What went through the minds of these new arrivals to Jamaica, as they
listened to predictions of their imminent demise? Renny does not say.

Figure P.1. *View of Port Royal and Kingston Harbours, Jamaica,* engraved by Peter Mazell, from Edward Long, *History of Jamaica,* vol. 2 (London, 1774), facing 138. Courtesy of the National Maritime Museum, London.

Perhaps the singing women reminded the new arrivals of plague songs chanted by children in England, which, long after the plague had exhausted itself, continued to live in popular memory in the form of innocuous rhymes, playful reminders of humankind's pitiful frailty in the hands of Nature and of God. More likely, the passengers heard the black women's song differently. Probably, they were reminded of Jamaica's popular reputation as the "grave of the Europeans." Indeed, that is probably exactly what the women intended.

Passengers to Jamaica had good reason to be afraid. Life expectancy for whites in Kingston, the principal port and largest town on the island, was nearly as poor as it was for Europeans in West Africa, where, decades earlier, more than 60 percent of newcomers died within a year and only one man in ten survived more than three years. Kingston had recorded nearly 18,000 funerals and just 2,669 baptisms among the white population from 1722 to 1774. Neighboring Port Royal, where Renny and his fellow "new-come buckra" dropped anchor some years later, could not have fared much better. Disembarking at Jamaica, Renny would have had to inhale the putrid stench of the slave ships, bloated with dead and dying Africans, to see the corpses of executed criminals dangling on the gallows, and to heed the incessant talk of disease and demise.[2]

At one level then, the morbid song of the market women simply commented on a well-known aspect of social reality: death was imminent. But more important, the women chanted their song in a highly charged context. Indeed, "buckra" was an epithet as well as a ubiquitous term of description for white people. It could mean "master," "he who surrounds or governs," or "demon" in its West African usage—a powerful evil being to be contained, manipulated, or driven from the world. The word could be interpreted as an honorific or a provocation, and its double-edged meaning keyed the women's refrain to Jamaica's turbulent political climate. Jamaica was a brutal and volatile slave society, contentious and unstable in the best of times. Slave rebellions and conspiracies of varying magnitudes occurred almost once each decade between 1740 and 1838. More than that, the social relations of slavery entailed constant tensions and power struggles. In both overt and subtle ways, the enslaved were ever trying to undermine labor discipline and white authority. Masters and colonial police constantly devised and revised strategies for control. Promoting the sanctity and value of white lives through law and ideology was an important part of their efforts. In an emphatically unequal society, where it was a capital crime even to "imagine the death of a white person," the market women evoked disease and death as a social leveler.[3]

Violating the spirit of colonial order and discipline, the black women taunted the fresh white recruits, by intimidating them with the reminder that whatever privileges white skin was supposed to confer in slave society, newcomers were likely to be brought low by disease. In this respect, the "he be die" chorus could have been a corollary to another chant Robert Renny heard slaves sing in the streets of Kingston:

> One, two, tree,
> All de same;
> Black, white, brown,
> All de same;
> All de same.

While both songs expressed rejection of the symbolic order that facilitated social control in slave society, the "He be die" song also implied a basic connection between social conflict and the morbid environment. Invoking disease and death to mock white authority, the women made an ally of an inscrutable and unpredictable force; the song may even have been a curse. Whichever way the women intended to deploy the lyrics, the occasion reminds us that the link between catastrophic demographic circumstances and communal strife went far beyond colorful jesting.

The song of the market women was a jeering reminder of the final end, yet at the same time an indication that the end was the beginning, that death arrived not only to finish the living, but also to cultivate important features of social life. Just as the Grim Reaper arrived to gather in the harvest at the end of the life cycle, he also sowed the seeds of social renewal. Death was as generative as it was destructive. In a society characterized by movement and uncertainty—arrivals and departures of migrants, precarious crop cycles, and market fluctuations—as well as by repressive hierarchy and tense negotiation, the activities surrounding death gave the volatile world a reliable axis.

The song introduced the newcomers to this world, where death structured society and shaped its most consequential struggles. The accumulation of property, the reproduction of family and social networks, and the meaningful representation of life all stemmed in significant ways from high mortality and the lingering presence of the dead. The demographic environment—where rampant disease, malnutrition, overwork, and violence resulted in frequent burials—ensured that the ideas, articulations, and rituals associated with death and the dead would play a fundamental role in conflicts among European fortune-seekers, who, betting against the demographic odds, jockeyed with each other for status and power, and also between the tiny minority of white slaveholders and the enslaved black and brown people over whom they ruled with virtually unlimited authority. Eventually, too, the outgrowth of death affected relations between reformers back home and their colonial compatriots. In various ways and with differing consequences, they all strove to fulfill communal desires and political ambitions through cultural practices that related the living to the dead. In this way, the story of death and slavery illustrates a premise common to many religious worldviews, that the dead are active participants in the living world. Encapsulated by the Akan adinkra (icon)

Figure P.2. "Nyame nwu na mawu" (God does not die, so I cannot die) is the Akan *adinkra* symbolizing the continuing influence of the dead in the affairs of the living.

"Nyame nwu na mawu" (loosely translated, "God does not die, so I cannot die"), which symbolizes the continuity of the human spirit in temporal affairs, this idea contemplates death as a transition between the physical and the immaterial states of being, with the dead remaining pivotal players in the societies in which they had lived (Figure P.2).[4]

Admittedly, it is a subject shrouded in uncertainty. One must accept the droll bit of wisdom offered by a religious leader on Africa's Gold Coast in the 1740s, who reminded a European Christian that lack of observable data prevented informed discussion of the hereafter. "I have never been dead and come back to life," he said, "to enable me to debate with such certainty about the other life, as *your* holy man did when he was here." Practices surrounding death are ultimately grounded in perceptions of the unknowable and ineffable. Yet this is a story that can be told without metaphysical speculation. Attitudes toward death often lie at the heart of social conflict, and the dead are frequently objects of contention and struggle. If research from the fields of demographic, cultural, and social history is drawn together, the practical ways that people make political meaning of death can be observed, described, and, ultimately, fashioned into a materialist history of the supernatural imagination.

⚜

Death and its meanings have historically been central to social order and tension. People have derived profound social meaning from the beliefs and practices associated with death, and they have employed those meanings—charged with cosmic importance—in struggles toward particular ends. I call such activity *mortuary politics*, employing a capacious general definition of politics as concerted action toward specific goals. Alongside more conventional political practices like policymaking and institution building, this broad definition allows me to consider how people justify actions, claim and dispute authority, or create and use the cultural categories that mediate social life. Mortuary practices may reflect historic changes, as intense disputes about custom, authority, and religion play out within final rites of passage. More significantly, relations between the living and the dead also generate historic changes when those relations emerge as the source of struggle.[5]

"Death is the quintessential cosmic issue," remarks the anthropologist Katherine Verdery, "one that brings us all face to face with ultimate questions about what it means to be—and to stop being—human, about where we have come from and where we are going." Because death is universal and the dead are universally meaningful, mortuary ideas and customs specific to different groups can be potent sources and arenas of momentous action. Relations with the dead, by virtue of their powerful symbolism and association with things sacred, have the ability to connect private and public concerns, by aligning individual experiences of loss and memory with the interests of community, church, or state. This linkage makes the dead integral to both social organization and political mobilization, and therefore vital to historical transformation.[6]

This was especially the case in Atlantic plantation societies, where death weighed heavily in people's considerations, at least from the time of the Spanish conquest of Native America, when the Caribbean Indian populations suffered perhaps the greatest collapse known to historians. "The new world, indeed, appears to be surrounded with the flaming sword of the angel," wrote Robert Renny, "threatening destruction to all those who venture within its reach." High mortality rates have been widely recognized as one of the most remarkable features of these societies, especially those committed to sugar cultivation, but less is known about mortality's social and political implications. Groundbreaking forays into the epidemiology of the slave trade and colonization have built up an impressive body of knowledge about the medical and demographic dimensions of slave societies, and historians have discussed the impact of mortality on the broad outlines of the social history of the Americas. However, few have seriously examined the way that death shaped daily life, or how, in the terms proposed by the psychiatrist Robert Jay Lifton, people symbolized "continuity in the face of death" in struggles over property, authority, morality, territory, and belonging. In other words, we know little about how the meaning of mortality motivated people to act or, as many would have understood it then, how the dead affected the history of the living.[7]

An explanation depends on the answers to four interrelated questions: In what ways (or by what means) did people formulate their relations with the dead? How did mortuary belief and practice respond to demographic, socioeconomic, political, and religious changes? How were ways of relating to the dead embedded in political conflict? Finally, how did mortuary politics shape the course of history for the contending groups in Jamaica's world of Atlantic slavery, where relations with the dead impinged on daily struggles, rebellious outbursts, and even parliamentary politics?

In *The Birth of African-American Culture: An Anthropological Perspective*, originally published in 1976, Sidney W. Mintz and Richard Price sketched out an influential method for historical ethnographers of slave societies, admonishing scholars to pay closer attention to the way institutional contexts shaped the cultures of people in slavery. They reminded students of cultural history generally, and early African-American history in particular, to examine carefully the ways in which material life shaped the evolution of the beliefs and practices that Africans brought with them to the Americas, to describe more precisely how Africans became African Americans. While many of the provisional conclusions Mintz and Price drew about patterns of group identification and belonging have been revised by subsequent scholarship, the outline of their approach, which called for an emphasis on the cultural creativity of the enslaved, remains compelling.[8]

Recently, acclaimed histories of slavery in the Americas have refined our understanding of how different New World contexts shaped black identities and generational experiences. But the cultural history of slavery in early America goes much deeper than characterizations of identity along a continuum from African to American (or, for that matter, assertions that identities are in fact hybrid) can capture. Cultural practices in American slave societies were deeply entangled. People of diverse origins readily borrowed, stole, and mimicked one another's behavior. For this reason, it can be misleading to attribute cultural traits to distinct "ethnic" groups, traced back to their places of origin, or to describe cultural change in terms of linear progress toward settled New World patterns. This kind of analysis also leaves the mistaken impression that people's sole aim was to achieve a distinct cultural identity. That may have been one important goal, but it was undoubtedly not the only one. Examining the politics of practical behavior, by contrast, calls attention to people's strategies for using cultural

practices to fulfill a variety of pressing needs in difficult and dangerous circumstances. Burial ceremonies, conceptions of the afterlife, inheritance
practices, and rites of commemoration, for example, all played a significant role in the political history of slavery, which goes beyond the cultural
history of identity. Rather than ask of a cultural practice or idea, "How
African is it?" it might therefore be more useful to ask, "What was it used
for? What were its consequences?" By themselves, African-ness and ethnicity do not tell us enough about how human beings struggled to remake
their worlds—about how in specific contexts particular cultural configu-
rations shaped political experience and action.[9]

Robert Renny and his compatriots may have heard the "new-come
buckra" song of the market women as a typical example of an expressive
black culture or as a peculiarly African form of play. But that matters little,
for surely, too, they understood it more as an intentionally provocative
dialogue with potential enemies—a warning, a threat, perhaps the
women's hope for things to come. In other words, it represented social
conflict more than cultural contact. Seen this way, the song is remarkable
more for its meaning than for its form. Diagnosing their world, the
women affirmed that Atlantic slavery was a deadly enterprise. In acknowledging that whites were equally subject to the dominion of death, they
also recognized that this world was an integrated one.

Europeans often thought of their colonies as fundamentally alien places,
atavistic spaces of degeneracy and violence constituting a "Torrid Zone"
beyond the boundaries of civilization. But whereas this imagined geography shaped European self-perceptions and even, to some extent, colonial
policymaking, it did not even begin to map the actual circuits of consequence in the world of Atlantic slavery. While it might have been convenient for Europeans to see the plantation colonies through the prism of
such invidious distinctions, thereby absolving themselves of moral responsibility for the nightmarish societies they had created, it was a vision calculated to obscure the actual depth of mutual engagement between colony
and home country, and to gloss over the precise nature of the relations
between the various peoples in their empires. It allowed them to believe
that empire existed on the margins of European progress.

Yet Jamaica was by no means peripheral to the British Empire; it was
the focus of concentrated attention. In 1756 the British naturalist Patrick
Browne accurately described the colony as a "necessary appendage to our

present refined manner of living." Browne acknowledged that if one considered the value of its agricultural products, the number of men and ships employed in its trade, or the quantity and value of its imports from Europe, Jamaica was "not only the richest, but the most considerable colony at this time under the government of Great Britain." It was in many ways the fulcrum of British Atlantic slavery. Comprising a diverse population of immigrants and their descendants and pivotal to the success of imperial enterprise, the colony was inextricably connected to its hinterlands in Africa, Europe, and North America. Consequently, the history of Jamaica is seen most clearly from an "Atlantic" perspective that describes the colony in relation to its wider web of connections and comparisons with other parts of the Atlantic basin. Following routes of cause and effect in this context requires a method akin to that of epidemiology, for it one must describe the movement of people, cultural practices, and social actions as an epidemiologist might analyze pathogens spreading through space and time—by examining both the causal agents and the conditions in which they take root, thrive, or degenerate. Such an approach illuminates the unlikely connections that often escape notice in more narrowly bounded histories.[10]

Just as Jamaica was geographically integrated into the larger Atlantic world, so its inhabitants were interconnected with one another. Whites depended for their livelihood on black slaves as surely as the institution of slavery constrained the life chances of Africans and their descendants. Social power may operate by enforcing boundaries between the weak and the strong, but the analysis of power must survey the dominant and subaltern within the same field of vision. The political history of slavery is the story of intertwined (if nevertheless distinct) destinies, of inseparable differences. Thus, it fails to fit strictly within the fields of British imperial, American colonial, Black Atlantic, or African diaspora history; each is braided together with the others.

The history of slavery is best understood by accounting for the social awareness, strategies, and tactical maneuvers of all contending parties, including the illiterate, the weak, and the nonwhite. Sifting through uneven sources to describe these multiple perspectives and many-sided struggles is a tricky pursuit, however, and raises acute problems of evidence and voice. From written records one can fix the thoughts and deeds of planters, merchants, and colonial officials with greater confidence than one ever can when interpreting these sources to discern the actions, meanings, and motivations of the enslaved. The latter requires difficult acts of triangulation, reading documents produced by slaveholders against what we know about African-American cultural and political history, as well as what political scientist James C. Scott has described as the "fugitive political conduct of subordinate groups." Though I have investigated a multitude of disparate and fragmentary sources, including tombstone inscriptions, wills, diaries, parish vestry minutes, plantation account papers, court returns, travelers' reports, assembly minutes, visual images, and the archaeology of burial sites, uncertainties remain. These ambiguities undermine the authority of the omniscient narrator's voice favored by historians. In its place, I offer only sincere engagement with the sources and a provisional analysis of a certain kind of politics.[11]

The signal themes in the history of Atlantic slavery have been the predicament of colonial societies in a global political economy, resistance to enslavement, and cultural transformation under extreme conditions. The political history of death in Jamaica informs each of these. The human consequences of the Caribbean political economy—high death rates, rapid demographic turnover, and social relations characterized by flux and instability—resulted in an unsettled slave society, in which social authority had to be continually rearticulated through the most imposing idioms.

When the transatlantic slave trade dragged African men, women, and children into the grinding mills of American slavery, it shattered networks of belonging that connected the newly born to the long dead. The survivors of millions of deadly journeys had to reconstitute their social worlds wherever they landed. In Jamaica, the lethal environment, the instability of estates, and the preeminence of slave masters made the task extremely arduous. Poised amid perpetual upheavals, Africans and their descendants struggled to conceive new relations out of kinship idioms that they already shared, learned from each other, or had forced upon them by their overlords. As they made a new social place for themselves in Jamaica, many sought to break free entirely of the constraints of slave society. Most struggled to negotiate more for themselves, their families, and their new clans than their rulers wanted to allow.

To achieve these political objectives, the enslaved needed compelling forms of communication to identify and rally new collectives. To govern a precarious and restless enslaved population with a transient white work-force, slaveholders had to send messages that everyone could comprehend. At least through the end of the transatlantic slave trade, the very flux that characterized the society confounded efforts to find common modes of communication and forced the population to achieve considerable dex-terity in negotiating intercultural complexity. Caribbean peoples developed "plural personas, command of multiple communicative registers, and mobile social forms" to navigate their heterogeneous societies.[12] The ability to manipulate sign systems and switch from one to another, to move rap-idly back and forth between several modes of communication, meant that the most impressive forms of authority would need to adopt forms of dis-course that could attach to the most universal aspects of experience.

Everyone dies. And in Jamaican slave society, death held everyone's attention. The omnipresence of corpses, mortuary commerce, and funeral rituals made death a vital subject of strife and debate. In the activities that joined the living with the dead, survivors in Jamaican slave society could fasten their political efforts to themes that were significant to everyone. Relations with death and the dead made the transcendent a tool in worldly conflicts. Awesome questions of spiritual existence could be transposed to temporal social struggles. As people interpreted and expressed material life in affecting spiritual practices, they manifested their beliefs about the supernatural in concrete economic, social, and political action.

Mortuary politics mediated group cohesion, property relations, strug-gles to give public influence a sacred dimension, contests over the colonial moral order, and efforts to politicize local geography and history. Black, white, and brown people engaged the dead to procure financial resources and to make land claims. Slaveholders and rebels bolstered governing and insurrectionary authority through symbolic manipulation of the dead. Religious figures from Jamaica to Great Britain articulated morality through pivotal references to death and the afterlife. Commemorations of the dead gave potent force to place making and memory.

These were general phenomena, which took on distinctive patterns over time. Between Jamaica's emergence as Britain's most profitable colony and the end of slavery, some aspects of the relationship between death and power were continuous and others changed dramatically. Throughout the era of slavery, confrontations with death produced intense activities—macabre calculations of interest, rites of passage, and inheritance practices—that helped make a society in the midst of a human disaster. But over the course of the period, demographic transformations, shifts in the imperial political climate, and local struggles over spiritual faith altered relations to death and the dead. Slave revolts, the antislavery movement in Britain, the rise of evangelical Christianity, and provincial claims on territory and history drew energy from an evolving mortuary politics and reshaped the character of that politics in turn.

Thus death and the dead were factors in high-stakes competitions to determine the course of colonial Jamaican history—and of Atlantic history as well, because Jamaica was more than the site of contests among its residents. The island was also the indispensable locus of British imperial ambition: it stood at the pinnacle of colonial wealth creation, and at the center of a vast web of trade, migration, and government administration. Still, though it was home to the United Kingdom's most powerful naval squadron, its wealthiest and most influential imperial subjects, and its largest slave population, Jamaica was a catastrophe.

CHAPTER ONE

❦

Worlds of Wealth and Death

By THE MID-EIGHTEENTH century, Jamaica was the vital hub of British
America, far and away Britain's most significant American colony. It was
also a death trap. Death was at the center of social experience for everyone
on the island during the eighteenth and early nineteenth centuries.
Throughout the eighteenth century, the death rate for the British in
Jamaica exceeded 10 percent a year. In 1740 Charles Leslie reported, "Once
in seven Years there is a Revolution of Lives in this Island . . . As many
die in that Space of Time as perfectly inhabit it; and no doubt the Multitude that dies would soon leave the Place a Desert, did not daily Recruits
come over from Great Britain." Blacks died at slightly lower rates, but in
far greater numbers. For enslaved Africans and their descendants, Jamaican
demographic conditions represented the continuation of the long death
march that had begun, for many, deep in the interior of the African continent, while for British arrivals the reality of imminent death came as a
shock. Together, they built a magnificent factory out of mortal crisis, and
prosperity continued to draw enslaved and free alike to the island. In the
transatlantic experience of Jamaica's inhabitants, death and wealth and
power were inextricably entangled.[1]

The Grave of the Europeans
The English were latecomers to the Caribbean, and Jamaica's fortunes as a
British colony had uncertain beginnings. Spanish naval power dominated

the region until the early seventeenth century, though Spain was more interested in her mining colonies on the Central and South American mainland. With Spanish power weakening as the sixteenth century closed, the English managed to settle several islands in the Lesser Antilles—Saint Christopher in 1624, Barbados in 1627, Nevis in 1628, Monserrat and Antigua in 1632. Working on the margins of an Atlantic economy dominated by the Spanish, Portuguese, and Dutch, the English began to develop plantations for export crops, first tobacco and then sugar.[2]

Sugar revolutionized the Caribbean. Though the Spanish had planted the crop on the island of Hispaniola from their first colonizing ventures, it was the Portuguese in Brazil who initiated the development of a full-blown American sugar industry. Since the first half of the sixteenth century, the Portuguese had been successfully growing the crop by relying on enslaved African laborers on plantations in the island of São Tomé, off the coast of West Africa. In the mid-1540s, however, they introduced sugar to Brazil, and production there rapidly grew to dominate the international market. Sugar planting was labor-intensive. As exports increased, the colony swelled with the importation of slaves. The English began planting sugar in Barbados in the 1640s, with help from the Dutch, who had occupied part of northern Brazil during its productive peak. The Dutch provided English planters with technical knowledge and capital, while their merchant fleet connected Barbados to sources of labor in Africa and hungry markets in Holland. The island's economy boomed: land prices increased nearly tenfold in the 1640s alone. Large-scale entrepreneurs grabbed up acreage, converted from tobacco and other crops, and brought in increasing numbers of enslaved Africans to replace indentured European laborers. When the British pried the large and uncultivated Jamaica from Spain's grip in 1655, sugar planters migrated, along with buccaneers, who used the island as a base for attacks on Spanish shipping.[3]

As the sugar industry metastasized, authorities in London took notice. Hoping to confine the newly recognized benefits of empire to the state and its subjects, they passed several navigation acts in the mid-seventeenth century to cut Dutch middlemen out of English trade and granted monopoly charters to English companies trading with Africa and the West Indies. These measures precipitated three Anglo-Dutch wars, from which England emerged as the dominant naval power in the Atlantic. To protect the plantations, the navy moved to suppress the pirates, now an impediment to legitimate trade. Indeed the Royal Navy was the guarantor of the whole system of British Atlantic commerce. A permanent squadron was established at Port Royal in 1695, followed by naval bases in Antigua in 1731 and Halifax, Nova Scotia, in 1749. Merchants thrived, as the volume of trade between England and America expanded over the course of the eighteenth century. By 1800 a quarter of the imports that Britain retained from abroad were produced in the Caribbean.[4]

Jamaica's sugar revolution peaked during the second half of the eighteenth century. Despite the abundance of arable land on Jamaica, its sugar industry grew slowly in the first four decades of the 1700s. Large landholders monopolized the best sugar-growing lands, without having the labor to exploit them, and a temporary decline in British sugar prices during the 1730s compounded the problem. Protracted war with the Maroons, bands of runaway slaves who harried frontier plantations, continued to prevent the expansion of industrial agriculture. The Maroon War ended by treaty in 1739, at the same time that prices rose again in the sugar market. In the three years immediately following the cessation of hostilities with the Maroons, the number of sugar works on the island more than doubled, from 180 to 377. Beginning in 1740 and lasting until the onset of the imperial crisis of 1776, Jamaica had an astounding period of economic growth. During that time, the total number of plantations increased by 45 percent and diversified to include coffee and other valuable crops; the aggregate value of Jamaica's annual exports rose from £650,000 to £2.4 million; the total value of the colony's economy increased fivefold; and the enslaved population nearly doubled, from about 100,000 to 197,000. The total population of the island mushroomed from 4,000 in 1661 to 255,000 in 1788. Before 1780 alone, 600,000 people migrated to Jamaica, as compared with fewer than 900,000 to all of British North America. The enslaved accounted for most of Jamaica's growth—226,000 people in bondage. Nearly 90 percent of the population was enslaved in 1788, and 93 percent of the inhabitants were visibly of African descent. By the time slavery ended in 1838, whites still constituted a small minority of a population that exceeded 370,000.[5]

From the mid-eighteenth century to the early decades of the nineteenth, immigrants to and sojourners in Jamaica arrived in the richest, or perhaps it is better to say the most profitable, single colony in the British Empire.

When people with great ambition dreamed of America, they imagined West Indian fortunes. A comparison drawn from probate inventories of private material wealth in 1774 in the empire shows why. For those who survived their first years in the new environment, British America was generally a good place to improve their fortunes. Whereas the average person in England or Wales had a worth of about £42 sterling, considering all assets and subtracting all debts, free whites in the American colonies averaged over £89. But this figure is skewed by the outsized hordes of West Indians. Free whites in the New England colonies averaged just over £42, those in the Southern plantation colonies nearly £93. Meanwhile, the average worth of a free white person in the British West Indies was an astounding £1,042 sterling. The largest and most productive British Caribbean territory, Jamaica was also the wealthiest colony in British America, with private wealth totaling about £24 million. The average property holder on the island held more than thirty-six times the assets possessed by his counterpart in the thirteen North American colonies.[6]

This wealth translated into real power and influence within the empire. West Indians formed the most powerful colonial lobby in London, deriving special consideration in tax and military matters. Wealthy Jamaicans sent their children to be educated at Eton, Harrow, and other elite British schools, and the graduates sometimes stayed on in the United Kingdom to represent West Indian interests. Absentee Jamaica planters and merchants were integrated into the British elite. They built magnificent homes in the English and Scottish countryside and mingled with key imperial administrators, and many served in Parliament. The Jamaica native William Beckford was a member of the House of Commons for more than twenty years and was twice Lord Mayor of London in the 1760s.[7]

Partly because Jamaicans were so influential in Britain, few called the island home. Jamaica was what today we might call an enterprise zone, a territory organized by the government on behalf of business interests, where profit taking prevailed over civic investment. Jamaica was a "Constant Mine," wrote Charles Leslie, "whence Britain draws prodigious riches." Jamaicans built few schools and no universities. Public works projects were conducted only for the benefit of commerce. Instead, people went to Jamaica hoping to win their fortunes as quickly as possible, living fast, and, if need be, dying young. The planter and historian Bryan Edwards remarked, "Even such of them as have resided in the West Indies from their birth, look on the islands as their temporary abode only, and the fond notion of being able to go home (as they emphatically term a visit to England) year after year animates their industry and alleviates their misfortune."[8]

Their misfortunes were legion. The white population of Jamaica during the years of slavery could not sustain itself by natural increase. Yellow fever and malaria killed off Europeans as fast in Jamaica as they did in other tropical locations. In fact, because Europeans did not possess even the limited immunities to these diseases that Africans enjoyed, whites died at a faster rate than blacks. In the first half of the eighteenth century nearly 50,000 European migrants were needed to increase the white population by only 5,000 or so. Through the middle decades of the eighteenth century, immigrants could not expect to survive more than thirteen years. Those native-born whites (Creoles) who survived childhood were likely to die before they reached the age of forty. Still, colonists kept coming to Jamaica. Laborers from Ireland, Scotland, and the Lesser Antilles arrived, alongside Sephardic Jews from Brazil and Suriname. The majority, though, were Englishmen seeking to build names, reputations, and family fortunes. Between 1739 and 1778, migrants nearly doubled the white population, which climbed from 10,080 to 18,420, despite the high mortality rate. In the late eighteenth and early nineteenth centuries, refugees fleeing the American War of Independence and the Haitian Revolution swelled the Jamaican white population even more rapidly. These trends ensured that Jamaica remained overwhelmingly an immigrant society throughout the eighteenth century. In contrast to the plantation colonies of North America, which experienced rapid growth in both white and black native-born populations, 80 percent or more of Jamaica's white population and some 75 percent of blacks had been born outside the island.[9]

Migrants who left Great Britain for Jamaica arrived under very different circumstances than the enslaved did. In 1717 Jamaica stopped the importation of convicts, who had been an important source of white migrant labor in the seventeenth century. Indentured servitude persisted on a limited scale until the mid-eighteenth century, but by the time Jamaica reached its peak prosperity in the 1770s, slaves had almost completely displaced white servants. The servants who arrived during the middle decades of the eighteenth century came largely from England and, to a lesser extent, Scotland. Free migrants arriving during the same period were a slightly more diverse group. Some 62 percent were English, 18 percent Scottish, 8 percent Irish, about 4.5 percent each from North America and other West Indian colonies, and the remainder from Wales, the European mainland, and Spanish America. Nearly half of the free English came from London. Jamaica's towns also swelled, thanks to a motley assortment of sailors and soldiers. Merchant-mariners were always present in Kingston; having deserted or been discharged from ships, they were awaiting passage elsewhere.

Because Jamaica's wealth invited war, the British army and the Royal Navy were permanent fixtures at the strategic garrison, though the troops' "dread of going to the West Indies" created persistent recruiting problems for military officers.[10] Many soldiers and sailors viewed Jamaica as little more than a vast infirmary and burial ground, where slaveholders played vainly at the pursuit of riches. In the late 1790s Lieutenant Abraham James of the Sixty-seventh Regiment sketched his own impressions of life on the island in a twenty-one-scene caricature of Johnny New-come, the folk icon for white sojourners in the West Indies (Figure 1.1). Arriving at an early age, ready to seek his fortune, Johnny is immediately set upon by mosquitoes. He falls ill at once, and half the remaining scenes are devoted to

Figure 1.1. "Johnny New-come," the folk icon for newly arrived white men, detail from *Johnny New-come in the Island of Jamaica,* by Abraham James (London, 1800). Courtesy of the National Library of Jamaica.

his sickness and death, much as foretold for the new-come buckra of the market women's chant. When he is not vomiting, shivering, and wasting away, Johnny valiantly acts the part of a sugar planter, hunting for game, beating a slave, and cavorting with his mulatto mistress. James clearly admired little about life in Jamaica, but his satire was right on the mark.[11]

Most of the whites who came to Jamaica during its rapid economic expansion in the latter half of the eighteenth century were free men seeking their fortunes. The 1773–1776 Register of Emigrants reveals some interesting social characteristics of British immigrants to the Caribbean. Emigrants from Britain to the West Indies tended to be men in their midtwenties. They were much more likely to be traveling without masters and without families than were emigrants to other American colonies. More strikingly, over half the emigrants who stated their occupations upon their departure claimed to be either gentlemen or merchants. These were often people from well-heeled families (though seldom the principal heirs) heading out to manage family properties or businesses. Most Englishmen who traveled to Jamaica, a wildly prosperous colony on the eve of the American Revolution, did so hoping to get rich working as planters, property managers, or commercial traders.[12]

These privileged young men were not escaping poor demographic or social conditions. Despite a significant spike in the 1740s, London's mortality rate declined and life expectancy improved steadily during the latter half of the eighteenth century. Throughout the eighteenth century, the perils of life in London were concentrated among the poor. Mortality rates in London were highest in the most crowded areas of the city, where people lived in conditions hospitable to contagious pathogens. People of means simply moved out of neighborhoods burgeoning with immigrants from the countryside and thus avoided the most dangerous bacterial infections, like bubonic plague and typhus. Newcomers to the Caribbean could not have known that mosquito-borne tropical viruses would be much harder to elude. Colonists, though well aware of the dangers of the tropics, expected that rank would protect them in Jamaica, as it had in London, just long enough for them to make their fortunes and return to Great Britain unscathed.[13]

Adverse social circumstances were a more important factor in emigration from Scotland. Of sixteen respondents in the Register of Emigrants who said they were escaping poor conditions, ten were Scots faced with

high rents or unemployment. In the mid-eighteenth century the aristocracy and the largest landholders, having consolidated their holdings, even
as the general population increased, had left less land for the growing populace and squeezed out those in the middle of the social hierarchy. More
than 6,500 Scots traveled to Jamaica between 1750 and 1800. The majority
of them were educated tradesmen or professionals who had fallen on hard
times, and they hoped to find greater opportunity in the West Indies than
was available to them in Scotland. From Scottish newspapers they learned
of opportunities in Jamaica for people with skills and training. More
important was that successful Scots who returned with wealth and influence fed the aspirations of others who were considering the risks. Why go
to North America to eke out a humble portion as a farmer, they might
have asked, when they could go to the West Indies and take a chance at
making themselves masters of the colonial world?[14]

Such eager and ambitious Britons came to Jamaica unprepared for the
demographic catastrophe they encountered. Greed and fear governed their
outlook by turns. Faced with chronic sickness and death, they often longed
to leave, but ambition or debt kept them from going. Like gamblers, they
put their faith in good luck, even as they came to recognize the dangers
they ran. "We are in Jamaica," one fictional character announced in the
1820s, "but though it should be our resting place, we must e'en take our
chance in't." They had to wonder about their odds of success (Figure 1.2).
"And what awaits me now sad Isle!" Jack Jingle inquired in the last stanza
of his poem, "Jamaica" (1824): "The boon thou givest all thy sons / An early
grave." Living daily under such apprehension, sojourning whites desperately hoped to get rich and get out.[15]

Only a small minority of these enterprising Britons actually made a fortune in Jamaica and returned home. Though they hoped to return to the
United Kingdom flush with property and power, most, of course, lived
and died in the world they built in Jamaica. Creole whites, native to the
island, also sometimes aspired to make their fortune and retire to Britain,
but they were more easily satisfied with prominent positions on the
leading edge of empire. By the mid-eighteenth century, profitable planting
required large capital investments in land and slaves, a prerequisite
ensuring that very few people could enter the upper echelon of Jamaican
society. During the "golden years" of the sugar industry, from 1750 to 1775,
wealth was narrowly concentrated among an elite oligarchy of planters
who dominated landholding as well as formal political and social life.

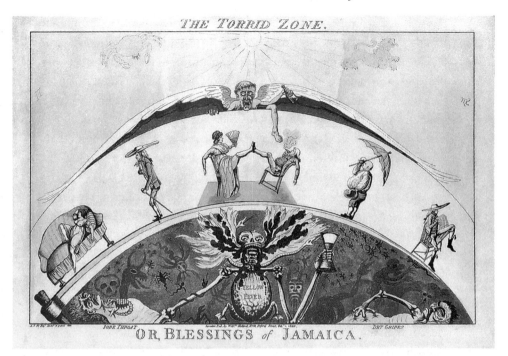

Figure 1.2. *The Torrid Zone, or, Blessings of Jamaica,* by Abraham James (London, 1800). This parodic cosmological diagram shows opposing aspects of life for white colonialists in Jamaica—the languorous noontide and the hell of tropical disease. James, who began his military career with the calamitous British occupation of revolutionary Saint-Domingue, was acutely aware of the power of death to shape social life. Here, he shows the luxuries of Jamaican colonial life to be literally resting upon Death's sickle. Courtesy of the Wellcome Library, London.

Their money and status kept them in close contact with colonial administrators, which enhanced their influence on imperial policymaking. Jamaica afforded them an opulent and intemperate lifestyle, yet most preferred to live in Britain and returned there as often as they could. While they were away from Jamaica, they entrusted their properties to estate managers and planting attorneys. These attorneys, often plantation owners themselves, could manage dozens of estates, and although their work kept them in Jamaica, they were among its richest occupants. In a class below them were the merchants and professionals, including a large contingent of Scots. Many of these people in the "middle class" of masters owned midsize plantations and managed to live quite comfortably indeed.[16]

Among the richest masters was Simon Taylor, born in Jamaica in 1740, the eldest son of Patrick and Martha Taylor. Simon's father had migrated from Scotland to become a wealthy Kingston merchant. After returning to the island from his schooling at Eton in the early 1760s, Simon himself became one the wealthiest men in the British Empire. In addition to owning and operating his own plantations, Simon Taylor was a leading planting attorney for absentee proprietors, like his childhood friend Chaloner Arcedeckne. Lady Maria Nugent, the wife of Jamaica's early nineteenth-century governor, described Taylor as "the richest man in the island." When he died in 1813, his estate, including 2,138 slaves, was worth an estimated one million pounds sterling. His yearly income had been as high as £47,000 at a time when contemporary economists estimated the incomes of the English nobility to be in the range of £5,000 to £10,000. Exceptionally rich, Taylor was also politically powerful. He served in Jamaica's House of Assembly continuously from 1768 to 1781 and again from 1784 to 1810, while variously holding the offices of Kingston Custos, chief justice of the Court of Common Pleas, and lieutenant-general of the militia. The economic historian Richard Sheridan fairly said of Taylor, "He may have exercised greater influence in Jamaica, and for a longer period, than any other individual." In spite of this distinction, Taylor had much in common with absentee owners back in England. Though he lived nearly his entire life in Jamaica, Taylor invested the great majority of his wealth in London. He felt himself to be the political equal, perhaps even the better, of his client Arcedeckne, who lived in Suffolk, England, and who served as a member of Parliament (M.P.) from 1780 to 1786. The voluminous letters Taylor wrote to business partners, friends, and family members in the United Kingdom reveal that he felt a deep identification with the fate of the entire British Empire, an interest inextricably connected with the island where he accumlated his wealth.[17]

Unlike Taylor, most whites began in low-status jobs. If people had no talent for agriculture, they could work as well-paid clerks for merchants or occupy the petty service and civil administrative jobs in town. Then, of course, they risked the famously high mortality of the major ports. On the plantations they were small farmers, keepers of livestock pens, overseers, bookkeepers, and artisans. These whites were more important for their role in the domination of blacks than for any laboring skills they possessed. Vastly outnumbered by a restless enslaved population, whites were deeply insecure about their ability to keep slaves in a state of subjection. Making whiteness—in personal and cultural practice—a coherent and inviolable social category helped Europeans and their descendants band together against the numerically superior enslaved blacks. The main function of working-class whites on the plantations, then, was to represent and maintain white supremacy. "Deficiency laws" stipulated that estates employ a minimum number of whites in proportion to slaves or pay taxes to support the maintenance of parish militias. These quotas were seldom met, but the social value of whiteness provided real opportunities for white men—opportunities facilitated by the high mortality rate. White workers were transient, often remaining on a single plantation for just a few months. Their scarcity put them in high demand, so they could command excellent wages. In a society stratified by color, the meanest of white men enjoyed opportunities for social mobility unknown in Europe. They may never have exchanged familiar letters with M.P.'s or challenged the hegemony of the great sugar planters, but neither were they bound by the same codes of deference that constrained them in Britain. With good reason, these whites believed fervently in the early American dream. If they worked hard enough and lived long enough, they might buy a few slaves of their own, hire them out in gangs, and finally acquire some small parcel of land, independence, and social respectability. Jamaica appeared to be the "best poor man's country in the world," according to the description in one fictional account of the nineteenth century: "For with industry and economy, every man here may prosper."[18]

Thomas Thistlewood, who kept a diary of his thirty-six years in Jamaica during the eighteenth century, certainly would have thought so. Born in 1721, the second son of a middling tenant farmer in Lancashire, England, Thistlewood faced poor prospects in the Old World. He arrived at Kingston in 1750 with fewer than fifteen pounds in his purse and died in 1786, worth over three thousand pounds. Thistlewood worked his way up by learning to drive slaves, initially as a pen keeper for the wealthy planter Florentius Vassall, then as overseer of the Egypt sugar plantation in the parish of Westmoreland. Violent and domineering, Thistlewood earned the nickname No for Play from those he ruled. By 1766, Thistlewood was able to buy a three-hundred-acre pen on Breadnut Island. He moved there with twenty-eight slaves of his own the next year. Thistlewood lived his last two decades as a member of Jamaica's landed gentry, becoming a local magistrate and lieutenant of the fort at Savanna-la-Mar, Westmoreland's principal town. After a remarkably long life in Jamaica, he died, having attained far more property and power than he could have ever hoped for in England.[19]

Thistlewood never entered Jamaica's most elite circles of power. But he, Simon Taylor, and other slaveholders were united in their aspirations. "The foremost characteristic of white Jamaicans," one knowledgeable historian has argued, "was an all-consuming ambition for wealth, an avaricious and aggrandizing self-interest." Self-interest nearly always meant the domination of others, for slavery was the basis of prosperity. All the slaveholders' hopes and dreams, their ability to possess things and to command prestige, depended on the black multitudes they held in bondage. The same was true for Thistlewood, Taylor, most whites below their rank, and indeed for the whole eighteenth-century British Atlantic system. If Jamaica was the linchpin of the British Empire in America, the slave trade with Africa made it possible. This was clear enough to the novelist, economic journalist, and empire booster Daniel Defoe when he argued the importance of England's Africa trade in 1713: "The case is as plain as cause and consequence: Mark the climax. No African trade, no negroes; no negroes no sugars, gingers, indicoes etc; no sugars etc no islands, no islands no continent; no continent no trade." Just as black slave labor had enabled Europeans to prosper throughout the Americas, it powered a massive engine of wealth—and of death—in Jamaica.[20]

Africans working in Jamaica had survived ghastly odds against reaching the island at all. Wherever in Africa they had started from, a near majority of those captured and sold into the Atlantic trading network died en route. They fell in large numbers at every stage of their enslavement: as slave raiders and warriors first captured them in Africa; as they marched, famished, to inland slave markets, and then again to the dank and overcrowded slave forts and the waiting European ships at the coast; as the heaving Atlantic twisted them in their chains and soaked them in their own filth; as they waited for buyers in Jamaican ports; and as they fanned out onto the plantations and fell in line with their harsh and unyielding work regimes. Even once they had "adjusted" to Jamaican slavery, they could not expect to live longer than two decades.[21]

Numbers for the Nameless

Though Captain John Hawkins had carried Elizabethan England into the African slave trade in the 1560s, English participation in the trade remained relatively insignificant until the mid-seventeenth century, when sugar planting brought its demographic and commercial revolution to the British American colonies. Nurtured first by freebooters, then by a succession of monopolistic companies with royal charters—the Guinea Company in 1651, the Company of Royal Adventurers Trading into Africa in 1663, and the Royal African Company in 1672—the British share of the transatlantic slave trade began its steady and relentless increase. Competing with the Portuguese, Dutch, and French, English merchants organized the forced migration of around 6,700 Africans in each year of the 1660s. As plantation economies grew in tandem with maritime commerce, the British slave trade, first opened to private businessmen in 1698, expanded to eclipse that of any other nation. Throughout the 1700s the British were the world's preeminent slave traders, during their peak in the 1760s embarking more than 42,000 Africans yearly.[22]

British ships from London, Bristol, and Liverpool followed winds and currents that Portuguese navigators had charted in the fifteenth century, south past the Canary Islands, then along the African littoral, where captains purchased men, women, and children from African traders situated between the Senegal and Zaire rivers. Each ship concentrated its efforts, usually gathering slaves from only one or two regions along the coastline. Closest to Britain was the area embraced by the Senegal and Gambia rivers, yet by the mid-eighteenth century this was rarely a favorite destination. The British traded more actively to the south and east, in Sierra Leone, the Gold Coast, the Bight of Benin, and especially the Bight of Biafra. Farther south they bartered for people along the Loango Coast of West-Central Africa. Having loaded their cargos, the slavers sailed west, first reaching Barbados, or the Lesser Antilles, where they replenished supplies and gauged regional markets, before proceeding downwind to the biggest slave bazaar in the empire, Jamaica, where they knew they could always sell the most slaves at the highest prices.

From 1740 through 1807, ships from the British Empire carried about 2.2 million men, women, and children away from the African coast. The period began around midcentury, when the Jamaican economy was entering its peak years, and concluded with the cessation of the British transatlantic slave trade. During this time more than 10 percent of the Africans died before they reached their New World destination; still, over 1.9 million arrived in the Atlantic British colonies. As the leading slave trade entrepôt in the empire, Jamaica received about 33 percent of them, more

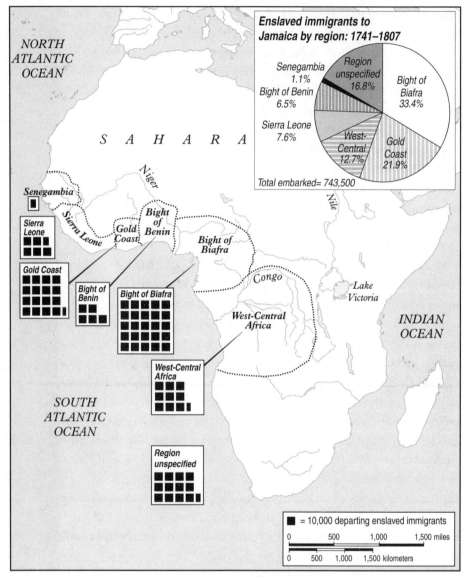

Map 4. Enslaved immigrants to Jamaica, by region, 1741–1807, drawn by Philip Schwartzberg

than 600,000 forced migrants. Between 1713 and 1739, when Britain had held the *asiento* contract to supply slaves to Spanish America, 33 to 50 percent of the Africans who landed at Jamaica embarked again for the mines and plantations of South America; but from 1740 onward only about 17 percent of the captives were reexported to other colonies. In total, the island absorbed more than any other single British colony did—more than

500,000 enslaved Africans—during that period, or 25 percent of all the African immigrants to Anglo-America.[23]

Though regions of embarkation are unknown for a large minority of the captive Africans, it is clear that there were shifts in regional migration patterns over time. Although the Bight of Biafra had been a minor source of slaves prior to 1740, it became the British Empire's single most important supplier of enslaved Africans from the mid-eighteenth century until the end of the transatlantic slave trade, so that a third or more of all those arriving at Jamaica from specified regions of Africa in the latter half of the eighteenth century came from the densely populated areas between the Niger Delta and the Cameroon River. Men, women, and children from the Gold Coast represented almost as significant a proportion, arriving in great and consistent numbers until Gold Coast exports fell off in the 1790s. Consistent imports from the nearby Bight of Benin similarly declined as the century drew to a close. Sierra Leone, which remained relatively insignificant for British slavers until the middle of the century, contributed sizable numbers of slaves to Jamaica from 1750 to the end of the century. The contingent of Africans drawn from West-Central Africa spiked into the tens of thousands in the 1790s, when the French and Haitian revolutions caused the collapse of French trading competition north of the Zaire River. These variations were patterned as much by supply as by demand.

British slavers were keen analysts of African markets, taking advantage of regions where local political institutions protected and facilitated foreign exchange, or where sudden disruptions provided windfall opportunities.[24] For the Gold Coast and Bight of Benin, militarized states like Asante and Dahomey ensured stability in the supply chain. Dotting the coastline were the castle factories established in the early years of the Africa trade. Their governors helped to maintain a stable business climate by negotiating with local authorities and by taking sides in local disputes to resolve them in favor of trading interests. The governors also warehoused captives, to help to expedite the loading of ships. In the Bight of Biafra, established African hinterland traders from Aro Chukwu controlled the flow of captives to ports. As British trade expanded there in the mid-eighteenth century, the Epke Society of merchants arose to manage the credit arrangements that governed trade in the region's Cross River estuary.[25] Where the British did not have an established institutional framework, they kept watch for favorable turns of events. Their trade at Sierra Leone exploded between 1750 and 1780, when the Futa Jallon holy wars reached peak intensity. Similarly, when revolutionary upheaval distracted the French from the slave trade, British traders rushed into France's former position in West-Central Africa. African political organizations of various sorts generally smoothed the progress of trade. Nevertheless, commercial order and social disruption went hand in hand. Fluctuations in social, political, and military conflict brought about the most massive forced migration in history. From the mid-seventeenth century to the abolition of the British slave trade in 1807, the British alone transported some 3.5 million people.

The numbers tell an impressive story, but it is easy to forget that they represent the logic of markets better than they do the experience of enslavement. Markets work by assigning value to units of exchange, to humans no less than they do the "widgets" of modern economic theory. Spanish and Portuguese traders had called young African males *piezas* or *peças*—pieces—as if they and their value as potential laborers could be counted like bolts of cloth. Women, young children, and the old were designated as fractions of pieces. British slavers numbered their captives outright, according to the sequential order in which they were purchased. Men, women, and children from myriad networks of belonging, each with their own terms of identification, fell into the commercial unit "Negro," when African merchants sold them to Europeans for textiles, copper, iron bars, cowrie shells, guns, and other goods. When British traders used regional and ethnic designations for groups of slaves, it was mostly to show their ports of embarkation and to reflect vague stereotypes. Such designations were mere product labels, meant to effect the reduction of humanity to the status of commodity.[26]

The facts derived from notations meant to represent only commerce threaten to obscure the humanity of the people they describe. They make it difficult to avoid thinking and writing in terms consistent with commercial accounting—"volumes," "distributions," "rates," and so on—which make commodified people appear nothing more than commodities. Statistical analyses of the slave trade can in this way seem to communicate the merchant's perspective, a discourse of exchange that seeks equivalences between units, flattening the social world by rendering it in the abstract. Gains that derive from elucidating general trends are offset by insensitivity to the experience of historical subjects. Considerations of scale, variation, and typicality trade the anguish and confusion of dimly discernible experiences for perceived mastery of the facts. It is somewhat unsettling, then, that business records have guided the best-known recent studies of the slave trade, in which recorded transactions affecting human commodities serve as data for forensic analysis.[27]

Nowhere has this been truer than in studies of slave-trade mortality rates, which have yielded important insights into causes of death, regional variations in cargo losses, and strategies for maintaining profitability in the midst of morbidity.[28] At the same time, such research renders the deadly migration of Africans somewhat like the chalk outline of a murder victim. The data delineate scale, proportion, and distribution quite well, but they cannot represent the wrenching personal trials endured by the enslaved, any more than an outline on the street can convey the passions that drove someone to kill, or the grief of the survivor who cries out from the scene of the crime to demand some measure of justice. Admittedly, there is no escaping the difficulty of reconstructing the experience of the enslaved, especially before they reached the Americas. Reliable descriptive sources are few and scattered. European slavers paid only an accountant's attention to the deaths of captives; records written by African merchants are extremely scarce; and recorded memories of the enslaved are even harder to come by. Even if extensive testimonial accounts by the enslaved could be found, we would still want to know if they were exceptional or if they represented common experiences. Undeniably, there were as many perceptions of the slave trade as there were people caught up in it. Nevertheless, by following the merchants' numbers, and by speculating on the cultural implications of death during forced migration, we may still learn much about the experiences of enslaved men, women, and children during their last days in Africa.[29]

Dislocation, Alienation, and Death

The booming Atlantic trade benefited Africans too—just not those who were enslaved. For them, the transatlantic system generated massive social disruption, terror, and death. Their experiences led them to associate the accumulation of wealth with the most malevolent forces in the universe. Over decades and centuries, all along the trade routes that penetrated Africa's interior, societies made themselves over, in order to meet the demands of the burgeoning Atlantic market. But the enslaved did not march inevitably toward European ships. As prices rose steadily throughout the eighteenth century, the scale of slavery within Africa increased along with the export trade. African slaveholders used slaves to perform household, agricultural, commercial, military, and reproductive labor. They also held them as status symbols, or even sacrificed them in sacred ceremonies. Slaveholding itself was widely accepted in Africa as a means of enhancing personal and communal wealth, and power accrued to those who commanded large numbers of dependents, including subjects, kinfolk, and slaves. European trade goods enabled a privileged few to acquire exceptional concentrations of enslaved wives, children, workers, and bearers of specialized knowledge. Wealth, power, and population accumulated among the select sovereigns and merchants who kept slaves moving toward the coast, in what one prominent historian of the slave trade has aptly characterized as "an alliance between European capitalism and African ruling elites, at the expense of the generality of Africans." Indeed European demands complemented the needs of African rulers, who preferred to retain women and very young children, to augment and reproduce their lineage, whereas Europeans valued young working-age males for plantation laborer. Roughly two-thirds of the people transported across the Atlantic were male. Most of them had been taken from some society other than that of the traders.[30]

The principal means of enslaving people for export were carrying out raids under conditions of open warfare, kidnapping the vulnerable, and condemning debtors and accused criminals. After interviewing scores of enslaved Africans in the Caribbean in the 1760s, one European concluded, "Most of them had been captured in the course of a declared war or in a surprise attack. A few of them were sold off because of debts that they owed, and a still smaller portion of them were caught on the open road." Summary accounts gathered in Sierra Leone around 1850 from a diverse group of 179 formerly enslaved Africans indicated that a similar pattern continued through the early nineteenth century. A third of them had been enslaved as war captives, and another third had been kidnapped. Just over a tenth of them were sentenced to slavery for real or bogus crimes, and the remainder had been sold by their social betters or by indebted relatives. The methods of enslavement varied somewhat by region. Greater percentages of captives from the Gold Coast, the Bight of Benin, and Sierra Leone had been captured in full-scale wars. Enslavement on judicial grounds was more likely in the Bight of Biafra, but all along the coast, people were sold as a result of witchcraft accusations. In some regions, especially West-Central Africa in the late eighteenth century, drought and famine made slaves cheap to acquire: desperate circumstances forced families into debt or drove unprotected members of the community to alien and hostile lands. Nearly everywhere, small bands of kidnappers, to ease their own debts or make their fortunes, took advantage of the high prices paid for slaves.[31]

Despite regional variations, common aspects of the experience of enslavement continued to affect the survivors who reached the Americas. The Africans who arrived in Jamaica all had a sharp sense of dislocation and rupture; they were all threatened by utter social alienation; and they all knew the proximity of death. Their shared experiences of death and dislocation ultimately formed the basis of common assumptions, idioms, and beliefs that would shape the worlds of meaning slaves used to stave off social annihilation.

The most common experience was of dislocation and movement. Enslaved men, women, and children moved from trader to trader, and from market to market. Along the way, they were assembled into larger groups for treks to the coast or sold off in small lots to domestic buyers. They marched up to a thousand kilometers from villages in the interior. 'Sibell, a woman who was kidnapped by her brother-in-law somewhere in West Africa, traded for gun and powder, and taken eventually to Barbados, emphasized her perception of movement and distance when she narrated her experience in 1799: "He take and carry, carry, carry, carry me all night and day, all night and day 'way from my Country." Alexander Falconbridge maintained that many of his captives from the Bight of Biafra, "upon being questioned relative to the places of their nativity, have asserted, that they have travelled during the revolution of several moons (their usual method of calculating time), before they have reached the places where they were purchased." As they traveled, the enslaved moved through different social contexts at a pace disorienting to all but long-distance traders. Time sped up as their awareness grew of the difference between themselves and the other peoples they encountered. This heightened sense of change and difference accompanied an enhanced fear of social alienation.[32]

As the world of Atlantic slavery drew people in, it tore them from the kin and communities that had thus far defined their social existence. For enslaved Africans the tragedy of the booming slave trade was most unmistakable in the winnowing of their social worlds, and in the loss of personal belonging and security. Historians and social scientists have described slavery as "a process of social transformation that involves a succession of phases and changes in status." At the point of capture or sale, individuals were stripped of social belonging and lost all claims to personal security and communal standing. This was equally the case for all enslaved prisoners, whether they were victims of war, kidnapping, debt, or judicial procedure. Yet this is too abstract a characterization. Even at the point of exchange, slavers considered whatever they knew of their captives' physical or personal attributes, in order to fix their value. These were already social judgments. Once acquired, however, an enslaved person began the socialization process anew, by building new personal relationships that held forth a potential advancement in rank. Slaves always sought to improve their positions. They often escaped or rebelled, to be sure, but they also made claims upon their masters. They again became family members, celebrated warriors, productive workers, even court officials. Yet as slaves they were perennially endangered by the prospect of resale and the resulting obliteration of their social selves. The Atlantic trade increased the number and frequency of alienating seizures and sales within Africa. Each time slaves might have hoped to be incorporated into new communities, the specter of the burgeoning markets on the coast haunted their efforts.[33]

Olaudah Equiano's description of his enslavement in the Biafran hinterland in the 1750s bears this out. Equiano's 1789 autobiography described his kidnapping as a young boy and his movement between different African slaveholders before being sold to the Europeans as part of a process of enslavement in stages. What stands out in his description, besides his hopes for escape, is his yearning for social connection. Enslaved along with his sister, he depicts their forced separation in his most emotional language: "I cried and cried continually; and for several days I did not eat anything." Yet his circumstances eventually improved: "After many days travelling, during which I had often changed masters, I got into the hands of a chieftain, in a very pleasant country. This man had two wives and some children, and they all used me extremely well." Equiano's "first master" was a metalsmith who began to teach the boy the skills of the trade. Already, he was much more than a commodity, though he was forbidden to eat with free children of his age. While he still plotted his escape and return to his family, even as a slave he began to feel a sense of belonging in his new circumstances. After the death of his master's daughter, however, Equiano was sold again, several more times in fact. He encountered progressively more alien peoples, "very much struck with this difference," until he was delivered to the Europeans, with whom he could imagine no connection at all. Along the way—during a short-lived surprise reunion with his sister, and as he learned "two or three different [African] tongues"—Equiano was constantly engaged in a struggle to enact his social personhood, in spite of his commodification. What he did not describe, perhaps because he was anxious to show Africa to his British readers in a favorable light, was the trail of death he trod as he moved along the coast.[34]

Perhaps one of every three captives destined for the Americas died before embarking on European ships.[35] In all the regions where Africans were enslaved, captivity made death seem imminent. Death came in a number of ways: famine, disease, war, and simple exhaustion devastated African captives before they even reached the coast. In the Bight of Biafra long journeys through pestilent waterways claimed untold numbers of lives. The Loango Coast of West-Central Africa received survivors from hinterland frontiers wracked by human and ecological calamity. The militarized states that fed the trade routes to the Gold Coast, the Bight of Benin, and Sierra Leone launched warfare that killed perhaps as many Africans as traders sold. Wherever the slave trade prospered, death took a dividend.

Most Africans from the Bight of Biafra who were sold to the British in the latter half of the eighteenth century came, as Equiano claimed to have come, from the populous areas near the coast, inhabited by Igbo- and Ibibio-speaking peoples. Captives were transported through a network of winding land and water routes. They moved through new and devastating disease environments at the slave fairs in the hinterland, and again at the swampy coastal trading outlets. Their journeys could last for months. Olaudah Equiano remembered traveling six or seven months, "sometimes by land, sometimes by water, through different countries, and various nations," before he finally arrived at an Atlantic port.[36]

Great numbers of other captives, seized from towns up to two hundred kilometers from the Atlantic Ocean, embarked on long forced marches, passing through many people's hands before they reached the Europeans. Slave ship surgeon Alexander Falconbridge reported in 1788 that the "black traders," who mediated the trade between the Europeans and the suppliers in the interior, generally bought their slaves at great fairs in the interior. Big hinterland markets had sprouted in the eighteenth century to support the increasing demand for slaves. "Several thousands are frequently exposed to sale, who had been collected," noted Falconbridge, "from all parts of the country for a very considerable distance round." From the fairs, coastal traders brought their captives downriver in canoes crowded with thirty to forty persons. It is certain that all along their route, the enslaved died in large numbers. Falconbridge made that assumption: "Even before they reach the fairs, great numbers perish from cruel usage, want of food, travelling through inhospitable deserts &c." Traveling downriver for several days, bound and tightly packed into canoes, the underfed captives shivered in the intermittent rains and made easy prey for tropical viruses and parasites. At the slave markets, disease ran riot. Speaking in the 1830s, one merchant sea captain remembered the crowded, noxious barracoons at one small town up the Bonny River. "They are built to contain from 300 to 700 slaves each. I have seen from 1,500 to 2,000 slaves at a time, belonging to the several vessels then in the river . . . I have known disease to make dreadful havoc in these places," he said. "Great numbers are carried off annually by diarrhoea and other diseases." Near the big markets and along the roads that connected them, slaves who died of exhaustion, disease, or suicide were thrown unceremoniously into what locals called the Ajo Ofia, the "bad bush."[37]

Death pervaded the swampy, malarial trading sites at Bonny and at Old and New Calabar. Inhabitants of the towns built large wood fires in their huts, to keep mosquitoes at bay; imported slaves, however, remained exposed and vulnerable. Along the coast and up the Cross River, dead slaves were commonly thrown to the sharks. The sailors who died each day were buried in shallow graves on a sandy point, just half a kilometer from the town. At high tide, water submerged the corpses, raising a stench that pervaded the marketplace. Captives loaded onto ships at the Bight of Biafra died more frequently than did those embarked from any other region. This fact was not lost on British slavers. "As to Old Callabar and the Camaroons," one Liverpool merchant grumbled in 1788, "I have allways declined sending to those two Rivers, as they are Sickly, and the

Slaves inferior to any other, very Weakly and liable to great Mortality." Africans loaded at Bonny, and at Old and New Calabar and other ports in the Bight of Biafra, had been traveling, undernourished, sick, and depressed, for months. No matter how robust they may have been when they started their journey, the traumatized survivors must have been shadows of their former selves.[38]

Beyond the Bight of Biafra, wars and raids killed as many as did disease and exhaustion. Slavery and warfare thrived off each other. Small, fragmented polities on the coast had been making war and capturing each other's subjects well before the Europeans arrived, but with Atlantic trade came the introduction of weapons that increased the scale of the violence. As slaves ebbed out of Africa, guns flowed in. Initially introduced in small numbers by traders in the mid-seventeenth century, guns increased in number, until 180,000 per year were purchased in the Gold Coast and the Bight of Benin by 1730. In the latter half of the eighteenth century as many as 50,000 guns arrived each year on the Loango Coast. From there they were distributed all over West-Central Africa. Whether to build powerful states, to leverage the position of merchants in the trade, or to protect kinfolk and subjects, European firearms were precious acquisitions.[39]

On the Gold Coast, by the beginning of the eighteenth century, the New World's demand for slaves and the Africans' desire for European weapons and other goods fueled a deadly cycle of wars, raids, and counterraids. By 1705 the region named for having exported great quantities of gold had, according to a Dutch West India Company official, "completely changed into a Slave Coast," where "the natives no longer occupy themselves with the search for gold, but rather make war on each other in order to furnish slaves." A Dutch account of 1730 explained the symbiotic relation between firearms and slave trading: "The great quantity of guns and powder which the Europeans have from time to time brought there has given cause to terrible wars among the Kings, Princes, and Caboceers of those lands, who made their prisoners of war slaves; these slaves were increasingly bought up by the Europeans at steadily increasing prices, which in its turn animated again and again those people to renew their hostilities." While the coastal Fantee Confederation flourished with the slave trade, the rising military power of the Asante kingdom gave its merchants an advantage in supplying the Europeans. From 1724 on,

Asante controlled the trade in gold, ivory, and slaves between the coast and the northwest hinterland. Expanding its dominion in all directions, Asante dominated nearly the entire region by the end of 1745, controlled the supply routes to the interior, and raided neighboring polities almost at will.[40]

Asante rulers generally protected their own subjects from the slave trade, meeting European demand largely with captives from the northern periphery of the Akan-speaking region. As a result, prisoners who survived Asante military assaults marched as many as three hundred kilometers to Gold Coast ports, arriving "very meagre," according to Captain John Adams, "in consequence of the fatigue experienced by them in their long journey from the interior." Arriving at the trade castles and forts on the coast, war captives were crowded into prison warehouses to await sale. Equiano's friend and fellow writer, Quobna Ottobah Cugoano, having been kidnapped near the coast as an adolescent in 1770, spent three days in a Gold Coast prison, where he "heard the groans and cries of many," before he was delivered to a British ship anchored at Cape Coast Castle. There he joined captives who had been transferred from the castle dungeon, a dark hole, where death rates had been so high earlier in the century that Royal African Company officials complained bitterly and repeatedly of the "great mortality" and the "number of them very much reduced and in a bad state of health."[41]

The initiatives of powerful states like Asante similarly shaped the experience of enslavement in the Bight of Benin, Sierra Leone, and the Windward Coast. From the late 1740s to about 1774 the kingdom of Dahomey, just inland from the Bight of Benin, operated as a middleman, supplying enslaved Africans who had been seized in the military raids of the Oyo kingdom to the northeast. After 1774, skirmishes between Dahomey and its neighbors supplied the majority of slaves to ships cruising between the ports of Whydah and Lagos. Captives of hinterland traders had marched as many as a thousand kilometers to the Bight of Benin, from as far away as the central Sudan. Even if prisoners had been captured near the coast, they marched westward for as many as two hundred kilometers to the principal trading forts. To the west of the Bight of Benin, the Futa Jallon holy wars began in the 1720s and reached their violent apogee from the 1760s through the 1780s. The fighting proved a boon to slave exporters when prisoners from the sub-Saharan savannas were sold to traders from Sierra

Leone. Royal Navy Lieutenant John Matthews, present in Sierra Leone in the mid-1780s, contended that "the prisoners made in these religious wars" comprised "great numbers," about 3,000 a year, and were "brought down, fifty or a hundred together, by the black slave merchants." Waiting offshore or canoeing upriver to small trading posts, Europeans bought refugee survivors in small lots from coastal dealers. African merchants took firearms, among the assorted goods procured in exchange, back into the interior, to sustain the business cycle.[42]

Africans collected from ports along the Loango Coast, just north of the Zaire River, had one of the deadliest journeys to the coast. By the end of the eighteenth century, commercial slave trading had reached deep into the interior and was drawing slaves largely from the central highlands or areas beyond the Kwango Valley. In communities previously at peace, the death rate among the children and young adults most threatened by the slavers increased dramatically with the advance of Atlantic commerce. In the 1790s and early 1800s, when the British recruited heavily from West-Central Africa, agents for coastal merchants at Loango purchased most of their slaves from areas several months' march from the coast. In the few remaining peaceful and fertile territories in West-Central Africa in the late eighteenth century, people drawn into the slave trade by indebtedness suffered the sharpest decline in life expectancy; their short-term odds of survival fell to 5 or 10 percent of life expectancy at home. At the slaving frontier whole populations suffered heavy losses from war, famine, and epidemics resulting from the violent disruptions brought by slave raids. A severe drought in the 1780s and 1790s made human life cheap and drew traders eastward to grab starving refugees. Shackled together in groups of about thirty, the newly enslaved headed west in caravans, passing through dense tropical forest and along the dangerous mountain slopes of the Mayombe Hills. One out of every four died en route. The greatest number expired just before they reached the trading towns, as hunger, dehydration, and sickness finally overwhelmed them. Another 15 percent died while waiting to be sold to the Europeans. A few of these were unfortunate enough to reach the coast at the Portuguese-dominated port of Luanda, a charnel house for the enslaved. At Luanda, European merchants dumped the bodies of dead slaves in an overflowing cemetery near the commercial center or into graves too shallow to keep the hyenas from picking them over. Captives who took more direct routes to Cabinda, the main port on the Loango Coast, were more fortunate, having partially recuperated at less deadly villages in the interior before coming down to meet the British camped along the shore. Still, by the time these Africans wedged themselves into the holds of slave ships, they knew that Atlantic Africa was a world of death.[43]

A Theater of Ghosts

In every region with a point of embarkation for America, the shattering experience of war, relocation, and estrangement shaped the way Africans understood their predicament. Having been witness to untold deaths, and to corpses scattered everywhere—in raided villages, along roads and riverbanks, and in rotting heaps at coastal depots—Africans undoubtedly fixed upon the association between slavery and death. Their first assessments of Europeans, their experience of the impact of commercial wealth on the coast, and their impressions and myths about the Atlantic economy reveal a way of seeing, speaking, and thinking that associated Atlantic slavery with murder, sorcery, and the alienated dead.

When at last Olaudah Equiano encountered white slave traders, he could only imagine that they intended to eat him. "When I looked round the ship," he recalled, "and saw a large furnace of copper boiling, and a multitude of black people of every description chained together, every one of their countenances expressing dejection and sorrow, I no longer doubted my fate, and quite overpowered with horror and anguish, I fell motionless on the deck and fainted." Sale to Europeans represented the ultimate alienation. With the Africans who had delivered him into British hands, Equiano still felt he shared some common human feelings. He asked them whether he was "not to be eaten by those white men with horrible looks, red faces, and long hair."[44]

Fear of white cannibalism was widespread. William Bosman, who traded around the Slave Coast more than half a century before Equiano's capture, claimed that Africans from the interior feared that "we buy them only to fatten and afterwards eat them as a Delicacy." These captives were more likely to attempt escape, or to kill their European captors and run the ship aground, "by which means they design to free themselves from being our Food." Slave ship captain John Newton noted much the same thing of captives taken from the Sierra Leone region. In West-Central

Africa, many believed that black bodies had been pressed to make cooking oil, that European red wines contained the blood of the enslaved, and that cheese had been pressed from their brains. Perhaps some Africans had heard rumors about actual cannibalism on slave ships. According to stories circulated by white slave traders, the English captain John Harding had one man killed in 1724 for plotting a rebellion. Harding had the man's heart and liver removed and cut into three hundred pieces, which he then force-fed to the remaining captives. How many Captain Hardings were there in the Africa trade? There did not need to be many, because Africans with little experience of European ways were inclined to believe the worst, that whites were alien predators who would use them as readily consumable goods. This was the extreme consequence of their dislocation, a sense that at the end of the odyssey, they would be delivered to cannibals.[45] As Equiano's testimony indicates, white slave traders were more likely than African ones to inspire fears of cannibalism.[46] At the same time, the enslaved interpreted the actions of the more familiar African slavers by correlating sorcery and death with accumulation of material wealth.

Commercial wealth in Africa was symbolized dramatically by elaborate funerals, which reached grandiose proportions in the militarized states of the Slave Coast and the teeming trading towns in the Bight of Biafra. In these places last rites for kings and persons of great wealth included the sacrificial slaughter of slaves. Great funerals often involved the executions of wives and servants, who in theory would continue to serve the deceased in the afterlife. While anchored at Anomabo in December 1790, Captain Hugh Crow heard of twenty-three women put to death at the interment of a local prince. Ashy, a Fantee native enslaved in Barbados, recalled in 1799, "If any of our Grandee people die, den all de head of his servants is cut off, and bury in de same place wid him." More might be killed at occasional ceremonies, as additional offerings or as messengers from the living, who hoped to secure the favor of the dead. The numbers of victims increased with the power and prominence of the honorees, and also with the affluence of those paying tribute. Increasing concentration of wealth on the coast resulted in a kind of "conspicuous consumption" in which slaves were sacrificed both in veneration of the dead and as a way of enhancing the prestige of the wealthy. In the militarized trading states, the sacrifice of war captives symbolized the power of the kingdom. As Atlantic commerce swelled the numbers of slaves in the great trade centers, ever more of these unfortunates were subjected to ritual execution.[47]

In Dahomey, royal funerals and annual ceremonies for "watering the graves" of deceased kings involved the sacrifice of hundreds of wives, slaves, and war prisoners. Some fifteen hundred were killed during more than two years of observances following the death of King Kpenga in 1789. In 1797 Asante hosted the sacrifice of fourteen to fifteen hundred persons for the funerals of princes. The scale of the killing was less excessive, but still great at the commercial towns in the Bight of Biafra. Sixty-five people were killed to honor Duke Ephraim, ruler of Old Calabar, in 1786. A spare first-hand account of the slaughter survives in the diary of the African merchant Antera Duke: "About 4 A.M. I got up; there was great rain, so I walked to the town palaver house and I found all the gentlemen here. So we got ready to cut heads off and at 5 o'clock in the morning we began to cut slaves' heads off, fifty heads off in that one day. I carried 29 cases of bottled brandy, and 15 calabashes of chop [food] for everybody, and there was play in every yard in town." One can only wonder how the sights and sounds of the killing affected those bound for America. During the sacrifices for Duke Ephraim, several hundred captives were aboard the *Preston*, anchored in the estuary. One hundred and eighty-six were sold at Kingston nearly a year later, fifty-five of them young children. What knowledge of death and power did these people bring with them from Old Calabar? We cannot know with any certainty. Yet we can assume that these Africans, like others passing through the hands of coastal merchants, associated the prosperity of the commercial coast with the ostentatious expenditures, a display of their wealth in people. In this way the enslaved might reasonably have equated extravagant affluence with massacre.[48]

More commonly, they saw accumulation of material wealth as the result of sorcery. Eighteenth-century Africans, not unlike other peoples, generally assumed that only a fixed amount of wealth was available in the world, distributed as much according to a precarious balance of spiritual forces as through human endeavor. They therefore considered the pursuit of prosperity a "zero-sum game," played in both the mystical and temporal realms, in which one could gain only at another's expense. This view formed the crux of holistic ideals for human affairs that linked economic equilibrium with the harmony of society, the health of individuals, and the play of good and evil. Concentrations of wealth resulted in social pathology and physical illness. By the same token, the presence of sickness and strife must prove the influence of some evil intent. In the absence of evil, no one would have too much or too little. Thus, extreme inequities were seen as the result of a great imbalance between the forces of benevolence and malevolence. If someone wanted to get rich or enjoy extraordinary vigor, that person would have to employ dark powers to take from another or might have to sacrifice his own health or that of a family member.[49]

While small differences in wealth and status could result from individual skill or good fortune, great riches, such as those the traders had accumulated, could be obtained only through nefarious magic. As Africans could witness all around them, the goods and people that enriched some had brought social distortion, pestilence, and death to others. In seventeenth-century Loango, for example, the Dutch traveler Olifert Dapper noted the belief that "no one dies except through the malice and enchantment of the enemy, who, by the same spells, revives him, transports him to deserted places, and makes him work there to enrich him." The character of the eighteenth-century slave trade only strengthened the widespread association between wealth and death, whereby malevolent sorcery provided the means to achieve prosperity. The great numbers of broken families, the men, women, and children dead before their time, the plagues of raiders all represented disruptions on a cosmic scale. Only collaboration with the dark forces of the universe could explain the profits reaped from this cascading tragedy. Only countervailing sorcery for the good of the community could combat the ill effects. Throughout the slaving regions, people formed protective associations, procured defensive talismans, and performed ritual cleansings and healings, while accusations of witchcraft proliferated. Many of the people convicted for witchcraft were, in punishment, themselves enslaved and sold. From every angle, then, enslaved Africans could see that the slave trade was suffused with evil and deadly magic.[50]

Africans integrated these views with supernatural conceptions of Atlantic geography and economy. The deaths of the enslaved were more than disappearances, absences, or extinctions; the deaths generated new stories and understandings to account for the enormity of the social disturbance. West-Central Africans metaphorically associated whites and their territories across the ocean with the afterlife. Knowing that the overland slave trade was a trail of death, they assumed that European ships continued on to a realm of the dead. Oral histories in early twentieth-century West Africa described Atlantic commerce itself in terms of death and accumulation. Cowrie shells, the currency so widely circulated in coastal West Africa, were believed to have fed off the cadavers of slaves thrown into the sea; thus, money issued from corpses.[51]

Such allegories of the Atlantic economy may have had literal referents. On the coast, Africans could see and hear of the European commercial activity that attended death. To keep trade moving smoothly, Europeans often provided gifts for the funerals of prominent Africans, thereby linking commercial operations with these final rites of passage. Similarly, when white traders died on the coast, ship captains and factors paid "death duties" to African leaders, presumably to cover rents for their burial plots. Europeans were careful, however, not to bury on their own initiative any Africans with known relatives who died within their forts and factories, out of fear of taking on the debts of the deceased. White grave robbers strengthened the association between death and the Atlantic trade. Africans were frequently buried with their possessions, and thieves recognized an easy opportunity. In 1738 British officials at Cape Coast Castle censured James Hope for "Clandestinely opening the Grave and Triffling the Dead" body of Mrs. Phipps, a wealthy local who had been interred with her gold. Hope, in his search for the shortest route to success in the lethal surroundings, had tortured some of Phipps's friends and relatives, in order to discover the location of the grave.

Whites died quickly in Africa, usually leaving debts to be settled. By the late eighteenth century, accountants for the Company of Merchants were retailing the effects of dead traders to pay their arrears. "The Salutary Effects of selling Dead Mens Property for ready Money already appears conspicuous," reported Cape Coast Castle Governor Richard Miles in 1782, "for by this Ship goes the Amount of two or three small Estates of persons lately dead." Elsewhere, one ship captain noted the practice in terse log entries: "Sold the Deceas'd people Cloaths; great part of which was damag'd and rotten." If this was not exactly cowrie shells feeding upon cadavers, these activities certainly suggested the tendency of slave traders to reap from death the benefits of commercial exchange.[52]

Throughout Atlantic Africa, people knew the dead to be active participants in the affairs of the living. As long-dead ancestors, they constituted a category of beings not unlike saints or demigods, capable of bestowing fortune upon their devotees; as recently departed kin, they watched over the family welfare; if they were the spirits of powerful leaders, they continued to command gestures of respect; if they were the ghosts of the wicked, witches, or outcasts, they could put a curse on the living, or do them bodily harm.[53] Just as removal from kinship networks represented a terrible crisis for the enslaved, so did the estrangement of the dead from their home territories and family roots.

Most of the Africans who died along their route to the Americas passed without communal care. The dead were devoured by animals, thrown into the bush along the way, heaped in piles at trading forts, or tossed unceremoniously into rivers and lagoons. Without relatives and compatriots to mark the passage, death threatened the deceased with eternal alienation. The absence of commemoration compounded the social disruption caused by capture and sale, constant movement along the trading routes, and high mortality. For most Africans, as for most people in general, death represented a rupture in social relations that required some form of ritual healing, even under normal circumstances. The groups captured and sold into slavery had limited means to adequately ritualize death, so they left restless spirits in their wake. All during the inexorable journey to the Americas, as Africans repeatedly made and lost fragile social connections, they trailed a lengthening column of displaced souls. This was a spiritual cataclysm, perhaps the most horrifying aspect of the experience of enslavement. Embarking for America, enslaved Africans had entered a theater of ghosts. Olaudah Equiano, for one, knew when he finally boarded a British slave ship that he "had gotten into a world of bad spirits."[54]

The Cargo Hold

Aboard the Guineamen, as the slave ships were called, the misery of enslavement was concentrated. The captives arrived in lots of various sizes over periods that stretched to several months. Only when the holds were full did the ships embark for America. They packed in anywhere between 150 and 600 or more people, depending on the tonnage of the vessel. The three-hundred-ton *Vulture* carried 646 people from the Bight of Biafra to Jamaica early in 1787; the much smaller *Commerce* brought just 161 from the Senegambia later in the year. Most ships held between 200 and 400. Belowdecks, men, women, and children each had separate compartments, divided by bulkheads. The men were generally shackled, for fear they might stage violent revolts, while the women and children were left without chains but scrutinized closely by nervous seamen. In separate groups they came up on deck for rudimentary exercise, meant to keep them healthy enough to fetch a suitable price at the next market.[55]

Captains raced to obtain their full complement before the slaves began to die in quantities. As they perished, the dead were commemorated in the ships' logs by numbered notations: "Depart'd this life one Man Slave of fever. N° 1 . . . 6th March 1 Man flux & 1 of a fever N° 6 Total on board 234." When the vessels neared capacity, sickness and death stalked the sweltering holds. "Now that the whole ship's cargo were confined together it became absolutely pestilential," Equiano wrote in his autobiography. "The closeness of the place, and the heat of the climate, added to the number in the ship, which was so crowded that each had scarcely room to turn himself, almost suffocated us . . . The wretched situation was again aggravated by the galling of the chains, now become insupportable; and the filth of the necessary tubs, into which the children often fell, and were almost suffocated. The shrieks of the women, and the groans of the dying, rendered the whole a scene of horror almost inconceivable." James Stanfield, an ordinary sailor in the Africa trade, concurred with Equiano, likening a slave ship to "a slaughterhouse. Blood, filth, misery, and disease."[56]

Unlikely as it may seem under such conditions, the captives again began the process of forming new social connections in these wretched cargo holds. Fragile relationships were found and lost as the ships filled up in stages and people adapted, or died. Those who shared a language or could find other ways to understand one another commenced the narration, interpretation, and assessment of their common experience. Crammed together, they could gauge their situation, even plan their escape. Rebellions were frequent, suicides even more so. More prevalent still was the laborious process of making a new common sense from the horrifying world of the dead. Nothing was more urgent for the passengers than the discussion of death, and if their differences led to disputes over the precise meaning of fatality or the proper rites of passage, they could all agree that they faced a comparable social and spiritual crisis.

Certainly, the trip across the Atlantic kept their minds focused on death. In the eighteenth-century British slave trade, mortality rates among captives during the crossing ranged between 10 and 15 percent. Those numbers improved over the course of the century, as the percentage fell in response to improvements in ship design, health, and medical care, as well as late eighteenth-century legislation that regulated the numbers of Africans carried on each ship and stipulated that bonuses would be paid to captains and surgeons who ensured better survival rates. Yet an African's chance of surviving the Atlantic passage depended largely on the fortunes of the particular voyage. Mortality on transatlantic voyages correlated most strongly with particular points of departure. Human cargoes from the Bight of Biafra had consistently lower survival rates than those from the Gold Coast, West-Central Africa, and Sierra Leone. Ailments acquired during travel to the coast overwhelmed the captives once they entered the deadly conditions of the ships. With the slaves jammed into impossibly close quarters, once the Atlantic passage was under way, each contagious person threatened all the others; each healthy one depleted the limited supplies of food and water. The enslaved suffered a variety of fatal maladies during the middle passage: they contracted diseases in the cramped, filthy holds, they starved, they grew dehydrated from lack of water and from chronic dysentery, and sometimes they simply yielded to despair. Smallpox, yellow fever, and cholera epidemics; unexpectedly long voyages that outlasted the provisions; or captors' negligence and cruelty could all sharply increase loss of life.[57]

The living were in constant and immediate proximity to the dead. During his time as a surgeon in the slave trade, Alexander Falconbridge saw instances in which dead and living Africans were found shackled together. During the weeks and months of the passage, the halting, dislocating journeys of enslavement in Africa had brought routine, almost familiar encounters with death. At any given time a slave might awake to find that the person with whom he or she had been desperately trying to communicate hours before was now lying lifeless nearby. These lifeless bodies—chained alongside the living, cast into the open ocean before scores of witnesses—became unforgettable icons of shared experience for those who survived the trip to America. Amid mortal crisis, they forged lasting relationships. Having been collectively threatened with utter alienation, the survivors claimed their fellow passengers as kin. In Jamaica, "shipmates" were treated as brothers and sisters. The term was, according to one contemporary observer, "the dearest word and bond of affectionate sympathy amongst the Africans." Indeed, shipmates remained a crucial part of fragile family networks throughout slavery, protecting one another's children, arranging funeral rites, and inheriting one another's property.[58]

These novel relationships were born during thousands of passages on ships like the *Ruby*. If no single slaving voyage could be considered typical, it was also true that few were unusual, and in many respects the *Ruby's* Atlantic crossing was comparable to countless others. One of the smaller ships in the trade, the *Ruby* embarked from Sierra Leone in late February 1792, bound for Jamaica with a cargo of 158 slaves. Thomas Walker, a co-owner of the vessel who resided on the African coast, was pleased to inform his partner James Rogers in Bristol that the *Ruby* had loaded 55 men, 26 women, 49 boys, and 27 girls (one was missing from this account), probably refugees from war-ravaged villages in the interior. On 22 March, after a passage lasting twenty-seven days, Captain John Kennedy reported to Rogers from Barbados. Infectious dysentery had plagued the voyage. His accounting showed "Eighteen Buried in the flux" and "24 Slaves very much Reduced by that Disorder," though he expected only 2 of these to die. He hoped to "Recover all the Rest fit for Market in ten days after my arrival in Jamaica," but 5 more died before he reached the island on 1 April, and another 3 while he was anchored in Martha Brae Harbor. Kennedy landed 131 of his original cargo, though 2 of these were too sick to sell, and so "was thrown in" free of charge with a parcel of 30 "refuse slaves" sold at cut-rate prices to Mr. Gillies, a retailer who turned his profit by nursing those he could back to marketable health. In total, the shipment grossed just over £7,957.[59]

This was a disappointing venture for James Rogers. The *Ruby* had left Africa some forty-six slaves short of its intended complement, owing to the sudden death of the resident trader, James Cleveland, with whom Rogers and Walker had contracted their business and to whom they had advanced large amounts of goods on credit. The cargo also contained too many children, and its 17 percent mortality rate was higher than average. Still, John Cunningham, the factor who sold the *Ruby's* captives at Montego Bay, explained that things could have been worse. "Considering the Cargo," he wrote, "the Average of £43 Sterl [after duties and fees] was more than I expected. There were 45 Boys & Girls under 4 feet 4 inches many not more than 8 or 9 years of age. I had plenty of purchasers and sold the first choice at £75 & Duty for Males & Females, then the next £70 for Males & £60 for females many of the small ones at £55 thereabouts."[60]

Despite Rogers's ill fortune, the voyage of the *Ruby* was in many ways consistent with general patterns. The presence of 2 males for every female in the cargo was ideally suited to the demands of Jamaica slaveholders and matched the sex ratio in the trade overall. The ship encountered no major delays on the Atlantic crossing, there were no serious shipboard revolts, and the death rate among the Africans, though high, was not financially ruinous. Though there were 54 children among the 129 slaves sold, nine of them were listed in Cunningham's accounting as "Man-Boys" and "Woman-Girls"—adolescents, who commanded good prices. The voyage could be reasonably described as having been "completed as intended." It was not a typical voyage, nor was it extraordinary, and there could have been nothing more matter-of-fact than the way the traders represented the twenty-five deaths on the mortality list.[61]

The "Mortality List of Ship *Ruby*" is a kind of memorial inscription for the captives who died on board. In neat columns and straight rows for easy tabulation, Captain John Kennedy recorded the number of deceased men, women, boys, and girls, with their place and date of departure. He also listed the cause of death, accounting for "disorders" in the most orderly fashion possible. Ten of the 25 captives accounted for (Captain Kennedy's number falls 2 short of the difference between the 158 he took from the coast and the 131 he landed) expired within a week of his having left Africa. Indeed, Kennedy was keen to emphasize that 13 of them had had the flux when he left the coast. There were several deaths in each of the following three weeks; all but one of them occurred at sea. The causes were monotonous: all but four died of dysentery, or the flux, and three of respiratory ailments, coughing fits designated as "consumption." One victim of dysentery followed another so closely that the disorder was most commonly represented by the repetitious "ditto," made even more efficient by the abbreviation "d°." Whereas Equiano had remarked in 1789 on children who fell into tubs of filth, the *Ruby*'s mortality list of 1792 merely notes the presence of the flux, neatly avoiding the image of dead children covered with shit.[62]

Then there is the curious, lone entry for 27 March. Just days before landfall, in the midst of his shipmates—future cane workers, domestic servants, runaways, and rebels—one young boy died of insanity. What could he have done to merit the distinction? Was he screaming? Crying uncontrollably? No, that would have been too commonplace. Was "insanity" simply a euphemism for "suicide"? Falconbridge maintained that some Africans could die of a "diseased mind."[63] Perhaps the boy emitted some baffling expression of grief all his own, too alien to be easily accounted for but too inconsequential to be worthy of further notice. Maybe for the young boy the distinction between sanity and madness had vanished somewhere during the passage. However the boy ended his life, finally, here in the mortality list, was something truly typical, though it was less a commentary on the experience of the slave trade than on its essential character as a business of death. The inventory was an elegantly distilled, formal mantra for the representation of dead commodities, intoned thousands of times over hundreds of years.

> Dysentery.
> Insanity.
> Consumption.
> Ditto.
> Ditto.
> Ditto.
> Ditto.

The Cost of Cultivation

On landing in Jamaica, African captives were exchanged again. Over a period of several weeks they were sold in small groups from shipboard or taken to great holding pens called guinea yards, where they were retailed to their eventual owners. Affluent planters and urban merchants might buy twenty or more in a single transaction, but large numbers of captives were bought singly, or in twos and threes, by smaller traders. The survivors of the *Ruby* were divided up among twenty-seven different buyers. Only seven of them, including the "refuse" trader Gillies, bought five or more people. Among the nineteen slaveholders who bought three or fewer was Simon Taylor's cousin, John Taylor, who purchased one little girl for £50. In all likelihood, John bought the girl for Simon. We might imagine that John Taylor's purchase was something like the one he had made for Simon Taylor only two years earlier, a problematic exchange that stymied one girl's hopes for a family reunion. Then, it seems, Simon thought two "refuse" girls, one with a swollen arm and another missing an eye, had been slipped into one of his parcels. He returned both of them to the market. John wrote back to say, "There is several very fine girls here. I wish you had seen them as I believe you might have got two such as you would like in place of those returned." For Simon Taylor, the dissatisfied customer, the dynamic market could provide easy redress, but the same market brought only further ruin to one of the children. "The Girl with one Eye I find has a sister at your Penn," John informed Simon. "She is crying most dreadfully." As with family ties, bonds of communion forged along the trek to the West Indies were tested yet again as the enslaved, dispersed throughout the island, became subject to new masters and found new occupations and social roles in Jamaica, a graveyard for blacks no less than for whites.[64]

When they first came into the hands of Europeans, as mentioned, alienated Africans had often believed that whites would eat them. As Africans were incorporated into plantation life, we can say, with little exaggeration, that this assumption was ultimately correct. American planters would exhaust the slaves' lives as productive capacity, grinding them into sugar, coffee, and other crops for export, primarily to Europe, where they would indeed be consumed—but only if they could survive their initial adjustment to slave society. For all its economic success as an outpost of empire, Jamaica routinely destroyed its black people.

The death toll imposed by the slave trade continued to mount in Jamaican ports. As the leading slave trade entrepôt in the British Empire, the island was a principal node in the circuit of Atlantic disease. Because the widespread use of inoculation did not begin in Jamaica until the early nineteenth century, each new slave ship that came to the island brought the threat of a smallpox epidemic. In 1732 Governor Robert Hunter appealed to the Lords of Trade and Plantations to approve "an act to Prevent the Landing or Keeping of Negroes Infected with Smallpox in any of the Three Towns of Spanish Town, Port Royal, or Montego Bay." The act proved inconvenient to merchants, who preferred more flexible quarantines, and it was allowed to lapse six years later. Despite the efforts of Kingston's principal traders to locate their "guinea yards" well away from the towns, smallpox remained a serious problem. When smallpox spread beyond the port area and swept through the plantations, the results were calamitous. In 1774 the Jamaican planter and historian Edward Long called smallpox "one principal source of depopulation" among the slaves.

"Sometimes they have been landed with this disease upon them; and this has proved so fatal, that I have known seven in ten [to] die of it." By comparison, Long noted that seventy deaths among a hundred slaves was "fifty-six more than the computation made of those who die in England by this disorder taken in the natural way." In 1787 Simon Taylor bought seven Africans for Chaloner Arcedeckne's Golden Grove sugar plantation, "but they brought the smallpox out of the ship with them." A third of that ship's cargo died of the disease shortly thereafter. By this time, however, planters had learned to inoculate vulnerable populations. "Whenever the smallpox breaks out," Taylor assured Arcedeckne, "we always inoculate all we have that has never had it, by that means it never now comes on as a plague, as it used to do formerly."[65]

The market had another way of taking the dangers of smallpox into account. Slaves who had survived the pox—or the deadly yaws—and had scars to prove their immunity drew higher prices. Sellers could claim that these people were "seasoned." The "seasoning" usually referred to a period of time, one to three years in most cases, during which enslaved Africans confronted a host of mortal dangers as they adapted to conditions in Jamaica. The captives first had to survive any maladies they had brought with them from Africa or contracted aboard slave ships. Caged in warehouses as they waited for buyers, the Africans were threatened by crowded and unhealthy conditions similar to those they had endured on the African coast.[66] Then the survivors began to adapt to the new disease environment in Jamaica, while simultaneously adjusting to the grinding labor routine. Like all slaves, "new Negroes" commonly lived in pestilential surroundings where they were overworked and underfed.

Too many enslaved Africans could not endure the trial. "Almost half of the new imported Negroes die in the Seasoning," Charles Leslie observed in 1740. Five decades later, an agent for another colony in the West Indies testified that little had improved: one of every two Africans that reached the islands still died within a few years. William Fitzmaurice, who worked as a bookkeeper and overseer in Jamaica between 1771 and 1786, told a committee of the House of Commons how precarious the lives of recently imported Africans were. "In the last four years I lived on the island," he testified, "I bought ninety-five; at the expiration of the four years I sold fifty-two, which were all that were living, and those fifty-two I did not sell as seasoned Slaves; if I had attempted to keep them till the usual time of seasoning, I should have had a greater decrease, and on this very account I sold them." In his diary entry for 3 July 1784, slaveholder Thomas Thistlewood mentioned the ill fortune of Mr. John Richardson, a planter who had bought 190 unseasoned Africans over the previous fourteen years and lost 141 of them. Richardson maintained that for keeping recently imported Africans alive, "prudence & Industry are highly necessary," but that "most succeed from a lucky combination of circumstances." Indeed, Thistlewood fared much better with his own purchases. Of the 27 people he bought between 1756 and 1778, only 3 perished within the three-year seasoning period.[67]

To protect their investments, planters took several steps to keep their new purchases alive. Fresh recruits were placed in the care of more experienced slaves, spared the most difficult tasks, and put instead to building houses and planting provision grounds. Recent arrivals lived and worked alongside the veterans, who taught their "inmates" how to negotiate the unfamiliar circumstances. As with shipmates, the inmate relationship could be the beginning of deep and lasting bonds in slave society. For instance, when Old Phibba died in 1763, her overseer noted that Old Sharper, whom she had first taken in as a new Negro, had her coffin made and presumably made the offerings to her spirit. But sometimes the mentoring relationship could turn abusive. According to some planters, established slaves contrived to exploit their "inmates" by cajoling the new Negroes into working extra time on veterans' own provision grounds, plots of land from which the enslaved drew most of their nourishment. The established slaves even used their "inmates" to cultivate a surplus that they could sell for cash, but of course planters were less concerned with the rights of unseasoned slaves than with the labor that crafty subordinates might commandeer for themselves. The primary issue, after all, was to turn labor quickly into profit, in the form of export crops, not local staples.[68]

The most profitable crops were also the deadliest. Sugar plantations were the most dangerous places to be enslaved. According to B. W. Higman's analysis of the demographic characteristics of Jamaican plantations from 1829 to 1832, slaves on sugar plantations recorded the highest annual death rate of any agricultural workers, 35.1 deaths per 1,000 enslaved. Close behind that was the mortality rate on the jobbing gangs of subcontracted slaves, who were often enlisted to do the heaviest work on sugar plantations. Chances of survival in the coffee, livestock, and pimento (allspice) industries were a bit better, but the mortality rate declined significantly only when slaves worked on plantations where cultivation of minor staples like pimento was combined with coffee growing or livestock raising. Enslaved men and women working on such properties were better fed and subject to lighter workloads than those on sugar estates.[69]

Unfortunately, between half and three-quarters of Jamaica's slaves worked in the sugar industry, where the labor regime was most intense. Planters commonly divided the workforce into three gangs. The first, generally called the great gang, did the heaviest work. This included holing and trenching the fields, cutting canes and feeding them to the mills, chopping firewood, boiling the sugar, and repairing wooden fences, stone walls, and dirt roads. On a well-functioning estate, about a third of the slaves worked in the great gang. The second gang, which consisted of teenagers, the aged, Africans in seasoning, and people temporarily relieved from the great gang because they were pregnant or ill, performed lighter tasks, such as weeding, bundling the cane for transport, driving the animals that powered the mills, and gathering cane trash to fuel the boilers. Young children, who made up the third gang, collected grass and weeds for the livestock and did other miscellaneous light work.[70]

The burdens that fell on the field gangs contributed heavily to the high mortality on sugar estates. Richard Dunn's analysis of slave labor patterns at the Mesopotamia plantation in Westmoreland parish, for example, shows that from 1762 to 1831, male field-workers were recorded as being sickly during 48 percent of their working years. Five percent of the time they were listed as nonworking invalids. They could labor only an average of 13.2 years in the field before their health broke down drastically and they "retired" to lighter tasks. They died at a mean age of just over forty-two. Women field-workers fared slightly better. On average, they could spend 2.4 years more in the field, and they outlived men by about 3 years. Yet despite these advantages, enslaved women were sick or disabled for nearly 60 percent of their working lives.[71]

Cane planting was so costly in slave lives that for the hardest tasks, such as digging holes to plant the fields, slave masters preferred to hire temporary workers—jobbing gangs that belonged to someone else. Mortality among the jobbers nearly matched that on the sugar plantations, because these gangs were so often employed to do the most grueling work in the industry. *Marly*, a kind of early ethnographic novel about Jamaican life, describes in detail the taxing first stage of sugar planting. Everyone in the field gangs commenced digging with hoes. "The black tradesmen were on the ground, together with the overseer and the two book-keepers, to assist in carrying the lines, so that the hole might be regularly dug," two and a half feet square and about six inches deep for each new plant. "This process of excavation was performed with the hoe alone, two negroes being placed to one hole as nearly matched as possible, a strong negro having for his partner a weak one; but all had to perform the same quantity of work, and in the same time, in order to keep them in line; consequently a female or weak person had to dig nearly as much as the strongest." As the workday advanced, the gangs weakened visibly. "After a week or five days of this kind of labour, very distressing to the people, few acres were indeed gone over, although there were rather more than a hundred negroes employed, one day with another, digging only those holes in the ground." Day after day of such toil exhausted the workers. Harvesting and processing were only slightly less arduous. During one excellent crop year on Golden Grove, Simon Taylor noted that the mill had been operating continuously for nearly nine months, "in which time the poor wretches of Negroes have not had above six hours of rest out of 24, & what with getting their little provisions etc. what time have they had to Sleep." He encouraged Arcedeckne to hire jobbers for the next rounds of holing and planting, for the estate could not keep up the pace "without murdering the Negroes."[72]

Seeking short-term profits, many slaveholders used the threat of the lash to push the gangs well beyond the breaking point. Dedicated planters like Simon Taylor often complained about unscrupulous overseers and attorneys who worked laborers to death, as Taylor put it, "to aggrandize an Overseer's name by saying he made such and such a crop for a year or two," and then moved on, before proprietors discovered the extent of the damage. In the early 1780s Taylor accused the overseer John Kelly of "driving every thing to the Devil to make a great crop to get himself a name" and then blaming future failures on events beyond his control. The enslaved had a common saying about men like Kelly: "Buckra make whip do every ting, but make life, and that it no able to do, but it make plenty dead."[73]

As difficult as the work was, it might have been physically bearable if the workers had been well nourished. Even when they combined their weekly rations with produce from their gardens, slaves achieved only marginally adequate nutrition. The caloric content of their diets barely matched their energy needs. In other words, they ate just enough to keep on working. In stressful times—during planting season, droughts, storms, or speedups in production—they often starved. Hunger and poor nutrition impaired plantation workers' ability to resist illness. Africans were already threatened when they entered infectious environments for which they had scant natural immunity. Densely populated plantation villages provided ideal conditions for the spread of dysentery and influenza. Personal depression, brought on by the harrowing migration and constant repression, further handicapped their immune systems and compounded the risk of illness. Poor diet also aggravated the effects of common bowel and respiratory diseases, which were among the most common causes of death.[74]

The farther slaves stayed from sugar-cultivating field gangs, the healthier they would be and the longer they could expect to live. When slaves worked in a task system, where they could accomplish their prescribed duties and then find extra time to cultivate their crops or to fish, hunt, and trade, they ate better. Slaves in towns had more diverse opportunities. Wharf workers had the lowest death rates of any slaves in Jamaica. If plantation slaves could secure lighter workloads or higher-status occupations like driver, craftsman, or stockkeeper, they could enjoy more food, rest, and longevity. But those jobs were difficult to obtain: women, commonly excluded from craft work and stock work, were often materially dependent on men; the position of driver was frequently reserved for older slaves who had already proved themselves and had gained the trust of their masters. Even so, the death rates for all these workers, as well as their friends and kin on the sugar estates, remained high enough to teach everyone that life was fleeting and that early death was a prominent feature of slavery.[75]

As long as slavery continued, however, the lethal conditions weighed most heavily on infants and children. The most common killer of infants was neonatal tetanus, commonly known as lockjaw. Children died also from maladies that afflicted adults: bowel disorders, sore throats, colic, whooping cough, measles, smallpox, yaws, worms, and others. Early nineteenth-century observers estimated that of all children born to slaves, between 25 and 50 percent died before their first birthday. On the Worthy

Park plantation there were 345 live births during the five years between 1787 and 1792. Within the same five-year period 186 of these children died. Absentee planter Matthew Lewis was astonished by the rate of child mortality when he visited his plantation in 1816. One woman who had recently lost a child "had borne ten children, and yet has now but one alive: another, at present in the hospital, has borne seven, and but one has lived to puberty; and the instances of those who have had four, five, six children, without succeeding in bringing up one, in spite of the utmost attention and indulgence, are very numerous." Infant mortality was probably even higher than 50 percent. Simon Taylor observed in 1789, "Four children out of five die within the first nine days after they are born." Planters often did not bother to record a birth before the baby had survived for at least nine days, however, a practice that makes more accurate estimates of infant mortality nearly impossible.[76]

Enslaved women shared the fatalism of planters; neither expected many newborns to survive. As one midwife told Matthew Lewis, "Oh, massa, till nine days over, we *no hope* of them." Once a child had survived its early years, however, a mother could give herself permission to hope. Abba, one of Thomas Thistlewood's domestic slaves, raised her son Johnie for six and a half years. When he took seriously ill early in 1771, she was, according to Thistlewood, "almost out of her senses." Johnie died within four days of having fallen sick; Abba, her master noted, was "quite frantic & [would] hear no reason." That night Thistlewood had another slave dig a grave near Abba's house, and Johnie was interred in a small coffin, as several people from Thistlewood's Egypt and the neighboring plantation sang ritual farewells.[77]

High child mortality meant that the Jamaican slave population would never sustain its numbers by natural means. By the late 1780s, West Indian planters were under pressure from officials back in England to do something about child mortality. In 1789 the Jamaican assembly voted to offer bounties to overseers for every enslaved child that survived to the age of one. Between 1790 and 1810, Simon Taylor's efforts on the Golden Grove plantation enabled thirteen or fourteen infants to survive each year, but on average during this time sixteen adults died annually. At the Mesopotamia plantation nearly twice as many deaths as births were recorded between 1762 and 1831. Attorneys at the Radnor plantation recorded thirty-two births and forty-one deaths between February 1822 and February 1826. At the Worthy Park plantation the slave population was self-sustaining for only six of the fifty-five years in the period from 1783 to 1838. From 1783 through 1792 alone, there were fifty-one births on the plantation and ninety-two deaths. Not counting the addition of newcomers, the enslaved Jamaican population as a whole suffered a rate of annual decrease averaging between 2 and 3 percent during the two periods from 1739 to 1787 and 1817 to 1832, for which reasonably good figures are available. Until the end of the transatlantic slave trade, Jamaican planters essentially externalized the costs of raising children to villages in Africa.[78]

Catastrophic events accelerated the steady wastage of human life. Famines and epidemics frequently accompanied wars and hurricanes. At the onset of the American Revolution, for instance, a sharp reduction in trade between Jamaica and North America initiated a food shortage. Then, on 4 October 1780, a massive hurricane tore through the western part of the island, killing more than a thousand people and destroying precious crops. William Beckford, a resident planter, described the devastation: "The stench that arose from the putrefecation of dead bodies, which remained for many weeks without interment . . . occasioned a kind of pestilence that swept away a great proportion of those who providently escaped the first destruction. Almost every person in the town and neighborhood was affected; and the [medical] faculty were rendered incapable, through sickness, to attend their patients many of whom perished from the inclemency of the weather, from want of attendance, or supply of food." Hurricanes battered the island again in 1781, 1784, 1785, and 1786, with similar effects. In August 1786, Simon Taylor reported a "Famine all over the Island," in which he believed "some thousand of Negroes" would die "for want of wholesome food by Fluxes & Dropsies." Planters during this period, in the midst of accounting for their total property losses, estimated that over fifteen thousand slaves had died from the resulting deprivations.[79]

Such disastrous demographic circumstances made the slave trade all the more important. Had it not been for fresh recruits from Africa, plantation slavery in Jamaica might have rapidly exhausted itself. In the 1760s Simon Taylor thought that sixteen to twenty new slaves were needed each year on Golden Grove. Yet given the prosperity of the time, he was able to assure Arcedeckne, "In three years time each Negroe will pay for himself."

Thanks to similar assessments on the part of slaveholders throughout the island concerning death and wealth, the slave population continued to grow until the end of the trade. Jamaica imported as many as 750,000 Africans between the late seventeenth and early nineteenth centuries, but on the eve of emancipation in 1838, just over 300,000 enslaved people remained.[80]

Over the Threshold

From the mid-eighteenth century through the end of chattel slavery, in one of history's greatest episodes of creative destruction, Jamaica's dynamic and profitable economy consumed its inhabitants. Death regularly struck down people no matter what their age, the lowly and the powerful alike. What implications did that fact have for the way people conducted themselves in Jamaican slave society? This is a question that demographic overviews cannot answer. Aggregates compiled from accounting records yield few insights into how people interpreted and experienced the high rate of mortality. Such summary reports tell us even less about how understandings of death drove people to take consequential action. Seen from a distance, the magnitude of the problem is clear, but to understand how the society developed as it did and how particular circumstances motivated people to make historic changes, we must imagine the situation from the inside, ascertaining as best we can how people made meaning of their experiences. How, in a frenzied, high-stakes game of chance, did white immigrants build a society on the ruins of human life and dignity? How did the enslaved make their way in a world where they were numerically superior but which others owned and operated for the benefit of the few? Jamaica's residents saw the story of Atlantic slavery, in its broad outlines, as a dramatic chronicle of evil and opportunity, in which death was both the central character and the guiding motif. The disheartening chant of the women who introduced Robert Renny and his fellow passengers to Jamaica, Abraham James's rough satirical portrait of sickness and dissolution, Simon Taylor's shrewd calculations of profit and loss, and the unquiet spirits of the children who died aboard the *Ruby* all demand that the history of slavery be told alongside the history of death.

In *Sugar and Slaves*, the classic study of the rise of the British Caribbean planter class, the historian Richard Dunn speculated, "the specter of death helps to explain the frenetic tempo and mirage-like quality of West Indian life . . . It was impossible to think of the sugar islands as home when they were such a demographic disaster area." Dunn's insight is the necessary starting point for any meaningful account of life in Jamaican society. For instance, it explains much of the reaction by the colonial elite. Lady Maria Nugent, who accompanied her husband to Jamaica when he went out to govern the colony in 1801, was immediately struck by the precariousness of life. Just one month after arriving she wrote in her diary: "Rise at 6, and was told, at breakfast, that the usual occurrence of a death had taken place. Poor Mr. Sandford had died at 4 o'clock this morning. My dear N. and I feel it very much, but all around us appeared to be quite callous." Indeed, long-term residents of Jamaica soon grew accustomed to short life expectancies. The "frequent occurrence" of death, another visitor remarked in the early 1830s, "renders it an object of far less solemnity than in England. The victims are almost immediately forgotten: another fills their office, and their place knows them no more for ever." Like many members of the wealthy elite, who never fully adjusted to life in Jamaica, Maria Nugent was eager to leave. Not long before she finally departed, she concluded that Jamaican social life had only three topics of conversation: debt, disease, and death. "It is, indeed," she wrote, "truly shocking."[81]

Lady Nugent consoled herself by reading William Dodd's *Reflections upon Death*. Six months into her sojourn she described it as her favorite book. She must have agreed fervently with Dodd's lament. "It is too commonly found," he offered, "that a familiarity with death, and a frequent recurrence of funerals, graves, and church-yards, serves to harden rather than humanize the mind; and to deaden rather than arouse those becoming reflections, which such objects seem excellently calculated to produce."[82] Yet Dodd's assumption was misleading. Familiarity with death and proximity to the dead may have removed the shock people felt on confronting mortality, but it did not render them inert.

Those who lived in Jamaica had to build their short lives and fleeting dreams on "demographic disaster." On the island they created new worlds of meaning in a politically charged "space of death." The inhabitants of colonial Jamaica were always on the threshold of death. Morbidity and the heightened ephemeral quality of life made all of them overwhelmingly aware of their mortality. Few could have had confidence in their odds of surviving. For people living in what was essentially a liminal state between existence and the afterlife, final rites of passage and relations with the dead took on added significance, generating some of Jamaica's most intense and significant political activity. As they articulated symbolic representations of death, ritualized the passing of life, and memorialized the dead, Jamaica's inhabitants struggled to fulfill desires inspired by convention and circumstance.[83]

Early colonial Jamaica was much more than a failed settler society; it was an abundant garden of power and terror. Demographic turmoil, rather than terminating social development and stifling cultural practice, was a seedbed for particular forms of being, belonging, and striving appropriate to this world of relentless exploitation. It is thus less revealing to see the extravagant death rate in Jamaican society as an impediment to the formation of culture than it is to view it as the landscape of culture itself, the ground that produced Atlantic slavery's most meaningful idioms. Death served as the principal arena of social life and gave rise to its customs. Africans and Europeans, whites and blacks, all tilled the same haunted ground, but they planted different seeds and reaped different harvests.

Some strove to turn the steady squandering of human life to profitable advantage, while others fought to strengthen the basic ligatures of social belonging. Adapting to the accelerated life cycle, people turned demographic flux into social order. They struggled to establish intelligible patterns for group cohesion, and the reproduction of family, hierarchy, and prosperity—however they defined these. In all their efforts, people translated their views of death into idioms of power and protest: funerals were occasions to articulate communal values, bequests served to buttress familial networks against future fluctuations, and claimants to authority made partisan use of the dead. The living regularly reached over the threshold to draw potency from the afterlife.

꘏

CHAPTER TWO

Last Rites and First Principles

FREQUENT DEATHS OCCASIONED regular funerals. Fittingly, Abraham James's satirical portrayal of life in Jamaica concludes with Johnny's humble burial in a cramped churchyard (Figure 2.1). Five or six pairs of legs, faintly visible at the top of the frame, represent anonymous and interchangeable onlookers at an all-too-common occurrence. Johnny's coffin lies next to an open grave. Three sets of figures dominate the scene: three men, three skulls, and three scavengers. The people—a slave, a lawyer, and a priest—confront three memento mori, death's-head icons urging viewers to be mindful of the transitory nature of temporal existence; natural decay and regeneration are represented by three crabs scuttling toward the burial pit.[1]

As an impressionistic interpretation of Jamaican society, James's closing image makes a provocative statement. The skulls hold the center of attention, indicating the ubiquity of death and the insistent presence of the dead. The icons are not all equal. In the foreground, one of them is etched into a handsome memorial stone, while next to Johnny's grave one set of skull and bones lies unburied. James clearly recognized that, contrary to fatalistic opinion, not all were equal in death. A man who has appeared in previous panels as the lawyer who drafted Johnny's will, Mr. Codicil, now appears as a sexton, standing beside the grave with a shovel, eager, perhaps, to bury the body and begin managing Johnny's estate. An enslaved man, standing where one might expect to see a family member, looks on, as the clergyman, barely in the panel, reads the service. Slavery,

Figure 2.1. Funeral of Johnny New-come: "Hic Jacet Joannes New-come" (Here lies John New-come), detail from *Johnny New-come in the Island of Jamaica,* by Abraham James (London, 1800). Courtesy of the National Library of Jamaica.

property, and the church are renewed, as torrid nature rushes to devour the individual.

Though James's satirical depiction does little to evoke the grieving process, so crucial to acknowledging and healing the disruptions caused by death, his sharp outline of Jamaican society, defined at the moment of Johnny New-come's interment, suggests a compelling way of perceiving the impact of death upon life. Burial ceremonies, as final rites of passage and ritual farewells, provide an outlet for anguish and an opportunity for commiseration. Yet they also shape social order. At each stage in a customary sequence—determining the cause of death, preparing the body for burial, accompanying the corpse to the grave site, eulogizing and sermonizing, celebrating life, mourning loss, and consigning the departed to the spiritual world—last rites for the dead help individuals and groups confront death as universal and final, while, even more important, encouraging them to contemplate publicly what it means to be alive. Death rites thus provide an opportunity for people to enact social values, to express their vision of what it is that binds their community together, makes its members unique, and separates them from others. That is why final rites of passage are a powerful source of moral guidance. As one of the most basic obligations, burial customs have a privileged role in determining ideals and standards of human conduct.[2]

Last rites in Jamaica articulated the first principles of slave society—the meaningful codes of conduct that organized public life and its categories of belonging. The precarious demography of tropical life kept families and communal institutions in flux.[3] But though demographic catastrophe could have rendered all social patterns transitory and fleeting, Jamaican society was partially structured by the ideals enacted in death rites. Participation in such rites of passing gave enduring form and pattern to Jamaican life, shaping the terms of social interaction by providing frequent occasions for people to indicate group boundaries and to act out their vision of social hierarchy. Demarcating the limits of affiliation and exclusion at ceremonies for the dead, Africans divided themselves into "nations"; the enslaved recognized internal distinctions; and whites delineated and underscored the supposed differences between themselves and "mulattoes" or blacks, as well as that most important division between free and enslaved.

Within the company of slaveholders, mortuary rituals symbolized wealth, rank, and white supremacy. Inquiries into cause of death, and the routine business of burial, ratified standards of governance rooted in property ownership and racial dominance. Even the established Church of England, nominally concerned with the passage of souls to the afterlife, owed its existence in Jamaica to the proceeds it took in from death services, relying on finely calibrated estimations of the material worth of the dead. Among Africans and their descendants in Jamaica, funeral rites shaped moral idioms that highlighted their common humanity and values, often transcending and challenging the dominant mores and imperatives of slavery. Evocations of kinship and ancestry during funerals yoked participants to their past, even in the accelerated world organized by slaveholders' expectant outlook. The skills involved in communing with the spirit world endowed select individuals with social authority, as well as a status that was not wholly determined by the power of masters. In the violent and volatile context of Jamaican slavery, the semiautonomous ideals of the enslaved could constitute a significant countervailing political force.[4] Though amassing property was the more urgent concern for whites, and community building was for the enslaved, no simple opposition existed between white materialism and black communalism. Rather, communal values and material exchanges were intertwined for everyone, as people used death rites to define and signify categories of belonging, measures of status, moral injunctions, and shared desires—the ordering principles that helped construct society from catastrophe.

Burial and Belonging

Everywhere in Jamaica, one could hear the sounds of black funerals. Because of the rate at which the enslaved expired and the depth of their ubiquitous experience with sickness and death, funerary rites were an urgent priority and were perhaps their most extensive basis of social communion. "Their principal festivals are at their burials," noticed the resident planter William Beckford, "upon which occasions they call forth all their magnificence, and display all their taste." They gathered in groups that could number into the hundreds, to weep, feast, joke, tell stories, dance, and sing. "The death beat of the gumbay," remarked Alexander Barclay, was "heard almost every night on some one or other of the plantations."[5]

For the most part, black people organized and managed funerals without white intervention. Slaveholders cared little about black customs, as long as they did not impair their slaves' capacity for labor. From time to time, the colonial state passed regulations to prohibit large gatherings or the use of loud instruments, which could be used to communicate over long distances, but enforcement was lax. Slaves outnumbered masters by more than ten to one, and slaveholders were acutely aware that they had to make some tactical concessions to keep the plantations working. In the eighteenth century, when their funerals were almost always held at night, the enslaved gathered outside the surveillance of the plantation regime to recognize powers that transcended the preeminence of their oppressors. Night after night, in slave villages or secluded clearings all over the island, diverse assemblies of mourning slaves showed contempt for the conditions of their enslavement by articulating their own ideas about the proper social arrangements in the temporal no less than in the spiritual world. As solemn rites, "on no account to be dispensed with," in Barclay's words, burials provided a focus for sacred practices and beliefs.[6]

From vast expanses of Atlantic Africa came people with specific ideas about how to ritualize the passing of life. Brought together in towns and on plantations, they argued over ways to put previously known principles into practice as their situations required. Various groups of Africans and native black Jamaicans—Christians, Muslims, and adherents of myriad traditional faiths—worked out appropriate funeral ceremonies. Olaudah Equiano maintained that Africans in Jamaica retained "most of their native customs," such as burying their dead with pipes, tobacco, and other grave goods "in the same manner as in Africa." Yet these were not the same people they had been in Africa. Drawn from hundreds of villages, scores of polities, and numerous linguistic groups, they recognized categories of belonging in Jamaica that had not had the same purchase in the Old World. During their dislocating migrations and the resulting desperate interactions, people from the environs of the Bight of Biafra or the Gold Coast congregated as Eboes and Coromantees, for example—new "nations" in the Americas. These and others forged alliances based on shared languages, similar principles of social organization, and similar memories of the African landscape and territories. In order to cohere, however, these groups had not only to recognize their similarities, but also to mark their differences from one another. In this undertaking, the funeral ceremony was a primary locus of belonging and exclusion, an opportunity to express and enact ideas about group membership and cultural distinctness.[7]

As people gathered to bury and celebrate the dead, they found some ritual practices to be mutually exclusive. In different parts of Africa ceremonial performances varied in duration and complexity. People from different regions had different ideas about how bodies were to be washed, shrouded, or clothed for interment. Some buried the dead beneath their houses or in family compounds; others used sacred grounds outside villages. Some laid grave goods in the tomb—buried the dead with jewelry, tools, or other objects of ritual significance. In Jamaica the enslaved identified distinct groupings according to their funeral practices. Yet in order to establish meaningful distinctions, people had to come together; they recognized the differences by meeting in common celebrations. Of necessity, narrower territorial identifications yielded to broader association, for enslavement and dislocation had fractured ancestral communities. At the same time, common participation in collective rituals produced new distinctions. The process was continuous. In specific locales around the island, cohorts of recent arrivals from Africa transformed the character of belief and ritual as their numbers and influence allowed.[8]

Some ideas and some ceremonial practices were relatively constant. Common perceptions of relations with the dead formed the basic elements of a moral discourse that Africans and their descendants used in an effort to regulate their interactions with one another and oppose the tenets of their masters. In Jamaican slave society, much as anthropologist Melville Herskovits recognized in early twentieth-century West Africa, relations with ancestors represented "the most important single sanctioning force for the social system and the codes of behavior that underlie it."[9] During funerals, enslaved blacks created a shared moral universe: they recovered their common humanity, they assumed and affirmed meaningful social roles, and they rendered communal values sacred by associating them with the dead.

Divided though they might be by language, regional identification, gender, or occupation, enslaved Africans nevertheless held some common assumptions about death. Throughout large areas of western Africa, people shared similar "cosmological orientations" and basic practices having to do with relations between the living and the dead.[10] Most Atlantic Africans recognized a supernatural hierarchy, from a high god to lesser territorial deities and down to ancestors and the spirits of the dead. With these otherworldly beings, most especially with the dead, they maintained active relations. From extensive interviews conducted among Africans in the Danish West Indies in 1767–1768, the Moravian missionary Christian George Andreas Oldendorp concluded, "There is almost no nation in Guinea that does not believe in the immortality of the soul. It is also understood by them that the soul continues living after its separation from the body, that it has certain needs, that it carries on various activities, and that it is capable of experiencing both happiness and misery." Physical death represented only the separation of body and spirit. The spirit—variously called the soul, life, breath, shadow, or double, for many Africans believed people to have more than one soul—then made its way to the spirit world or lingered, sometimes ominously, around its dead body or homestead. During his first year in Jamaica, through conversations with the enslaved, Thomas Thistlewood learned of *duppies,* the spirits of the dead, who could harm or (sometimes) aid the living. He was also told of evil spirits that could lure people to their death by posing as friends and relatives. The appropriate burial of the body was necessary to send spirits properly on their way to the other world, both as a precaution against haunting and to ensure their benevolence toward the living. Burial rites generally involved sacrifices and offerings: the blood of animals, sacrificed to protect the living from the angry dead, and foodstuffs, tobacco, and drink to nourish the spirit on its journey. "Their treatment of the deceased," observed Oldendorp, "reveals the fact that they consider their condition to be little different from that of the living, attributing to the former the very same needs whose fulfillment was necessary for them when alive." Funerals also involved ritual song, dance, and percussive rhythm, the means of communicating with spirits of all kinds. Such communication and offerings were necessary because most if not all Africans believed that the dead played an active role in worldly affairs.[11]

Spirited Inquests

Before burial, on the way to the grave, a dead person could admonish wrongdoers and shape communal values. Europeans frequently remarked upon the way that funeral processions included supernatural inquests into the cause of death. The enslaved seldom considered untimely demise to be "natural." Consequently, the first requirement in laying the dead to rest was to divine what malevolent forces were responsible for the killing. As pallbearers carried the body, laid upon an open bier or—less frequently— in a coffin, they became mediums for the departing spirit. They were directed one way or another by the spirit, which made a point of stopping at nearly every home in the slave quarters to demand reparations and atonement from debtors and enemies. Described in similar ways over a century-long period, the procession appears to have remained pretty much the same in character from the mid-eighteenth to the mid-nineteenth century (Figure 2.2).[12]

"When one is carried out to his Grave," observed Charles Leslie in 1740, "he is attended with a vast Multitude, who conduct his Corps in something of a ludicrous Manner: They sing all the Way, and they who bear it on their Shoulders, make a Feint of stopping at every Door they pass, and pretend, that if the deceast Person had received any Injury, the Corps moves toward that House, and that they can't avoid letting it fall to the

HEATHEN PRACTICES AT FUNERALS.

Figure 2.2. Afro-Jamaican funeral procession. *Heathen Practices at Funerals,* engraving, in James M. Phillippo, *Jamaica: Its Past and Present State* (London, 1843), facing 244, depicts a coffin divination ceremony from the early nineteenth century, at once a spirited inquest into the causes of social discord and a curative ritual for enslaved communities. Courtesy of Harvard College Library.

Ground when before the Door."[13] Over a hundred years later, Baptist missionary James Phillippo published a similar but more detailed account:

> When on the way with the corpse to interment, the bearers, who were often intoxicated, practised the most strange and ridiculous manoeuvres. They would sometimes make a sudden halt, put their ears in a listening attitude against the coffin, pretending that the corpse was endowed with the gift of speech—that he was angry and required to be appeased, gave instructions for a different distribution of his property, objected to his mode of conveyance, or refused to proceed farther towards the place of burial until some debts due to him were discharged, some slanderous imputation on his character removed, some theft confessed, or until they (the bearers) were presented with renewed potations of rum: and the more the effectually to delude the multitude, and thereby enforce their claims, to some of which they were often instigated by the chief mourners, they would pretend to answer the questions of the deceased, echo his requirements, run back with the coffin upon the procession, or jerk with it from side to side of the road; not unfrequently, and the most trivial pretence,

they would leave the corpse at the door or in the house of a debtor or neighbour indiscriminately, resist every importunity for its removal, until his pretended demands were satisfied.[14]

The supernatural inquests originated in West Africa. Viewing the rite in the Danish West Indies, Oldendorp claimed inaccurately that it was exclusive to the "Amina" Africans from the Gold Coast. There, the practice seems to have been employed to help discern the worthiness of the body for proper burial. If the bearers could not "move forward, but rather are pulled backward, even after exerting all their physical strength," it was thought that the deceased "did not belong to God." In such an event, the body would be "thrown into the bush, far from the graves of honourable people." The naval lieutenant John Matthews observed "the ceremony of interrogating the corpse" in the Sierra Leone region in the 1780s, though the inquests were carried out with a different aim there. The rituals reported by Matthews were conducted to find murderers or witches. According to Olaudah Equiano, Africans in the Bight of Biafra held similar consultations with corpses if foul play was a suspected cause of death.[15]

The origins of cultural practices did not determine their uses. In Jamaica, the spirited burial processions probably served a number of purposes. Just as interrogations of the dead had varying functions in Africa, various groups of slaves in Jamaica certainly attached different meanings to similar rituals. In the context of such ceremonies, people probably employed distinctive ritual procedures and goals to mark their group differences, even as they established general mores on which most could agree. Whether the spirit spoke out to accuse or to convey its own moral essence, the funeral also provided an occasion for social persuasion.

In the course of placating the dead person and sending the soul on its way, the supernatural inquest shaped values among the enslaved in a very significant way. As the pallbearers, in their role as mediums for the deceased, passed each house in the slave quarters, they demarcated a community by reminding everyone of the part he or she had played in the life of the late man, woman, or child. Acting as the focus of community memory, the dead had enormous power to enforce communal values. The corpse, the physical link between human life and the spirit world, was a potent material symbol of a group's cohesiveness. It evoked a sense of fellowship considered by funeral participants to be timeless—at least for the duration of the ritual—an eternal sense of belonging in a transcendent moment.[16]

When the corpse (or its mediums) spoke, it invested communal principles and codes of conduct with a significance that transcended material time and space, giving eternal importance to the collective precepts expressed. Offenses that had been committed against the deceased had to be atoned for before the spirit could leave the community. The threat of spectral revenge was supposed to be the severest moral sanction against thieves, debtors, and witches. Justice would be enforced, if not by the living, then by the dead. The coffin procession also promoted harmony among the enslaved. When friends and relatives acted as mediums for the deceased, they not only made criminal accusations on behalf of the dead, but also complained about petty conflicts—"treachery, ingratitude, injustice, slander"—that threatened the peace of the slave quarters. These complaints articulated the ideals of the enslaved: loyalty, gratitude, justice, and adulation. For slaves in Jamaica fundamental mores were expressed most forcefully at the intersection of life and death, during funeral processions and burial ceremonies. These principles were meant to govern relations between the living and the dead, no less than those among the living. Thus individuals, families, social groups, and ancestors could share a moral universe that revolved around the final rite of passage.[17]

Call and Response

The enslaved recovered a sense of their common humanity at funerals. Though national groups formed the core of the gatherings, burial ceremonies were generally open to all who chose to attend, excepting, in most cases, whites and their offspring. Blacks affirmed their common connections to the dead through participation in intensely emotional ritual practices. Interment of the dead usually involved feasting; sharing among the mourners was an essential activity. For favored slaves, planters provided rum, Madeira, sugar, or flour for the feasts and offerings, but most of the contributions—chickens, a hog, fruits and vegetables—came from provision grounds or petty thefts. Leslie wrote, "Cool Drink (which is made of the *Lignum vitae* Bark) or whatever else they can afford, is distributed among these who are present" after the burial; "the one Half of the Hog is burnt while they are drinking, and the other is left to any Person who pleases to take it."[18]

Building their ceremonies around dance and rhythmic music, Africans and those close to them stressed their cultural similarities, even as they reinforced the distinctness from nonblacks. Whites and persons of mixed heritage who identified with whites rarely shared the rapport that Africans found in graveside musical celebration. Just before Mulatto Will died on Thomas Thistlewood's plantation in 1758, he specified that he wanted to "be buried at . . . his Mother (Dianah's) right hand, and that no Negroes Should Sing &c." Unwelcome at most slave burials, Thomas Thistlewood scrawled sparse notes about them from within his overseer's house: "All last night & today, a vast of company, with singing & c. at the Negro houses, with Franke, for the loss of her husband, Quashe. She killed a heifer, several hogs, &c. to entertain her company with. Delivered Franke a jug of rum, 8 gallons or more."[19]

Europeans, in commenting on slave funerals, rarely failed to remark on the communal production of the music. With little admiration, Edward Long noted that "every funeral is a kind of festival; at which the greater part of the company assume an air of joy and unconcern; and, together with their singing, dancing, and musical instruments, conspire to drown all sense of affliction in the minds of the real mourners." The slaveholders' advocate Alexander Barclay included an eyewitness account of similar orchestrations in his 1826 apology for West Indian slavery. One night, only a few weeks into his sojourn in Jamaica, Barclay was awakened by what he described as "a strange and unearthly sound of music." From his window, he saw "a large body of negroes, two of them with a coffin on their heads, with which they were wheeling round and dancing." The others carried torches as they danced and sang, "yelling unlike anything human," in Barclay's untutored opinion. Black funeral music made such an impression on him that he attempted a crude twelve-bar notation for the benefit of his readers (Figure 2.3). "Probably African," offered Barclay, who judged the music as follows: "To me it appears strikingly wild and melancholy, associated as it is in my mind with such recollections, and heard for the first time sung by savages interring their dead at the midnight hour."[20]

Call-and-response singing accompanied burial parties to the grave site. There, close family members of the deceased joined in singing with the

Figure 2.3. Afro-Jamaican funeral music, in Alexander Barclay, *A Practical View of the Present State of Slavery in the West Indies* (London, 1826). That the notation is an actual attempt to describe African music is suggested by the pentatonic (five-note) scale, common to African but not European composition of the time. Barclay appears to have assumed mistakenly that the melody was the most meaningful aspect, as was customary in European music. In choosing to represent a single vocal line in his notation, he ignores the polyphonic character of African musical arrangements. He also appears to have simplified the rhythm (tapped out on a bell or maintained by clapping of hands), in translating the time signature from 12/8 (common in Atlantic Africa) to 6/8. Curiously, he described the tune as "melancholy," though he emphasized that the melody was in a major key, whereas Europeans generally agree that sadness is conveyed by the minor. Courtesy of Harvard College Library.

gathering crowd. "All the while they are covering [the body] with Earth," Charles Leslie wrote, "the Attendants scream out in a terrible Manner, which is not the effect of Grief but of Joy; they beat upon their wooden Drums, and the Women with their Rattles make a hideous Noise." Drumming, dancing, and singing could continue all night. "The instruments resound, the dancers are prepared," recounted William Beckford, "and the night resounds with the chorus of contentment; and the day only rises to awaken in their minds the regret of a necessary departure, and to summon them to their expected work." At such celebrations, sacred rhythms, reconstituted from diverse memories of African ceremonial music, established a fragile but vital concord among the enslaved.[21]

Of course, funerals did not eliminate social distinctions; in important ways, they reinforced them. Burial ceremonies affirmed the social status of the dead. Only well-liked or prominent slaves drew large crowds to their funerals. The most eminent could draw assemblies of more than a thousand, but for many, perhaps most, burial was completely unceremonious. Certainly those who died shortly after arrival, before they had time to form a significant network of social ties, received minimal honors at death. Slaves who had few friends or relatives were interred quickly and simply: an overseer would dispatch a couple of available men to bury the corpse in a crude pit. For others, the extravagance of the ceremonies, as

well as the size of the gathering, would indicate the popularity and importance of the deceased. "The expense with which the funerals of the better
sort of negroes upon a plantation are attended, very often exceed the bounds
of credibility," commented Beckford. Men and women with fruitful provision grounds knew they would be able to supply for their own ceremonies
when the time came. For well-liked people in difficult circumstances, others
made contributions. The character and intensity of the music and dance
also varied according to the status of the deceased. Bryan Edwards observed,
"At the burial of such as were respected in life, or venerable through age,
they exhibit a sort of Pyrrhick or warlike dance, in which their bodies are
strongly agitated by running, leaping, and jumping, with many violent and
frantic gestures and contortions. Their funeral songs are also of a heroic or
martial cast." Long wrote that funeral dirges were "filled with encomiums
on the deceased, with hopes and wishes for his happiness in his new state."
Funerals provided a ceremonial occasion to separate the good and great from
the cursed and mean. The magnificent tributes to favored departing spirits
also demonstrated to everyone present that whites did not determine blacks'
ways of valuing individuals.[22]

Just as ritual participation helped delimit categories of belonging, it also
exhibited internal hierarchies among the enslaved. Quite apart from their
functions in the plantation economy, slaves assumed a meaningful social
role during the performance of ritual obligations. Planters generally did
not care who among their slaves were the best dancers, drummers, or
singers, though they might be amused by their perfor-mances. Black
people, on the other hand, recognized the indispensable contributions of
these performers. In the context of a burial ceremony, musicians and
dancers bore the responsibility for structuring emotions and communicating with the spirit world. Their skills managed what blacks generally
viewed as the most important stage in the life cycle. A gendered division
of labor organized ritual music production. Drummers were always men;
women generally led the singing and accented the rhythm with hand claps
and rattles. Both men and women danced, but each group performed a
different style of movement. Establishing gender distinctions at ceremonies was but one aspect of a larger process of assuming meaningful
roles that could counter the degradation of abject bondage. By establishing
communication that transcended language, according status through ceremonial participation, and valuing skills unconnected with commercial

imperatives, mortuary rituals provided the most profound context for the social differentiations that distinguished the universe of black values from the values of white slaveholders.[23]

In the course of their mortuary obligations, the enslaved also defined familial belonging. Preparations for burial reinforced the significance of kinship and friendship. Family and friends were responsible for wrapping the body in linen, when they could afford it, and decorating it with possessions that the deceased had valued in life. The nearest relation of the deceased bore the responsibility for killing the sacrificial animal. Between a month and a year after interment, select friends and family returned to the grave to sacrifice, feast, and sing again, "congratulating the deceased on her enjoyment of complete happiness," according to Charles Leslie's account. "This was supposed to terminate their mutual obligations." In turn, as a nineteenth-century missionary reported, "each of the party then expressed his wishes of remembrance to his kindred, repeated benedictions on his family, promised to return to them, repeated promises to take care of her children, and bade the deceased an affectionate farewell." Sometimes the sacrifice consecrated explicit lines of descent to underline the authority of fathers and elders. Planter Bryan Edwards described one such sacrificial rite among Africans from the Gold Coast. "Every family has a peculiar tutelar saint, who is supposed to have been originally a human being like one of themselves and the first founder of their family," he explained. At the anniversary of this ancestor's burial, "the whole number of his descendants assemble round his grave, and the oldest man, after offering up praises to [the high gods] Accompong, Assarci, Ipboa, and their tutelar deity, sacrifices a cock or goat, by cutting its throat, and shedding the blood upon the grave." The elder man's sacrifice was followed by offerings from every head of household among the Coromantees in attendance.[24]

The integrity of enslaved families was extremely fragile: the slave trade severed close ties to African ancestors; child mortality blocked lines of descent that might have extended into the future; and the dictates of plantation managers trumped the authority of parents. Yet there is reason to believe that high mortality in Jamaica strengthened affective ties among kin, both genetic and "fictive." Long noticed that "filial disobedience, and insulting the ashes of the dead," were offenses exceeded only by murder. To curse a father, mother, or direct ancestor was "the greatest affront that

could possibly be offered" to Creoles. Edwards appreciated the "high veneration in which old age is held by the Negroes in general." He noticed
that younger blacks often referred to the elderly with the appellations "*Ta*
and *Ma*, signifying Father and Mother, by which designation they mean
to convey not only the idea of filial reverence, but also of esteem and fond-
ness." Moreover, the role of blood relations in funeral ceremonies reestab-
lished some small measure of stability in the organization of families, at
the same time that they accepted intimate friends and "shipmates" into
the family as members.[25]

Even as death tore communities apart, it brought the enslaved together.
Black people did what they could to honor their friends, relations, and
countrymen, though life was fleeting and time was short. Funeral ceremonies, which had been perhaps the most important occasions for communal association in Africa, became still more significant in the context
of demographic calamity in Jamaica. Rapidly changing societies of the
enslaved therefore found enduring patterns—if not traditions—in ceremonies for the dead. Here again, death was productive, stimulating a continual cycle of destruction and renewal: the greater the catastrophe, the
more intensive the regeneration.

The Reverse of "Our" Ceremonies

Slaveholders paid little attention to the deaths of slaves, noting them,
rather, principally as commercial losses or things to be paid for. Planters
performed their most important last rites for slaves when they jotted down
the year-end tallies of estate property, an act of notation as a final commemoration. Simon Taylor talked of "negroes destroyed" and estates
"falling back," but only in a few rare instances did he remark on the implications of black deaths for anything but his worldly ambition. Likewise,
Thomas Thistlewood "seldom expressed strong emotions when his slaves
died," according to his biographer, "even if he had spent considerable time
in their company. He noted dispassionately the deaths of many slaves,
seldom adding to the recognition of their deaths any appreciation of their
particular human qualities."[26]

When whites—slaveholders and nonslaveholders alike—commented on
black funerals, it was generally to express their disdain. European descriptions of expressive styles of movement at funerals as "wild," "frantic," and

"ludicrous" "gesticulations" distinguished appropriate—in other words "white"—decorum at funerals from "negro" lack of restraint. Descriptions of polyrhythmic music as "hideous noise" effectively denigrated one of the most important activities that Africans participated in together. Such disparaging depictions of African sound and movement, used often to characterize a host of other African and black cultural practices as well, played an important role in distinguishing what it meant to be "white" from what it meant to be "Negro" and so helped to secure in the minds of Europeans a general image of "Negro" degradation. In his description of slave funerals, the planter Edward Long eagerly concluded, "Their funerals are the very reverse of our English ceremony." If he knew of the customs in the northern English borderlands—where mourners were compelled to touch corpses because of the belief that the body would bleed at the touch of one guilty of foul play—he was careful not to say (though he did compare black funerals to Highland Scottish and Irish wakes). Characterization of one of the most sacred and emotionally fraught rites of passage in human experience as an uncontrolled manifestation of inherent savagery placed black cultural practice firmly at the bottom of the hierarchy of religion and culture.[27]

Whites saw the slaves' way of mediating on behalf of the dead while carrying the coffin to the grave site as the most outlandish feature of black mortuary practice in Jamaica. The supernatural inquests received disparaging scrutiny in numerous published accounts: Charles Leslie's in 1740, Edward Long's in 1774, Matthew Lewis's in 1816, James Stewart's in 1823, Alexander Barclay's in 1826, and James Phillippo's in 1843. As these authors recycled one another's descriptions or interpreted what they had seen in the light of their predecessors' accounts, they described a funeral procession that remained formally consistent over an extended period of time. They also reproduced and circulated a consistent set of bigoted assumptions about black spirituality. The common language of observers itself says something about their view of African relations with the dead. The words "pretend," "superstition," "ludicrous," "wild," "frantic," "gesticulations," recurring in each of the six published descriptions, indexed the agenda within which whites interpreted slaves' death rites. Their characterizations of "Negro" funerals reflected a comparative framework for thinking about religion, one that encouraged them to despise deviations from Protestant English religious practice.

Europeans commonly understood the mediations of the pallbearers as mere pretense. Of the six authors, only the gothic novelist and absentee plantation owner Matthew Lewis resisted using the verb "pretend" to describe the activity of the pallbearers. Instead, perhaps facetiously, he made the corpse the subject of the action: "If, as is frequently the case, any person is suspected of having hastened the catastrophe, the corpse will then refuse to go any road but the one which passes by the habitation of the suspected person, and as soon as it approaches the house, no human power is equal to persuading it to pass." For the others, identifying "pretense" in the ritual was their way of interpreting the procession as an excuse for fraud. In his account, James Stewart related an anecdote meant to reveal "fraudulent extortion" as the goal of the ritual. "A negro, who was to be interred in one of the towns had, it was pretended by some of his friends, a claim on another negro for a sum of money. The latter denied any such claim; and accordingly, at the funeral of the deceased, the accustomed ceremonies took place opposite the door of his supposed debtor; and this mummery was continued for hours, till the magistrates thought proper to interfere, and compelled the defunct to forego his claim, and proceed quietly on to his place of rest." Understanding the ceremony as little more than a pretext for greed allowed whites to fit the ritual comfortably into their assumptions about the relation between individuals, property, and the dead. Avaricious planters were projecting their own values onto the enslaved, viewing black customs in terms they could well understand.[28]

As capital investments and as chattel, enslaved men and women held value that could, in some circumstances, be redeemed when they died. For instance, slave owners received monetary compensation whenever state intervention resulted in a loss of human property. To construct public works, the parish vestries requisitioned workers from slave owners in the area. Building roads and clearing land was dangerous work, and owners were reluctant to risk their property on public development projects. To encourage compliance with civic duty, the vestries paid owners at least part of the value of any slave killed on such projects.[29]

The public also had more compelling reasons to compensate owners for dead slaves. The perpetual instability of Jamaican society necessitated constant vigilance against slave crimes and uprisings. To quell insurrections, the colonial state often compelled enslaved blacks to help white militias track down runaways and rebels. When slaves died performing military service, owners were again compensated. In one 1745 case, the Kingston vestry requisitioned "30 able Negro men" from William Austin to accompany a party of soldiers when they went out to suppress a band of rebel Africans. According to procedure, the vestrymen assured Austin that "they shall be Valued by any three of the Justices and Vestry and in case of their being kill'd or Maimed they shall be made good Answerable to Valuation." Planters who pursued rebels on their own initiative also filed petitions with the assembly to recover the value of lost slaves. In 1755 a widow, Anne Bennett of Saint Thomas-in-the-East, filed a petition on behalf of her infant son, George Rosewell Bennett—a slaveholder by inheritance—to recover the value of an enslaved man who had been killed in pursuit of a band of runaways. The assembly paid the infant forty pounds for his loss. Public institutions also compensated owners whenever slaves were convicted of serious crimes, executed, transported, or imprisoned for life. Because individual owners wanted to protect their property and therefore had a strong incentive to shield their slaves from prosecution, the assembly passed the 1717 "Act for the more effectual punishing of Crimes by Slaves," though it initially limited the recoverable value to forty pounds, paid by the island treasury. Early on, the policy invited abuse by unscrupulous slaveholders. In 1739 an assembly committee discovered that several slaves had been executed for petty thefts and other "crimes of no account," that their owners had had them prosecuted "for the sake of lucre, and in hopes of being paid for the said negroes."[30]

If slaveholders imagined that black funerals were an opportunity for personal material benefit, they were probably projecting their own intentions, their grasping efforts at monetary gain. Black people, in affirming their own sense of belonging and social value, rather than commercial worth, held celebrations for their dead that were in fact the very reverse of slaveholders'.

"By the Visitation of God"

The last rites of whites played a comparable key role in establishing communal values and shaping social order. Alongside the requisite tributes to ancestors and deities, socioeconomic and racial distinctions were determined. Whereas burial ceremonies for the enslaved helped articulate nationhood, advocate harmony, and celebrate black talents, white funerals enshrined the pursuit of wealth and white supremacy as society's first principles. White solidarity in the face of an overwhelmingly black population was crucial to the social order of colonial slavery. Accordingly, national and ethnic differences were not permitted to create invidious divisions among whites. Scots, English, and even Irish, French, and Spanish people, shared a social station in relation to the mass of enslaved blacks. Indeed, despite great disparities in fortune, whites were able to maintain surprisingly egalitarian relations with one another—at least by comparison with norms of behavior current in Europe.[31] They did, however, signal their achievements, aspirations, and claims to status through final rites of passing, in the process enacting and affirming hierarchical principles of social value. In state investigations into causes of death, in the way the established church valued and honored the dead, and at funerals that expressed the aspirations of the deceased and marked the desired boundaries of community, white society established distinctive patterns in the midst of Jamaica's demographic disarray. In ways appropriate to an aggressively materialistic society, whites in Jamaica marked social distinctions with fee schedules for burial services, symbolic displays of rank, and rituals of belonging and exclusion.

Just as last rites among the enslaved included inquests, the colonial state required coroners to investigate mysterious fatalities. Black supernatural inquests were a matter of curiosity and puzzlement to white observers, who rarely understood the role of these rituals in articulating the first principles of enslaved communities. Had they noted the social purpose of the slaves' divinations, they might have recognized that black and white inquests performed a similar function: both laid out the axes, boundaries, and values of community. What the extravagantly energetic movements of the pallbearers did for communal values in fractious and embattled slave villages, state inquests did for the slave masters—specifically, by inscribing white supremacy into official accounts of death.

Administered at the parish level, the office of coroner was usually held by men of respectable standing who were elected or selected by the freeholders of a local community. Following English precedent, Jamaican law required coroners "to take inquisitions on the bodies of all persons who shall die in gaol, or be found dead in other places," and to "issue warrants for summoning jurors." Coroner's juries consisted of white men from nearby farms and plantations. Jamaica's Act for Regulating Fees (1711) provided that coroners be paid three pounds "out of the estate of the person deceased, and where no estate is found, then to be paid by the churchwardens of the parish where the inquisition is taken." Coroners had an obvious financial stake in performing investigations into the deaths of slaves, but they also shared their peers' desire to safeguard the value of whiteness in slave society, one of the principal instruments of social control over the enslaved population. The inquests applied roughly the same racial distinctions to the dead that ordered the society of the living.[32]

The law was vague about inquests for slaves, and coroners often had trouble collecting their fees for such inquiries. The churchwardens often refused to pay for inquests involving enslaved blacks, on the assumption that there was little purpose or public benefit in determining the cause of a slave's death. The high mortality rate placed a heavy burden on coroners, who traveled incessantly throughout the parish to perform their duties. They complained frequently of the burdens of their employment and petitioned to recover compensation for inquests into the deaths of slaves. To resolve their difficulties, in 1770 the assembly passed "An Act for Settling the Proceedings and Fees of the Coroners." It stipulated that coroners should be paid the customary three pounds for an inquest "on a white person or a person of free condition, out of the goods and chattels of the person found dead; but if no goods or chattels of the deceased shall be found, or such person be a slave," the parish churchwardens would pay the fee.[33]

The churchwardens, who remained reluctant to assign the same value to inquests into the deaths of whites and blacks, often neglected to pay for seemingly worthless information on the deaths of blacks; but absolute neglect became more difficult in the late eighteenth and early nineteenth centuries, when inquests on corpses of the enslaved acquired political urgency. As the antislavery movement in England increasingly heaped criticism on the plantocracy in the 1780s, at least one legislator attempted to limit sadistic abuses against the enslaved by requiring stricter inquiries into their causes of death. A Jamaica assemblyman, concerned that slaves frequently "came to their Deaths by hasty and severe blows, and other improper treatment of overseers and book-keepers," and then were buried immediately "to conceal the truth of the cause of the death," proposed adding a clause to the "consolidated Negro bill" being considered by the assembly in 1787.

Though the clause did not become law, his proposal raised expectations that coroners should investigate deaths of the enslaved in the public interest. Coroners, who had mainly been responsible for inquests into the causes of white deaths, now claimed a greater responsibility to investigate the deaths of blacks. Vestrymen mitigated the outrage planters felt, once they actually began to pay the three pounds for blacks, by voluntarily raising the fee for white bodies to five pounds. The difference in fees was henceforth based on race rather than slave or free status. The graduated value of inquests for blacks and whites, by reinforcing the imagined hierarchy of black and white personhood, strengthened white supremacy in concrete terms. Only with the Coroner's Act of 1817 did an actual law establish a clear and unambiguous requirement that coroners perform inquests into the deaths of slaves, also stipulating that slaveholders could not be jurors at inquests concerning their own slaves. A belated response to antislavery pressure, the act established that, in principle, the deaths of black people merited serious investigation.[34]

Yet a story recounted by Benjamin McMahon, who spent eighteen years in Jamaica working as a bookkeeper on several plantations in the nineteenth century, indicates that most whites considered inquests concerning slaves to be an annoying interruption in the prerogatives of white supremacy. This was true even of coroners, whose loyalties were divided between their legal obligations and the patronage of prominent slaveholders. McMahon described one coroner's role in the case of an enslaved man who had been poisoned and buried clandestinely on a small property called Phillip's Valley. In June 1821 Dr. Craig, the plantation doctor in the area, accused Mr. Levy, the proprietor of Phillip's Valley, of committing the crime. As McMahon learned the circumstances, "the man often came to the hospital complaining of sickness. Mr. Levy said it was nothing but skulking, and on this occasion said he would cure him of it, and for this purpose he gave him six grains of tartar emetic which brought on excessive retching for several hours, until he died." Shortly after the man's death, Dr. Craig arrived and recorded in the hospital book that the victim had been killed by an overdose of tartar emetic. In response, Levy expelled Craig from the property. Craig then wrote to the authorities in Kingston, who ordered an inquest.

Three weeks later, the coroner Charles Austin arrived and gathered a jury to hear the case. McMahon accompanied Dr. Craig to the inquest and watched as Mr. Levy ordered Craig to withdraw until called for.

When Craig protested, Austin supported Levy. McMahon became suspicious of the proceedings, for "when the jurors were sworn," he "observed them all laughing and shaking their heads at each other, as if in ridicule of their oaths; and it appeared to me," he wrote, "that their oath only served as a cloak to their abominable designs." As it turned out, the coroner "was a particular friend of Mr. Levy, and he, of course, took care to have everything his own way." The inquisition was a farce. "It was easy to see that they did not desire to hear the truth," McMahon concluded, "but just to smother up the case." When the "sham investigation" was over, the jury returned the customary verdict: "Died by the visitation of God," the contemporary idiom for "died of natural causes."[35]

Several weeks after the inquest, Craig was discharged from practicing medicine on every plantation in the district. But that was not vengeance enough for Levy. He sued Dr. Craig for defamation of character and won a judgment for one thousand pounds in damages, "from a jury of planters like himself." According to McMahon, "The jury were quite exasperated at the idea of any white man daring to expose another, merely for being the cause of the death of a common negro." The judgment ruined Dr. Craig, who "had not one thousand pence," and he died in penury soon after.[36]

White juries denied the very notion that a slave's demise counted for much at all. Whatever the aim of the laws establishing coroner's inquests in Jamaica, the practice and execution of postmortem inquiries had less to do with establishing the cause of death than with demarcating boundaries between free and enslaved, thus signaling the limits of public worth and belonging. A crucial aspect of such border control was the maintenance of white supremacy; even dead bodies were ranked according to hierarchies of color and power. The murder of slaves by whites could therefore be deemed a natural consequence of enslavement. As a community ritual, state inquests enforced racial principles of social organization to the grave and beyond.

Signals of Status

Among the masters, funerals helped to establish a more finely calibrated hierarchy than that between free and enslaved. For fortune-seeking whites, especially those at the top of the social ladder, materialist attitudes toward death were more meaningful than religious ones. After all, it was largely the promise of riches that lured enterprising young Britons to Jamaica. William Hickey, the spoiled and freewheeling son of an affluent London attorney, came to the West Indies to seek his fortune as a lawyer in the Jamaican courts. As he approached Jamaica aboard the *New Shoreham*, Hickey recalled that the island was "considered as one of the most unhealthy in the West Indies, or in the world." His thoughts had been troubled by the ship captain, Surman, who had been telling stories throughout the voyage from England about death in Jamaica, "saying that several of his best friends had been carried off after only an hour's illness." When the ship steered into Kingston harbor, he pressed the theme more directly. Surman told Hickey to take note of "a dapper little man, dressed in black, with a spruce curled bob wig, who upon my landing would shake me by the hand, wishing me health and long life upon the island."

"But watch him closely," said the captain, "and you will perceive that whilst bowing and paying his compliments to you, he is, with a small ruler, measuring your height."

"And pray what is that for?" Hickey inquired.

"In order to have a coffin for you, which, he being the principal under-taker, he will immediately get ready, hoping to bury you tomorrow."

"Monstrously provoked" at the thought of such effrontery, Hickey anx-iously scanned the docks, resolved to give the undertaker "a kicking" as soon as he met him. Hickey never saw the man, however, and at length he recognized that he had fallen for one of Captain Surman's favorite old jokes.[37]

Hickey's career plans turned out to be more illusory than Captain Surman's imaginary undertaker, for though Hickey failed to find work, that "dapper little man" was plausibly representative of a firmly established sector of Jamaican society: the unhappy commerce and related social rit-uals that attended death. The basic demands of burial and memorial required a certain amount of economic activity. Shrouds used to wrap bodies varied greatly in quality and cost. The wealthiest whites were some-times wound in silk sheets, while enslaved Africans often went to their graves naked. Coffins were generally reserved for whites. Graveyards were valuable and productive lands for Jamaican parishes, and the "public" vied with private landowners to find places to put them. Signaling and reifying the social and financial status of the deceased, burial was as much a civil and economic event as it was a personal and familial one.[38]

Among public establishments, religious institutions are commonly designated to oversee death rites. For whites in Jamaica, small contingents of Jews, Catholics, and Protestants of various persuasions held their own ceremonies. It was the Anglican Church, however, that serviced the richest and most powerful of Jamaica's elite. So, though the institution was relatively weak, membership in it brought standing in the white community. In a land of fluid possibilities, acquisitive and opportunistic people of all faiths looked to the established church to set the overall social tone, even when they did not share its tenets on spiritual belief and even when they resisted its authority. Whereas people might not have shared conventional Anglican views of God as a remote presence in a mechanistic universe, most approved of the pragmatic Anglican approach to power and personal fortune as something of this world, produced by humankind. If various denominations in Jamaica had their own funeral rites, those of the established church were most suited to represent the materialist social order. Indeed the church was rarely challenged, unless it tried to assert its spiritual authority over Jamaica's material elite.

The Church of England in Jamaica was supported in large part by the fees it charged for various burial services. Through the late eighteenth century, Jamaican churches toiled with meager resources and suffered low attendance. Peter Mardsen, writing in 1788, acknowledged, "There are churches in every parish of this island; yet, except in the towns, I fear they are little frequented but on that awful occasion of the burial of the dead." Most whites in Jamaica were too bent on the pursuit of material well-being to contribute much to the maintenance of the established church; the church had to wait until they died to draw significant support from them (Figure 2.4). Anglican rectors garnered yearly salaries from parish vestries, but the majority of their income came from surplice fees—commissions they earned for baptisms, marriages, and funerals.[39]

In 1746 the parish vestry of the town of Kingston ordered that the rector William May was to receive, in addition to his yearly income of £240, 10 shillings for the burial of each Kingston inhabitant who used the parish palls. Anyone who was not conveyed to his or her grave draped in the official coffin cover but who was interred in Kingston's West Burying Ground yielded 5 shillings to the Reverend William May. A return made in 1751 by John Venn, the rector of Saint Catherine parish, showed that May's salary had increased to £250, but he earned £600 in surplice fees,

The Soul & Body of John are consigned to the Priest | *The Body of John is pack'd up for the Penn.*

Figure 2.4. Death and burial preparations for Johnny New-come: "The Soul & Body of John are consigned to the Priest" and "The Body of John is packed up for the Penn," details from *Johnny New-come in the Island of Jamaica,* by Abraham James (London, 1800). Courtesy of the National Library of Jamaica.

at least a third of which probably derived from funeral services. John Newson, clerk to the minister in mid-eighteenth-century Kingston, acted as the official parish undertaker, drawing the majority of his income from burials. The vestrymen fixed his salary at £30 for 1746 and ordered that he be paid 3 shillings and 9 pence for each funeral he attended, except those ceremonies conducted wholly at public expense. He gained a more lucrative commission from making coffins and taking care of the parish palls. For each coffin that Newson manufactured, the parish granted him 1 pound, 3 shillings, and 9 pence. In addition, Newson collected the following fees from each ceremony that made use of the parish palls:

> For a NonResident's use of the Velvett Pall: two pounds and ten shillings.
> If Borrowed out of the Parish: three pounds, ten shillings.
> For the Use of the White Pall: one pound.
> If borrowed out of the parish: one pound, ten shillings.
> For the Use of the Black Cloak Pall: twelve shillings and six pence.

In total, John Newson earned more than £152 for "Sallerys and Parish Coffins" in 1746, about 80 percent of his income. Simon Monk, the Kingston parish sexton, earned his entire income from burying the dead. For digging a grave and attending a funeral, he received 7 shillings and 6 pence. The more hallowed the grave site, however, the more money Monk could make. For preparing a tomb in the churchyard, he earned £1; for "Laying a Tombstone or any other Ways Inclosing a Grave in the Church Yard" he earned £4; and for digging a grave in the church itself, he collected £10. When people borrowed the velvet pall, Monk was paid an additional 7 shillings and 6 pence to attend to it.[40]

The graduated fees for progressively more prestigious burial palls and grave lots gave the parish and the church a stake in the reproduction of social hierarchy. Rectors were paid more for burying whites than for burying people of color, and nothing for slaves. In the parish of Saint Ann in 1796, for example, the rector earned £1, 6 shillings, and 3 pence for burying a white, and just 6 shillings and 8 pence for presiding over the interment of a free person of color. In death, as in life, suitable accoutrements signaled people's social station. The vestrymen accordingly kept the parish palls in good repair, ordering occasionally that "the Old Velvett Pall be New Lined and Flounced and that a new White Pall be made." Only the wealthiest whites in Kingston paid to have their deceased loved ones carried to a church crypt in the velvet pall. More often, Anglican parishioners rented the more modest white or black cloak pall and paid the church for a space in the enclosed churchyard or one of the larger parish burial grounds. Yet even outside the churches, the wealthy could still distinguish themselves with marble headstones and elaborate monuments. Such ostentation could attract unwanted attention, as when the authorities in Saint Ann parish had to post a reward of 2 doubloons for information leading to the detection of "some VILLAIN or VILLAINS" who had stolen a marble headstone from a churchyard tomb.[41]

Church burial rites did not attract unanimous respect. Just as the differences in fee schedules reflected and reproduced social hierarchies, they also became subjects of contention. The profiteering of the clergy sometimes figured in sharp disputes. In his *History of Jamaica* (1774) the planter-historian Edward Long described one such altercation at a funeral between a rector and a group of sailors. When the funeral party called the rector to preside over the interment of three deceased seamen, according to Long, "he thought to make quick work of it by only one reading of the burial-service." Either he assumed that since he would recover only one fee, he ought only to perform one reading or, with inexcusable hubris, he hoped to assess three charges for one service. The "brother tars" insisted that the rector honor the dignity of their comrades by reading the service over each individually. When the rector refused, the ceremony collapsed in acrimony, and a heated argument turned into a brawl. "The parson, the clerk, and all the congregation, engaged pell-mell. Nor long the battle raged; for divinity proved victorious, after hurling two of the three of the combatants headlong into the very grave that had been prepared for their inanimate friends."[42]

On another occasion, someone directly challenged the sacramental authority of the clergy, by explicitly designating their fees as obnoxious. In 1796 rector John Barton filed a formal complaint to the Lord Bishop of London against the wealthy and well-born James Wood for interrupting a funeral service in the town of Port Royal. At dusk on the evening of 1 February, the mourning party proceeded to the wharf, from where they were to take small boats to the narrow point called the Palisadoes, the place of interment. As night fell, however, one of the mourners remarked on the inconvenience of traveling by boat in the dark and suggested that the burial service be performed on the wharf instead. The clerk of the church liked the proposal, adding that funerals on the wharf were common in Port Royal, and the group decided in favor of it. They gathered around the coffin in silence, and Barton commenced the ceremony. But before Barton could finish the first prayer, James Wood demanded that they put the boats to sea and "broke out into the most execrable and blasphemous expressions against the Ordinance of the Church."[43]

"Damn you and Buggar Your Prayers!" he cried. "We want none of your Prayers; I'll be Damn'd if you shall get your Fee." He continued cursing throughout the prayer, and when it ended, the service came to a halt. "When challenged for his presumptuous assault on a Clergyman in the discharge of his sacred Function," Wood flouted Barton's authority entirely, fulminating, "I put you to Defiance, what can you do to me Sir? I have been better bred, better educated than ever you was." Finding little satisfaction in the Jamaican assize courts, "where Religion is too superficially taken into account," Barton protested to Bishop Porteus in London: "This Man has been for a long time an atrocious disturber of the Peace, and is well known to have been guilty of repeated Offences against the order of Society, he piques himself upon his purse, and confident of possessing the powerful means of buying out the Law, goes on to multiply his Offences against God and Society." Barton hoped that pursuing his case with the authorities at home in the British Isles, "where the Laws and Administration thereof will maintain the Reverence due to the Ordinances of God, the Dignity of the Church, and its Members," would bring punishment to the offender, but there is no evidence that Wood ever suffered any penalty. He was protected, as he doubtless expected, by his wealth and status.[44]

Outside Kingston and Port Royal, parish vestries and the established church had a weaker grip on the business of burial: the parish palls generated less revenue, and fewer residents were buried in the official graveyards. In the outlying parishes, where large plantations dominated the landscape, whites generally conducted their funeral ceremonies and buried their dead on private estates. John Stoney served for just half a year as rector of Saint John's, where there was no church building; he made only ten pounds in surplice fees in 1751. More commonly, rectors in outlying parishes earned from fifty to a hundred pounds in surplice fees, nowhere near the six hundred pounds reaped by William May in Kingston. Prominent planters in rural areas who wanted to have their ceremonies certified by the established church obliged ministers serving the rural parishes to travel widely among the estates to collect their fees. Lower down the social ladder the ministers were less welcome. The semifictional *Marly* suggests that in the early nineteenth century white workers on the estates generally tried to save the fee incurred when clergymen were present at their funerals. Instead, neighborhood whites formed funeral companies and performed the religious duties for themselves. At the funeral of an overseer described in *Marly*, "the burial took place in the garden of the estate, the usual place wherein they bury the white people who belong to the plantations." A common man read the funeral service, "to prevent incurring the charge which the clergyman of the parish would have made, had he been desired to attend."[45]

Of course, the clergy's concern with death was not wholly monetary. Churchmen sought to organize the business of burial as best they could around contemporary notions of piety and prudence in mortuary practice. In 1745 the Kingston vestry ordered that "the Great Bell be not Wrung on

Any Person's Death or Funerall." The tolling of parish bells to signal a death was a post-Reformation holdover from Catholicism. As such, it was deemed a controversial practice among Protestants throughout the seventeenth century. While Bishop Humphrey Henchman of London explained in 1664 that tolling bells warned the living to "mediate of their own death," dissenting clergy condemned it as a "heathenish practice." By the mid-eighteenth century the Church of England had absorbed the criticism and sought to ban death knells. The church also moved to prevent burials within the cathedrals. Removing and replacing masonry inside a church caused inconvenient disruptions in religious activity. More important, rotting corpses accumulating beneath the floor were noisome and unsanitary. In 1789 the Jamaican House of Assembly passed an act to "prevent the burying of the dead in the churches of this island" and further enabled the "justices and vestry of certain parishes to purchase lands for burial-grounds," while compensating the clergy for lost revenues. Despite the law, the assembly often made exceptions for the most prominent. Just two years after passing the act, it voted to allow the former governor, the Earl of Effingham, to be buried in Saint Catherine parish church at public expense. To ensure decent ceremonies for all Christians, the church prevailed upon the colonial government to pay for burials of the poorest commoners, who populated the ever-expanding public cemeteries.[46]

A Jamaican Farewell

Although the outward forms of funerals for white residents were considerably different from those for blacks, their social purposes were similar. In fundamental ways, contrary to what Edward Long believed, the aspirations of blacks and whites were alike. They all wanted to be celebrated in death for their achievements in life. Like the Africans, whites tried to re-create traditional rites in Jamaica, and, though whites had vastly more power to perpetuate their ceremonies, conditions in Jamaican slave society constrained their ability to do so.

Jamaican newspapers published long and detailed descriptions of the funerals of great men in England. Readers might also aspire to have coffins adorned with beautiful palls and silver plates inscribed with their name and age. They would imagine the majesty of the processions, vast concourses of people following designated mourners of unquestionable distinction to some desirable patch of hallowed ground. Even those who wanted humbler ceremonies hoped their burials would proclaim their status in life. Yet the desire to have a quintessentially English or Scottish funeral was frustrated in multiple ways by the exigencies of the West Indian context. The tropical climate did not allow for long open-casket viewings; therefore, interments had to take place much more expeditiously than they did in Britain. When Sir Hans Sloane, the naturalist and founding collector for the British Museum, toured Jamaica in 1689, he noted, "The Air here being so hot and brisk as to corrupt and spoil Meat in four hours after 'tis kill'd, no wonder if a diseased Body must be soon buried. They usually bury twelve hours after death at all times of the day and night." Another difference was that in a frontier society people were usually buried on family property. Large processions of white mourners could rarely be assembled in a land where white people were few in number and dispersed over a great distance. Whites, though they did not face the severe limitations imposed by enslavement, were everywhere surrounded by the enslaved. The overwhelming presence of slavery meant that alien and despised black people were generally on hand at sacred ceremonies for whites. Just as certain aspects of their burial rites demonstrated their commitment to British folkways, their ceremonies also exemplified the impact of local circumstances.[47]

Powerful people aspired to elaborate funerals, send-offs that would affirm their exalted status in life. By organizing their burial ceremonies around rank, wealthy slaveholders hoped to enshrine their own preeminence as a principle of social order. The greatest of planters and merchants, having fulfilled their aspirations in the West Indies, died in England and were buried with great fanfare. The affluent patriarch Thomas Hall, having made his fortune in Saint James parish before retiring in splendor in England, died in 1772. The expenses for his grand departure celebration were to cover "six men in deep mourning to bear in the said coffin," "30 men with branches to light the funeral," and "beer for the men as usual."[48] In their wills, people of means in Jamaica similarly stipulated the number of mourners they wished to attend their bodies and the amounts of food and drink to be distributed to guests, one last act of noble generosity by which to be remembered, before volleys of gunfire, commensurate with the age and rank of the departed, sounded the final farewell. The most prominent of the resident planters might still wish to be buried in Britain, even if they had their funerals on the island. Florentius Vassall, a friend and patron of Thomas Thistlewood, made arrangements to have his body sent back to

England when he died, although he had enjoyed a long and exceedingly prosperous planting career in Jamaica and though several members of his family had been buried on the island.[49]

As Vassall's funeral would attest, burial ceremonies were generally less exalted than had been hoped. Vassall had desired that Thistlewood attend the funeral, the only invited guest who was not a pallbearer, as Thistlewood proudly recorded in his diary. Early on the morning of the seventeenth, Thistlewood set out for Vassall's estate, to accompany his friend's remains from the house to the wharves. From there, Vassall's body would be transported by ship to England. First, "his bowels, &c. were took out, he was enclosed in a wood coffin & then in lead soldered up." After these preparations Vassall "was brought out and placed in the hall with the pall over him, & part of the funeral service read over him by Dr Bartholomew & the Clerk." Then the funeral procession began. The pallbearers were "Mr Cope, Mr Meyler, Mr Haughton, Mr White, Mr Antrobus & James Williams," but theirs was a symbolic office. White pallbearers did not actually carry coffins in Jamaica—slaves did, as servants would have done for the gentry in England, thus marking the gulf separating physical labor and social esteem. Encased in lead, Vassall was "carried on Negroes shoulders to the seaside, with great difficulty & very slowly." The slaves bore the burden by turns, but "though often spelled with fresh hands," the coffin "was twice, or oftener, thrown down in the road." Wearing black gloves and hatband, Thistlewood joined the parson, the clerk, and the doctor, as they followed the chief mourner and the bearers. "We stopped in the road almost every minute," Thistlewood complained, but the party nevertheless arrived before midday. The body was put in yet another "strong wooden coffin" and "immediately put in a boat which directly set off for the shipping." As the ship set sail for home, more than seventy rounds of minute guns heralded Vassall's departure. The planter had lived that many years, a remarkable feat in such a deadly environment. Yet though the "torrid zone" had failed to shorten Vassall's life, it did hasten his postmortem decay. Thistlewood noted in his final remarks, "His smell was very offensive, some defect being in the lead coffin."[50]

Even those buried abroad, like Vassall, who did not deign to be interred in Jamaica, had to settle for what might be called creolized funerals. Whatever whites' sense of mortuary convention, and despite the persistence of formal British rites and symbols, Jamaican slave society had a transformative effect on funerary practices. Just as slaveholders were dependent on black labor for most other things in life, so they required the attendance of "alien" and "outlandish" people at the rites to mark their final passing. Black participation made its presence felt. Thistlewood was annoyed by the black pallbearers, who dropped Vassall's coffin, stopped frequently, and proceeded slowly. And perhaps it was more than the weight of the coffin that stalled their procession. One might ask whether these were deliberate acts of disrespect—whether Vassall's slaves took this final opportunity to pull their master down from his high position and lay him in the dirt. Or might the bearers, more surprisingly, have been carrying out an aspect of their own customary rites? Thistlewood certainly believed they had conducted Vassall's corpse in "something of a ludicrous manner," a phrase that recalls Charles Leslie's portrayal of African funeral parades. Is it possible, in short, that they performed their own ritual inquest? Did they, could they, act as mediums for the spirit of Florentius Vassall? It is a tantalizing but unanswerable question. What is certain is that English ways could not continue unchanged in Jamaica, despite all the power and wealth the world of Atlantic slavery had to offer.

⊰⊱

Abraham James of the 67th Regiment did not witness Florentius Vassall's funeral, but he would not have been surprised by it. It would have only confirmed what he knew of Jamaica, that it was a society made by death, in which funerals demonstrated the order of things. Though its dominion was universal, death did not equalize; it provided occasions to mark distinctions and hierarchies of communal belonging, race, and affluence. Vassall's sparsely attended burial would bespeak his greatness as a sugar planter, even as enemies and aliens dishonored his dead body. A corpse might go to the crabs, but the living would make use of the dead to institute meaningful social arrangements. Again and again, all over the island, last rites encouraged the articulation of first principles—the basic assumptions about belonging, status, and power that were to regulate slave society. Through these, the chaos of Jamaican demography yielded order. This was not, however, a structure that perpetuated itself. It was a pattern suffered, shaped, and directed by the living in association with the dead. As such, it had to be reproduced not only through repeated demonstrations of group coherence and personal standing, but also in the struggle to shape the lives of future generations and the attempt to ensure that the accomplishments of the dead would be carried on in accordance with their wishes. Final rites were the prelude to bequests and legacies.

CHAPTER THREE

Expectations of the Dead

JAMAICA'S INHABITANTS PERPETUATED and regenerated slave society partly by bequeathing property from the dead to the living. By this means, they attempted to pass down their hopeful vision of the social order, beyond the limit of their lifetimes. Leaving legacies to their descendants enabled the dead to continue the struggle for mastery and dignity that had occupied their lives. Legacies bolstered both family status and material resources, ensured that favored friends and relatives would be rewarded for their fidelity, and enabled fragile institutions to survive. Alongside constant immigration and frequent funerals, family inheritance was a major tributary to Jamaica's strongest social currents.

Within the corrosive conditions of Atlantic slavery, kinship networks allowed people to imagine communal integrity over time. Even while demographic disaster hacked at budding family trees, kith and kin sutured Jamaican society. Built on complicated arrangements for mutual aid—or exploitation—families helped people survive slavery or sustain it, disperse property, and concentrate wealth for the benefit of future generations. Family ties extended beyond "blood" relations. Marriage and biological descent were at the core of open and complex familial associations that included in-laws, shipmates, and friends: precious sources of support in a turbulent world. Through these relationships people struggled to fulfill their desire for affection, status, and material well-being. Most important, kinship networks offered mutuality that did not end with death. The living expected legacies, and the dead, through their bequests, expected to wield continued influence in the society they left behind.[1]

Shaped by contending forces within slave society, inheritance was inevitably the focus of negotiation and conflict. For fortune-seeking whites, especially those at the top of the hierarchy, the most important legacies of the dead were the ceaseless struggles over their estates and the consequences of transfers of ownership. But for trusted domestic slaves and the brown children of mixed unions, the death of their owners could also mean manumission, and perhaps some continued financial support. Even among the great masses of enslaved Africans and their descendants, many expected to receive material support from the dead. Inheritance rights for the enslaved, though never secure in law until the last years of slavery, were won through the consolidation of ambiguous customary rights and the occupation of territory claimed as family land.

The Will to Wealth

The artist and soldier Abraham James, perceptive critic of Jamaican society that he was, acknowledged the frequency and importance of bequests by creating the figure of Mr. Codicil, who arrives to record Johnny New-come's last will and testament. Crouched over a simple desk, as Johnny's mistress weeps in the background, Codicil records the will, his face betraying a faint grin (Figure 3.1). "All in a day's work," he seems to say. Mr. Codicil was, indeed, a stock character in Jamaican life, for legal arrangements surrounding death and property were a fundamental aspect of social organization.[2]

Inheritance entailed more than a simple transfer of property. It was a means of affirming familial bonds and expressing expectations for the future. White people in Jamaica spent a lot of time thinking about what impact the death of friends and relatives would have on their fortunes. They spoke often of wills. They wondered where they stood in the affections of kinfolk. They considered how future testators might judge their behavior, and they held future legatees accountable to their wishes and demands. Such concerns had considerable immediacy, for, despite all the productivity of Jamaica's plantation economy, great wealth and status were largely inherited. For the Jamaican elite, inheritance law generally followed English custom. Realty (property in land) passed to the eldest son, a practice known as primogeniture, while personalty (most other assets) was divided among the survivors—spouse, children, extended kin, and friends.

Figure 3.1. "John sends for Mr. Codicil and bequeaths his Kit," detail from *Johnny New-come in the Island of Jamaica,* by Abraham James (London, 1800). Courtesy of the National Library of Jamaica.

Among the most established families, holdings in land—and sometimes slaves—might be entailed at the direction of a testator, meaning that the property had to pass down through male heirs in perpetuity and that none of the heirs was free to designate future recipients of family realty. This system preserved great estates as family dynasties, directed by the will of distant ancestors. But in the case of both great estates and more movable properties, Jamaican mortality rates focused people's minds on how succession would play out, how each death, marriage, and birth, each act of fealty or betrayal, would affect the continuity of family and society.[3]

Perhaps three-quarters of whites belonged to a class of craftsmen, bookkeepers, and overseers, who generally died intestate—that is, without having made a will. In such cases, property was expected to pass on through primogeniture, though many disposed of their assets by informal arrangements with friends or family. The poorest became the subject of state concern. When clergymen died, for instance, their irregular earnings presented a problem for their surviving relations. "Here the son of a deceased clergyman hath nowhere to lay his head," lamented Edward Long, when he wrote to advocate establishment of a public fund for the benefit of widows and orphans. One was ultimately established late in the eighteenth century. People who did leave formal wills were likelier to own large estates, which, when reorganized to pay debts and provide shares to inheritors, caused great disturbance to society. By occasioning frequent and potentially disruptive transfers of property, the deaths of wealthy whites affected people at all social ranks, for whom the death of the powerful was a source of tremendous anxiety and insecurity, but also opportunity.[4]

The outstandingly wealthy Simon Taylor thought often about inherited property. In 1759 his father, Patrick Taylor, had left the sizable fortune that he had accumulated as a Kingston merchant to his son. That made Simon responsible for upholding his family's status. As Chaloner Arcedeckne's attorney, Taylor, always aware of how property determined a man's position within his family, offered advice on the tricky business of securing and consolidating an inheritance. Taylor had defended Arcedeckne's interest against the claims of his cousins when Chaloner's father, Andrew Arcedeckne, had died in 1757. To prevent these relatives from obtaining the family legacy in the future, Taylor urged Arcedeckne to marry and produce "Heirs enough of your own to inheritt your Estate," lest his cousins' children should profit by his demise. Meanwhile, in 1773 Taylor vowed to ensure that Arcedeckne received his due portion of his aging mother's property: "Depend in case of the Old Ladys death I will do every thing for you as if I was acting for my self."[5]

Taylor himself did not expect to live long—certainly not to his eventual age of seventy-three years. Born in Jamaica, he knew its dangers well, and he recognized that each bout of illness could be his last. In anticipation of his death, he incessantly rewrote his will. In December 1782 Taylor was afflicted with, as he put it, "Disorder in my bowels and a burning Fever which reduced me exceedingly." When he recovered, he turned immediately to discussing wills with his younger brother, Sir John Taylor. Simon had previously received and examined a copy of Sir John's will, and he now passed along his own for comparison. Simon Taylor's thoughts on the future of the family property indicated clear priorities. First, he wanted to provide for his recognized blood relations; next, he aimed to reward loyalty and service.[6]

Simon urged Sir John to think often of his legacy, reminding him that a will "must be altered every year as you have Children," and that it was necessary to make some explicit provision for "any Child your Wife may be [pregnant] with at the time of your Death." In his own will, as Sir John would see, while most of his estate would go to his brother's children, Simon had also provided for the two girl children of his younger sister Anne. As they were already quite well off, Taylor left them a fixed amount of money, £10,000 apiece. He did not want to give them more, fearing that they would then be more "liable to the prey of any Sharper or Fortune hunter." To Anne's husband, Robert Graham, the girls' father, Taylor left only a ring, but, he said, "leaving £20000 Stl. to his family I think it a very handsome Legacy indeed and he has got a very good Fortune already out of our Family." It was well earned, though, by Graham's "kind and Affectionate Behaviour to Poor Anny." If Sir John had had no children, said Taylor, he would have given the greatest share of his own fortune to Graham and the girls. He urged Sir John to think along similar lines: "I hope if you should die without Children or Grand Children which God Almighty forbid that you never will forget Anny's offspring."[7]

Robert Graham was favored as a loyal in-law, but Taylor also arranged a legacy for a faithful servant. "You will say I have made a great provision for the Woman who lives with me." Taylor wrote defensively because he was referring to Grace Donne, a free woman of color who served as Taylor's housekeeper and consort for more than thirty years. "I own it but she has been a faithfull servant to me and I never had occasion to call her twice for any thing or awake her in any of my very severe fitts of sickness." To Grace, Taylor would leave a gift of slaves, furniture, an annuity of fifty pounds per year, and a house for life; however, the house would properly belong to Sir John, and Simon hoped he would not object to Grace's occupancy. He promised to buy her another one, if he should live long enough, thus freeing his brother of any obligation to show altruism. In the event, Grace Donne did not survive Taylor. She died of an illness in 1804, leaving Taylor to lament, "I am like a Fish out of Water by her loss, as she managed everything in the House for me."[8]

In the case of his nieces and nephews, Taylor expected his bequests to extend his protection to his white family members, those who could claim to belong within his official lineage (Figure 3.2). He made no mention of the several children he had with women of color—Lady Maria Nugent was told that he "had a numerous family, some almost on every one of his estates." Having no white children, he chose his namesake, Sir John's son Sir Simon Richard Brissett Taylor, as his principal heir. Whereas young

Figure 3.2. Portrait of the Taylor family, from a photograph of *A Portrait of John and Simon Taylor Family,* c. 1784, pastel by Daniel Gardner. Simon Taylor is seated at left. His brother, Sir John Taylor, is standing at right by the side of his wife, Elizabeth Haughton, and their children. Simon Taylor's nephew and heir, Sir Simon Richard Brissett Taylor, is at the bottom of the frame, with his hand raised. Courtesy of the National Library of Jamaica.

Simon could expect to become fabulously wealthy when his uncle died, Simon Taylor expected to reproduce himself by using the promise of his bequest to mold the nephew according to his own ideals.[9]

When Sir John Taylor died in 1786, he was deep in debt, and his son was just a baby. As the head of the family, Simon Taylor assumed financial responsibility for his brother by paying his debts and providing for his children. From Jamaica he directed resources toward their education and training, but he took a special interest in his nephew and chosen heir and intended to make him, as he boasted to Lady Nugent, "the richest Commoner in England." Repeatedly, over the course of two decades, Simon the uncle used the threat of disinheritance to compel Simon the nephew to embrace the masculine ideals of the Jamaican planter class: vigor, shrewdness, and mastery. The uncle worried that his heir would follow his late father, John Taylor, in "Indolence, Love of Pleasure, Dress, Vanity, self Importance, and high Ideas of the Fashionable World" and prove unable to assume responsible command of the family fortune. Monitoring young Simon's behavior through contacts in England and castigating him often, the patriarch pushed the nephew to learn habits that would enable him to reproduce the uncle's success. "I think every person should dedicate the Whole of the Morning from the Hour he rises Untill He goes to dress for Dinner to the Study of some thing usefull," Taylor advised, "looking over his own Affairs inspecting his Accounts writing & conserving letters and seeing all his Accounts entered in to proper Books avoiding all debts whatsoever never giving way to Idleness or Dissipation nor leaving that to be done tomorrow that can be done today."[10]

Despite years of obsequious pandering, Simon the nephew was a disappointment to his patron. The uncle was seldom satisfied with his nephew's conduct and was easily offended by his letters. In 1806 Taylor resolved to disinherit his brother's son in favor of the son of his sister and Robert Graham. In 1811 Taylor notified Sir Simon that he would "alter everything in my Will which was in your Favor." Taylor did not appear to change his mind, even after his nephew unexpectedly turned up in Jamaica to curry favor. Rather, he complained that his nephew was a "nuisance," "fitt for nothing," who would never be able to manage sugar plantations—or any other properties—in Jamaica. "What shall I do with the boy?" Taylor asked his attorney John Shand. "Forgive him," said Shand, to which Taylor merely grunted, "Hmmph!" He instead prepared a decree to tie up his properties, allowing them to accumulate on their own, rather than passing to family. But Shand ultimately prevailed on Taylor to "destroy the obnoxious paper" and reinstate Sir Simon as his heir, just before the patriarch died in April 1813. Sir Simon Richard Brissett Taylor now controlled one of the largest fortunes in the British Empire. "I am truly glad that my Uncle did not leave the world with a sentiment of displeasure against me," he announced, "glad that his memory has been rescued by a natural bequest of his property from the stain that would have attached to it had that property been consigned to a hoard, or scattered amongst strangers." Sir Simon did not enjoy his inheritance for long. In two years he was dead, and the property went to his sister, Anna Susannah Watson, and her husband George, who both took the Taylor name.[11]

Just as the Taylor family did, the Ricketts family sought to perpetuate itself through inheritance, anxiously expecting the family name to reverberate through well-placed legacies. In September 1760 Colonel George Ricketts, a sugar lord in the parish of Westmoreland, died in possession of a profitable plantation called Canaan and several other properties, totaling nearly three thousand acres. In his last will and testament Ricketts bequeathed Canaan, "with all the negroes, stock, and cattle of all kinds, and their increase," as well as the other land, to his eldest son and heir, William Henry Ricketts. To his other children he left various sums of money, goods, and chattels.[12]

A few years before George Ricketts died, William Henry's newlywed wife, Mary, wrote to her husband, complaining because his father's wealth required them to stay so long in Jamaica. She did not like the island, feared the climate, disliked the local whites, and felt revulsion for slavery and the enslaved in equal measure. She reflected bitterly on waiting patiently for her father-in-law to die, meanwhile wasting her youth in Jamaica's rude society. "I think it Cruel such fine Prospects as we have that we shou'd be Buried alive here," she lamented. She continued in this manner, referring to Colonel Ricketts: "As to Staying for the Dissolution of a Certain *Person*, we might Punish ourselves this 10 years, for now he is Recover'd. If he has no Return of his Disorder he may Live so Long, that we Shou'd have But Little relish Left for any thing—our being here Reminds me of Pope, who Compares a Disappointing Life, to a Lingering Death; & yet he never knew this Country & Consequently cou'd not with half the Justice apply It that I Can." She hoped that George Ricketts's death would liberate her from an island that offered her neither personal security nor refinement and manners.[13]

Mary Ricketts's sentiments, cynical as they were, expressed a common predicament of Jamaica's white women. In a society dominated by patriarchs, who frequently took women of color for companions, white women were rarely recognized as vital participants. And contrary to contemporary popular opinion, which held that widows could succeed quite well by simply "marrying and burying," elite white women were fairly vulnerable to financial misfortune. As a result, they were often eager, like Mary Ricketts, to retire to Britain, where their prospects would be more promising. Few enjoyed the success of Teresa Constantia Phillips, the fashionable woman from London society who once served as Jamaica's Mistress of the Revels. She was nicknamed the Black Widow, for having married and survived a series of wealthy, short-lived men in rapid succession during the 1750s and '60s. Though she profited handsomely from their wills, her own wealth did not secure reliable status for her. When she died in Kingston in 1765, almost no one attended her funeral.[14]

The precariousness of life on the island resulted in perpetual financial insecurity. Even when women married as well as Mary Ricketts had, the death of their husbands could leave them in uncertain circumstances. In their wills, Jamaican men commonly placed limitations on women's economic status and generally favored children and friends over wives. Even dower rights, which by common law allowed women the use of one third of personal property and use for life of a third of freehold land upon the death of their husbands, were not respected in all cases. Moreover, the assembly placed a severe restriction on women's inheritance in 1775, when it passed a law to "prevent the severing of estates and plantations, lands, slaves, tenements, and hereditaments, by way of dower." This law increased women's dependence on male heirs or estate administrators, for whom women's interests were not always a priority.[15]

William Henry Ricketts would administer and dispose of his properties and provide for the family as he saw fit. In 1770 Ricketts petitioned the assembly concerning four unprofitable parcels of land not attached to Canaan, asking that he be permitted to vest the land in trustees who would dispose of it for his benefit and that of the other beneficiaries of his father's will. Just after the assembly assented to his request, Ricketts moved to enhance his position by making arrangements with Mr. Downer, the gravely ill proprietor of Walling Ford estate, to exchange some slaves and land. Downer "surrendered fifteen fine Negroes this Day besides those some time ago," Ricketts reported to his sister Polly. Both Ricketts and Downer negotiated in the expectation of a death. "Commiserating his Condition, together with the intimate Friendship that formerly subsisted between his Father and mine," Downer induced Ricketts "to sell him one valuable Fellow who did not have to quit his Children and other connections, give him in Fee three women about 55 years of age, also grant him for Life four more, which are to revert to me and my Heirs." The deal was closed by Downer's "giving Security that they shall be forthcoming at his Death, or pay the value for which he conveys the liquidity of Redemption of all the Negroes and lands." "By this," Ricketts wrote with evident satisfaction, "I have secured a number of valuable Negroes to my Estate worth at least £1500, also the lands of five or six hundred pounds value, besides the other four Negroes on Reversion." The acquisition of working-age slaves and land would help keep his properties productive and profitable, so that Ricketts could support a family that extended across the Atlantic; nevertheless, this and similar dealings did not settle the family's affairs for long.[16]

While William Henry Ricketts could depend on his business acumen, the other heirs of George Ricketts continued to wrangle over the inherited assets for three more decades. During the 1790s one of Colonel Ricketts's female grandchildren fretted to her aunt that her brother George, the executor of their mother's will, still had not given her her due. "My brother and myself were left one Thousand pounds by my grandfather Ricketts, and he left another by my Father, with the Interest from the Age of thirteen. Likewise all my Mother's Arrears of Dower which was near £2000 Sterling, and every other claim of hers, Alex told me Crawford had twelve Negroes which were my Mother's consequently they are mine." Apparently, the young woman was overly optimistic about her birthright. Her brother George wrote to say that the arrears on his sister's annuity only totaled a few hundred pounds. Moreover, she had misunderstood the legacy of her mother, Anne Ricketts. "By a Notorial copy of my Mother's will," George G. Ricketts explained, "You will perceive that my Sister is mistaken in thinking that my Mother devised to her any Negroes. I think she is also greatly mistaken in the amount of arrears due to my Mother."

As executor of the estate, he had enormous power to influence his sister's well-being, but also the welfare of the enslaved men and women who counted as the assets of the estate. Estate executors wielded so much influence, in fact, that they became the subject of intense political scrutiny.[17]

Executors

The executor stood at the center of transfers of wealth and, therefore, of status and social continuity. Executors were responsible for administering estates once a testator had died. They oversaw extensive properties and commercial transactions; they took care of dependents and took charge of slaves. Most children born on the island lost one or both of their parents before they reached adulthood, and so for them executors were parental figures. In choosing an executor, a testator bestowed considerable trust in that person's character and expected honor and competence in the execution of his or her wishes, as well as loyalty to any descendants. As the key figure responsible for implementing the will of the dead, the executor managed the continuity of property and family. Although people often preferred to appoint successful family members as executors, they frequently had to select from among friends or prominent businessmen. Ideally, executors took control of the deceased's property, paid off creditors, and executed the last will and testament. For these services estate executors earned a significant commission. Typically, they charged between 5 and 10 percent of the net value of the estate. The commission alone was enough to make executorship an attractive service, but the control of properties and assets made it even more so. Judging by the frequent complaints of legatees, executors often managed properties for their personal enrichment.[18]

In the 1770s Simon Taylor took it upon himself to defend Chaloner Arcedeckne's interests when Arcedeckne's aged and weakening mother, Elizabeth Kersey, appointed among her executors Charles Kelsall, a man whom Taylor deeply mistrusted. In 1773 Taylor wrote to warn Arcedeckne that Kelsall was "as damned a raskall as ever lived" and "as great a Villain as ever was hang'd." Taylor urged Arcedeckne to come out to Jamaica in order to prevent Kelsall from possessing his "house, papers, & effects." In Arcedeckne's absence, Taylor assured him that "in case your Mother should be taken ill," he would go immediately to her home in Spanish Town "in case of her death [to] take possession of the House, and every thing in and about it," and "as your Attorney turn Mr. Kelsall out of Doors." At stake was nothing less than the material integrity of Arcedeckne's family tree. "If I have at any time the Acct. of your Mothers being sick, and gett to Town before she dies, I defy him to hurt you."[19]

When Elizabeth Kersey did die, in 1777, Kelsall moved to "take away or place such papers &c. belonging to Chaloner Arcedeckne" and to "take and secure such Bonds Notes &c. belonging to the deceased Mrs. Kersey as her Executor." Taylor and two other attorneys for Arcedeckne's family acted quickly to block Kelsall's design. "We shall Judge it improper to admit you into Mr. Arcedeckne's house," they wrote, "until we can be fully assured whether matters will be carried on amicably or adversedly." They further cautioned Kelsall against "intermeddling." Stung, Kelsall pleaded his case by invoking his service to Mrs. Kersey. He detailed uncompensated expenses and unappreciated efforts stretching back to 1771, when he had begun managing Kersey's livestock pen. "I say I have been most faithfull to Mrs. Kersey and expected she would have left me a thousand pounds which I deserve, but make a charge of 100 per annum as she could not have got a person to have taken such Care and maintained him for that sum." He would be willing to relinquish his executorship, but only, he said, "if I am paid £700, and Mr. T and Kelly will give me one negroe and a receipt for the money I may owe her [Elizabeth Kersey] which is about £300." Taylor and his colleagues agreed to the settlement. "Had I not interfered," Taylor reminded Arcedeckne a few years later, "I assure you he would have given a very Extraordinary Acct. of her Effects."[20]

In 1740 the Jamaican assembly had attempted to remedy abuse in fiduciary commissions, in passing an "act for preventing frauds and breaches of trust" by, among others, trustees and executors. The law directed anyone who managed an estate on another's behalf to render to the island secretary a yearly written account of "all the rents, profits, produce, and proceeds" arising from the properties under his care. Failure to provide an inventory would result in forfeiture of the executor's commission for each year of dereliction, and a fine of a hundred pounds. The law's effectiveness in limiting abuses is questionable. Executors followed a narrow and self-serving interpretation of the law, by duly reporting inventories, while retaining broad discretion in the execution of the estates. Moreover, the assembly, made up of the wealthiest men in Jamaica, later undercut the

1740 regulations by opting to protect their flexibility in business administration over the rights of inheritors, many of whom lived in Britain. The
body acted in 1775 to defend executors from lawsuits by forcing creditors
to present their own proof of "actual receipt" of credits, rather than relying
on the general-issue statements of estate assets and debits that executors
often used in order to keep various creditors at bay. The act preserved the
right of executors to protect estates in their charge by protesting their
debts, without allowing creditors to use such statements against them. By
preserving the latitude of executors in this and other ways, the political
establishment safeguarded executorship as a business enterprise and a pillar
of the elite community.[21]

Charged with carrying out the will of the dead with regard to material
possessions, executors occupied a powerful position in the social structure;
consequently, they protected their privileges, and others avidly sought out
the job. For those who stood below merchants, sugar barons, and imperial
officials in the colonial hierarchy, executorship could be an easy route to
prosperity. "However poor a man may have previously been," reflected
former plantation bookkeeper Benjamin McMahon in the nineteenth century, "upon his appointment as executor to a wealthy individual, nothing
is more common in Jamaica, than for him at once to become rich." In
Marly, the semifictional account of a petty Jamaican planter, the anonymous author related the risible tale of Mr. Wogan, a would-be executor
who attended the funeral of a relatively wealthy overseer. Wogan was a
member of the deceased overseer's funeral company, and after they
interred the body, he went with the rest of the party to the "buckra-house"
to hear the reading of the will. When Wogan discovered he had not been
named as executor, he left abruptly. Riding out with Marly, Wogan, "who
it seems had anxiously expected the appointment to the executorship, in
the bitterness of his disappointment, addressed Marly in a language similar
to the following: 'It is no wonder I am a poor man. I have never yet been
appointed to an executor, while that fellow (meaning him who was named
for the office,) is always nominated: We have no reason to be surprised,
therefore, at seeing him get rich, while I, who am passing honest, and have
been five and twenty years in the island, am still poor—simply because I
have never been appointed to an executor.'" For his part, Marly wondered
how honest the man could be, "for he could not conceive how such a trust
could have a tendency to enrich him who did his duties justly."[22]

Benjamin McMahon, who devoted an entire chapter of his memoir to the habits of executors, held the opinion that they seldom fulfilled the trust placed in them. He enumerated a variety of corrupt schemes perpetrated by untrustworthy executors. "Cases are constantly occurring in the island," McMahon charged, "of the particular friends of the deceased, having come into possession of the property, appropriat[ing] the greater part of its proceeds to their own use, by virtue of their executorships, and then tak[ing] the benefit of act, and then leav[ing] the unfortunate children, with the miserable remnant." McMahon also accused executors of seducing young female heirs under their care. "They have no sooner arrived at the age of puberty," he alleged, "than every flattering and seductive charm will be presented to the mind, to induce them to live as mistresses with the man, who was bound, by every principle of honour, to protect them." This McMahon asserted to be "the general practice throughout the island." Corrupt executors, he maintained, had inspired the popular saying: "When a man dies in Jamaica, he is ruined for ever."[23]

Even the most faithful executors, acting in the normal exercise of their duties, could wreak havoc with the lives of the enslaved. Slaves suffered for both a live master's profit and a dead master's debts. When a slave-owner died in arrears, executors made hasty arrangements to sell enslaved men and women. As satisfactory collateral for the payment of debts, slaves were also subject to levies from creditors. Often, especially in the major port towns, where auctions brought good prices, the marshals seized slaves by writ and confined them in jail until the appointed day of sale. Even Edward Long, who was a vehement defender of Jamaican slavery, condemned the depredations executors often committed when restructuring an estate's assets. "I do not know any thing in the colony system of slavery so oppressive and detrimental to the Negroes, as this practice of levying upon them, and selling them at vendue," Long avowed. "What severer hardships can befall these poor creatures," he wondered, than to be suddenly "divided from each other, sold into the power of new masters, and carried into distant parts of the country . . . ? Numbers doubtless have perished by these arbitrary removals." Hercules Ross, having frequently during his three decades in Jamaica (between 1751 and 1782) witnessed men and women being seized and sold to pay debts, appreciated the bitter irony of such episodes—"that any class of human beings should be sold for debts which they did not incur."[24]

Both Long and Ross believed that slaves should be attached to the soil—Long because he could not bear to see "flourishing" plantations ruined, as much as from concern about the well-being of black families. Yet slaves were simply too valuable as liquid assets to be conjoined with real estate. Except when they were entailed to a property by will, they provided the most flexible means of asset management. When the assembly did pass an "act to regulate the devises of negro, mulatto, and other slaves, in wills" in 1775, the law did nothing to attach slaves to plantations. On the contrary, it allowed executors to sue for recovery of slaves belonging to the deceased who were held by "a stranger, or other person having no legal or just title thereto." At times, slaveowners might reward favored slaves with a degree of autonomy or make casual business agreements with other masters to allow enslaved men or women to work on other properties, where they could be closer to kin. The law now annulled these types of arrangements when an owner died, by allowing executors to recall to the estate or to the auction block men and women who had been hired out or informally manumitted by the testator. In such cases the act of 1775 entitled an executor to act as deus ex machina, able to rend or restructure social relations on behalf of dead owners with the stroke of a pen.[25]

While there is no government record to indicate the extent of such displacement in the eighteenth century, Long estimated in 1774 that 400 slaves were seized by writ and forcibly relocated each year. The rate of dislocation accelerated when the Jamaican economy declined in the early nineteenth century. Even in the best of times, planters operated their factory farms on credit, given in anticipation of income from the next crop. When the plantations ran effectively and when the prices for colonial produce were high, planters could always gain access to more capital. But when disaster struck individual properties, as it often did, and when the prices for most West Indian products fell in the early nineteenth century, credit evaporated, mortgage holders seized the assets, and a planter's title to his estate ended with his death. What happened next was described by the reform-minded planter Gilbert Mathison in 1811: "The Negroes are sold in lots, families are torn asunder, a complete dispersion takes place, and all the horrors of the African trade are again repeated." From the cessation of the transatlantic slave trade in 1807 until 1827, when Jamaican planters generally were struggling with mounting arrears, over 22,600 enslaved men and women were seized to pay debts. In all, they brought over £1.6 million sterling at auction. A substantial number were sold to settle dead people's estates. When an indebted slaveowner died, then, the enslaved could expect to lose many of their social connections and to have their families scattered about in a final act of domination. Here, again, the dead continued to shape the society they left behind.[26]

The Will to Freedom

The anxiety that most slaves surely felt upon the death of white masters was tempered, for a select few, by the hope of receiving a legacy. Slaveholders sometimes made provisions in their wills, giving instructions to executors or heirs to free enslaved concubines or those who had provided some other devoted service.[27] Manumission and legacies in these cases depended as much on the will of the legatee as on that of the testator: enslaved people had to struggle to acquire their bequests. Yet the rare instances when they did were not insignificant. The number of people who acquired legal freedom by devise increased incrementally, and along with their children and further descendants, they came to form a substantial and vocal community of free people of color by the nineteenth century.

Enslaved women were subject to frequent, and often violent, sexual violation. No law or moral scruple prevented white men from forcing themselves on black females, women and girls alike. Resistance to a white man's predations could get a woman beaten, tortured, or killed. Some women negotiated this predicament by subjecting themselves to patrons, yielding to some white man who could protect them from the rest. In such relationships, men continued to dominate and exploit their consorts, yet prolonged intimacy allowed the women to make some claims on them. Just as women could lobby for their own protection, they could secure some advantage for their children; in rare cases, this meant receiving a legacy of freedom, money, or property when their patrons died.[28]

When he made out his will in 1786, Thomas Thistlewood desired that his longtime mate, Phibba, be freed and given property. After his death, "as soon as is convenient," he stipulated, his executors should "purchase the freedom of a certain Negroe woman slave named Phibba the property of the Honourable John Cope and who has been living with me a considerable time past." He also intended to provide Phibba with the economic means for relative independence—land and slaves: "I give devise and bequeath unto the said Phibba my Negroe woman slave named Bess and her child named Sam together with the future issue and increase of the said Bess to hold the said slave named Bess and her Child Sam together with her future issue and increase unto the use of the said Phibba her heirs and assigns forever." Phibba's autonomy would be guaranteed by the continued enslavement of others. Thistlewood also directed his executors to set aside a hundred pounds in Jamaican currency for Phibba to purchase a plot of land of her choosing and to build a house "suitable to her station." Thistlewood offered to buy Phibba's freedom and establish her independence, only provided that "no more is required for such freedom than the sum of Eighty Pounds current money of Jamaica." If her owner demanded more, then she would simply receive an annuity of "£15 per annum during her life." The balance of Thistlewood's estate, less £50 each to two of his acquaintances, went to his nephew and niece in England, his official family. As it turned out, Phibba received her manumission six years after Thistlewood's death. And it is not certain that Phibba received the rest of her inheritance, for at the time that Thistlewood's will was proved, executors, beneficiaries, and the law commonly thwarted the wishes of testators when it came to blacks.[29]

Apprehending that poor freed people, released from the financial responsibility of masters, might burden the parishes, the Jamaican assembly passed an act in 1774 to require slaveowners to pay an annuity of five pounds to the parish churchwardens for manumitted slaves. Until the assembly bowed to pressure from England and voided this regulation in 1816, the primary beneficiaries of wills often refused to pay the annuity, thereby condemning the manumitted slaves to continuing bondage. Moreover, as most whites died intestate, bequests of freedom from lesser slaveowners were routinely ignored. Before the 1816 Slave Act, manumissions by legacy required a proved will "executed with all the Solemnities essential for passing real property." The 1816 act relaxed this requirement through a provision that allowed bequests of freedom to be legitimated by any document sufficient to pass along personal property. Nevertheless, manumission by legacy was still a remote possibility, and when it did occur, it was mostly an opportunity for plantation managers to rid an estate of aging or recalcitrant workers. In nearly all cases, the heirs who held the slaves tried to implement manumission as a business transaction, by seeking reimbursement for manumitted slaves, in order to buy replacements.[30]

Frequently, slaveholders left their own children enslaved. At the Mesopotamia estate in Thomas Thistlewood's Westmoreland parish, white fathers manumitted only twelve of the fifty-two enslaved interracial children who lived on the plantation between 1761 and 1833. Some found this state of affairs amusingly pitiful. Elsewhere, in 1768 overseer John Scott wrote to Thomas Hall, an absentee proprietor in England, concerning Hall's son William, who had recently been on the plantation. Scott combined reports of William's activities with inventories of the slaves, making special mention of "Zipporah's Child, which is the second she has had since you was gone, the first was a Girl that died. The 2nd is really a fine boy and is quite sensible for his age, which is near 15 mo.s old." Scott continued in a comic tone: "I can't say whether you've heard who the Father is. He's very much like him and is more fair then some white women's children: Mrs. Scott has had him Christened and his name is William. So I leave you to guess who the Father is: It's a pitty he should be a slave."[31]

Even when whites sought to free their enslaved children, often someone else owned them, making for a protracted and complicated process. In 1771 Simon Taylor wrote to Chaloner Arcedeckne, urging him to manumit a woman named Catherine Chaplin and her children. The children were the three sons that Catherine had had by a Dr. Collins, who had once resided on Golden Grove estate. Before Dr. Collins died, he directed his executor, John Archer, to buy the children's freedom, but Archer kept the money allotted for their purchase and did nothing before he in turn died. Archer "gave himself no trouble about it in his life time," Taylor explained, "but by his Will he mentioned it & desires that they may be bought." Arcedeckne was reluctant, despite the intervention of both Taylor and Arcedeckne's mother, Elizabeth Kersey. The children were part of an entailed legacy—their ownership would revert to Arcedeckne's in-laws at his death—and he could not compromise the longevity of the family properties.[32]

Catherine and her children were still enslaved in 1783, when Arcedeckne received a letter from Timothy Penny, an acquaintance of Arcedeckne's late mother. Penny again interceded on behalf of "Old & Faithful" Catherine, "now Growing in years, but very desirous of having her, & her Children's Freedom." By now, Chaplin had survived another white companion, Jacob Gutteres, whose will had directed his executors "to Purchase of & from Chaloner Arcedekne, Esq. His heirs or Assigns the freedom of a Sambo

Woman Slave named Catherine Chaplin & her three Children named John Collins, Edward Carvalo Collins & Isaac Chaplin." If the manumission could be purchased for £350 Jamaican currency, then Gutteres's estate would also provide an annuity of £12. Penny, who claimed that Elizabeth Kersey had often promised "that she would use her endeavours" to free Chaplin and the children, had been asked by the executors to approach Arcedeckne—and this nearly seven years after Gutteres's death. Having taken surnames for herself and the children, Catherine certainly expected to be distinguished from common slaves, who rarely had more than a forename and a nickname, and to signify that she belonged to a legitimate family, deserving of public recognition. Surnames notwithstanding, they remained enslaved. Over more than twelve years' time, at least three testators demanded freedom for Catherine, John, Edward, and Isaac. Nothing indicates that Arcedeckne ever freed them.[33]

Matthew Gregory Lewis recorded the slightly happier story of Nicholas Cameron, a mulatto carpenter enslaved on Lewis's Cornwall plantation. Cameron's white father had charged his nephew and legal heir to purchase the freedom of his natural son. "The nephew had promised to do so; I had consented," Lewis wrote in 1816. "Nothing was necessary but to find a substitute." Before the nephew could fulfill his uncle's wishes, however, he died suddenly, and the estate went to a distant relation. Lewis appealed to the new owner to pay Cameron's manumission price, but to no avail. "I felt strongly tempted to set him at liberty at once," Lewis wrote, but he decided instead to protect his business interests. "If I were to begin in that way, there would be no stopping; and it would be doing a kindness to an individual at the expense of all my other negroes—others would expect the same; and then I must either contrive to cultivate my estate with fewer hands—or must cease to cultivate it altogether." Nicholas Cameron continued to pursue his own freedom, hiring his labor out to neighboring planters. Almost two and a half years later he had managed to gather the £150 necessary to finance his escape from slavery.[34]

An 1832 letter from the planting attorneys on the Chiswick sugar plantation to absentee owners in London shows familiar calculations by the attorneys in a situation similar to that in which Cameron and Lewis found themselves. In accordance with common practice, the late overseer of Chiswick had "formed a connexion with one of the Women on the Estate, and by her, had two children." In his will the overseer directed that the woman be freed, but the attorneys felt less compelled by the last wishes of the overseer than by the practical needs of their enterprise. Cognizant of the customary reluctance of managers to release productive slaves, the woman knew she had to stage demonstrations to gain her release. "As in all cases of this kind," the attorneys acknowledged with chagrin, she "had been much indulged for several years before his death, and naturally became troublesome soon after that event; we therefore deemed it prudent to free her." The attorneys received £200 for the woman and her two children, presumably from the overseer's estate, and resolved to "invest in the purchase of a family of much more value, and more effective for the purposes of the property." Anticipating a larger-than-usual harvest, they purchased seven slaves for £315 as substitutes. This woman had been able to play the system to her personal advantage. During her years as the overseer's companion, she had convinced him that when he died he might reach back from the grave and touch his "illegitimate" family. In return for the most intimate subjection, she finally received freedom for herself and her children from her dead patron.[35]

Gradually, frequent unions of this kind between white men and black women produced a growing population of people of color who, if they could procure freedom at all, often gained it by legacy. In 1774 there were approximately 23,000 people designated "mulattoes" on the island; only 4,000 of them were free. The closer to white in color and the higher the social status of the father, the greater the chance that a brown man, woman, or child would not be enslaved. As Edward Long noted, "the lower rank of miscegenous unions remain in the same slavish conditions as their mother; they are fellow labourers with the Blacks, and are not regarded in the least as their superiors." As people of the lower rank were usually the darker in color, across generations there was an incentive for people of color to "breed up," by mating with whites to increase the fortunes of their descendants. In this way, whiteness had real economic value, the benefits of which could accrue upon the death of patriarchs.[36]

Despite all the difficulties, free people of color who were descended directly from whites eagerly sought (and sometimes gained) shares of their progenitors' property. In 1761 the assembly found that mulatto children held property valued between £200,000 and £300,000 in Jamaican currency, devised by their parents. This included "four sugar estates, seven penns, thirteen houses, besides other lands unspecified," according to

Edward Long, who defended restrictions on such devises passed by the assembly in 1761. The law banned what it called "exhorbitant grants and devises made by white persons to Negroes and issue of Negroes," those of real or personal estate valued at over £2000. Many property holders objected to the restriction, incensed that it violated "their right to dispose of their own effects and acquisitions, in the manner most agreeable to their inclinations." Long admitted that the act of 1761 was "repugnant to the spirit of English laws" but argued that it was a practical necessity for the general good, which depended on clear and unambiguous white supremacy. He hoped that limiting bequests to mulatto children in Jamaica, as English law excluded "bastards" from inheritance, would encourage white men to "abate their infatuated attachments to black women" and form racially pure families. Looking with disgust upon what he called the "vicious, brutal, and degenerate breed of mongrels" peopling the Spanish Americas, Long expected that white Jamaicans could best uphold the interests of British colonial society by "raising in honourable wedlock a race of unadulterated beings."[37]

Long did nonetheless approve of allowances for cultural assimilation. Where the "polish of good education, and moral principles" could be proved, wealthy property owners could still apply to the assembly for exceptions. In 1790 George Bedward of Westmoreland parish petitioned the assembly for permission to bequeath a large share of his estate to his natural grandson, George James Bedward, "a free quadroon infant of tender years, who hath been baptized, and will, when of sufficient age, be brought up and instructed in the principles of the Christian religion." Recognizing that the light-skinned child would be brought up according to English religious and secular customs, the assembly assented to Bedward's request and passed an act authorizing him to dispose of his estate "in such manner as he shall think proper." In this case, it was clear that George James posed little threat to the racial hierarchy of slave society. The assembly continued to make similar exceptions for "respectable" people of color through the early nineteenth century, as long as it was clear that white supremacy could be maintained through assimilation.[38]

Still, whites were anxious about the free colored population, and for some good reasons. Even as young G. J. Bedward grew to adulthood, a growing and increasingly vocal group of free people of color protested the restrictions of the act of 1761. Between 1790 and 1820 the free colored population more than tripled in size, expanding from under 10,000 to nearly 30,000. By the second decade of the nineteenth century, free blacks and coloreds made up over 40 percent of the rank and file in the Jamaican foot militia. Working in service occupations, some had amassed impressive assets, and feeling a swelling sense of their power, they commenced petitioning campaigns to ease restrictions on their social activity. In 1813 they won the revocation of the legacy constraints. As a result, John Swaby was able to bequeath two large estates to his mulatto son James in 1826. Listed in the *Jamaica Almanack* of 1828, James Swaby owned 217 slaves and 331 head of stock and held a commission as a lieutenant in the British army. Slavery could certainly coexist with a man like Swaby, but his success did throw white supremacy open to question.[39]

But James Swaby was a rare exception. Many people of mixed ancestry remained slaves. In 1832 about 10 percent of the total enslaved population consisted of people of color who had white forebears. Most free people of color remained poor, working as artisans, bookkeepers, or petty entrepreneurs. More important, white supremacy remained one of the society's central organizing principles, giving aid and cover to people who would cheat nonwhites of their inheritance, even when it was legally due. "Of all the robberies committed in the island," Benjamin McMahon wrote of corrupt executors, "none have ever affected my mind more deeply than those which are practised upon the poor, young, innocent brown people who are thus thrown from affluence into penury and want." Free people of color lived in such poverty in early nineteenth-century Jamaica that they often died without any money at all and were buried at the expense of the church or the parish.[40]

Black Market Bequests

Very few enslaved men and women could hope that posthumous intercession by dead whites would alter their lives for the better. Yet a few more could expect bequests from fellow slaves, because they sometimes held property and, within close limits, disposed of it at death according to their wishes. Struggling for some small measure of social continuity, with help from reformers in England, over time the enslaved turned informal and extralegal arrangements for property transfer and land tenure into customary rights and legal victories.

Within Jamaica, the enslaved carried on a dynamic internal commerce. On larger plantations slaves were allowed houses, gardens, and provision grounds. Imported food was expensive, so planters compelled the slaves to feed themselves by farming small fruit and vegetable gardens adjoining their houses and larger plots of land set aside for growing food. On the one day during the week allotted for them to provide for themselves, enslaved men and women raised livestock, tended food crops, and applied their skills to petty manufactures, hoping to produce more than they needed to survive. Then they marketed their goods among the estates or took the products of their labor to great Sunday markets. There, amid animated socializing, the best-supplied—and most energetic and shrewd—could generate profits to support their families.[41]

Edward Long contended in 1774 that slaves held 20 percent of Jamaica's circulating specie. "They have the greatest part of the small silver circulation among them," claimed Long, "which they gain by the sale of their hogs, poultry, fish, corn, fruits, and other commodities, at the markets in town and country." In this way, in spite of their masters' preeminence, the enslaved established tentative economic distinctions among themselves and fragile social hierarchies that reflected their own efforts. Although most had to spend whatever they earned on essential staples, some managed to save enough by the time they died to provide for their own funerals and make bequests to friends and family members. Long asserted that some had "been known to possess from £50 to £200 at their death" and that the "industrious and frugal" often laid up £20 to £30. Long surely exaggerated the amounts, but he nevertheless pointed to a widespread informal system of intergenerational transfer. Whatever status they had managed to achieve among their fellows, enslaved men and women hoped they could pass it on to their descendants, or use it in death to provide support to their friends in bondage.[42]

One might be surprised that slaveholders allowed slaves to have property at all. Independent economic activity had the potential to sustain autonomous social power and threaten slaveholders' hegemony. On the other hand, masters were simply too stingy to provide for the total welfare of their slaves. Even in conditions of land scarcity—Simon Taylor told an associate in 1801 that the only chance he had of obtaining land for provision grounds was "when a person dies that has a spot of one or two hundred Acres and orders his Executors to sell it"—planters valued these grounds as crucial to the survival of the workforce. To the extent that the enslaved provided for their own welfare, owners had more capital available for investment or personal consumption. However, though the slaves' economy figured in slaveholders' self-interest, it was, paradoxically, the product of negotiation and struggle. To acquire and defend customary privileges, slaves had to press masters to see that such economic arrangements were part of the cost of doing business; slaves led masters to recognize their mutual interest. As slaveholders allowed slaves to hire out their skills, market their crops and livestock, and keep their profits, the enslaved came to view their internal economy as a right.[43]

Just as masters conceded the right to slaves' semiautonomous commercial life, they allowed informal inheritance rights. Enslaved men and women made their last wishes known verbally to trusted kin, friends, or authority figures, who administered the deceased's effects without the sanction of law. Legators passed on currency and livestock to whomever they pleased and, over time, even began to will gardens and provision grounds, provided that the devisees lived on the same estate. "They are permitted to dispose at their deaths of what little property they possess," Bryan Edwards wrote in 1793, "and even to bequeath their grounds or gardens to such of their fellow slaves as they think proper." And Cynric Williams observed on his tour of the island in 1823, "They are allowed by courtesy, in all cases, to leave what property they may acquire to their children or friends upon the same estate, but not to strangers." The master's definition of a stranger was likely to be different from that of his slaves, and for those who had relatives on other estates the restriction was a severe impediment to the reconstitution of family lines. The restriction also compounded the injury done to slaves who were sold away from estates where they had relatives. Yet despite the limitations, enslaved men and women retained some ability at their deaths to preserve, stabilize, and re-create relationships with kin and friends through material legacies.[44]

Willingness on the part of a master to leave it up to the enslaved to determine their own rules of inheritance did not preclude participation in disputed claims. Sir Henry Thomas De la Beche, the pioneering British geologist and absentee landlord of the Halse Hall estate, wrote in his *Notes on the Present Condition of the Negroes in Jamaica* (1825) that custom "gives the negro the power of disposing his property as he may think fit; the nearest of kin generally bury the deceased, and take possession of his grounds, house, & c." However, "those who wish their property to be left divided in any particular manner, make a will for that purpose." As evidence, De la Beche reproduced the will of an enslaved "mulatto" man named Richard Sadler:

> This is the last will and testament of me, Richard Sadler, of Halse Hall. I give and bequeath unto my dutiful wife, Frances Bell, (for her good conduct and attention towards me during my illness) my house, and my household goods, and my wearing apparel, my mare, and furniture, and as to all the rest, residue, and remainder, of my property and effects, of which I may die possessed or entitled to. I devise and bequeath, that, after my burial, that neither male nor female is to trouble the said Frances Bell about my property and effects. And I hereby nominate, constitute, and appoint James Butler to settle my affairs, for the said Frances Bell, of this my last will and testament. Taken this 2nd day of July 1824, signed in behalf of Richard Sadler.

The document was signed by James Butler, one of the Halse Hall book-keepers, and marked by four enslaved witnesses: Frances, Thomas, Black, and Nelly. The overseer and attorney for the plantation, Valentine B. Cock, certified that "every thing of which he may die possessed shall belong solely to Frances Bell." Despite Sadler's wishes, his other relations laid claim to his estate, persuading De la Beche to read out the will in public, "after which they were contented, and the widow took possession of all that was left her."[45]

One must use caution in interpreting Richard Sadler's will. De la Beche, like most others who commented on slavery in the midst of abolitionist political agitation in Britain, had an agenda. Although he was not a proslavery ideologue, he was keen to render a sympathetic portrayal of his family's business. He thought that abolitionists had exaggerated the sufferings of the enslaved, though he also condemned the casual brutality of many Jamaican slaveholders. Most important, he was among those enlightened reformers who thought of the enslaved as subjects of both the British Empire and their masters. As British subjects, even slaves would theoretically be entitled to certain rights—and the right to property figured prominently in such considerations. De la Beche, like many slaveholders, was eager to show that his own subjects enjoyed such rights by custom, lest he be found to be a tyrant, and Parliament encouraged to intervene against him. In publishing Sadler's will, De la Beche thus tried to represent plantation slavery as a civilized institution. On the other hand, the fact that De la Beche published the will for a reason does not mean that he fabricated it. De la Beche, who directed the world's first geological survey, was, after all, more attuned to empirical than to polemical considerations. In the light of other evidence concerning bequests among the enslaved, it is likely that the will reproduced by De la Beche corresponded in large measure to the one prepared by Sadler.[46]

Treated as an actual testament, then, Sadler's will suggests several things about the family legacies of the enslaved. Most important, legacies were contested among the enslaved as well as among the free. This meant that whatever principles of inheritance existed among them, competing claims required an appeal to social authority. Slaves sought to give their bequests the greatest possible weight, including, when possible, the sanction of law. Witnessed by Frances, Thomas, Black, and Nelly, the signing of the will was an event that invited acknowledgment from the enslaved community. By appointing the bookkeeper Butler as executor, Sadler invoked the authority of white supremacy and plantation hierarchy—a form of ratification reinforced by the certification of the overseer. When a dispute arose, the existence of the written document allowed De la Beche, Halse Hall's ultimate judicial authority, to settle the matter by intoning Sadler's last wishes. "Although the attempt at legal form may cause a smile," wrote De la Beche with mocking condescension, "the instrument answered every purpose for which it was intended." Perhaps most significant was that as a man with a white parent, Sadler had more access to and facility with the tactics and tools of formal authority. Closeness to the cultural practices of the powerful bred in him an expectation of successful familial continuity.[47]

The overseer Thomas Thistlewood, who had facilitated a similar transaction in March 1758 for an enslaved "mulatto" man named Will, made a note of Will's last wishes in his diary. "Tuesday, 21st March: Write a memorandum, how Mulatto Will's goods are to be disposed of at his death. His wife's shipmate Silvia to have his cow; her daughter Hester, the heifer; Damsel his wife (Jimmy Hayes's wife) the filly & rest of what he has. He desires to be buried at Salt River at his mother Dianah's right hand." A week later, on Easter Monday, Will died; his final wishes regarding his effects allows a brief glimpse into his network of intimate relations. His desire to bequeath a cow to his wife's shipmate highlights the crucial importance of that peculiar kin relationship to families as a whole and not just to the individuals who endured the middle passage together. The women in Will's life were at the center of his last thoughts. His mother, his wife, and her daughter were all to receive legacies, but his white father, possible male children, and friends are not mentioned. Most surprisingly, perhaps, his wife Damsel still receives the greatest portion of his effects, though it appears he had to share her affections with Jimmy Hayes, a white man on the plantation, who claimed her as a consort. Despite this most intimate intrusion, Will nevertheless sought in his last gesture to aid his wife and the other women in his family. Will's bequests may indicate his inclination toward principles of matrilineal descent, but more certainly they show a determination to brace a fractured lineage, of whatever kind. Thus, his last wishes echo a hard fight against the fleeting nature of life, connection, and legacy in Jamaica.[48]

As the testaments of Richard Sadler and Mulatto Will illustrate, the genealogical principles that governed inheritance among the enslaved were open and adaptive; in other words, they reflected the flux that characterized social life. The perpetual movement of people, from Africa to Jamaica, to various properties, and to the afterlife, required, as anthropologist Jean Besson has explained, that families create "networks of mutual exchange and aid, elaborating biological ties on both parental sides." The enslaved drew fictive kin and intimate friends into familial relationships that extended through time. Cynric Williams recognized this network in the early nineteenth century, when he compared inheritance practices among slaves to "the present laws of France on wills, which restrain a testator from bequeathing away his property to the exclusion of his relations and children, though illegitimate."[49]

Most eighteenth- and nineteenth-century commentators described inheritance from the standpoint of male testators and never discussed devises made by women. Yet most also recognized the relative openness of inheritance practices among slaves. Long recognized the authority of "the black grandfather, or father, [who] directs in what manner his money, his hogs, poultry, furniture, cloaths, and other effects and acquisitions, shall descend, or be disposed of, after his decease." William Beckford, writing in 1788, argued, "Negroes absolutely respect primogeniture; and the eldest son takes an indisputed possession of his father's property immediately after his decease." However, contrary to Beckford's assertion, there is scant evidence that primogeniture was the general practice. Indeed, more evidence suggests that family land passed on to "all descendants in perpetuity, regardless of gender, birth order, and legitimacy." The same year that Beckford published his descriptive account of Jamaica, Hector McNeill described a more open system of inheritance that also took into account the intervention of plantation managers: "The possessions belonging to old Negroes are commonly bequeathed by the deceased to his relations, or they are bestowed by the superintendant on the most deserving and the most needy; but more particularly on those who possessed the greatest share of affection of the deceased—an excellent institution to insure attention and comfort to the aged." John Baillie, who was the resident proprietor of the Roehampton estate from 1788 to 1826, observed that when testators died without children, the parceling out of inheritance adhered to African ethnic lines and affective ties. When a House of Lords committee asked him in 1833 what became of the property of deceased slaves, Baillie told them, "They have all connexions more or less; the Africans, they call one another brothers and sisters, and so on. Those who are their countrymen, they claim it; the master never gets it at all events."[50]

The rare descriptions of enslaved family inheritance patterns available from nineteenth-century records suggest that the importance of daughters as heirs equaled or exceeded that of sons. In 1823 one old man who had worked in a livestock pen decided to leave five pounds to his daughter's husband, the manservant to the pen's owner. He did this not because he felt obliged by the marriage to do so, but because the man "had behaved so well to her." The rest of his effects "he left to his daughter for herself." An incident that Matthew Lewis recorded in his diary in 1817 also hints that daughters and their children were important inheritors of slave property. Old Damon had two daughters, one married to a man named Pickle, the other to Edward. Damon planned to split his effects between the two women when he died, but Edward had declared publicly that "his wife would remain sole heiress of the father's property." Shortly after Edward's declaration, Pickle's wife had a miscarriage. It was her third, and she now suspected witchcraft as the cause. Pickle and Old Damon came to Lewis, who granted them a hearing. They told him that "in order to prevent a child coming to claim its share of the grandfather's property, Edward had practised Obeah to make his sister-in-law miscarry." Lewis dismissed the charge as groundless, even "foolish." It is possible that if Old Damon had

had living sons, they might have been exclusive heirs; Lewis does not say. Nor does he divulge how contingent the inheritance of Pickle's wife was on her having her own children. But the incident he described does at least suggest that the right of women to inherit the property of their progenitors was strongly established, especially when they did have children. It also indicates the vital importance of the patronage grandparents tried to bestow on their grandchildren.[51]

Clearly, slaves tried to retain or reconstitute familial links that stretched as far across time as they could manage. Indeed, just two months before Old Damon accused Edward of trying to truncate the family bloodline, Lewis heard a request from another of his slaves for help in maintaining good relations between ancestors and descendants. Neptune came to him "to request that the name of his son, Oscar, might be changed for that of Julius, which (it seems) had been that of his own father." Neptune's son had chronically poor health, and Neptune feared that the child's condition resulted from his deceased grandfather's displeasure over Neptune's failure to name the child after him. Lewis concluded: "They conceive that the ghosts of their ancestors cannot fail to be offended at their abandoning an appellation, either hereditary in the family, or given by themselves."[52]

Land and Lineage

Veneration for ancestors derived from traditions rooted in Africa. It also provided the basis for a struggle between masters and slaves over the inheritance of Jamaican land. While precise inheritance patterns among the enslaved are difficult to distinguish, it is possible to discern the increasing importance of land claims in struggles to establish and maintain family lines. Edward Long rather cynically assumed that the veneration blacks had for their elders and for ancestry was stimulated by the goods they "enjoyed by devise." Yet with respect to land, it is more accurate to say that Africans and their descendants valued it and sought to possess it, in order to manifest a preexisting respect for their ancestors. As anthropologists Sidney Mintz and Richard Price have put it, they used land "as a means of defining both time and descent, with ancestors venerated locally, and with history and genealogy both being particularized in specific pieces of ground." Africans in most areas of the continent that fed the Atlantic slave trade owned land corporately and had the right to farm and own the products of their labor, but rarely to sell, alienate, or rent their land. Indeed, common views on landholding established ancient ancestors, who had settled the territory on behalf of their descendants, as the true owners of land—an arrangement Britons might have likened to entail. This belief might explain why slaves paid great attention, as so many planters observed, to the genealogy of plantation ownership. Long noticed that "their attachment to the descendants of old families, the ancestors of which were the masters and friends of their own progenitors, is remarkably strong and affectionate." William Beckford insisted that "they reverence a master who claims from inheritance." As soon as Matthew Lewis arrived on his plantation from England, he said, "Twenty voices at once enquired after uncles, and aunts, and grandfathers, and great-grandmothers of mine, who had been buried long before I was in existence, and whom, I verily believe, most of them only knew by tradition."[53]

Africans in Jamaica revered ancestral lands partly because they were burial sites and places of social attachment and incorporation, where forebears afforded spiritual protection from evil and chaos. Slaves, when forced to move from the land where their kin were buried, lost that protection, as well as the limited security afforded by temporal social connections. The predicament provided a powerful incentive for the enslaved to learn how they could stay close to their burial grounds and force masters to respect their land rights. Older Africans and Creoles born and raised in slavery therefore learned to adapt corporate ancestral claims to accord with familial inheritance claims. Just as Africans tried to stay close to their ancestral burial grounds, they tried to pass them on to their children. As one commentator noticed, "they bury their Relations adjoining to their own House, which makes the House go to the Family as it were." For the enslaved, the staking of greater claims to territorial property was one strategy for avoiding dislocation and social isolation. On family land, slaves could found family lines and anchor widespread kinship networks. This was no easy or ordinary achievement. Older survivors of slavery and Creoles could clearly claim a more secure right to land, but only those who lived long enough to have children, and whose children survived the ravages of the colonial economy, could authoritatively link land with lineage.[54]

In 1783 Simon Taylor wrote to Chaloner Arcedeckne concerning a piece of land claimed by an elderly man named Philander, formerly a cooper on the Golden Grove estate. Philander was comparatively privileged, having earned from Arcedeckne an annuity of five pounds upon his "retirement" some years before from plantation labor. Now, he wanted to leave a legacy. "It is a piece of land at the End of the Garden and which is entailed, he has been twenty times told he could not have it, but nothing Satisfies him, or indeed any Negroe, when they think that by importunity they can get a thing," Taylor recounted. "It is not for the Sake of the Children that are buried there that he wants it, but to give it away to some other Children after his Death for he lives there now unmolested by any one whatever." Philander certainly knew that he was testing the limits of Taylor's indulgence by insisting that the customary right to pass on goods and livestock extended to include the right to bequeath land. Indeed, he was claiming land under entail—land that Arcedeckne was legally forbidden to sell to anyone—so there is little possibility that he achieved his aim. But there is little doubt that Philander was determined to pass down the hard-won concessions gleaned from a life spent in slavery. Taylor's frustration with Philander highlights a complex and dynamic process of sharp negotiation that ultimately resulted in slaveholders' informal respect for the land claims of the enslaved. Struggles such as Philander's probably played out all over the island, for in the 1780s William Beckford noticed how reluctant slaves were to "resign those houses that were built by their ancestors, forego those grounds that were settled by their forefathers, and which have been handed down for years, and become the inheritance of the same family." In effect, Beckford was describing a system of two parallel land tenures: a formal one, regulated by force of law, and an informal one, supported by the determined negotiations of the enslaved.[55]

These slaves' efforts coincided with pressure from Britain for systemic reform, which eventually obliged slaveholders to take slave land claims somewhat more seriously. Slaveholders in Anglo-America had largely been left to run their own affairs, until the expansion of the British Empire that followed the United Kingdom's victory in the Seven Years' War, and the imperial crisis wrought by the American Revolution, provoked serious engagement with questions of imperial governance on the part of imperial policymakers. But beginning in the 1770s and with mounting intensity after the rise of the antislavery movement in the 1780s, officials in London began to consider how the empire might more effectively rule its overseas subjects, who included a great many slaves. Edmund Burke, who was among the most influential writers of the time, became convinced that the enslaved should not be left "under the sole guardianship of their Masters, or their Attorneys and Overseers." In 1792 he sent a seventy-two-point "Sketch of a Negro Code," originally drafted in 1780, to Home Secretary Henry Dundas. The plan suggested more stringent imperial oversight of slavery and the slave trade but also elaborated on how the enslaved might become suitable subjects. Along with religion, family, and morality, Burke believed, "the means of acquiring and preserving property" were essential to preparing slaves for their eventual assumption of British liberties and responsibilities. To this end, he suggested they be given testamentary rights to "devise or bequeath" any "lands, goods, or chattels" acquired during their lifetimes. Should a slave die intestate, Burke suggested—always assuming a male testator—his property should be distributed among "his wife and children." It is not apparent that Burke knew anything of the ongoing struggles to obtain inheritance rights in the Caribbean, and his concept of family made no allowance for cultural difference, but his own thoughts on bequests complemented the efforts of the enslaved them-selves, and by the 1790s gave them influential allies among imperial policy-makers.[56]

Slaveholders, in this context, felt pressure from above and below. Cer-tainly, by the end of the eighteenth century the customary right to bequeath land had been won. "They are permitted," observed Bryan Edwards, a longtime resident of Jamaica, in his 1793 history of the British Caribbean, "to bequeath their grounds or gardens to such of their fellow slaves as they think proper." Edwards told his British reading audience what they wanted to hear but also, just as important, what he had been compelled to notice himself. "These principles are so well established," he explained, "that whenever it is found convenient for the owner to exchange the Negro-grounds for other lands, the Negroes must be satis-fied, in money or otherwise, before the exchange takes place. It is univer-sally the practice."[57]

Legacies of Struggle

Though the inheritance claims of the enslaved could provide the basis for a social cohesion that might challenge slaveholders' power, slaves also had an incentive to work within the established hierarchy of the slave society to achieve and consolidate their inheritance rights. In time, as the enslaved pushed the boundaries of their internal economy, they selected people of increasing prominence in the plantation hierarchy as trustees and executors of their "estates." When Edward Long wrote of bequests among the enslaved population in 1774, he noted that legators nominated "trustees, or executors, from the nearest of kin, who distribute them among the legatees, according to the will of the testator, without any molestation or interruption, most often without the enquiry of their master." Only when the people who died had no close relations did the superintendent, usually the overseer, divide the property as he saw fit. However, by the nineteenth century enslaved blacks chose as executors people who held positions in the social hierarchy that were more secure than their own. Recall that Mulatto Will deputed Thomas Thistlewood as his executor, presumably because he thought only a white man had the authority to carry out his last wishes properly. Similarly, Richard Sadler made the white bookkeeper James Butler his executor. As men of mixed parentage, Will and Sadler were more likely to have access to white patrons. Yet among enslaved blacks too, men whose social authority was bestowed by plantation managers came to occupy a greater role in the administration of bequests.[58]

On smaller properties or for domestic work, where masters and slaves labored in close proximity, the executor might even be the proprietor. Mr. Klopstock, the owner of a modest livestock pen, became the executor for one of his slaves. The man made Klopstock responsible for parceling out his property and for arranging his funeral, so "that he might be consoled in his dying moments with an assurance of the honours he should receive after death." On large plantations, where blacks generally lived isolated from whites, they turned to the black managers on the estates. John Baillie told the House of Lords in 1832 that in case of any disputes over legacies, he was content to leave their resolution to these head people, constituted by the driver, the head cooper, the head mason, the head carpenter, the head blacksmith, the head pen keeper, and the head watchmen. "If there is any dispute," explained Baillie, "they bring their Evidence of Connection, and it is arranged among the head people what proportion belongs to one and what to another; sometimes they say Tom shall have such a fruit tree, and Bessy another, and it is understood among their family before their death." By co-opting head people as arbiters of inheritance claims in this way, slaves conceded the structure of plantation authority in order to implicate it in the protection of their claims.[59]

The enslaved kept shrewd account of what they considered to be their land and its agricultural products. Cynric Williams once heard from a slaveowner that his slave had come to claim compensation from him after the master had cut off a branch of a calabash tree in his own garden. "The negro maintained that his own grandfather had planted the tree, and had had a house and garden beside it," wrote Williams in 1823, "and he claimed the land as his inheritance, though he had his own negro-grounds elsewhere as a matter of course. The gentleman was so amused by Quaco's pertinacy and argument, that he bought the land and tree, right and title, of him for a dollar."[60]

By the end of slavery, the enslaved had turned customary usage into near-legal rights wrested from the Jamaican plantocracy. Responding to insistent recommendations from London, the Slave Act of 1826 finally codified the right of slaves to own chattels and to receive bequests, though the law did not authorize lawsuits for the recovery of legacies until 1831, when slaveowners were given the right to sue for the recovery of legacies made to their slaves. The act of 1826 formally sanctioned the executorship of masters such as Mr. Klopstock on behalf of their slaves when it authorized a slave's "owner, manager, or possessor" to act as trustee of slave bequests. The reforms stopped short of mandating full protection and were careful to subsume slave property rights under the ultimate sovereignty of slaveowners, but enslaved men and women conveniently ignored the finer points and provisos of the law. As William Burge, a coffee planter, Jamaica agent, and former attorney general of the island, explained to the House of Lords in 1832: "A slave being once put into possession of his provision grounds considers them completely his own property, and he is allowed to dispose of them to such of his family as he pleases. Those acquainted with Jamaica know," Burge continued, "that if from any cause it becomes necessary to remove the slaves from one property to another, or even change their provision grounds on the same property, the greatest difficulty is found in reconciling them to the removal or change." Indeed, planters paid what Burge thought to be "considerable sums" to enslaved landholders in compensation for lost grounds. "A person having to remove slaves must first of all furnish them with new

Houses, and plant new grounds for them, and give them a compensation for the grounds they have already, independently of their being at liberty to go back and take all the provisions remaining in those grounds." As an example, Burge cited an anecdote told to him by Simon Taylor. "Adjoining the houses and gardens of the negroes on one of his estates were some cocoa-nut trees which had grown up, and were supposed to render their Habitations unhealthy," Burge recounted, "but it was with the greatest difficulty, and after a length of time, and by giving them money, he could prevail upon them to allow him to cut them down." In the face of ever greater intervention by London into colonial affairs and of imminent emancipation of the slaves by Parliament, Burge clearly wanted to represent slavery as a relatively mild institution and probably overstated the actual control that slaves had over their property. At the same time, it is clear that the enslaved forcefully asserted their right to own and exchange property according to their wishes.[61]

Some among the enslaved had apparently grown so confident of their property rights that they loosened the old African prohibitions against selling or alienating land. Vice-Admiral C. E. Fleeming, who visited Jamaica for several periods in the 1820s as the commander in chief of the naval force in Jamaica, told the House of Lords that slaves conducted "transfers of property among themselves," including exchanges of huts, houses, and grounds. "I have known of persons who have acquired property by inheritance passing it to others," said Fleeming, "for, when the people are in little communities, they are very particular about their own boundaries." Similarly, Edmund Sharp, who was an overseer on seven different properties between 1811 and 1832, where he was in charge of between 150 and 600 slaves, reported that blacks sold, exchanged, and willed their houses and provision grounds "to any one upon the same estate, and that without any objection, that I ever heard of, upon the part of the master."[62]

Slaveholders' indifference had limits. Some families were so successful at claiming possession of and passing on their land that planters felt compelled to intervene. In 1817 Matthew Lewis complained that some enslaved men and women on his Cornwall plantation had come by inheritance to be "owners of several houses and numerous gardens in the village, while others with large families were either inadequately provided for, or not provided for at all." Reasserting his own dominion, while flattering himself on his benevolence, Lewis decreed that "henceforth no negro should possess more than one house, with a sufficient portion of ground for his family." Lewis implemented his commands with little delay: "The following Sunday the overseer by my order looked over the village, took from those who had too much to give to those who had too little, and made an entire new distribution according to the most strict Agrarian law." Lewis's draconian land reform surely reminded his slaves that it was only determined effort, rather than the generosity of any slaveholder, that enabled them to demand and defend some limited but crucial collective self-determination—and that, even then, no gain made within the confines of slavery was ever secure.[63]

Though death inspired active and dynamic practices of social reconnection, scholars have often followed Orlando Patterson in positing a metaphorical "social death" as the basic condition of slavery. In language echoing the theses of Robert Park and E. Franklin Frazier—that the enslaved had been culturally stripped by slavery's rigors and terrors—Patterson described social death as the absence of inheritance. "Formally isolated in his social relations with those who lived," Patterson wrote of the archetypal slave, "he also was culturally isolated from the social heritage of his ancestors." Patterson was certainly correct in arguing that slaves "were not allowed *freely* to integrate the experience of their ancestors into their lives, to inform their understanding of social reality with the inherited meanings of their natural forebears, or to anchor the living present in any conscious community of memory."[64] Yet everything in this assertion hangs on the word "freely," and nothing was free in Jamaican slave society. Recognition of actual inheritance practices among the enslaved should therefore caution historians and others against viewing "social death" as an actual state of being, while the history of slave bequests also reminds us that social connections and communities of memory had to be created through struggle.

⪥⪥

Death in Jamaica destroyed individuals, while generating a society. In the midst of catastrophe, people anxiously imagined the future, expecting the dead to assist them in their endeavors, just as they expected to play a continuing role in the lives of their own descendants. Legacy and inheritance were crucial features of slave society, less through precise rules of intergenerational transfer than as an inspiration to purposeful will and action. The practices for managing financial transfers from the dead to the living were embedded in struggles over the nature and future of the society.

The deaths of powerful whites created opportunities for material gain that coincided with the risk of massive social disruption. People grappled with both risks and opportunities partly by struggling over the legacies of the dead. With families, institutions, and the social order itself subject to constant threat from demographic conditions and political insurrections, bequests and legacies molded the character of Jamaican social life. A personal bequest—for free and enslaved alike—represented a means to stabilize families and angle for social position. Executors were the crucial mediators in this process: they could strengthen families or tear them apart, implement the wishes of the deceased person or use their power for private enrichment. Executorship was a means to great wealth but also a socially disruptive force in a debt-burdened economy, where the death of a property owner might occasion the dislocation of scores of men and women. In order to maintain the profitability of their properties, all slaveholders, but especially the landed planters, had to contend with the communal aspirations of their slaves. Inheritance claims, reflecting proprietary, familial, and emotional attachments to land and goods, formed a significant part of those aspirations. To gain recognition for those claims, the enslaved continually had to test, challenge, and negotiate the authority of slaveholders, and in this sense the politics of inheritance formed a critical aspect of the politics of slavery. The expectations of the dead thus shaped social hierarchy and conflict over time.

Social patterns do not betoken social stasis. Relations between the living and the dead helped stabilize tumultuous lives, but they were also agents of change. People allied themselves with the dead not only to give some regularity to the chaos of slavery, but also to engage in battles to preserve, reform, or end it altogether. Although death and power in Jamaica were embedded in a larger transatlantic history, they also shaped and directed that history. In other words, the dead had afterlives of consequence.

CHAPTER FOUR

Icons, Shamans, and Martyrs

IN DECEMBER 1806, toward the end of the British transatlantic slave trade, Captain Hugh Crow brought his cargo of 393 captives from the Bight of Biafra into Kingston Harbor. The Africans were crowded onto the deck of the *Mary* when she steered past the sandy lowland keys of Port Royal, where they witnessed a human sacrifice. Ten or twelve sailors, executed for some breach of discipline aboard a warship of the Royal Navy, were hanging on the gibbets that festooned the shoals. For the crew of the *Mary*, familiar with the rough nature of military justice, the spectacle of fellow tars dangling lifeless in chains and iron cages "excited more of pity for their fate than of abhorrence for their offence," which, according to Crow, "few persons believed was deserving of so awful a punishment." The Africans, who had already seen nearly a hundred of their number die during their seven-week passage, "became dreadfully alarmed, lest they should be sacrificed in the same manner," and the crew had "much difficulty in preventing many of them from jumping overboard, and in allaying their apprehensions."[1]

Crow did not use the word "sacrifice" lightly. By the time his memoir was published in 1830, its readers could congratulate themselves on the abolition of the slave trade. He meant to suggest to them that the trade was no more savage than the punitive customs of military rule. Indeed, he indicated that human sacrifice, with all its atavistic connotations, was the price of imperial order. The authority of the Royal Navy depended in no small measure on its willingness to kill the disobedient and make a

Figure 4.1. Executions of convicted rebels, engraving by Joshua Bryant, in Bryant, *Account of the Insurrection of the Negro Slaves in the Colony of Demerara on the 18th of August, 1823* (Georgetown, Demerara, 1824), plate 12. The illustration depicts the punishment of three slaves implicated in the uprising. A man hangs on the gallows, and two heads mark the road to the plantation in the distance. Similar scenes characterized the Jamaican landscape throughout the era of slavery. Courtesy of the British Library.

public spectacle of their corpses. Such demonstrations were a frequent occurrence in Atlantic ports, especially during times of war, when naval discipline was at its strictest. But similar spectacles were even more common on the island, where slaveholders employed the most terrifying tactics of state control (Figure 4.1). Though Crow may have meant merely to salvage his own reputation by establishing a comparison with the reputed cruelties of slave traders, he also highlighted an important aspect of the operation of power throughout the world of Atlantic slavery: necromancy, the conjuration and manipulation of the dead for the purpose of shaping actions and events. To put it another way, naval officials and Crow's crew knew just what the Africans knew, that the dead were ever present and could be conscripted for political service. By yoking the dead to claims of authority, not only the Royal Navy, but all those who contended for power could forcefully invoke the revenants of the departed. In effect, those who used the bodies of the executed to proclaim their dominion were, just as surely as shamans, who claimed to hold influence over the dead, practicing a politically potent form of necromancy— enlisting the transcendent to affect the outcome of worldly conflicts. By invoking the power of the dead, whether as an admonition to rebels, as a force from the other world, or as an example of martyrdom, the living made the haunted and terrifying landscape of spiritual existence apply to temporal social struggles.[2]

Icons

In his history of the British West Indies, the planter, poet, and politician Bryan Edwards admitted that "in countries where slavery is established, the leading principle on which the government is supported is fear: or a sense of that absolute coercive necessity which, leaving no choice of action, supersedes all questions of right." Yet slave masters did not achieve the fear requisite to maintain control over the enslaved by physical force alone. They asserted their right to rule by trying to terrorize the spiritual imaginations of the enslaved. To do so, slave masters projected their authority symbolically through punishment wreaked upon the bodies of the dead. As anthropologist Katherine Verdery has noted, dead bodies carry great symbolic weight: "They evoke awe, uncertainty, and fear associated with 'cosmic' concerns, such as the meaning of life and death." Moreover, when dead bodies are managed with political intent, "their corporeality makes them important means of *localizing* a claim." The physical presence of a corpse connects its meaningful associations with its tangible location. Using dead bodies as symbols, masters marked their territory with awe-inducing emblems of their power.[3]

The use of terror to capture the imaginations of the enslaved was a staple feature of social control in slave society. Slaveholders supplemented physical coercion with even more menacing "government magic," as they harnessed the affective power of the dead and people's awe of the afterlife in an attempt to transmute legal mastery into sacred authority. Yet though their intent was to dominate the imagination, the routinization of terrifying spectacles only enhanced the importance of practices that associated dead bodies and haunting spirits with political authority, practices that could also reinforce the influence of slaves who were willing to resist or to rise up and strike their masters. Both masters and slaves tried to boost their authority by drawing the connection between it and the transcendent. In other words, they attached otherworldly significance to worldly concerns.⁴

Slaveholders faced a persistent threat of dispossession through slaves' suicide. The harshness of the labor regime, social isolation, and diminished status, as well as the longing to return to ancestral lands, prompted many among the enslaved to destroy themselves. Henry Coor, who worked for fifteen years as a millwright in the Jamaican parish of Westmoreland, observed that unbearable workloads, physical punishment, and incessant hunger led many Africans to cut their own throats or hang themselves. "I remember fourteen Slaves," he told a British House of Commons committee in 1791, "that it was generally said, and I believe it was, from bad treatment, that them [*sic*] rise in rebellion on a Sunday, who ran away into the woods, and all cut their own throats together." For some, harsh treatment only aggravated the general indignity of lost social status. One plantation doctor who served in Jamaica from 1755 to 1765 told the same committee about an African "man of consequence" who reportedly refused to work for any white man. Even after being punished by his overseer, the African told the overseer to warn his owner that "he would be a slave to no man." Fearing that the man was an incorrigible rebel, the owner ordered him removed to another plantation. "His hands were tied behind him; in going over a bridge, he jumped headlong into the water, and appeared no more." Even Africans held in lower esteem still faced the kind of disorienting social isolation that could lead to irremediable depression. The same plantation doctor owned a boy who "detested the idea of slavery so much that he refused all support, which brought on a dropsy, and terminated in his death." New African immigrants were known to kill themselves more often than seasoned slaves; Creoles (those born on the island) only rarely committed suicide. Commenting on the death rates for newly arrived men, higher than those for women, former overseer William Fitzmaurice testified in 1791 that women, who were able to enter into relationships and work as domestic servants, had access to social roles and protection unavailable to men. Consequently, he surmised, men were more depressed and committed suicide in Jamaica more often than women. Recently arrived Africans "constantly told me," he said, "that they preferred dying to living."⁵

Perhaps many Africans were sanguine about the prospect of suicide because they believed they would return home to their ancestral lands after death, there to be reunited as spirits and ancestors with lost kin and friends. Mark Cook, a clerk, schoolmaster, and small planter in Jamaica, knew of several men and women, all Africans, who had hanged or shot themselves. Claiming to be acquainted with African funerals, he recognized that the enslaved made "great rejoicings on those occasions, because, as I have understood from them, they thought their countrymen were gone back to their own country again." When Lieutenant Baker Davidson of the Seventy-ninth Regiment testified before a House of Commons committee in 1790, he was asked if he knew of any cases of Africans "expressing themselves with affection of their native country, and desiring to return to it." Davidson replied, "I did, . . . as I brought a Guinea woman to England who wished much to be sent back to her own country; and it is very common for Negroes when they are sick to say, they are going back to their own country." "Do they say it with apparent satisfaction?" the committee asked. "They certainly do," Davidson said, "as they express always a great deal of pleasure when they think they are going to die, and say that they are going to leave this Buccra country."[6]

Slave masters throughout the Caribbean used spiritual terror to deter Africans from self-destruction. At least as early as the mid-seventeenth century, British West Indian planters hoped that mutilating the dead would impress Africans with the slaveholders' power over the spiritual fate of the enslaved. Africans, lamented Richard Ligon, a seventeenth-century chronicler of slave society in Barbados, "believe in a Resurrection, and that they shall go into their own Country again, and have their youth renewed. And lodging this opinion in their hearts, they make it an ordinary practice, upon any great fright, or threatening of their Masters, to hang themselves." A planter acquaintance of Ligon's, Colonel Walrond, had in a short time lost three or four of his most valuable slaves to suicide. Fearing that they had set a costly example to others, Walrond ordered that one of their heads be chopped off and fixed to a pole a dozen feet high. He marched all his slaves around the icon, commanding them to gaze at the severed head, and he asked them to acknowledge that this was indeed the head of one of the self-murderers. As they did, Walrond told them that "they were in a main errour, in thinking they went into their own Countreys, after they were dead; for, this man's head was here, as they all were witnesses of; and how was it possible, the body could go without a head." As Ligon remembered it, the Africans were convinced by the "sad, yet lively spectacle." They apparently changed their convictions, and hanged themselves no more.[7]

Though Walrond may have been spared further losses of that sort, Africans continued to kill themselves with distressing frequency in the Caribbean, and slaveholders kept resorting to grisly techniques of deterrence. In the eighteenth-century Danish West Indies, C. G. A. Oldendorp reported that "the head and hands of such suicides have been put in a cage on public display—a measure not without effective results." In prerevolutionary Saint-Domingue, French slavers mutilated the body of the first Ebo slave to die of suicide in a given shipment: they beheaded the corpse or sliced off its nose and pried out its eyes, to prevent losses among other captives from the Bight of Biafra, who were widely reputed to be prone to suicide. With a similar objective, Cuban merchants and masters in the early nineteenth century incinerated corpses of other Africans.[8]

In Jamaica, such practices were widespread throughout the eighteenth-century. Just before midcentury, an anonymous Jamaican planter wrote that to prevent Africans from believing that they could escape the island through death, their bodies were "often hanged up" by their masters to show the living that the dead remained in Jamaica. It was around this time that masters began to apply the punishment for outright rebellion—burning of bodies to ash—to suicides as well. And to dramatize the impossibility of their repatriation in death, masters threatened to deny suicidal slaves last rites. In 1751 the Anglican rector of Westmoreland parish wrote to his bishop that "to deprive them of their funeral Rites by burning their dead Bodies, seems to Negroes a greater Punishment than Death itself. This is done to Self-Murderers." As late as the final decade of slavery, John Stewart remembered a time when newly arriving Africans committed suicide to "return to their native country, and enjoy the society of kindred and friends, from whom they have been torn away in an evil hour." He also recalled the "dismal and disgusting spectacle" of their heads adorning poles along public roads, and their bodies "sometimes consumed by fire."[9]

Whether such mutilations in fact constituted an effective deterrent is open to question. Dismemberment certainly represented a compelling metaphysical threat to English Protestants, but there is little or no direct evidence that Africans believed that losing their head or a limb would prevent their return to ancestral lands. Many Africans had surely seen severed heads taken as trophies by warring state authorities in Africa. Indeed, in parts of West Africa, slaves were routinely beheaded after the death of nobles, so that they could continue to serve their masters in the spiritual world. European masters in Jamaica, only dimly aware of African parallels, beheaded and dismembered their own slaves with a similar desire that the dead continue their service. Through the treatment given dead bodies slaveholders attempted to seize and manipulate the African vision of the afterlife, to govern the actions of the living.[10]

Mutilating the bodies of Africans who committed suicide was only part of a broader agenda that made use of ritual execution to lend to worldly authority a sacred, even supernatural, dimension. As with the punishment of suicide, punishments for rebellion were meant to inspire terror in the enslaved about their ultimate fate, in this case by visiting extraordinary torments on their bodies before and after death. By the late seventeenth century, slave rebels were being burned alive. Sir Hans Sloane, who visited Jamaica just before the turn of the eighteenth century, described the grisly tortures meted out to slaves and the meticulous method of executing rebels, "by nailing them down on the ground with crooked Sticks on every Limb, and then applying the Fire by degrees from the Feet and Hands, burning them gradually up to the Head, whereby their pains are extravagant." Only two weeks after Thomas Thistlewood arrived in Savanna-la-Mar in 1750, he watched his host William Dorrill order the body of a dead runaway dug up and beheaded, with the head to be fixed on a pole and the body to be incinerated. Just months later Thistlewood "saw a Negro fellow nam'd English belonging to Fuller Wood Tried, lost, and hang'd upon ye 1st Tree immediately (for drawing his knife upon a White Man), his head Cutt off, Body left unbury'd." Once he assumed the post of overseer on the Egypt sugar plantation, Thistlewood also had occasion to use the dead to enhance his authority. In October 1752 he was pleased to receive a letter, two returned fugitives, and "also Robin's head, who was hanged yesterday for running away with those two boys." As a warning to others he "put it upon a pole and stuck it up just at the angle of the road in the home pasture."[11]

Lady Maria Nugent passed just such a signpost on her way to church one day in 1803. If the members of her party had not already promised their attendance to the clergyman in Kingston, she protested to her diary, "I would not have gone, for we were obliged to pass close by the pole, on which was stuck the head of a black man who was executed a few days ago." Placing the bodies of the condemned along well-traveled paths served to haunt those places with memories and narratives of crime and punishment. Once, while touring western Jamaica in 1816, Matthew Gregory Lewis was inspired to ask "to whom a skull had belonged, which I had observed fixed on a pole by the roadside, when returning last from Montego Bay." As it turned out, the severed head had been there for five years, since about 1811, when "a Mr. Dunbar had given some discontent to his negroes in the article of clothing them . . . This was sufficient to induce his head driver, who had been brought up in his own house from infancy, to form a plot among his slaves to assassinate him." The recycling of such stories reintroduced past proof of white power into the present and fastened marks of it to particular places, in the form of remains of criminals like Mr. Dunbar's rebellious driver. At times, the colonial state even tried to convert the oppositional discourse of the enslaved into narratives of slaveholder power. Jamaican authorities hanged Eboe Dick in 1816 for "making use of singing, propagating and disseminating seditious and rebellious words, songs, and expressions." Placing his head in "the most public place at Lindhurst" plantation, officials hoped to make him sing a different song. Yet in their attempts to inscribe their power on the landscape, slaveholders also animated memories of resistance among the enslaved. Before the executions of Dunbar's driver and his co-conspirators, while they were imprisoned and awaiting trial, a woman on a neighboring plantation rose up against her overseer, grabbed him by throat, and called out to her fellow slaves, "Come here! Come here! Let's *Dunbar* him!" Dunbar's killer had become a role model, and a single act of resistance had become a verb. How many other slaves, seeing the skulls of Dunbar's killer or of Eboe Dick, heard their stories in subsequent years and thought, Here is where a hero died?[12]

That is not what slaveholders hoped for. They wanted the ghoulish displays to serve a clear purpose. Dead bodies, dismembered and disfigured as they were, would be symbols of the power and dominion of slave masters. In their view, the severed heads standing sentry over the plantation landscape conveyed a warning to potential rebels and reassurance to supporters of the social order. Such symbols were thought to be effective because they had emotional power: they harnessed the otherworldly and the sacred to specific bodies, places, and narratives, which in turn bore witness to the social power of the rulers. Mostly, Jamaican slaveholders brought these conventions from the British theater of social control, but in the Caribbean those who were running the show had to restage several elements of the exhibition.

Courting the Supernatural

Elaborate tortures and postmortem humiliations were standard punishments in early modern Europe and England. As in Jamaica, they served to graft sacred and social power onto the bodies of condemned criminals. Disfiguration and scorching gave criminals a foretaste of the punishments their souls would receive in hell. Thus, human beings brought the wrath of God to bear on enemies of the state. Dismembering corpses or exposing them to be "consumed by the air and the birds of the sky" protected living communities from the evil that criminal spirits might continue to work in the world. Incineration of criminals' corpses effected complete physical and metaphysical annihilation. Denial of a decent burial for the remains arrested the spirit's passage into the other world and profaned the memory of the dead, by fixing the attention of the living upon the rotting body. Throughout Europe public exposure of bodies at places of execution and at crossroads "formed part of a dual system which maximized display . . . The executions themselves were primarily meant as an example to the inhabitants. Exposure of corpses along the roads was a special warning directed at non-residents coming in." Indeed, late seventeenth- and early eighteenth-century English guidebooks often mentioned gallows and gibbets as landmarks.[13]

The fear and submission induced by such measures depended in part on an understanding held in common by the rulers and the ruled. To a degree, the populace and the overlords shared a religious idiom concerning death and the afterlife, though they surely interpreted the lexicon differently, in accordance with their experience of material life and social hierarchy. Also, they shared an understanding of the religious ramifications of courtroom protocol and public execution.

Assize judges, who descended on the English countryside twice a year during the eighteenth century, carefully tailored their rhetoric to connote godly paternalism, as well as the power and passion of righteous vengeance, as a means of legitimating the rule of law. When the time came to pronounce a death sentence, "the powers of light and darkness were summoned into the court with the black cap which was donned to pronounce sentence of death, and the spotless white gloves worn at the end of a 'maiden assize' when no prisoners were left for execution." The rites of legal practice likened judges to God, and thus they seemingly derived their authority from the divine. A death sentence, then, represented a supernatural judgment, merely mediated by the state. At the place of execution, dramatic pageants of sin, redemption, and damnation organized the scaffold ritual. The widespread sale of pamphlets containing the "last dying speeches and confessions" of the condemned created common expectations for the drama of the executions. Recurring forms and ceremonies drawn from religious narratives and regional history played to "generations highly literate in emblematic meaning." The gallows itself simultaneously proclaimed that a given place was a "city of law" and heralded the majesty of the authorities who enforced the laws. Symbolic authority was enhanced by the judicial exercise of mercy and personal patronage. Judges wielded broad discretion in the matter of waiving death sentences. The intervention of well-heeled, influential men often saved the lives of convicted felons. The effect was to deliver people threatened by execution (who were disproportionately poor laboring folk) into the custody of the propertied elite, who generally controlled the legal institutions in the first place. In short, to enhance their power, authorities drew on a common discourse about legal ritual, symbolic authority, and death produced by local historical precedents relating to personal and cultural interaction.[14]

Such common forms of discourse were scarcer in Jamaica. Africans and their descendants, schooled to understand very different and disparate emblems of sacred power, replaced the "visually literate audience" that had been educated to interpret the sacred signs of English legal authority. One can only assume that similar rites of terror read quite differently to an audience in Jamaica than they did in England. In Douglas Hay's conception, "Justice, Terror and Mercy," managed with delicacy and circumspection, tutored people to respect the authority of the elite in England. The Jamaican plantocracy, which initially shared few cultural idioms with slaves, and perhaps none with Africans, ruled largely through magistrates' exercise of terror. Slaveholders, though they drew on the cultural resources of England, had to adapt them to the Jamaican situation.[15]

Unlike the English common folk, Africans and their children were cultural outsiders. When Edward Long evaluated Jamaican slave laws in 1774, he opined that "the Africans, first imported, were wild and savage in the extreme." In expressing this view, he merely echoed the language of the 1661 Barbados slave code, which condemned "negroes" as a "heathenish, brutish and an Uncertaine dangerous Kinde of people," who could not be adequately governed by English law. Early in the life of the colony, lawmakers in Jamaica had drawn on the legal experience of both England and Barbados. By the eighteenth century, the legislators had adapted their slave codes to local conditions, chief among them the persistent threat of open rebellion. The legal system was in place, but a belief system was not.[16]

Rapid demographic turnover in the sugar islands meant that the implementers of social order could never count on having people know or internalize the rules. Moreover, the meanest enforcers of plantation discipline, the "petty whites," shifted about constantly from plantation to plantation, from colony to colony, and from life to death. The "new-come buckra" regularly confronted "new Negroes" of diverse origins. Jamaica was perpetually threatened by its fluctuating and restless enslaved population. As Long put it, expressing the characteristic negrophobia of the planter class, "their intractable and ferocious tempers naturally provoked their masters to rule them with a rod of iron." Their masters also struggled to conjure an effective symbolic discourse to legitimate their rule, similar to the harsh punishments of the military, but based on principles and practices possessing features peculiar to slave society, quite different from those operating in England.[17]

In 1664 the Jamaican assembly established parallel courts specifically for the trial and sentencing of slaves. In her study of the slave courts in Saint Andrew's parish from 1746 to 1782, the historian Diana Paton has convincingly argued that judicial practice in Jamaica "emphasized the difference between slave and free, and valorized the slaveholder's private power," rather than "representing the supposed common discipline of all to a single rule of law, as did the contemporary English spectacle of trial and punishment." Throughout most of the eighteenth century, crimes committed by slaves were tried before informal and irregularly scheduled tribunals composed of three freeholders and two magistrates, who were usually prominent planters. Until 1788 there was no jury, and even after the law provided for nine-man juries (paid two pounds each by the parish vestries to attend), and then twelve-man juries in 1816, the defendants never had any opportunity to appeal. At any rate, there would have been no time for appeal because, as the planter William Beckford remarked, "a negro is often condemned in one hour, and receives execution in the next." Rather than trying to instill in slaves the idea of a uniform system of justice, slave courts demonstrated to the enslaved that in most cases the will of their masters and the law were one and the same.[18]

It followed that the punishments decreed by the court resembled those routinely meted out by slaveholders. Much more frequently than courts in England, slave courts ordered corporal punishment, featuring use of the whip, that enduring symbol of plantation authority. Mutilation for noncapital crimes—the chopping off of ears, noses, feet, and so on—continued long after European courts had discontinued such abuses. For the capital crime of "assault on a white person" or "rebellious conspiracy," postmortem punitive measures were common. The frequency of mutilations and aggravated death sentences, which in eighteenth-century England were reserved for traitors, signaled the expansion of the very concept of treason to include almost any crime committed by slaves; for any act that could be interpreted as resistance to their absolute subjugation could be defined as betrayal.[19] Paradoxically, a population that had fewer reasons to be loyal to the ruling elite than had English common folk was more regularly defined as traitorous. Slave codes and courts in Jamaica operated on behalf of a narrowly conceived public interest comprising little more than the collective interests of slaveholders. Planters and merchants may have been convinced of the moral legitimacy of such a system, when they bothered to justify it, but they needed only to compel the enslaved to respect the authority of fear.

The centerpiece of legal terror was punishment and execution used to set an example. Yet unlike the regular, carnivalesque demonstrations of state authority in England, Jamaican executions consisted of sporadic, localized dramas. When groups of rebels were hanged or burned after failed uprisings, crowds certainly gathered, but at most times, in most parts of the island, public executions were used more to dramatize the power of masters than to construct a community governed by recognizably just laws and punishments. After a 1766 uprising in Westmoreland parish, Thistlewood noted, "2 of the Rebel Negroes were tried yesterday and one of them burnt with a slow fire (alive) near the gallows at Savanna la Mar, yesterday evening; and the other, this morning at Cross-Path, where they killed Gardiner." Killing the second rebel at the same place where the white man had been slain certainly represented an attempt to reclaim the place for white authority. This was common practice, as Thistlewood remarked some years later, when "the head of Gold, the Rebel, [was] carried to Leeward this evening, to be put up as a terror." After landing in Saint Ann's Bay, Jamaica, in 1779, Captain Thomas Lloyd of the Royal Navy saw a man and a woman "in irons, bound together, leading to trial, and attended by very few people." He was told that they were runaway slaves. At the time Lloyd was on his way to dinner at a plantation in the interior but when he returned in the evening to his ship, the *Hercules Victualler*, he inquired about the couple. An officer from another ship in the harbor who had been ashore described what had taken place: "They were both executed on the wharf, in the sight of the ship's company . . . The sister of the woman who was executed, bewailing her loss, the owner came to her, and said, Take care of yourself, you B—, you see how your sister is served. Upon enquiring of some of the Planters, the man had been hanged for running away, and the woman for secreting him."[20]

In the late eighteenth century, constables or deputy marshals were paid to attend trials and carry out executions. In 1794, for example, the Saint Thomas-in-the-Vale parish vestry paid the deputy marshal, George Coward, two pounds for the trial and ten pounds for execution of Frank, a black horse thief. Coward collected one pound, twelve shillings for "the Hire of a Horse and Cart to convey Frank to his gallows at Bog Walk." The vestry also reimbursed him five pounds for providing a party of light dragoons with refreshment. The soldiers had been ordered to attend the execution. The dragoons provided security as well as a reminder of the imposing presence of the colonial state, but apparently they, along with sailors in Saint Ann's Bay, constituted most of the audience for the execution of the enslaved couple. Perhaps the military officers and the slaveholders conspired not only to keep the enslaved in subjection, but also to warn the long-suffering rank and file not to challenge military hierarchy. After all, the West Indian garrison had an extraordinarily high mortality rate; according to historian Roger Norman Buckley, the soldiers "were driven to misconduct by the danger of their new lives." To control them, officers were encouraged to "treat them all like slaves." Common soldiers may have watched such executions with conflicting feelings of pride and anxiety: but for the grace of colonial power, they might be standing under the gallows themselves.[21]

The enslaved were often tried, sentenced, and executed in towns, but postmortem punishments usually took place on the plantations where slaves had committed crimes or hatched their rebellions. Planters even preferred that the entire demonstration of authority occur locally. In 1731, landowners in the Carpenter's Mountains in Saint Elizabeth parish sent a petition to the Jamaican assembly requesting permission to set up a court nearby, so that they would not have to travel the "near forty miles to give an account of their white people, slaves, and cattle, in order to be assessed." They also complained that the usual custom of trying slaves in the town of Lacovia, at such an inconvenient distance, allowed many of them to escape "just punishment." Planters proposed that they be allowed to try slaves "nearest the place where any facts are committed." They reasoned, "The example of such a trial, and the punishment ordered by the justices and freeholders, in the neighborhood, must strike a greater terror in the other slaves than their bare hearing of its being acted at a distance, although, if condemned to death, the head may be ordered to be put up at the place where the fact was committed." The petitioners hoped to harness the whole judicial ritual to local authority, thereby making their private rule synonymous with public power. Whether they got their way in this instance is unknown; by a century later, though, it seems clear that while slave trials took place in towns, the executions had been relocated to the countryside, to the scene of the crime. In the wake of the 1831 Baptist War, the Methodist ministers Thomas Murray and Henry Bleby watched as thirteen convicted rebels were taken from the town of Lucea into the Hanover parish countryside for execution. In any case, the planters of the Carpenter's Mountains already possessed the ability to deploy perhaps their most fearsome token of authority: relics that haunted the landscape.[22]

Diana Paton has shed light on the "detailed and finely calibrated language" of the sentences involving mutilation in the Saint Andrew parish slave court records. Not only was the court specific about which body parts would be removed at what time from each individual criminal, it often ordered that the severed pieces, especially ears, be nailed to significant landmarks. For example, magistrates ordered that ears be nailed to the gallows, to watch hut gates, or quite often to great trees. Jamaican authorities employed a "symbolics of mutilation," by trying to impress on the enslaved the meaning that such punishments had carried in Great

Britain a century earlier. They also innovated. The court often ordered lashings to occur beneath large silk cotton trees and body parts to be nailed to the trees. Black people in Jamaica reportedly believed that the spirits of the dead dwelled in and around such trees, sometimes by choice, but more often because they had been caught and trapped by magical means. Jamaican whites were aware of this belief—some probably shared it—and tried to manipulate it. In effect, they co-opted African understandings of spiritual capture.[23]

When European visitors and missionaries in Africa described Africans' spiritual world, their biases often led them to misrepresent African religious ideas and practices. Nevertheless, they correctly acknowledged the prominent place the spirits of the dead held in African social thought. In the mid-eighteenth century the first British missionary to the Gold Coast, Thomas Thompson, noted that Akan-speaking Africans believed that "the soul, after death, keeps haunt about the body, and is latent in, or near its repository." All across West-Central Africa in the seventeenth century, missionaries observed that "those who had died violent deaths, outcasts, or people who were not buried . . . formed a category of ghosts and other wicked spirits . . . Religious precautions were taken to prevent them from doing harm." But people could also harness and manipulate such spirits. Among Africans shipped to Jamaica from the Loango Coast, who comprised as many as a quarter of enslaved immigrants during the last two decades of the transatlantic slave trade, *minkisi*, or spiritual charms, could be used to effect one's will in the world. According to Robert Farris Thompson, "the *nkisi* [was] believed to live with an inner life of its own. The basis of that life was a captured soul . . . The owner of the charm could direct the spirit in the object to accomplish mystically certain things for him." By the late eighteenth century, whites certainly knew that such techniques of spiritual capture made a strong impression on slaves. Similarly, whites knew that blacks often feared and shunned the spirits of the dead. Matthew Lewis observed in 1816, of the beliefs of slaves on his property, "The duppies of their adversaries are very alarming beings, equally powerful by day as by night, and who are *spiritually terrific*." Lewis learned that an African man hospitalized with fits had been stricken by the specter of a recently deceased white man whom the African had formerly offended. He had received what Lewis called "the ghostly blow" when passing through a burial ground used exclusively by whites.[24]

Lewis's story highlights a curious congruence between the spiritual beliefs of the enslaved and the disciplinary techniques of the plantocracy. At Half-Way Tree in Saint Andrew, the old cotton tree that gave the spot its name and that commonly bore the bodies and relics of maimed and executed blacks lived next to a well-populated (and potentially dangerous) church graveyard. In 1752 the Kingston parish vestry erected a public gallows at Spring Path, on the same site as a "negro burying ground." The evidence that the slave courts intended to domesticate the dead in accordance with their understanding of African cosmology is inconclusive. Yet the rituals of sentencing and punishment, resulting from rapid and irregular trials before few spectators, were no doubt less fearsome to the enslaved than the lingering presence of body parts and mutilated corpses or, more precisely, the presence of the spirits that hovered around them. Recall the unfortunate Mr. Dunbar's head driver, who, Matthew Lewis learned, had been above suspicion until investigators searched his house. There, they found not only Dunbar's watch, "but with it one of his ears, which the villain had carried away, from a negro belief that, as long as the murderer possesses one of the ears of his victim, he will never be haunted by his spectre."[25]

Shamans

The way in which Africans and their descendants in Jamaica harnessed the dead to promote political authority was not fully apparent to the plantocracy until after Tacky's Revolt in 1760, though some knew that Africans brought magical talismans and medicines with them when they crossed the Atlantic and that they tried to use them against their captors. Cruising off the Windward Coast of Africa in 1751 aboard the *Duke of Argyle*, Captain John Newton discovered that nearly twenty of the captive Africans belowdecks had broken their chains. The slavers barely averted an insurrection, but days later the Africans tried another tactic: "In the afternoon we were alarmed with a report that some of the men slaves had found means to poyson the water in the scuttle casks upon deck," Newton recorded in his journal, "but upon enquiry found they had only conveyed some of their country fetishes, as they call them, or talismans into one of them, which they had the credulity to suppose must inevitably kill all who drank of it." Relieved, Newton nervously congratulated himself on his own "superior" spirituality: "If it please God thay make no worse attempts than to charm us to death, they will not much harm us, but it shews their intentions are not wanting." Earlier in the century, some Englishmen showed a greater concern with the efficacy of African spiritual power. Thomas Walduck, an army officer stationed at Barbados in the early 1700s, wrote, "White men, overseers of plantations and masters have been forced to leave this island by being bewitched by the Negroes." Yet most Jamaican planters seemed as unconcerned as Newton.[26]

When they wrote in diaries or in published accounts, whites in Jamaica often referred casually to the magical practices of the enslaved. Before 1760 whites considered these practices to be a generally harmless and bizarre feature of slave life, not unlike witchcraft and conjuring in Europe. In the spring of 1753, Thistlewood watched as Guy, from the nearby Salt River plantation, "acted his Obia, &c. with singing, dancing, &c. Odd enough"— odd, but not serious. Early the next year, Thistlewood noted with amusement that Jinney Quashe, a well-known obeah man, was "pretending to pull bones, &c. out of several of our Negroes for which they was to give him money." Somehow, Jinney Quashe's clients discovered that he was a fraud, and "they chased him out of the estate, frightened enough." The event reminded Thistlewood of a scene he had witnessed in Yorkshire when a noted conjurer from Wakefield, Black Lambert, was chased out of the town of Acworth. Such innocent comparisons ended a few years later when an islandwide slave conspiracy in Jamaica brought the alarming aspects of black shamanism to the forefront of planter concerns.[27]

In the 1760s, two bodies of spiritual practice, obeah and myal, came to the attention of Jamaican authorities. Often conflated in the minds of whites and in their descriptions, these two spiritual arts held a supernatural political authority among the enslaved. Obeah and myal were used both to mediate conflict and to instigate it; they were both a threat to communal equilibrium and a powerful social discipline. Sometimes too, they provided an axis for insurrectionary action, for, as John Newton discovered in 1751, supernatural power emboldened slaves to resist the dominion of their masters and allowed blacks to believe more generally that they could challenge whites.[28]

"Obeah" (or "obia") was the catchall term used to describe a complex of shamanistic practices derived from various parts of Africa and conducted by ritual specialists working largely outside formal institutions.

Practitioners of obeah operated as herbalists and sages tending to physical, social, and spiritual needs, though whites generally mischaracterized obeah as simple witchcraft, thus failing to see its larger role in social and spiritual healing and protection. Throughout most of the eighteenth century, it was almost exclusively Africans who mastered obeah, but one of the earliest reports to the House of Commons on Jamaican shamans claimed, "The Negroes in general, whether Africans or Creoles, revere, consult, and abhor them; to these Oracles they resort, and with the most implicit Faith, upon all Occasions, whether for the cure of Disorders, the obtaining of Revenge for Injuries or Insults, the conciliating of Favour, the Discovery and Punishment of the Thief or the Adulterer, and the Prediction of Future Events." The term "obeah" also referred to the charms that carried spiritual power and could be placed strategically around an individual who was to be cursed or protected. These were made of a variety of materials thought to have sacred significance, including blood, feathers, parrot's beaks, animal teeth, broken glass, eggshells, and dirt from grave sites.[29]

Haunting and spiritual cure were central to Jamaican shamanism. In 1799, for example, Mr. Graham, a free black man and a Christian, reportedly sought out an obeah man because "his first Wife, who was dead, came into his ground and troubled him." The obeah man prepared "Guinea Pepper and red head Roots," which Graham was to put above his door to drive away the spirit of his former wife. Graham paid the obeah man a rooster and a dollar for his services. One critical skill possessed by obeah practitioners was "shadow catching," the ability to capture souls. In 1826 Alexander Barclay claimed to have been present at the trial of a "notorious obeah-man, driver on an estate in the parish of St. David." One of the witnesses against the driver was another slave on the same plantation. When asked if indeed he knew the accused to be an obeah man, the witness replied, "'Ees, massa, shadow-catcher, true . . . Him ha coffin, (a little coffin produced) him set for catch dem shadow.'" The court asked for further clarification and the witness complied: "'When him set obeah for [somebody], him catch dem shadow and dem go dead.'"[30]

Like obeah, myalism addressed spiritual danger, though in the more institutional setting of a religious sect. As first described by Edward Long in 1774, the "myal society" revolved around a ritual dance, performed to manage the activities of spirits in the social world. The rite of initiation involved a symbolic enactment of death and rebirth, in which the initiate danced under the influence of a narcotic potion until passing out, seem-ingly lifeless. "In this state he continued," as Long described it, "no pulse, nor motion of the heart, being perceptible," until the initiate was provided with an antidote, at which point "the body resumed its motions, and the party, on whom the experiment had been tried, awoke as from a trance, entirely ignorant of any thing that had passed since he left off dancing." Thomas Thistlewood was angry when he discovered in 1769 that his con-sort's daughter, Coobah, had twice hosted the myal dance on the Paradise estate, where "Egypt Dago, and Job, who are both Myal-men attend these dancings." Soon after, he "reprimanded Coobah severely." The society was supposed to offer protection from the workings of malevolent forces, but especially from the unsettled spirits of the dead. Suffering under the evils of enslavement, sickness, and social disharmony, the enslaved turned to such tactics to negotiate a path in the world.[31]

People employed obeah men and women privately to treat disease and to manipulate human behavior by harnessing spirits; they brought in myal men (literally, "spirit men") to hold collective ceremonies of healing and communion. These practices played an important role in explaining mis-fortune and mediating disputes over illegitimate concentrations of posses-sions or power among the enslaved—such as the privileges accumulated by drivers and others who collaborated with slaveholders—but under some circumstances, such necromancy also enhanced the political influ-ence of ritual specialists and their patrons, when they rose to challenge the plantation regime. If obeah and myal often acted to counter the power of slaveholders, as some scholars have maintained, both were most authori-tative when engaging with the problems presented by the presence of the dead. Such practices offered people power over the most fraught and per-ilous feature of life in slave society: the permeable frontier between life and death. Rampant death made such arts of the spirit critical at all times, but as masters recruited dead bodies and parts of bodies to demonstrate their power, the political significance of necromancy acquired paramount importance for the enslaved. Many joined the myal society, as Long rec-ognized, because initiates would supposedly be "invulnerable by the white men; and, although they might in appearance be slain, the obeah-man could, at his pleasure, restore the body to life." During the 1770s, Long described obeah as "a sort of witchcraft of most extensive influence . . . The authority which such of their old men as had the reputation of wiz-

ards, or Obeah-men, possessed over [slaves], was sometimes very successfully employed in keeping them in subordination to their chiefs." In fact,
Long was looking back to 1760, trying to explain the role of such "wizards"
in the most extensive slave revolt in the eighteenth-century British
Caribbean.[32]

Tacky's Revolt, named for one its principal African leaders, threatened
British control of Jamaica for the first time since the Maroon Wars of the
1730s. Taking advantage of the opportunity presented by troop redeploy-
ments during Britain's Seven Years' War against France and Spain, more
than a thousand slaves revolted in the first phase of the uprising, which
began on 7 April 1760 and continued until October of the next year. Over
that time, rebels killed sixty whites and destroyed thousands of pounds'
worth of property. "Whether we consider the extent and secrecy of its
plan, the multitude of the conspirators, and the difficulty of opposing its
eruptions in such a variety of places at once," wrote Long in his 1774 *History of Jamaica*, Tacky's Revolt was "more formidable than any hitherto
known in the West Indies."[33]

During the revolt and the repression that followed, more than five hundred black men and women were killed in battle, were executed, or committed suicide, and another five hundred were exiled from the island for
life. Tacky, having been shot by Maroons allied with the plantocracy, was
decapitated, and his head was displayed on a pole on the road to the capital, Spanish Town. The warning sign did not mark the highway for long;
Tacky's head was stolen, Long supposed, "by some of his country men
who were unwilling to let it remain exposed in so ignominious a manner."
Captured rebel leaders were liable to be burned alive. Bryan Edwards later
described the stoicism of one man at the stake: "The wretch that was
burnt was made to sit on the ground, and his body being chained to an
iron stake, the fire was applied to his feet. He uttered not a groan, and
saw his legs reduced to ashes with the utmost firmness and composure;
after which one of his arms by some means getting loose, he snatched a
brand from the fire that was consuming him, and flung it at the face of
his executioner." Other Africans reportedly cracked jokes in the hour of
death. The diaries of Thistlewood, who successfully defended his plantation when the uprising came to his parish, confirm Edwards's published
accounts. Shocked planters and colonial officials responded to Tacky's
Revolt by tightening social control, updating their slave codes, and urging

more vigilant enforcement of existing regulations. In 1761 the Jamaican assembly considered, but ultimately did not pass, a bill to increase the import duties on enslaved recruits from the Gold Coast, whom planters blamed for the revolt and who comprised more than a quarter of all Africans arriving in Jamaica. We cannot know whether this measure would have calmed the aftershocks. Coromantees and their allies rose up again in 1765, 1766, and 1767.[34]

The aftermath of the rebellion threw the direct competition among different forms of sacred authority into stark relief. Tacky had planned and instigated the uprising with obeah practitioners as his closest counselors. He and his co-conspirators called on the shamans to use their charms to protect the rebels from bullets and to administer binding loyalty oaths, which required the plotters to consume a concoction made up of blood, rum, and grave dirt, which they believed to have sacred significance. In the wave of executions that followed the rebellion, none were more impressive than those of the shamans. Revealingly, colonial authorities felt that they needed to resort to more awesome displays than they normally projected. In a report to the House of Commons, one witness described the scene: "At the place of execution he bid defiance to the Executioner, telling him that it was not in the Power of the White People to kill him; and the Negro Spectators were astonished when they saw him expire. On the other Obeah-men, various Experiments were made with Electrical Machines and Magic Lanthorns, which produced very little Effect; except on one who, after receiving many severe Shocks, acknowledged his Master's Obeah exceeded his own." Jamaican masters could not abide sources of authority they did not wholly control. After Tacky's Revolt, Jamaican law called for the death, imprisonment, or exile of "any Negro who shall pretend to any Supernatural Power"; and the aggressive prosecution of enslaved necromancers remained a prominent concern in slave court trials of the late eighteenth and early nineteenth centuries. Executions of shamans took place with sufficient frequency (especially in turbulent times) that Thomas Thistlewood could note matter-of-factly in his diary, "Hear Stompe, the Mial Man, was burnt alive this evening, and his wife (Dr Frazier's Pollu, a mulatto) hanged," without further comment on the merits of the case.[35]

Whites both believed in and doubted the efficacy of black supernatural power. They continued to regard it as "superstition," but of a peculiarly threatening kind. Most important, from the standpoint of the Jamaican plantocracy, obeah could motivate the enslaved to direct political action. In 1784 Judge John Grant rejected a master's appeal to stop the transportation of a convicted obeah man for the following reason: "If granted in this instance," warned the judge, "application with equal reason might be made, while a rebellion might be raging throughout the country." Judge Grant clearly worried about obeah's political potential, but in his notes on the case he defined obeah as the "pretended exercise of witchcraft or sorcery, a crime which the new negroes bring with them from Africa, and which does infinite mischief among their fellow slaves." Such ambivalence toward black necromancy characterized the colonial state's persecution of its practitioners right through to the end of slavery and beyond. As long as people believed in its power, governing authorities would have to punish its practice. The consolidated slave act passed in Jamaica in 1823 clarified the real issue at stake: "Obeah practised with intention to excite rebellion, or endangering the life or health of a slave, shall be punished at the discretion of the court." As far as colonial officials were concerned, the ban on obeah was a ban on alternative authority and social power.[36]

As long as obeah's spiritual power remained credible, black men and women, free and enslaved, wielded it to combat the worldly power of whites. Authorities received periodic reminders that the enslaved continued to look to "wizards" for political guidance. The notorious rebel Three-Fingered Jack, who led an outlaw band of West-Central Africans in 1780, was reputed to be an obeah man. A conspiracy to revolt on the Orange Vale plantation in Saint George parish in 1807 revolved around the participation of Captain, reportedly a skilled obeah man who was to administer loyalty oaths to the rebels and advise them on strategic maneuvers. Captain was an experienced and revered military sage. Colonial authorities discovered, a decade after the fact, that he had also counseled the Charles Town Maroons in the War of 1795–96. Less dramatic, but still cause for concern, were more routine attempts to employ obeah against whites. In a report to his cadre of evangelists back home, John Shipman, the Kingston district chairman for the Weslyan Methodist Missionary Society, described a fascinating encounter between a plantation overseer and a free black man armed with an obeah charm. One night, about midnight, the overseer heard someone digging not far from his house. When he looked out the window, he spotted a man whom he recognized digging a hole and "depositing something which he knew to be an Obiah-Spell." The overseer said nothing at the time, but the next morning "he sent for the person who had done it and opened the hole and took out the deposit (intimating that something extraordinary had informed him of it) and found it to consist of a Bottle filled, I believe, with rain water, and some feathers and cat's teeth." As Shipman put it, "This Gentleman got to understand that it was intended to remove him from office, by death of course." The overseer harangued the man, "informing him that he could *Hang* him for what he had done" but then let him go, "charging him to escape to America or some other place."[37]

Though missionaries like Shipman emphasized the spiritual harm caused by "communication with evil spirits" and with "the Devil" (as had prosecutors in seventeenth-century European and American witchcraft trials), Jamaica's colonial government was more concerned with different products of the supernatural imagination, particularly practices that undercut the ability of the plantocracy to harness the influence of the dead to bolster its own authority. Because black shamans drew their most impressive power from the management of spirits and death, the prohibition amounted to a strategy to limit the prestige the enslaved could derive from association with the spirits of the dead, while maximizing the power of the colonial government's "magic." In this sense, power in Jamaican slave society operated through various sorts of necromancy that would influence the course of social events by invoking, reanimating, or placating the dead.

Political authority nearly always has a transcendent—that is, a sacred—dimension. The dead, as representatives of an existence beyond time, carry a mystical influence that can be put to decisive use by the living. In eighteenth- and early nineteenth-century Jamaica, sacred spiritual authority resonated with the practical demands of domination, on the one side, and of the struggle for survival under enslavement, on the other. Supernatural beliefs and the machinery of the colonial state were inextricably enmeshed. Colonial masters confronted African spirituality, while black shamans wielded a (sometimes) countervailing political influence. In practice, neither masters nor slaves recognized a distinction between material and spiritual power. As a political phenomenon, then, colonial necromancy forces us to turn our attention to strategies for manipulating cultural practices in a world where the dead were an active social presence, and where domination, dissent, and the threat of incredible violence plagued every interaction.[38]

Martyrs

This haunted world extended well beyond the slave societies of the Americas. The iconic power of deaths of black rebels and shamans reverberated across the ocean, where death meant other things and generated other political possibilities. Historians have often gazed in horror at such gruesome scenes, finding them reprehensible, or have averted their eyes, moving quickly past the grisly events to focus on deeper structural analyses. But they have seldom seen them as transitions, liminal moments in the human progress toward the afterlife. In such moments, African rebels became transatlantic spirits, and those spirits played a generative role in the political history of slavery. The rebellions of the 1760s, which brought state power and popular necromancy into open conflict in Jamaica, also inspired a significant moment of empathy back in the United Kingdom—one that preceded a rising tide of antislavery sentiment that would also draw strength from the continuing presence of the dead in the temporal world. Here, too, the dead enjoyed an afterlife as a subject of contention and an emblem of power, invoked by claimants to the mantle of the sacred. Executed slaves became important symbols, entering history in a way that masters could not control and making history in ways that have often escaped notice. According to Africans' prevailing beliefs, the spirits of executed rebels, at least those who were born in Africa, probably returned to Africa. Bryan Edwards acknowledged as much when, in 1760, he penned a eulogistic poem from the perspective of a condemned insurgent looking forward to his repatriation: "On those blest shores—a slave no more!" Yet the spirits of these rebels also continued to move through the Atlantic world, fighting slavery, as they engaged with anxious investors, sentimentalizing authors, and vigilant masters, as well as successive generations of the enslaved.[39]

North American readers of the *Pennsylvania Gazette* could follow the aftermath of Tacky's Revolt closely and ponder its implications for their French and Indian War. As ships from Jamaica arrived in ports along the eastern seaboard, passengers brought news of rebellion and reprisal. The paper carried details of the executions: Scipio, Harry, and Cuffee, for example, were executed at Spring Path, "first hanged, then their Heads struck off, and fixed on Poles, and their bodies burnt." Readers learned how four women named Sappho, Princess, Sylvia, and Doll, "who it appeared had some Knowledge of the Conspiracy, were conducted to the Place of Execution, with Halters round their Necks; and, after Quaco and Anthony were executed, were re-conveyed to Gaol, from whence they are to be transported from this Island, and to suffer Death if they return." As late as 1763 readers learned from a gentleman arriving in Boston from Jamaica that several conspirators had been executed just before he left the island.[40]

The rebels haunted the enterprising families of Great Britain more than they did the North Americans, however. From across the Atlantic, anxious colonial investors could follow the trials of the Jamaican plantocracy in the *Gentlemen's Magazine*, where in 1760 readers also found articles concerning "the duration of man's life," necessary "data for calculating annuities on lives," and a discussion "on the intermediate state of souls." In June they first learned of Tacky's April rebellion: fifteen overseers killed, four plantations in Saint Mary's burned and destroyed, and most distressing, the commercial convoy that had been set to sail on 1 May delayed. In July the magazine reported that Tacky and his chief lieutenant had been killed and that the plantocracy had vanquished the insurgency. August brought news of fresh uprisings in the prime sugar parishes of Westmoreland and Hanover. It would be another year before gentlemen could read, in August of 1761, the good tidings that the Jamaica fleet had arrived under convoy of the *Lively*, which had £70,000 on board "for the use of the merchants." At last, interested parties must have believed, the public executions and the macabre icons of planter power had finally worked their magic on the minds of the enslaved and brought them back under control.[41]

Even as Jamaica seemed to grow quiet, the spirits of the rebels animated English literature, generating sympathetic affinities between slaves and freeborn Britons. Tacky's Revolt and its aftershocks coincided with the United Kingdom's overwhelming victory in the Seven Years' War, after which the empire acquired vast new territories and assumed sovereignty over an unprecedented number of diverse and far-flung peoples. The immensity of the conquered territory provoked widespread discussion on how hundreds of thousands of new subjects could be incorporated into a single orbit of imperial allegiance. In this context, many whites began creatively to imagine affiliations with aliens, including the enslaved, that were based on their own deeply felt way of identifying with other Britons. The existing style of speech and narrative of belonging briefly brought the dead rebels into the fold. News of the executions circulated amid prevailing sentimentalism and popular Christian martyrology, which helped the British to envisage their nation as a moral community founded in persecution, death, and religious virtue. As this imagined community expanded, however briefly, to include the enslaved, the political killings of African rebels were understood according to the same conventions used to describe the passion of Jesus Christ and the political executions of later martyrs. In a bizarre appropriation, perhaps mirroring the way that the enslaved made spiritual sense of official homicide, the deaths of African rebels became the subject of an empathetic poetry of death and righteousness, emerging in sentimental scenes of suffering and fortitude that argued in favor of the possibility of a united polyglot British nationality.[42]

Inspired by tales of heroic suicides, the first major antislavery poem, Thomas Day and John Bicknell's *Dying Negro* (1773), posited a union between blacks and whites, cemented by Christianity. Claiming to be based on a true story, it presented the lament of an enslaved black man in England, newly baptized and betrothed to a white servant, awaiting transport to the dreaded West Indies. Preferring death to life in the Caribbean, the man prepares a suicide sonnet for his intended wife and then fatally stabs himself. To his master, he proclaims the superiority of Christian death to the prerogatives of property ownership.

> And thou, whose impious avarice and pride
> the holy cross to my sad brows denied,
> Forbade me Nature's common rights to claim,
> Or share with thee a Christian's name;
> Thou too farewell! for not beyond the grave
> Extends thy power, nor is my dust thy slave.[43]

The poem helped to establish a recurring pattern in abolitionist literature, glorifying the African who chooses Christian redemption in death over servitude in life.

Remarkably, even slaveholders participated in propagating this trope. Bryan Edwards was so moved by the sight of the executed rebels of 1760 that he wrote one of his first poems in the voice of a condemned African who faces his executioners with dignity and defiance. Edwards, whose fortune depended on slaveholding, nevertheless found in the death of Alico, his allegorical African rebel, a way to evoke a sacred struggle for liberty, the rallying standard of Britishness. "Firm and unmov'd am I," declares the African at the stake. "In freedom's cause I bar'd my breast—In freedom's cause I die." Africans might even represent sacred national virtues better than slaveholding Britons. "Now, Christian, glut thy ravish'd eyes," challenges Alico; "I reach the joyful hour / But know, pale tyrant, 'tis not thine Eternal war to wage / The death thou giv'st shall but combine / To mock thy baffled rage." Finally, Alico salutes death, "how welcome to th' opprest!" for it brings liberation: "Thy kind embrace I crave / Thou bring'st to mis'ry's bosom rest / And *freedom to the slave!*" Tacky's rebels were martyrs, the poem contended, in an ironic twist of fate; here, a savage pagan plays the role of the savior of humanity and embodies the virtues dearest to British hearts. But this moment of empathetic identification arrived too soon to have a significant impact on imperial policy. Evocations of martyred rebels served writers who wanted to show their political sensitivity to the question of imperial sovereignty, but outbursts like Samuel Johnson's notorious toast "Here's to the next insurrection in the West Indies!" notwithstanding, statements by literary men did not convince the metropolitan elite to support such rebels against British slaveholders—not yet anyway.[44]

Tacky and his fellow conspirators, shamans, and martyrs provided more direct inspiration to the enslaved in Jamaica. These rebels arguably enjoyed their most significant afterlife when they entered popular history. In 1807 Simon Taylor told his cousin, "I believe we are on the eve of a rebellion breaking out." Several newly arrived Africans on Taylor's plantation had risen up and attempted to stab their driver. Taylor apprehended them, interrogated them, and made a startling discovery. There had been "some improper Communication" between his own slaves and those on a frontier estate, "the Negroes of which Estate have always been the foremost in all Insurrections from the year 1760, 1765, & 1767." As a consequence, Taylor learned, "all new negroes know of the insurrection of 40 years ago." He asked rhetorically, "If something were not going on, for what reason would they tell these New Negroes who have not been four months in the island of what happened before any of the negroes sent there were born?" Taylor himself had sharp memories of the events of the 1760s. He had returned from his sojourn at Eton just in time for the 1765 revolt. Taylor's own overseer was killed and decapitated by the rebels, who set fire to several sections of cane field, as they called their fellows to arms by "singing their war song." Given the turnover in Jamaican population, he must have expected the revolts to have been long since forgotten by the enslaved. But apparently the latest rebels on Taylor's plantation had been inspired by lessons from the Jamaican past. Taylor caught a glimpse, reflected in his letter, of an oppositional political history, taught and learned on Jamaican plantations, a radical pedagogy of the enslaved. In surreptitious conversations and certainly in sacred rituals, the dead figured in the goals, strategies, and outcomes of slaves' political activity. The spirits of generations past indicated what might have been possible in the 1760s, and what might still be, in Jamaica.[45]

By the time Taylor discovered this subversive school of historical thought, the imperial context was quite different than it had been in the 1760s. Whereas patriotic Britons were able to feel themselves favored by God in the outcome of the Seven Years' War, many felt cursed by events of the 1770s, 1780s, and 1790s, and this perception would contribute to the emergence of a different approach toward dead slaves, which presented them less as symbols of irrepressible liberty than as evidence of national sin. Although slave rebels could be seen as embodying British virtue in the midst of national triumph and conquest, the intervening decades had brought the American, French, and Haitian revolutions; rare was the Briton who could celebrate violent resistance in such dangerous times. In fact, martyred rebels never made so great an impression on the British imagination as would the more passive victims of slavery, the heaps of men, women, and children who died unheralded. Whereas black martyrdom illustrated the transoceanic availability of the dead to serve political purposes, martyrdom was not so influential as deaths that could be summoned without raising the specter of retributive violence, those which allowed the projection of sentimental concern and the possibility for imperial renewal, without admitting the justice of slave revolution. The black casualties of Atlantic slavery would affect political history less as icons of sacred authority than as the focus of arguments about national morality. Heroic rebels would influence imperial politics less than would the black victims of ordinary murders, which, happening to occur at a more opportune time than Tacky's Revolt, had extraordinary consequences.

❧❧

CHAPTER FIVE

The Soul of the British Empire

IF THE TIME was not yet right in the 1760s for martyred slave rebels to win posthumous battles in the imperial capital, by the 1780s, changing conceptions of the proper relation between the living and the dead had helped advance the antislavery movement in Great Britain considerably. Beginning in the mid-eighteenth century, as rising evangelicalism, popular sentimentality, and the fashionable genre of graveyard literature focused British public attention on the relation between death and moral values, the high mortality rate in Britain's Caribbean slave colonies became a central focus of a massive movement for colonial reform.

Between the 1780s and the end of slavery, as partisans debated the causes of high mortality, they made the dead central players in the politics of antislavery. The antislavery movement, particularly in its evangelical Christian incarnation, drew strength from a new rhetoric about slave mortality; what had earlier been described principally in economic terms became a moral problem of vital importance to the "soul" of the British nation. Nevertheless, arguments about deaths among the enslaved showed an interpenetration of feeling and reason, of sentiment and calculation, that blended new styles of thought and speech with very old—indeed, one could say, unenlightened—impulses. Discussions of the sin of slavery were intertwined with consideration of judgment and the afterlife. Fear of damnation thus helped spur legislation to abolish the slave trade, register all slaves on colonial plantations, and finally end slavery in British colonies.

Goods Thrown Overboard

Late in the summer of 1780, five Liverpool merchants, including William and John Gregson, the former and future mayors of the city, outfitted the *William* to trade for slaves in West Africa. When the ship reached the Gold Coast early the next year, its captain, Richard Hanley, found another ship for sale, a recently captured Dutch prize, the *Zorgue,* or *Zong.* He bought the vessel for his employers, dispatched the fortunate news, and transferred the *William*'s surgeon, Luke Collingwood, to the *Zong* as captain. Collingwood and a crew of seventeen immediately commenced purchasing slaves to sell in Jamaica. As battles with the Dutch erupted along the coast, Collingwood cruised the trading forts, managing to acquire 440 captives. He also took aboard the outgoing governor of Anomabo, Robert Stubbs, who had been suspended for instigating a dispute with local chiefs.[1]

On 6 September 1781, the *Zong* left West Africa. The length of the Atlantic voyage stretched unexpectedly to eleven weeks; mortal sickness gained on the crew and cargo. By the time the ship was in sight of Jamaica on 27 November, seven members of the crew and more than sixty enslaved Africans had died. The epidemic promised to kill more before long. Sickness aboard the slaver would surely cause wary port authorities to quarantine the *Zong* in the harbor, thus alerting potential buyers to defects in the cargo.

Collingwood steered the ship away from the island (he would later claim that he had mistaken it for Hispaniola), pushed back into the encircling sea, and called a meeting of his officers. He told them that the ship's fresh water supply was low, that the sickest slaves below would surely die, and that when they did they would lose all value, cost the owners dearly, and diminish the expected remittance to their employees; but "if they were thrown alive into the sea, it would be the loss of the underwriters." His briefing held special appeal for the officers, who were promised the "privilege" of a certain number of slaves upon sale of the whole lot. The value of the officers' share would be determined by averaging the sale price of the entire cargo. Every sick and dying African who brought a low price at auction would reduce the officers' commission.[2]

Collingwood showed a clear familiarity with the maritime insurance policies then applicable to the slave trade. Indeed John Weskett's *Complete Digest of the Theory, Laws, and Practice of Insurance*, published earlier that year, provided a calculated justification for the actions Collingwood was about to take: "Whatever the master of a ship in distress, with the advice of his officers and sailors, deliberately resolves to do, for the preservation of the whole, in cutting away masts or cable, or *in throwing goods overboard* to lighten his vessel, which is what is meant by jettison or jetson, is, in all places, permitted to be brought into a general, or gross average: in which all concerned in ship, freight, and cargo, are to bear an equal or proportionable part of what was so sacrificed for the common good, and it must be made good by the insurers in such proportions as they have underwrote."[3] Backed by sound financial rationalization, Collingwood ordered the slaughter of the sickest and weakest Africans for "the preservation of the whole," averring also that it might be crueler still to let them linger without water until they died of their illnesses.[4] It would be better, he might have said, to end their worldly suffering and resurrect them as part of a "gross average." The chief mate, James Kelsal, initially opposed the plan, or so he later testified in court, but he did not resist the order.

On 29 November, crewmen came into the dark and suffocating hold, selected fifty-four ailing men, women, boys, and girls, and took them above into sunlight and fresh air. Then they bound their hands and cast them overboard. The next day they came for forty-three more. Certainly, not all of these people were terminally ill, for one African man had the strength to grab hold of a rope that hung overboard, drag himself up to a porthole, and clamber back into the ship, where crew members found him hours later. Momentarily shielded from Collingwood's surveillance, the sailors sympathized with the man and returned him to the hold. Maybe they suspected that they and their own sick mates might have been similarly dispatched, if only they had been worth something dead.

The next day it rained, and the crew collected enough fresh drinking water to add a three-week supply to the ship's store. Then, on Collingwood's orders, they came below to take 36 more Africans. The crew managed to bind and jettison 26 of them before the last 10 leapt unfettered into the sea and escaped to drown themselves. In just three days, Collingwood and his crew had caused the deaths of 132 Africans.

The captain and crew conducted this business as they watched the terrified Africans thrashing about helplessly, choking and sputtering as the sea swallowed them whole. Remaining in his cabin below, Robert Stubbs, former governor of one of the busiest slave-trading posts in the

Atlantic world, saw and heard the drowning slaves from his portal. He was only a passenger, he said later, and had nothing to do with the transaction; perhaps he also thought it beneath him to sully his hands with the business. Housed beneath Governor Stubbs's quarters, the Africans could hear only the screaming and splashing, as they waited in the darkness for their turn. Whether from disease, dehydration, or sheer fright, thirty more of them died in the hold before the ship made landfall. On 9 December the *Zong* came within sight of Jamaica again. The slaver made harbor by 22 December, docking in time for Collingwood, Stubbs, and the crew to celebrate Christmas on land.

On 28 December the merchant firm Coppells & Aguilar offered two hundred survivors of the massacre for sale, advertising them as "choice young Coromantee, Fantee, and Ashantee Negroes" (Figure 5.1).[5] What became of them? How did they narrate the experience to others in Jamaica? At present, historians do not know who bought the Africans or where they may have gone, much less with whom they commiserated, who retold their stories to others, or how they resolved to live with the certain knowledge that whites were willing to murder them, methodically and systematically, without apparent purpose. We do know, however, that many Britons told and retold the story, in the vocabulary of evangelical moral sentiment, because they were certain that Collingwood, his crew, and the courts of Great Britain had grossly distorted the meaning of death.

"Death More Dreadful Made"

The moral outrage exemplified by the reaction of evangelical Christians to the *Zong* massacre animated emerging abolitionist sentiments. The event provided a graphic example of the primacy of economic calculation over human life in the system of slavery. In the context of eighteenth-century conceptions of death and the dead, the articulation of this moralistic trope motivated a passionate politics. Antislavery campaigners superimposed the image of slavery that crystallized in the *Zong* case on the major parliamentary inquiries into the material and spiritual well-being of the enslaved in the British Caribbean. Making the high mortality rate in the Caribbean a focus of committee hearings in 1791 and of the slave registration legislation of 1815, Parliament regarded slave mortality, the accumulation of dead black bodies, as an important dimension

141 4   Kingston, 27th December, 1781.

STOLEN or STRAYED from the CAMP at *Up-Park*, a DUN HORSE, marked on the shoulder MB in one. Whoever will bring him to the Store of *Thomas Adrien* in Port-Royal Street, shall receive HALF A JOE Reward.

Kingston, 23th December, 1781.

RUN away from the subscriber, the 24th instant, a Negro Boy named *GEORGE*, of the *Congo* country, about 14 years of age, 4 feet 10 inches high, smooth faced, very much in of the right knee, had on when he went off a blue coat with yellow and blue lace, and a long white shirt; he was seen the next morning at Spanish-Town Bridge, in his shirt with no coat on. He was formerly the property of Mr. George Shore, Tavern keeper, in Kingston. Whoever will give information of the above Negro being harboured or concealed by a white person, on coviction thereof shall receive *Ten Pounds* reward, if by a free negro or mulato *Five Pounds*, and if apprehended or secured in any of the Goals, or brought to me at the Barracks in Kingston, shall receive *Two Pistoles* reward and all reasonable charges paid.

141   J. WATLING, Lieut. 39th Regt.

141—2   28th December, 1781.

FOR SALE at *Black River*, on Wednesday the 9th day of January next, on board the Ship ZORGUE, *Luke Collingwood* Commander, from the Gold Coast of AFRICA, 200 choice young *Coromantee, Fantee,* and *Ashantee* NEGROES, by

Coppells & Aguilar.

Figure 5.1. The survivors of the *Zong* massacre, advertised for sale by the merchant firm Coppells & Aguilar. *Supplement to the Royal Gazette* (Kingston), 28 December 1781.

of debates over the abolition of the Atlantic slave trade and colonial slavery. At the moral center of antislavery concern was a figure—indignation at the triumph of greed over human life—that found expression in rhetoric about the deaths of slaves. This was more than propaganda; moralistic evocations of the enslaved dead grew out of deep convictions. They also relied on conventions of discourse that stemmed from profound transformations in the eighteenth-century Anglo-Atlantic world.[6]

As Britons struggled to come to terms with revolutionary changes in their demographic, economic, political, and religious experience, concern for the fate of Africans and their descendants, at a remove from the immediate upheaval at home, impelled abolitionists to articulate idealized notions of the British moral order at home and abroad. The dead became a symbol, a rhetorical device that abolitionists could bring to bear on political life. Detailed narratives of pain and death, and later the humanitarian use of demographic statistics, gathered power at the intersection of British idealism, sentimentalism, and evangelicalism.

In eighteenth-century Britain a dramatic increase in life expectancy accompanied the onset of the industrial revolution. The ravages of the plague, which had reduced the population of England from about 5.25 million to less than 4.9 million between 1657 and 1686, yielded to steady population growth by the middle of the eighteenth century. Once inoculation and vaccination had brought smallpox under control, Britons saw the first signs of a population boom. However, steady progress in life expectancy did not lead directly to the spread of more secular or "rational" ways of viewing death. In fact, at midcentury the perception was that Great Britain had experienced a dramatic *decline* in population.[7]

Many writers in Britain shared the view that the population of the "civilized" world had fallen, morally as well as numerically, since ancient times. Many also believed that the spread of commerce was to blame for the decrease. In a well-received essay, the Reverend John Brown argued that excessive commerce "brings Superfluity and vast Wealth; begets Avarice, gross Luxury, or effeminate refinement among the higher Ranks, together with general Loss of Principle." In his explanation, "Vanity and Effeminacy" reduced the desire to marry among the elite, and "Intemperance and Disease" rendered the "lower Ranks" partially impotent. "This Debility is always attended with a Shortness of Life, both in the Parents and the Offspring; and therefore a still further Diminution of Numbers follows on the whole." Two bills introduced in Parliament in 1753 and 1758 sought to determine the extent of the supposed decline, by establishing a national register of births, marriages, and deaths. Both bills failed when they ran up against popular fears that "numbering the people," King David's great sin (Sam. 24:1–25), would incur divine wrath. Most viewed death and demography not through the lens of medical science but through the apocalyptic visions of Christianity. Indeed, men and women of feeling—especially authors and dissenting evangelicals—eschewed disenchanted rationalism in favor of emotionally charged public interactions with the dead.[8]

In the early eighteenth century, orthodox Protestantism held that death severed all meaningful communion between the living and the deceased. Unlike Catholics, in whose view the prayers of loved ones and the intercession of the Church could improve the state of passing souls, Protestants knew that their fate was fixed at death. As the historian Philip Almond has put it: "On the last day, the judgement would be made by God. And when this life was done with, and this world passed away, there would remain only a state of total blessedness and a state of interminable misery in the stark symmetry of contrasts between heaven and hell." The only proper approach to death, then, was lonely and anxious preparation for eternity. Popular guides to the *ars moriendi* (art of dying), such as William Sherlock's *Practical Discourse concerning Death*, first published in 1689 and appearing in thirty-two editions by 1759, urged, "This ought to be the Work and Business of our whole Lives, to prepare for Death, which comes but once, but that once is for eternity." Such convictions isolated individuals from eternal communities—communities in which the living and the dead interacted across the boundary between the physical and metaphysical worlds—and distanced the dead from the routine concerns of the living.[9]

By midcentury, the increasing currency of Enlightenment philosophy tended to reduce the emphasis on eternal damnation and suffering, at least among the literate upper echelons of British society. The image of God commonly took on a more benevolent, detached, and rational aspect. For many, the idea of "natural death" replaced notions of death as a "transcendental trauma." As the historian Roy Porter has explained, "Death ceased to be the ultimate enemy, requiring heroic acts of will, faith, purgation, and penitence. Instead dying came to be widely treated as an easy transition to a more blessed state, a natural metamorphosis to be accepted, even welcomed." It was not so for everyone. For members of the rapidly growing evangelical sects, only a grateful fixation on the death of Jesus Christ could afford the assurance of ultimate salvation.[10]

Beginning in the 1730s and 1740s, the Protestant revival washed up on nearly every shore of the Anglo-Atlantic world. Distressed by what they saw as spiritual torpor, the decline of clerical authority, and the spread of rationalism, George Whitefield, Charles and John Wesley, and many other Protestant ministers resolved to rouse people's faith with passionate homilies about the death of Christ and his gift of salvation. Ministers abandoned the previous century's difficult and uncertain preparations for death and advocated instantaneous deliverance through faith and repentance. Though the evangelicals scorned Enlightenment skepticism, they did adapt to new currents of thought and expression that stressed the validity of personal experience and induction; the *experience* of faith in Christ's sacrificial death came to determine individual confidence in salvation.[11]

Yet despite the assurance offered to believers in the martyred Christ, evangelicals generally subscribed to a providential worldview according to which hell's terrible punishments would be visited on entire nations. Not only was the individual sinner at risk of eternal damnation, but whole societies risked awful retribution if they refused to renounce their sins and amend their ways. Eighteenth-century evangelicals conceived the world as a divinely sustained moral order. In this view, Providence was also "their inescapable summons to mould the world to a righteousness which would avert deserved national disaster, relieve the mundane sufferings of men, and pave the way for the salvation of their eternal souls." Thus, the terrors of the afterlife were brought to bear upon the social and political world. By making the death of Jesus the crux of both personal and national redemption, evangelicalism put death at the center of its vision of moral renewal and moral order. Evangelical religion supplied a nearly irresistible motivation for purposeful moral action, and new conventions for expressing moral sentiments and for representing relationships linking the dying, the dead, and the living helped shape the moral impulse at the heart of abolitionism.[12]

As the evangelical movements attracted ever-larger followings, their themes converged with those of popular writing about death. In 1732 a London printer produced an inexpensive new edition of John Foxe's *Book of Martyrs, containing an account of the sufferings and death of the Protestants in the reign of Queen Mary*, originally published in 1563. Its graphic depictions of the executions of the Protestant faithful confirmed the dignity of suffering and dying for religious principles. Published in cheap installments throughout the century, the *Book of Martyrs* was among the most widely read and most affecting texts of its time. As the historian Linda Colley has observed, "Foxe's martyrs could stand for Everyman. They included women as well as men, the poor and insignificant as well as the eminent and prosperous, and all ages from the venerable old to the most vulnerably young." They helped create a sense of nationhood founded on persecution, death, and Christian righteousness.[13]

Graveyard poetry, which emerged from the classical elegy in the early eighteenth century, paralleled the popularity of martyrology. Graveyard poets gained an audience throughout the century by inviting readers to reflect on the meaning of death as they joined self-conscious narrators on descriptive tours of church vaults and night walks through burial grounds. Appearing first in the 1740s and '50s, Robert Blair's work *The Grave*, Thomas Gray's *Elegy Written in a Country Church Yard*, and Edward Young's *Complaint or, Night Thoughts on Life, Death and Immortality* were among the most widely published writings of the latter half of the eighteenth century. Young's poetic address to a "worldly infidel" went through twelve editions in the 1750s alone. "What is this World?" Blair asked his readers. "What? but a spacious Burial-field unwalled . . . Sin has laid waste, Not here and there a Country, but a World." The narrator of Young's *Complaint*, pining by the grave of his stepdaughter, pleads for the strength to quit a living death of sin, to break the "Thread of Moral Death that ties me to the World." Similar sentiments governed Elizabeth Rowe's *Friendship in Death*, originally published in 1728, and then followed by seven more editions up through the 1750s. In a series of imaginary letters from the dead to the living she cautions readers to be mindful of the afterlife and turn away from sin, so that they could look forward to experiencing the ineffable pleasures promised to the faithful. Emotionally affecting in tone, the work also signaled the ascendance of moral sentimentalism as a discourse of advocacy. "Nothing teacheth like death," wrote William Dodd in his popular reflections on the subject, which were reprinted frequently between 1763 and 1822 (Figure 5.2).[14]

The convergence of elegy and evangelicalism often reflected personal connections between poets and preachers. Robert Blair had a personal

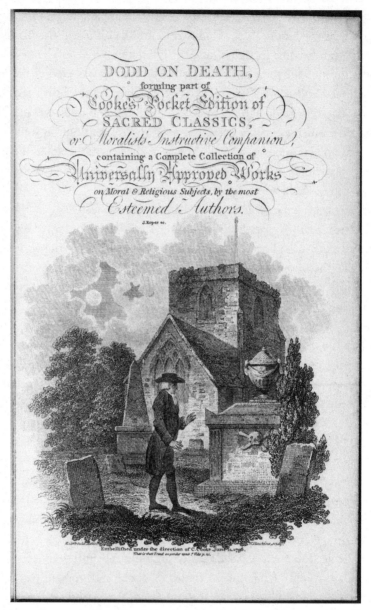

Figure 5.2. Graveyard ethics. Frontispiece, *Dodd on Death,* in William Dodd, *Reflections on Death* (London, 1796), engraving by W. Hawkins. This image shows a minister walking through a graveyard, drawing lessons on mortality from his meditations there. "What is that I read on yonder tomb?" reads the caption below the illustration. Courtesy of Houghton Library, Harvard College Library (2003J-EC109).

relationship with the dissenting minister Philip Doddridge, whose *Rise and Progress of Religion in the Soul* (1745) had a formative influence on evangelical thinking. James Hervey, himself an evangelical preacher, taught pious lessons in the hugely popular *Meditations among the Tombs* (1746), written in the tradition of graveyard poetry. Hervey and the Wesley brothers appreciated Edward Young's *Night Thoughts* because it dovetailed with fervent Christianity in highlighting the depravity of man and affirming the reality of the supernatural, while stressing the authority and authenticity of personal feeling. Upon Hervey's death in 1758, William Romaine, an associate of George Whitefield and, like him, an evangelist to the poor, composed and published a sermon in Hervey's honor, *The Knowledge of Salvation Is Precious in the Hour of Death*. It went through twelve editions before the end of 1759.[15]

The popularity of such writing served to keep death at the center of moral sentiments, given more secular expression by Edmund Burke and Adam Smith. In *A Philosophical Enquiry into the Origins of Our Ideas on the Sublime and Beautiful* (1757), Burke argued that pain, danger, sickness, and death give rise to the strongest human passions. Such passions were also at the heart of Smith's *Theory of Moral Sentiments* (1759). In the suffering and death of another, a person could discover empathy, the prerequisite for all moral concern. "We sympathize even with the dead," wrote Smith, especially with the victims of malign intent. Empathy could "animate anew the deformed and mangled carcass of the slain," inspiring, in Smith's account, the "horrors which are supposed to haunt the bed of the murderer, the ghosts which, superstition imagines, rise from the grave to demand vengeance upon those who brought them to an untimely end." Of course, where Smith and Burke offered reasoned worldly accounts of the relation between pain, death, and sentiment, the torments of hell and the possibility of eternal salvation weighed more heavily on the moral imagination of evangelicals and other Christians. Indeed, religiously inspired mortuary writing had set the stage for a much broader concern with the moral sentiments that connected the living with the dead.[16]

In early eighteenth-century Europe stories about death and pain among ordinary people proliferated, narratives that linked the concerns of readers to the experiences of others. Realistic novels, autopsies, and various social inquiries all made the dead and the dying available for representation and interpretation beyond the traditional realms of religion and family. Perhaps more important, such accounts introduced complex causal explanations for death. Gothic and Romantic narratives, revolving as they did around evocative images of pain and death, helped build a morally charged aesthetic around mortality that directed sentiment toward the mortal trials of others. These novel literary forms worked with emerging religious discourse to encourage new spiritually charged narratives of cause and consequence. Increasingly, and with greater effectiveness, the moral weight of the suffering or lifeless body could be used as leverage in a partisan dispute.[17]

In the late eighteenth century, British views about the radical changes wrought by the rise of industrial capitalism and the expansion of empire were couched in this idiom. The booming commerce in the Atlantic region enhanced the public profile and political prestige of the merchants and planters involved in West Indian trade, even as Britons began to experience dislocations and disorienting new work environments. From what they could learn about colonial slavery, most people understood large plantations to be the analogue, perhaps even the archetype, of the novel forms of production sprouting up around them. As Robin Blackburn has put it: "The novelty of the slave plantation, the commercial megapolis, the proto-industrial village, the capitalist factory posed fundamental questions about the relations between production and reproduction, and about the compatibility of new productive forces with a stable configuration of family and state."[18]

Just as many feared that the new economic organization would disrupt traditional life, they also worried that the same commercial values that fueled the Atlantic slave trade and fed the plantations would upset more sacred relationships. Did the absolute power that masters held over their slaves confirm that property rights included the license to dispose of a slave's life? Under such circumstances, could death itself remain sacred? Did the new materialism have its own designs on the meaning of death? Mortuary writing emphasized that earthly wealth was no guarantee of eternal salvation; in fact, it could prove to be quite the opposite. "Leisure is our Curse," wrote Young in *Night Thoughts,* the bitter fruit of "Art, brainless Art! our furious Charioteer [who] Drives headlong towards the precipice of Death / Death, most our Dread / Death thus more dreadful made."[19]

An appreciation for elegy and the literature of suffering similarly distinguished men and women "of feeling" in Jamaica, though they could not share the British public's anxiety over slavery. When Thomas Harrison, the attorney general and advocate-general of Jamaica, heard *Night Thoughts* read aloud by the Reverend William Jones in 1779, he reacted with fashionable sentiments but hard-nosed practicality. In tears, he protested, "Were I to indulge in reading much of such books, I should be extremely fond of them, but it wou'd absolutely incapacitate me for attending to my Business." Bryan Edwards, the planter, politician, and historian, was also a graveyard poet. His 1764 "Elegy on the Death of a Friend" featured a "poor Libyan slave" pining "with accents wild" over his master's grave. And Edwards was not above feeling sympathy for the enslaved. He acknowledged the injustice of slavery in several poems, including "Ode, on Seeing a Negro Funeral," published in 1773. "Why triumph o'er the dead?" he asked the reveling mourners. Because death had carried an African home: "'Tis now the hero lives, they cry, / Releas'd from slav'ry's chain: / Far o'er the billowy surge he flies / And joyful views his native skies / And long-lost bow'rs again." Yet Edwards's encomiums for dead slaves did not signal antipathy toward slavery. Like Thomas Harrison, Edwards had business to attend to; he owned more than fifteen hundred slaves in Jamaica.[20]

Englishmen at home generally reacted to the immorality of slavery with a greater sense of urgency. In the conspicuous materialism of West Indian planters, moralists discerned something that epitomized their greatest anxieties. Evangelicals in particular saw in colonial slavery an example of the existential struggle between the "dark bondage of sin and the light of Christian liberty that was carried on in each individual soul." As the working public of Britain saw in slavery a dystopian vision of their own future, many evangelicals saw in slaveholders the height of individual conceit and disdain for the promise of salvation. In *Thoughts upon Slavery* (1774), John Wesley cautioned slaveholders that if they did not change their course, they risked losing the only thing that truly mattered. Adopting the language of moral sentiment and alluding to the image of the crucified savior, he asked, "Do you ever feel another's pain? Have you no Sympathy? . . . When you saw the flowing eyes, the heaving breasts, or the bleeding side and tortured limbs of your fellow creatures, was you a stone, or a brute?" He accused slave traders and West Indian planters of murder. "Thy hand, thy bed, thy furniture, thy house, thy lands are at present stained with blood," he charged. "Surely it is enough: accumulate no more guilt." And "Regard not money!" Wesley warned. "All that a man hath will he give for his life! Whatever you lose, lose not your soul: nothing can countervail that loss." It was common for evangelicals of all denominations to see themselves as God's special prosecutors. So when the evangelical Gustavus Vassa, formerly the slave and sailor Olaudah Equiano, approached fellow evangelical Granville Sharp in 1783 with news of 132 Africans killed for their insurance value, a mighty rhetorical weapon came into Sharp's hands, one he knew he had been chosen by God to wield.[21]

Granville Sharp was, by the 1780s, the most prominent antislavery campaigner in Great Britain. Sharp had taken up the advocacy of enslaved blacks in 1765, after he met Jonathan Strong, who had come to Sharp's brother William seeking medical aid for deep lash wounds inflicted by his West Indian master. In 1770, having already worked for several years to prevent masters from forcibly removing their slaves from England, Sharp began to advocate for James Somerset, a recaptured runaway slave whose master intended to send him to Jamaica. Immersing himself in English property and slavery law, Sharp prepared the winning brief for Somerset's defense of his right to remain in England. In 1772 Chief Justice Lord Mansfield ruled that while nothing prevented slaveholders from owning human property, no positive law sanctioned the removal of slaves from England. Though Mansfield stopped considerably short of ruling slavery on English soil to be illegal, his decision was widely misinterpreted as doing just that. Granville Sharp thus gained the reputation as the man who had reaffirmed that England was by definition a "free" country.[22]

Sharp's political energy derived from his belief in Providence and his concern with the moral governance of the world. In 1776 he argued that slavery violated the moral law of universal benevolence, on which righteous government ought to be based. "Upon the gospel Dispensation, all mankind are to be esteemed our brethren," Sharp wrote in *Just Limitation of Slavery.* "Especially are we bound, as Christians, to commiserate and assist to the utmost of our power all persons in *distress,* or *captivity.*" Not only did Sharp undermine the religious endorsement of slavery, but he argued that antislavery agitation was an imperative of evangelical Christianity. In keeping with prevailing evangelical themes, Sharp raised the specter of divine judgment, suggesting that slaveholders might even be eternally condemned by their own slaves. "Let Slaveholders be mindful of the approaching consummation of all earthly things," he warned, "when, perhaps, they will see thousands of those men, who were formerly esteemed mere *chattels* and *private property*, coming in the clouds, with their heavenly Master, to judge tyrants and oppressors, and to call them to account for their want of brotherly love!" He extended a similar warning to the nation and the empire in *The Law of Retribution, a Serious Warning to Great Britain and Her Colonies, Founded on Unquestionable Examples of God's Temporal Vengeance against Tyrants, Slave-holders and Oppressors*. Perhaps Sharp was drawing directly on the rhetorical strategies of Philip Doddridge, whose influential *Rise and Progress of Religion in the Soul* (1745) acknowledged that people must imagine the execution of divine law, and "feel something of the Terror of it," before they could be convinced to turn to the Gospel for deliverance. That would explain why Sharp ended his *Just Limitation of Slavery* in the voice of God: "Depart from me ye Curs'd into everlasting Fire, prepared for the Devil and his Angels (Matt. XXV. 40,41)."[23]

Throughout *Just Limitation of Slavery*, Sharp singled out as most accursed the "TYRANNY *in America*" where "the abominable plantation laws will permit a capricious or passionate master, with impunity, to deprive his wretched slave even of his life."[24] Such outrage at the convergence of property rights and the right to kill foreshadowed his response to the *Zong* massacre.

Portents of Doom

The *Zong* case came before the English courts under the name *Gregson v. Gilbert*, as a dispute over an insurance claim. Upon learning of their loss, the Gregsons and their partners promptly filed a claim with their insurer, Thomas Gilbert, for 132 slaves, each valued at thirty pounds sterling. Gilbert refused to pay. The ensuing lawsuit was first heard at Guildhall, London, on 6 March 1783. Gilbert argued that the defendants were not liable for the incompetence of Collingwood's planning and navigation. The Gregsons asserted that the *Zong* had been put in distress "by the perils of the seas, and contrary currents and other misfortunes," and that the captain's actions were sensible. For his part, the first mate and chief witness James Kelsal (Collingwood having died by time of the hearing) confirmed that it was the captain's right and responsibility to make such judgments. However, at least one observer in the courtroom was frustrated by the boundaries of the legal arguments. In an anonymous letter to the *Morning*

Chronicle and London Advertiser, one that surely caught Gustavus Vassa's attention, a spectator testified, "I waited with some impatience, expecting that the Jury, by their foreman, would have applied to the Court for information how to bring the perpetrator of such a horrid deed to justice." Instead, the jury found in favor of the ship's owners, and the court ordered the insurers to pay for the slaughtered property.[25]

Still refusing to pay, Gilbert appealed to the Court of King's Bench for a new trial. The appeal was heard on 22–23 May 1783, before a panel of three judges presided over by Chief Justice Lord Mansfield, who had adjudicated the *Somerset* case more than a decade earlier. Granville Sharp was in the courtroom. He may have come hoping to hear that no positive law sanctioned the willful murder of slaves; instead, he listened as the judges recognized Solicitor General John Lee's arguments in favor of the owners. Lee insisted: "It has been decided, whether wisely or unwisely is not now the question, that a portion of our fellow-creatures may become the subject of property. This, therefore, was a throwing overboard of *goods*, and of part to save the residue." Mansfield agreed in principle: "Though it shocks one very much, the case of slaves was the same as if horses had been thrown overboard." Nonetheless, Mansfield ultimately did order a new trial to reconsider the *necessity* of the jettison and the contractual liability of the underwriters. The ten Africans who jumped into sea of their own volition were excluded from consideration; by asserting their agency, Mansfield ruled, these had voided their insurance value. The result of that new trial, if it ever was held, remains unknown. In any event, the case moved abruptly from the Court of King's Bench to the court of Christian opinion, where Granville Sharp proved to be an expert litigator.[26]

Through a tireless letter-writing campaign, Sharp highlighted the moral stakes involved in the case, by emphasizing the incommensurability of the Christian and the commercial views of death. Outraged that, rather than require that a criminal judgment be rendered, the authorities had ordered a new trial "concerning the *value* of those murdered Negroes!" Sharp first wrote to the Lords of the Admiralty, requesting that they initiate a murder trial. "The most obvious natural right of human nature is at stake," Sharp wrote, "the right even to life itself." He continued, "A *right to live* ought by no means to have been suppressed in favour of a mere pecuniary claim in the most doubtful species of property." As the cultural theorist Ian Baucom has recognized, the "horror and outrage" inspired by the massacre was compounded by the recognition that it was in itself "a financial trans-action." Advocates for the owners had convinced the court, and thereby established in legal precedent, that "in drowning the slaves Collingwood was not so much murdering them as securing the existence of their mon-etary value." In doing so, the British nation itself became implicated in the intentional killing of human beings for financial gain.[27]

In Sharp's view, this could only bring a terrible judgment upon the entire country. "For the sake of national justice, that the blood of the mur-dered may not rest on the whole kingdom," he urged the Lords of the Admiralty to take action: "The only pleas of necessity that can legally be admitted, or are worthy of being mentioned in this case, are—1st, A neces-sity incumbent upon the whole kingdom to vindicate our national justice, by the most exemplary punishment of the murderers mentioned in these vouchers;—2nd, The necessity of putting an entire stop to the Slave Trade, lest any similar deeds of barbarity, occasioned by it, should speedily involve the whole nation in some such tremendous calamity as may unquestion-ably mark the avenging hand of God, who has promised to destroy the 'destroyers of the earth.'"[28] Sharp supplied them with a 138-page hand-written packet of material, including his letter urging that they conduct a murder investigation, a brief account of the massacre, and his own tran-script of the trial at the Court of King's Bench. He also provided them with a copy of a letter he would send the first Lord of the Treasury and a copy of a petition sent from the insurers to William Pitt, the chancellor of the Exchequer. Without waiting for government action, Sharp consulted with the legal scholar Dr. Thomas Bever and at his own expense enlisted attor-neys to prepare a criminal prosecution. Nevertheless, the Lords Commis-sioners of the Admiralty never initiated a murder trial. In fact, there is no evidence that they even opened Sharp's letter.[29]

In another letter, to the Duke of Portland, first Lord of the Treasury, Sharp enclosed the same materials he sent to the Admiralty. This time he invoked the threat of personal damnation, quoting an earlier letter he had sent to Lord North. "I only wish, by the horrible example related in the enclosed papers, to warn your Grace, that there is an absolute necessity to abolish the Slave Trade and the West-India slavery; and that 'to be in power, and to neglect, as life (and I may add, the tenure of office) is very uncertain, even a day, in endeavoring to put a stop to such monstrous injustice and abandoned wickedness, must necessarily endanger a man's eternal welfare, be he ever so great in temporal dignity or office.' This was my warning to Lord North eleven years ago."[30]

Sharp sent a full account of the massacre to the newspapers, and he continued writing to influential men to repeat his description of "that horrible transaction," which, if not for its appearance in a business dispute, "might have been known only amongst the impious slave-dealers, and have never been brought to light." The reaction extended well beyond evangelical circles. Responding to Sharp's entreaties, the bishop of Peterborough admitted, "Were religion and humanity attended to, there can be no doubt that the horrid traffic would entirely cease; but they have too small a voice to be heard among the clamours of avarice and ambition." Dr. Porteus, bishop of Chester, but soon to be bishop of London, acclaimed Sharp's efforts: "Your observations are so just, and so full to the purpose, that I can add nothing to them but my entire approbation . . . I hope the attention of the public will be excited by your efforts." But public agitation would not have to depend on Sharp's efforts alone. Most important, he inspired other writers, who from his description of the *Zong* massacre crafted an indelible image of the enslaved dead both as the victims of English greed and as portents of national doom.[31]

In the wake of the *Zong* incident, antislavery activists fashioned parables (planters accused abolitionists of spinning pure fictions) that featured greed, slavery, and death as fixed points on a triangle. The stereotype reflected the widely held view that the only ethical approach to death and to the dead was to envision the moral progress of the individual soul. Evangelical abolitionists charged that in the commercial arrangements that defined slavery and the slave trade, money replaced the soul as the ultimate desideratum in death. Moreover, the murder of heathens was a compound crime, extinguishing not just the living body but also the eternal soul before it could know Christ and be assured of salvation. For antislavery writers, prepared by sentimental and evangelical discourse on death, the *Zong* massacre became the archetypal impression of slavery, one that had everything to do with their opinions about appropriate relations with the dead. Most important, as historian David Brion Davis remarked, their accounts "fixed an unforgettable image in the mind of the reading public," one that outlined an enduring moral critique.[32]

Abolitionist writers began retelling the story of the massacre almost immediately, and they very quickly turned the *Zong* into a metonym for colonial slavery. In his *Essay on the Treatment and Conversion of African Slaves in British Sugar Colonies* (1784), James Ramsay, an Anglican vicar and former slaveholder in the West Indies, affected shock and near disbelief at the case, calling Collingwood a "sick monster." In the minds of other writers, there was nothing anomalous about the *Zong* murders. Quobna Ottobah Cugoano, a radical antislavery activist from the Gold Coast and author of *Thoughts and Sentiments on the Evil of Slavery* (1787), cited the *Zong* massacre as only one example of the "vast carnage and murders committed by the British instigators of slavery." He took care to highlight the economic rationale behind the killing of slaves, "a very shocking, peculiar, and almost unheard of conception: They either consider them as their own property, that they may do with as they please, in life or death; or the taking away the life of a black man is of no more account than taking away the life of a beast." In 1788, John Newton, the evangelical rector of Saint Mary Woolnoth and a former slave trader, recounted the *Zong* case as one of the principal "specimens of the spirit produced by the African trade." But it was Thomas Clarkson who did more than anyone to secure the association of slavery with death, and the untimely death of slaves with greed.[33]

In his celebrated *Essay on the Slavery and Commerce of the Human Species*, published in 1786, then revised and expanded in 1788, Clarkson presented killing for profit as a common custom of slavers. Prefacing his essay with praise for the "pious endeavors" of Granville Sharp, Clarkson proceeded to "lay open the feelings of the reader" with tales of atrocity and avarice meant to illustrate the very antithesis of the Christian approach to life and death. He identified Collingwood's decision to "jettison" the Africans, those "victims, which avarice had determined to sacrifice to her shrine," as a "diabolical resolution." And though Clarkson called the massacre "unparalleled in the memory of man, or in the history of former times," he also made it representative of colonial slavery in general.[34]

He supplemented his account of the *Zong* massacre, "an authentic specimen of the treatment which the unfortunate Africans undergo," with other stories, including one about the killing of a sick child. Buyers offered such a low price for the weak and emaciated boy that the officers feared his sale would bring down the average sale price of the cargo and cost each of them about six shillings. They ordered the surgeon to throw the boy overboard. When the surgeon refused, they "came to the horrid resolution of starving him to death." They confined him, withholding food, water, and human contact, but for that of the chief mate, "who was continually going backwards to see if he was yet dead." After eight days, the boy died, "to the joy of the impious" slavers, according to Clarkson.[35]

Having made his moral point with such illustrations, Clarkson reinforced it with numbers. He found slave traders "guilty of the charge of having been accessory to the destruction of no less than twenty-five thousand of their fellow-creatures," positing calculated callousness as the cause of the high number. "It is conjectured," he asserted, "that if three in four survive what is called the *seasoning*, the bargain is highly favourable." Clarkson did not limit his discussion of the murderous nature of the slave trade to the deaths of Africans. Having personally interviewed thousands of sailors in London, Bristol, and Liverpool and examined muster lists for slave ships, he went on to observe in his *Essay on the Impolicy of the Slave Trade* (1788) that mortality rates for white sailors in the Africa trade were even higher than those for the enslaved. The slave trade was not a "nursery for [British] seamen," as elite opinion maintained, but "a Grave" destroying "more in one year, than all the other trades of Great Britain when put together destroy in two."[36]

Uniting the economic reasoning behind the *Zong* murders with general statistics in this way enabled Clarkson to argue convincingly that colonial slavery "cannot be carried on without the continual murder of so many innocent persons!" As for slavery's beneficiaries, he admonished them, "Exult in riches, at which even avarice ought to shudder, and which humanity must detest!" Reading Clarkson, Britons could hardly avoid interpreting his image of murderous slaveholders in the light of more general anxieties about ill-gotten gains in a rapidly changing social order. In another society, or at another time, Clarkson's indictments might have taken the form of an accusation of witchcraft; in late eighteenth-century England the means of expression for condemning the nefarious accumulation of riches derived from moral sentiment, evangelicalism, and the rhetoric of death.[37]

Echoing Granville Sharp's rhetoric, Thomas Clarkson wondered how the "sin" of the slave trade might be judged in heaven. "If the blood of one man, unjustly shed, cries with so loud a voice for the divine vengeance, how shall the cries and groans of an *hundred thousand* men, *annually murdered*, ascend the celestial mansions, and bring down that punishment which such enormities deserve!" He suspected he already knew the answer. The success of the North American rebels and the resulting rift in the British Empire seemed to prove God's displeasure, even as it provoked widespread anxiety over the proper course of imperial governance. During the 1780s a ruinous series of hurricanes had thrashed the West Indies, compounding the economic distress caused by war. Storms and earthquakes, "the violent and supernatural agitations of all the elements," could be seen only as the "awful visitations of God for this inhuman violation of his laws." After all, as Ottabah Cugoano had asked a year earlier, "What wickedness was there ever risen up so monstrous, and more likely to bring a heavy rod of destruction upon a nation, than the deeds committed by the West Indian slavery and the African slave trade?" Africans were victims of "improvident avarice," Equiano wrote in his 1789 description of the deadly holds of slave ships, and this could spell only a disaster of biblical proportions for Great Britain.[38]

Abolitionists worked with feverish intensity to avert the impending apocalypse. In April 1787 Granville Sharp and Thomas Clarkson joined a dedicated group of Quakers to help initiate a broad-based nationwide movement with evangelical rhetoric as its motor. Between 1787 and 1794 Clarkson worked tirelessly to distribute damning information about the trade, lobbying members of Parliament and traveling all over England to help set up local abolition committees. James Phillips, a successful bookseller and member of the London committee, published reams of pamphlets and book-length studies, including Clarkson's essays and abstracts of parliamentary debates on slavery and the slave trade.[39]

Novels, plays, and poetry concerning slavery also attracted a wide audience in the late 1780s and early 1790s. The emergence of the antislavery movement coincided with an explosion in printed material, and suddenly Africa and colonial slavery were hot topics. Personal connections between influential authors and West Indian colonists, along with the improved circulation of news from around the empire, contributed to a growing awareness of the conditions endured by colonial subjects, enslaved and free alike.[40]

As sentimental fiction sharpened the sensibilities of British readers, stories of suffering in slavery became test cases for moral feeling. Hannah More, an evangelical and one of the most prolific "sentimentalist" writers of the period, also wrote *The Black Slave Trade* (1788). Abolition committees scored important propaganda victories by publishing and distributing William Cowper's *Negroe's Complaint*, a melancholy poem written from the point of view of an enslaved African. Cowper, an evangelical poet, had earlier expounded on the role Providence played in punishing national sins. Inviting readers to empathize with his own trials as a slave, Olaudah Equiano published his antislavery autobiography in 1789, taking every opportunity to remind his readers that he had often prayed for death to emancipate him. The reading public already understood African suicide as a political condemnation of slavery—even an act of martyrdom—a reaction that Equiano acknowledged by referring to his own reading of Foxe's *Martyrology*. Situating his yearning for death within the contemporary genre of spiritual autobiography, Equiano reminded his audience that the truest desire of a Christian ought to be spiritual freedom from temporal bondage, but also that earthly masters who failed to respect that wish were undoubtedly sinful.[41]

The literature also dramatized the stakes in popular struggles that convulsed industrializing England. The broad dissemination of colonial morality tales about greed and indifference to human suffering spurred nationwide petition campaigns against the slave trade in 1788 and 1792. As Robin Blackburn has observed, "abolitionism as a movement derived strength from its association with the critique of the operation of pure market forces . . . West Indian planters were attacked for working their slaves to death and making profits from an inhuman, immoral and irreligious system." The populace in English industrial towns used antislavery rhetoric to assert that "where they conflicted, humanitarian and familistic values should prevail over business and property interests, and that capitalism and industrialism should be obliged to adjust to a self-reproducing human order." It should come as no surprise, then, that the first petition drives were incubated in burgeoning and fractious industrial towns. Manchester, which occupied the center of the spreading commercial and industrial networks but still had no parliamentary representative or municipal corporation, took the lead in circulating public petitions against the slave trade. Other industrial towns, including Birmingham, Sheffield, and Leeds, followed suit. By June 1788 over a hundred antislavery petitions had arrived at the House of Commons. Drawing their tenor of righteous indignation from evangelicalism, they generally subjected the slave trade to moral judgment, referring to it as "repugnant," "reproachful," and "inconsistent with the Profession of the Christian religion."[42]

The movement benefited from the involvement of a network of well-connected Anglican evangelicals centered around Clapham in South London. The Clapham Sect, or the Saints, as they were sometimes called, took up the abolitionist cause as part of an "international spiritual agenda" that aimed to bring spiritual renewal to the world by cleansing it of individual and national sins. It was in consultation with these influential evangelicals that, in July 1787, the London Committee had made the decision to concentrate its efforts on abolishing the slave trade through parliamentary legislation, thereby deferring an attack on slavery itself, which would be widely construed as an attack on property rights. Granville Sharp opposed the concession, declaring, "My own opposition is not merely against the slave trade, but also the toleration of slavery itself." But the leading role in the antislavery campaign had by then shifted to the most influential member of the Clapham Sect, William Wilberforce.[43]

William Wilberforce, a young, wealthy, and charismatic M.P., had converted to evangelicalism in 1785 during a protracted "spiritual crisis" provoked by his reading of Phillip Doddridge's *Rise and Progress of Religion in the Soul*. As he considered the implications of his awakening, he consulted closely with John Newton, who had ascended in the esteem of pious Christians from the hated occupation of slave trader to the status of revered spiritual tutor. Newton surely influenced Wilberforce's revulsion for the slave trade, and over the next two years Wilberforce also began to consult James Ramsay and Thomas Clarkson. Early in 1787, in the course of conversations with his friends, Foreign Secretary W. W. Grenville and William Pitt, the reformist prime minister, Wilberforce resolved to introduce a bill in the House of Commons to abolish the slave trade. He considered it his "sacred charge."[44]

At Pitt's suggestion Wilberforce agreed that there should first be hearings to gather more "factual" information about the trade. On 11 February 1788 Pitt appointed a committee of the Privy Council to consider the state of the slave trade. As the council gathered testimony, Wilberforce and Clarkson worked to ensure the presence of compelling witnesses for abolition, to counter the influence of West India lobbyists and Liverpool merchants. After compiling 850 pages of evidence, the Privy Council published its report in April 1789. Wilberforce brought a motion for abolition to the floor on 12 May that year, but as a result of heavy pressure from proslavery interests, the House of Commons delayed consideration until after it could hold its own hearings and gather its own evidence. By mid-1790, the House of Commons had gathered another 1,300 pages of testimony and reportage, yet because proslavery witnesses had dominated the process, Wilberforce had to call for still more examinations, to begin early in 1791. Finally, on 20 April 1791 at half past three in the morning, and after a two-day debate, the House of Commons voted on Wilberforce's measure. The poll resulted in defeat for the abolitionists, 163 votes against the bill and 88 in support.[45]

Enlightened Self-Interest

In Jamaica, Simon Taylor read the news of metropolitan abolitionism with alarm. In 1788 he began to complain bitterly to his business partner, the former M.P. Chaloner Arcedeckne, about the "people of England," who were so "willing to represent us as Devils incarnate." The antislavery activists were "mad Enthusiasts," Taylor wrote, "miscreants," "fanaticks," and "villains." He wondered what had become of sound English judgment. "All of this madness respecting of the African trade is of the most serious nature & is an axe to the root of their most valuable Commerce," he warned. "Such a Phrenzy I believe never struck any people but madmen before and none of Don Quixoti's exploits are to be compared to it."[46] After all, the reasonable arguments were on the side of the slaveholders, for their defense of slavery did not rest on visions of the afterlife, spiritual progress, or the rhetoric of moral sentiment. Taylor could take comfort in the fact that abolitionist images of slavery had as yet failed to overcome the influential discourse of proslavery advocates, witnesses, and writers. Testimony and opinions favorable to West Indian interests dominated the Privy Council report and had already begun to explain the deaths of enslaved Africans as an unfortunate consequence of individual management failures and as a result of African maladies. Apologists offered seemingly rational, rather than religious, explanations for the lethal nature of Atlantic slavery.

As early as 1774, writers who owed their fortunes to slavery were shaping the explanations that slavery's apologists would continue to use until emancipation sixty years later. Edward Long, the slaveholding planter and celebrated author of the three-volume *History of Jamaica*, responded to Granville Sharp's earliest indictments of slave mortality by asserting that homicidal avarice ran patently counter to slaveholders' self-interest: "The more mercenary a planter's disposition is, the stronger must the obligation grow upon him to treat his labourers well, since his own profit, which he is supposed alone to consult, must necessarily prompt him to it." His fellow Jamaican planter William Beckford followed Long's logic in his *Remarks upon the Situation of the Negroes* in 1788, extending this reasoning to encompass the motivations of the transatlantic slave traders: "Suppose a cargo should consist (as many do) of six hundred slaves, and one half of them should perish from neglect, or from want of the common necessities of life; and the remainder be reduced by inanition to skin and bones; what advantage can this large cargo boast, thus conditioned, over one of half that number, out of which the loss has been small and the passengers healthy?" Hector McNeill employed a similar approach in his *Observations on the Treatment of the Negroes in the Island of Jamaica* (1788). He argued that a fortuitous rise in the price of slaves had inspired greater interest in their longevity. "Times and circumstances have altered wonderfully," he wrote. "The value, or more properly speaking, the original price of the Negro, has, in the course of thirty years, risen upwards on one third . . . The proprietor is therefore led to view the Negro Property as an object of great concern, and consequently is disposed to preserve it by every prudent method." This connection between the fortunes of planters and the well-being of slaves also underlay the argument that enslaved blacks were better off than English laborers, who, being without invested owners, "must pay or starve." The argument still made sense to many, but by 1788 many others believed that the potential consequences of such thinking had already been demonstrated by Captain Collingwood of the *Zong*. The simple equation of the contentment of slaves with the contentment of their masters had grown increasingly less convincing to broad sections of the British public.[47]

Slaveholders had to admit to the high mortality suffered by the enslaved. Not only was it was obvious to most observers; more important, it served masters' argument that the slave trade should continue. In 1788, speaking of one parish in Jamaica, Edward Long told Parliament, "There are some Sugar Estates which have sustained their population by annual births, and are not under the necessity of buying Recruits. But I never heard of more than Eight such Estates; and they are, in proportion to the rest in that Parish, only as 1 to 70." Similarly, in 1788 William Beckford acknowledged, "No man, who is acquainted with the West Indies, can suppose it possible that the average upon estates in the islands, can preserve a given number of negroes, without the aid of foreign purchase. Some plantations bury more than others; and it is natural to suppose, that where the labour is disproportionate, *there* will be the greatest mortality." Planters granted that slaves sold to pay debts or those who labored hard on insolvent properties suffered enormously, but Long thought this situation could be solved simply by attaching them to the land. The *reasons* for high mortality, however, were generally attributed to aberrant features of colonial slavery and causes beyond the control of planters.[48]

Long ascribed mortality in the slave trade to accidents and errors. "The objection, that many die in transportation to the colonies," he maintained, "does not bear against the trade itself, but against some defect or impropriety in the mode of conducting it." A reduction in death rates awaited only "efficacious remedies." Blaming abuses on lower-class overseers, Long excused plantation owners altogether. In cases of willful cruelty, only the strict application of the law was wanting; for example, "a white person, found guilty of wantonly murdering a Negroe, should be adjudged a felon, and suffer *death*." In any case, he attributed most mortality in the islands to exotic African diseases or the difficulty of adjusting to changes in climate.[49]

Long also initiated the oft-repeated accusation that blacks were largely responsible for their own demise. He blamed infant mortality on enslaved women, who he said spread venereal diseases, practiced abortion widely, and maintained poor child-rearing habits. Suicide he blamed on Africans' inordinate fear about European intentions. Oddly enough, he identified African judicial practices as the reason for this panic. "Their edicts are mostly vindictive," he surmised, without the benefit of any knowledge or expertise on the subject, "and death or slavery the almost only modes of punishment." Claiming falsely that 99 percent of enslaved Africans were criminals in their own countries, Long maintained that it was natural that they would "entertain horrid notions" about sale to the Europeans "and often struggle for relief before they quit the coast." Given these conditions, Africans were better off enslaved in the colonies, where a mere few might "perish by casualties," than at home, where "all should die by the hand of the executioner."[50]

Following Long, Beckford argued that the anticipation of death among Africans subjected at home to "a worse slavery than they will experience in our colonies" offered the best evidence that blacks were better off in Jamaica. Beckford added that suicide was a cultural problem, an ethnically specific practice. "The Eboe negroes," he explained, "are particularly addicted to suicide." In this he only represented the widespread prejudices of Anglo-Atlantic planters. James Pinnock, a Jamaica barrister and slave-holder, recorded privately in his diary in 1781 that, "Hope, the Sail Maker, a very good Negroe generally but an Eboe, hung himself on a quarrel with Friends." But Beckford extended to an absurd extreme the claim that Africans were largely accountable for their own high mortality rate. Put-ting forward a view shared by many planters, he argued without evident irony that Africans killed themselves by attending the funerals of their friends and relations. "It is notorious," he insisted, "that more slaves are ruined in principle and health, at those dances which are allowed at the burials of their dead, than by any other intercourse or occupation what-ever." Chaloner Arcedeckne heard much the same when he queried a plan-tation doctor with twenty-five years' experience in Jamaica. "With regard to the mortality of slaves," Dr. William Wright explained, "it is not in general owing to severity or oppression," but "to their going to distant Parts to Negroe Plays in the night where they dance immodestly drink to excess, sleep on the cold ground or commit many acts of sensuality and intemperance." Such explanations for deaths in bondage, similar to what might today be recognized as a "culture of poverty" argument, were to form the core of the defense of the slave trade and slavery right up until emancipation in the 1830s.[51]

The Jamaican plantocracy responded to the abolitionist petitions in Great Britain primarily in the terms used by Edward Long. In two com-mittee reports sent by Jamaica's House of Assembly to the House of Com-mons at the end of 1788, slaveholders argued that the decrease in the slave population was due largely to various "causes not imputable to us, and which the People in Great Britain do not seem to understand." The reports attributed most deaths to an imbalance in ratio between the sexes, which inhibited the birth rate, and to epidemic diseases from Africa. To explain mortality in Jamaica, the planters offered tortured calculations that subtracted an inflated number of runaways, Maroons, and free blacks from the total numbers of Africans imported since 1655, to conclude that only 26,491 slaves had "decreased" in well over a century. Fifteen thousand of these, they proposed, had died between the years 1780 and 1787, when war, a series of violent hurricanes, and famine had wrought havoc on the island. Slaveholders thus sought exoneration by referring to the same catastrophic events that Granville Sharp had taken as evidence of God's judgment.[52]

To blunt the charge of murderous cruelty, the reports enumerated the recent adjustments to the legal administration of slavery, among them stricter punishments for the wanton murder of slaves and accountability on the part of overseers. Simon Taylor rushed to send a copy of one of the new laws to Chaloner Arcedeckne, "to show to the people we are not such inhumane beings as those wicked Enthusiasts represent us to be & that people cannot murder or destroy Negroes as they do Dogs at home." The assembly produced statistics on capital punishment showing that very few slaves had actually been executed. "In order more effectively to prevent the Destruction of Negroes by excessive Labour and unreasonable Punishments," a new law required the surgeon of every plantation, "to give an annual Account of the Decrease and Increase of the Slaves of such Plantation, with the Causes of such decrease, to the best of his Knowledge, Judgment, and Belief." Infant mortality would be arrested by the offer of financial incentives to overseers, "Twenty Shillings for every Slave born on such Plantation, Penn, or other Settlement." In short, and in sharp contrast to the spiritual discourse of the day, calls for slight modifications in civil administration and appeals to the self-interest of the propertied classes encompassed nearly the entire rhetorical explanation of the death of slaves by apologists for slavery. By distancing themselves and their business from the deaths they caused, slaveholders and their allies sought to remove as many of the dead as possible from the growing debate over slavery, and thus reduce the legions of dead slaves arrayed against them by abolitionists to a small band of spectral aberrations. Slaveholders hoped to kill symbolically those whom slavery had already killed physically.[53]

An Abstract of the Evidence

Carefully coordinated by Jamaica's principal lobbyist, Stephen Fuller, proslavery testimony carried the day when the M.P.'s voted on Wilberforce's first abolition bill in 1791. Nevertheless, the moral figure of slavery as murder occasioned by greed took more definitive shape in the testimony of the witnesses for abolition. Despite the failure of the 1791 motion for abolition, the testimonial evidence gave abolitionists another opportunity to frame and publicize slavery as a moral problem that revolved largely around the deaths of the enslaved. Late in 1790 Wilberforce managed to have an abstract of the abolitionist testimony published and distributed to each M.P. In 1791 the abolitionist publisher James Phillips printed fifteen hundred copies of a second edition, and within two weeks abolition committees had distributed it widely.[54]

The questions asked by the House of Commons committee in 1790 and 1791 and the testimony given at the hearings revealed that slaves' deaths and their moral implications now occupied an important place in the consideration of slavery and the slave trade and showed also the persistence of the imperial moral crisis kindled by the captain of the *Zong*. Ostensibly set to collect information only about the slave trade, the hearings brought life in the sugar colonies under close scrutiny, allowing abolitionists to draw as damning a picture of the institution of slavery itself as they had already drawn of the trade. The slave trade was becoming synonymous with massacre, and slavery with unnatural and untimely death.

The parliamentary hearings of 1790–1791 did take into consideration the intricate details of trade and economy, but Wilberforce and his co-counsel William Smith spent considerable time inquiring into the human toll levied by the slave trade and colonial slavery. The hearing investigated the whole of the British Caribbean, but as Britain's most populous and profitable colony, Jamaica featured prominently in the testimony. The witnesses went a long way toward establishing that the cruelty of overseers and the hardened avarice of slaveowners caused the high mortality in the West Indies. Testimonial evidence confirmed the impression that many M.P.'s had formed from the proposed preamble to a clause of Jamaica's Consolidated Slave Law (1787), which sought to make plantation overseers more accountable. Reported in the *Cornwall Chronicle* and reprinted in the preface to *Abstract of the Evidence*, the language disclosed "the *extreme cruelties* and *inhumanity* of the managers, overseers, and book-keepers of estates" and asserted, "It *frequently* happens that slaves come to their death by *hasty and severe blows*, and other *improper treatment.*" Wilberforce's and Smith's questions focused on the callous disregard for black life, for example: "Have you ever known persons who were known to have been guilty of great severities to their Negroes, and who were commonly reputed to have murdered them?; Have any instances fallen within your notice, wherein, besides regular punishments, Negroes have been treated by the overseers with capricious cruelty?"[55]

Men who had experience in the sugar colonies answered with illustrative stories meant to excite sentiment over episodes of suffering and death. Dr. Jackson, who had practiced medicine in Savanna-la-Mar in the mid-1770s recalled an instance where a flogging had killed an enslaved man. Asked if there had been any attempt to punish the killer, Dr. Jackson admitted that he was aware of none. Yet there had been public concern. "People said that it was an unfortunate thing, and they were surprized that the man was not more cautious, as it was not the first thing of the kind that had happened to him; but what they chiefly dwelt upon was the loss that the proprietor sustained."[56] Several others reported similarly unpunished murders. Robert Cross, a former bookkeeper, overseer, and soldier in Jamaica, told of another overseer who, "by severity," had "destroyed forty out of sixty" of the slaves in his power in the course of just three years.[57] Henry Coor, who resided fifteen years on the island as a millwright, described punishments for the enslaved in evocative detail to show just how severe overseers generally were:

> I have known many of these poor creatures, who have been whipt upon the ladder to the number of 100 to 150 lashes, and sometimes to the amount of two cool hundreds, as they are generally known by the overseers; I have known many of these poor creatures returned to the place of their confinement, and in the space of one, two, or three days, at the overseer's pleasure, have been brought out to the ladder again, and have received the same complement, or thereabouts, as before; and they generally make a point never to take these tortured creatures off the ladder till all their skin, from their hams to the small of the back, appears to be nothing but raw flesh and blood, and then they went over the whole parts with salt pickle, which, while the pain lasted, appeared to me, from the convulsions it threw them into, to be more cruel than the whipping.[58]

Coor also told specific stories that emphasized how inured to suffering and death whites in Jamaica had become. He told the parliamentary committee about Old Quasheba, who had been brought to the overseer as a runaway while Coor sat dining with him. After dinner, the overseer summarily hanged Quasheba with the aid of one his clerks. Coor heard her choking and screaming for several hours. When the clerk came, "apparently in great spirits," to brag about the deed, Coor reproached him. But the clerk retorted, "Damn her for an old bitch, she was good for nothing, what signifies killing such an old woman as her." The plantation manager sent for Coor the following morning to find out what had happened, incensed that Coor could see his "master's Slaves murdered in that manner, and not let him know of it." Coor simply responded that it was not his business, "cruelties of that kind were so common in the plantations, that I had thought no more about it." The plantation manager was furious over the loss of property, but not angry enough to dismiss the overseer, who had produced very profitable crops in the past. Evangelical audiences who read the published testimony later could not fail to see that nowhere in the story had anyone spoken of concern for Old Quasheba's immortal soul.[59]

Coor did observe, however, that "cruel treatment" had driven many enslaved men and women to suicide. Substantiating the common awareness that Africans believed they would return home after they died, stories of suicide confirmed the misery of slavery and countered proslavery testimony suggesting that Africans might be happier under colonial slavery than at home. Their performance at funerals also provided evidence of their readiness to find escape in death. Several witnesses testified to the "the great joy which is discovered at their funerals by their fellow-slaves, and which joy is said to proceed from the idea that the deceased are returning home." By contrast, at least one witness reported that funerals in Africa were more sorrowful affairs. When Wilberforce and Smith put the question to several more witnesses—"Did you ever know Negroes to commit suicide, and under what circumstances?"—the responses corresponded to popular Romantic descriptions of suicides as heroic tragedies for which the fault lay with a corrupt and unfeeling world. As such, suicide functioned as the ultimate proof of oppression, much as the decisions of the ten Africans who leapt freely overboard from the *Zong* indicted the venality of Captain Collingwood and his officers.[60]

As had been the case with the *Zong* massacre, the parliamentary testimony on slavery set up an equation linking slavery, death, and money, the willful substitution of financial gain for the fate of the soul. Slaves were routinely worked to death. "Hard work," as well as severe punishment, "certainly occasions a constant decrease in the able Negroes," explained former overseer William Fitzmaurice. "I am very sorry to say," he acknowledged, "that a great number of Negroes are hurried to their grave" by having to keep up an unbearable pace on work gangs. He spoke on good authority. During the last four years that Fitzmaurice lived in Jamaica, he bought ninety-five slaves and sold fifty-two of them. These "were all that were living, and those fifty-two I did not sell as seasoned Slaves; if I had attempted to keep them till the usual time of seasoning, I should have had a greater decrease, and on this very account I sold them." Seizing on such estimates of death and devaluation, Wilberforce and Smith asked, "Did you ever hear any calculation made concerning the time which an African Negro would be required to last in order to repay the price of his purchase?" Fitzmaurice admitted only that there had been an old saying in the parish of Saint Thomas-in-the-Vale, Jamaica, "that if a negro lived seven years he paid for himself." But slaves could not always be kept alive long enough to secure a return on the investment.[61]

Fitzmaurice told a story about one gentleman's plantations in Saint Thomas-in-the-Vale, where, "by over pushing, the most part of his Negroes were destroyed while he was in England, and when he returned he found his estates almost without Negroes, and judgements against him to the amount of a large sum of money to various people, and those Negroes that lived were taken upon writs of Venditioni; I purchased myself, at a public sale, fifty odd to cover a debt for a house in Kingston." In such a volatile market, few owners could be concerned about the family lives of the enslaved. Dr. Harrison, a former plantation doctor in Jamaica, told the committee that there was no "encouragement given to bring up families; the general opinion being, that it was better to purchase new Negroes, than to rear Negro children." Witness after witness came before the House of Commons committee to confirm Ottabah Cugoano's allegation that "the great severities and oppressions loaded upon the wretched survivors are such that they are continually wearing out, and a new annual supply wanted," to replace "the great multitude of human souls that are actually deprived of life by carrying on that iniquitous business." Against Cugoano's ideal image of all individuals' having an essential existence as souls precious in the sight of God, the testimony to the House of Commons in 1791 gave an impression just like that held by Captain Thomas Lloyd of the Royal Navy: to slaveholders, enslaved men and women "were very generally considered as black cattle, and very often treated like post horses."[62]

An Abstract of the Evidence concluded by invoking Hercules Ross, who
resided in Jamaica from 1761 to 1782. In the early 1770s Ross attended a
series of meetings in Kingston called by Thomas Hibbert, the most eminent Guinea factor, or slave dealer, in Jamaica, who wanted to debate the
wisdom and morality of the African slave trade. At these meetings, Ross
delivered the opinion that the trade was contrary to both "sound policy"
and "the laws of God and nature," and that it ought to be abolished. He
voiced this conviction no more than a few years after he had seen a particular group of slaves sold in Kingston's public square, survivors of an
event eerily similar to the *Zong* massacre. Before they arrived at auction,
these thirty-odd men and women had been packed, along with about four
hundred others, into the hold of an unnamed English ship that had sailed
from the coast of Africa. One night, it struck the reefs surrounding the
Morant Keys, three small sandy islands clustered just southeast of Jamaica.
The officers and crew took their boats ashore with provisions and arms.
They left the Africans shackled aboard the slaver. Through the night, the
captives wrenched free of their irons and fashioned life-rafts from pieces
of the vessel. The next morning, from the shore half a league away, the
officers and crew watched as the African women and children floated
towards them upon the rafts, attended by the men who could swim.
Fearing that the Africans would soon come after their food and water, the
officers and crew resolved to kill them. "As the poor wretches approached
the shore," Ross recalled, "they actually destroyed between three and four
hundred of them." Only thirty-three or thirty-four survived for sale in
Kingston. Perhaps the details of this massacre, a decade before the voyage
of the *Zong*, convinced Hercules Ross that the slave trade was a source of
"great destruction and great misery to the human race." Perhaps also, the
others holding the academic debate in Kingston were aware of the event
or were convinced by Ross, for they finally decided in the majority "that
the trade to Africa for slaves, was neither consistent with sound policy, the
laws of nature, and morality." In spite of that, the most profitable days of
the slave trade to Jamaica were still to come.[63]

When *An Abstract of the Evidence* circulated among the public, it helped
inspire half a million Britons to sign petitions calling for the abolition of
the slave trade in 1792. In April of that year, the House of Commons
responded to public pressure by voting to end the slave trade by 1796. But
the abolition bill met vehement opposition when it reached the House of

Lords. Though they were not beholden to popular opinion, the lords avoided voting the measure down directly; instead they stalled it once again, by demanding that the evidence collected by the Commons be presented anew to them. One motion away from victory, frustrated abolitionists would wait another decade before Parliament sanctioned their cause again.[64]

The abolitionists' disappointment in Parliament was not total. A few modest reform measures, of the kind acceptable to the more enlightened slaveholders, became law in the 1780s and 1790s. In 1788 Sir William Dolben, one of two M.P.'s for Oxford University, sponsored a regulation act to ameliorate the lethal conditions aboard slave ships. To alleviate shipboard overcrowding that generated "putrid disorders and all sorts of dangerous diseases," the act sought to limit the number of slaves that could be carried per ton and to provide piece-rate financial incentives to ship captains and surgeons for slaves landed alive. A decade later, in 1799, a similar act regulated the carrying capacity of slavers in relation to their physical dimensions. A 1790 statute responded to the *Zong* massacre by prohibiting the insurance of slaves, except for narrowly defined risks; a law passed in 1794 explicitly banned the recovery of losses incurred by throwing slaves overboard. But by 1793 antislavery rhetoric had lost some of its allure for many M.P.'s, who were now more touched by the tales of killing and chaos emanating from the French and Haitian revolutions. When the London Corresponding Society, formed in 1792 by such radical "British Jacobins" as Thomas Hardy, declared their support for abolition, many began to suspect that the *Abstract of the Evidence* might be as dangerously subversive as Thomas Paine's *Rights of Man*, a strident defense of the French Revolution.[65]

Chains of Meaning

The deluge of sentimental antislavery narratives in the 1780s had begun to lose some of its emotional force by the end of the century, as people recognized the limits of sentimental politics. As the literary historian Adam Lively has argued, "The enormous actual gulf between European and enslaved African was bridged in the imagination by projecting onto slavery conventional melodramatic scenarios. The anti-slavery aesthetic spoke more of the reader and of his (or very often her) existence than it did of that of the slave, its ostensible subject." Even antislavery testimony, based on first-hand experience, offered its narratives in the sentimental terms that the English found convincing at the time. The literary enthusiasm for victims of suffering drew sharp criticism in the 1790s, and even the most sentimental writers began to feel they had been self-indulgent. According to the cultural critic Debbie Lee, Romantic writers continued to write powerful moral critiques of slavery, albeit more oblique ones. "Since the topic had been made so explicit for so long," Lee says, "such writers considered it most powerful when least obvious, most familiar when unfamiliar, and truly intimate when seemingly distant." Relying more heavily on allegory, Romantics evoked antislavery sentiments in "traces," symbolic substitutions that could still be read for their political meanings.[66]

There was a similar, though less subtle, development in the way people applied graphic arts and statistics to further antislavery aims. The circulation of abolitionist anecdotes abetted by the enormous growth in print media in the latter half of the eighteenth century gave pictures and numbers a new power to sum up and signify antislavery themes. Both visual images and demographic figures acquired the ability to stand for sentimental stories whose moral was already understood. Empathy and abstraction converged in the combination of representations of dead and dying slaves and recitations of unnatural decreases in population. The guiding spirit of Edward Young, the poet of *Night Thoughts*, who inspired readers to draw moral lessons from relations with the dead, and of John Foxe, whose *Martyrology* appeared in five new printings between 1784 and 1800, continued to inform the public, as it learned to interpret increasing quantities of numerical and pictorial information. "For over a century Young was the poet of Christian sensibility par excellence," the literary historian Stephen Cornford contends, "and his poem signaled the beginning of an era when the search for truth, certainty and knowledge tended to find answers in idealism rather than empiricism, in enthusiasm rather than pragmatism."[67] In fact, during the antislavery campaigns, idealism and empiricism were dramatically united. Demographic data combined with visual imagery allowed people to survey and grasp immense amounts of information about events that they could never experience, yet traces of moral sentiment remained attached to these abstractions. Chains of meaningful association bound the *Zong* massacre to future discussions of slavery, and the ethical outrage that crystallized in its wake could be provoked in a flash by an image or by a recitation of numbers. Both could function as empirical proof of an ethical argument.

William Blake's antislavery engravings, for example, encoded the evangelical approach to death in macabre detail, along with the condemnation of colonial slavery. In 1791–92, as Britons considered the evidence of inhumanity in their West Indian colonies, Blake worked on his engravings for John Gabriel Stedman's *Narrative of a Five Years' Expedition against the Revolted Negroes of Surinam*. When the book appeared in 1796, antislavery activists scoured it for anecdotes and imagery that could excite abolitionist feeling, though Stedman himself had fought a bitter campaign against the Maroons and was an apologist for colonial slavery. From original watercolors by Stedman, Blake fashioned scenes of torture and death that were powerfully evocative but also, through the viewing conventions of the period, taken as accurate representations of objective truth. One of the images, *A Negro hung alive by the Ribs to a Gallows*, brought traditional iconography of death, horror, and evangelicalism together to create an enduring emblem of antislavery sentiment (Figure 5.3). The image depicts a man suspended from a gallows by a hook run through his rib cage. Around his body, skulls adorn sticks and bones litter the ground. Evoking the traditional memento mori, Blake announces the universal approach of death, made specific in the black man's imminent fate. The man stares directly out of the page without expression; perhaps he is already dead. But the open eyes of the man, suspended alive like Christ, also signify spiritual redemption and everlasting life. He embodies Blake's radical Christian vision. Blake's efforts to represent those killed for revolting against their status as chattel probably influenced his *Visions of the Daughters of Albion* (1793), which David Erdman has described as an "indictment of the 'mistaken Demon' whose code separates bodies from souls and reduces women and children, nations and lands, to possessions."[68]

After he finished his engravings for Stedman's *Narrative*, Blake took other opportunities to make moral images of death. He produced more than 537 watercolors and 43 engravings for the 1797 edition of *Night Thoughts*, and in 1805 he began drawing the images of death, judgment, and the afterlife that would appear in the 1808 edition of *The Grave* by Robert Blair. Soon after, he painted his impression of James Hervey's *Meditations among the Tombs*. Blake's engravings of the tortured body of the

A Negro hung alive by the Ribs to a Gallows.

Figure 5.3. *A Negro hung alive by the Ribs to a Gallows,* engraving by William Blake, in John Gabriel Stedman, *Narrative of a Five Years' Expedition against the Revolted Negroes of Surinam,* vol. 1 (London, 1796). This image was based on a 1773 eyewitness description from Suriname. The victim hung there alive for three days, until he was finally bludgeoned to death by a sentry he had insulted. Blake gave the scene the iconic status of a crucifixion and arranged the memento mori death's-heads to draw attention to the ship off the coast, implicating overseas empires in the execution. From the collection of the James Ford Bell Library, University of Minnesota, Minneapolis.

black man thus exemplified his larger concern with death, redemption, and the moral government of the world.[69]

Other artists made the connection between death, slavery, money, and politics more explicit than did Blake. Though British satirists generally accepted the prevailing contempt for blacks, they sometimes mined the topic of colonial slavery in order to lampoon greed, political corruption, and the degeneracy of elite society. The 1791 House of Commons debate and the petition campaign that followed it provoked more direct reflections on slavery. The satirist James Gillray engraved *Barbarities in the West Indies* (Figure 5.4), based on an incident reported by Sir Philip Francis to the Commons that April. The caricature shows a sinister-looking overseer stirring a slave in a boiling vat of sugar cane juice. Nailed to the wall behind him are some small animals, a severed black arm, and a single pair of black ears. As J. R. Oldfield has pointed out, this image, like similar caricatures, expresses ambivalence about the merits of abolition. Gillray may well have been satirizing what proslavery advocates saw as the excesses of antislavery testimony. Nevertheless, such images gave vivid form to the connections linking death, greed, and slavery and lodged them in the visual imagination of the viewing public.[70]

The best-known abolitionist image of the period (perhaps excepting Josiah Wedgewood's kneeling slave) showed the plan and sections of a slave ship, modeled on the *Brookes* of Liverpool, which, like the *Zong*, carried Africans from the Gold Coast to Jamaica. In late 1788, when abolitionists in Plymouth published an image of the packed lower deck of a slaver, it quickly came to Thomas Clarkson's attention. He had a more detailed version published in the spring of 1789, which he distributed to members of both houses of Parliament in advance of Wilberforce's first motion for abolition. The icon also appeared more widely in myriad antislavery tracts and pamphlets, posted in the streets of Edinburgh or even framed and displayed in private homes, and in the first edition of the *Abstract of the Evidence*. The London committee arranged for the printing and distribution of eight thousand additional copies in 1788–89.[71]

The image of the plan and sections of a slave ship encapsulated moral censure of the commercial way of death, rendered emblematically rather than anecdotally (Figure 5.5). "Here, in diagrammatic form," explains Oldfield, "were human beings reduced to the level of inhuman objects, treated as so much merchandise and stowed on board ship in the most appalling

Figure 5.4. *Barbarities in the West Indias,* drawing by James Gillray, 23 April 1791, in *The Works of James Gillray* (London, 1849). A plantation overseer uses a whip handle to stir a black body into a vat of boiling sugar, as he exclaims, "B—t your black Eyes! What you can't work because you're not well?—but I'll give you a warm bath to cure your Ague, & a Curry-combing afterwards to put Spunk into you." Nailed to the wall in the background are several dead animals, a black person's severed arm, and a pair of human ears. The caption refers to the parliamentary debates of 1791: "Mr. Frances relates, 'Among numberless other acts of cruelty daily practiced, an English Negro Driver, because a young Negro thro sickness was unable to work, threw him into a Copper of Boiling Sugar juice, & after keeping him steeped over head & Ears for above Three Quarters of an hour in the boiling liquid, whipt him with such severity that it was near Six Months before he recover'd of his Wounds & Scalding.' Vide Mr. Frances speech corroborated by Mr. Fox, Mr. Wilberforce & c. &c." Reproduced by permission of the Huntington Library, San Marino, California.

conditions."[72] Perhaps more important, it was impossible to escape the impression that the *Brookes* was a tomb, a mass grave that yielded handsome rents to its owners.

If the story of the *Zong* symbolized the Atlantic slave trade as a moral dystopia, the plan of the *Brookes* refined the abstraction. "Designed," according to Thomas Clarkson, "to give the spectator an idea of the sufferings of the Africans in the Middle Passage," the image effected a subtle

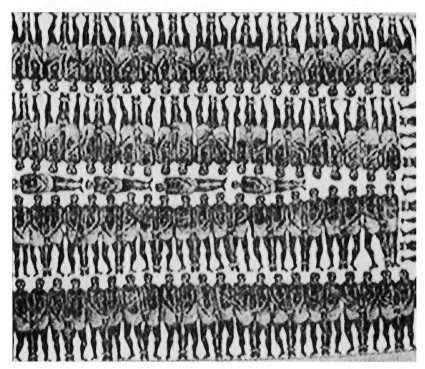

Figure 5.5. Detail from *Plan and Sections of a Slave Ship*, frontispiece to *An Abstract of the Evidence Delivered before a Select Committee of the House of Commons in the Years 1790 and 1791* (London, 1791). Originally published in 1789 (printed by J. Phillips), the image, which has been reproduced frequently down to the present, represents the cargo hold of the *Brookes*, a Liverpool slaver which traded in Jamaica in the 1780s. One of the larger ships in the trade, the *Brookes* carried as many as 609 enslaved Africans in its hold. Courtesy of the Rare Book, Manuscript, and Special Collections Library, Duke University, Durham, North Carolina.

shift in evocative technique, inspiring horror not through the details of suffering, but through its lack of detail. Although close inspection of the image would reveal gender distinctions, shackles, and bodily contortions, nothing indicated the anguished cries, or the blood and filth in the hold. For viewers trained by moral sentimentalism and gothic fiction to see authentically human experience in such details, the revelation that slavers could coolly reduce human bodies to such neat, lifeless patterns was in itself horrifying. Viewers who knew the stories of suffering and death contained in the *Abstract of the Evidence* had to notice the absence of such stories, the absence of humanity, from the plan of the slave ship. Indeed, the generic

nature of the image forced them to seek stories of suffering and death in
the accompanying text. As an abstract rendering of the confluence of death
and calculation, the image both summarized the traces of various sentimental and evangelical ethical narratives and foreshadowed the emergence
of the demographic debate on the enslaved population of the West Indies.
That debate only intensified after the abolitionists had finally brought a
halt to the British transatlantic slave trade. In the rhetoric that attended
that victory, the *Zong* again played a role. As Ian Baucom has recognized,
the story of the *Zong* massacre assumed a truly generic form in the House
of Commons abolition debate of 1806. During the debate "the story of the
massacre was retold: though now not as the story of a particular historical
event . . . but as one in a series of equivalent stories."[73]

Of course, the general understanding of the slave trade as commerce in
death was only one factor in the ultimate success of the abolition bill that
year. Recent evidence indicates that West Indian planters, especially in
Jamaica, faced a crisis of overproduction in the early years of the nineteenth century that severely eroded confidence in the sugar industry
among imperial policymakers. As Robin Blackburn has wryly observed, it
was only after the threat of Jacobinism and the French Revolution had
faded, and once a majority of M.P.'s were "convinced that abolition did
not contradict 'sound policy,'" that "knowing it to be dear to the heart of
the middle-class reformers, they allowed themselves to be shocked by the
appalling brutalities of the Atlantic slave trade." Nevertheless, by pro-
voking anxiety over God's judgment of the British Empire, the generic
representation of the slave trade had inspired passionate and crucial political action and would continue to frame the terms of the succeeding
episodes in the debate over colonial slavery.[74]

"An Arithmetical Proposition"

Following the abolition of the transatlantic slave trade in 1807, the old
theory that a decline in population could result from an immoral economic bargain formed the underpinning for the movement to bring about
registration of slaves, an amelioration in their living conditions, and their
eventual emancipation. Debates in Britain about the correlation between
the magnitude of the population and its moral welfare, which had begun
in the mid-eighteenth century with the earliest attempts to "number the

people," now focused on colonial slavery. The first nationwide census in 1801 had demonstrated that the British population was not, in fact, in decline, but the moralists were not satisfied; they transposed their argument to the slave colonies, where it appeared to be justified. In 1815, again backed by a mass campaign, parliamentary abolitionists pressed for a register of the enslaved populations in the West Indies. The proposed bill was meant to ensure, through carefully monitoring of patterns of birth and death in the colonies, that no new slaves were smuggled in from Africa. Though the intercolonial slave trade was still legal, strict enforcement of the ban on the African trade was intended to encourage planters to *breed* rather than *buy* their workforce. Merchants and planters in the colonies were hostile to the proposed legislation, rightly fearing that such a census might reveal embarrassing statistics. It was common knowledge that slaves failed to reproduce themselves naturally in the sugar colonies and that their numbers had decreased since the end of the transatlantic slave trade, but slaveholders hoped to hide the extent of the demographic debacle. Following the path hewn by Long and Beckford, they again blamed the decrease on factors beyond their control. The Jamaican assembly protested in 1815 that after the abolitionists had abused them "in detail," with anecdotes of cruelty and barbarity, "we are [now] attacked in the mass, and told, that although we have refuted the items, the general charge of cruelty and oppression must be just, because the slaves have not increased, but diminished, in number." The colonial assemblies' protests were enough to obstruct the imposition of a central register, administered from London, but there was enough pressure to persuade them to establish colonial registers under local control. The registration returns continued to document a profound demographic crisis. Confronted by the numerical "facts," advocates on both sides of the slavery issue again invoked the dead in spirited debates.[75]

Planters and merchants reprised the arguments laid out by Long: rogue underlings were beyond their control, and the bad habits of the enslaved were responsible for their poor life expectancy and low birth rate. Immorality, superstition, abortion, and even witchcraft served as convenient scapegoats for the demographic decline. The gothic novelist and slaveholder Matthew Gregory Lewis summarized planters' sentiments perfectly in his diary: "Say what one will to the negroes, and treat them as well as one can, obstinate devils, they will die!" Such sarcastic reasoning could not undo the ordinary conflation in the popular mind of slavery, avarice, and death that had been established in the 1780s and 1790s. As long as this simple chain of associations remained intact, abolitionist arguments continued to be morally convincing, even when they no longer relied on sentimental discourse. As incriminating statistics were reported in from the West Indies, antislavery activists in Britain came to see them as an index of the basic inhumanity of slavery.[76]

The recorded statistics acted as seemingly "rational" analogues to detailed stories of physical suffering. Thomas Fowell Buxton spoke for many humanitarians when he told an 1832 parliamentary committee on the state of the West Indies that the decrease in the slave population was "the best of all tests of the condition of the Negro." Basing his argument on his understanding of Malthusian population theory, he asserted that barring "great convulsions . . . increase can only be prevented by intense misery." In this way Buxton folded a generic argument, about the immorality that caused demographic deterioration, into what seemed a scientific truism. He justified his argument in terms appropriate to an age in which the influence of sentimental rhetoric was yielding to bureaucratic rationality. He cited population decline, he said, "because it cannot be liable to the imputation of any excitement of feelings; it was a purely rational argument, it was addressed only to the understanding, it was an arithmetical proposition." The statement was sly. Such numbers certainly excited feeling, but sentiment now came cloaked in the authority of reason. The ethical corollary to John Weskett's gross averages, demographic statistics carried narratives of suffering with them. Despite the transition from moral sentimentalism to humanitarian empiricism, emotional weight attached to the dead remained a fundamental feature of British morality. For the devout, redemption for the British Empire could only come with the cleansing of the national soul through the restoration of proper attitudes toward death and the dead, and this required expiation for the sin of slavery. The moral climate that developed in response to the death of slaves was an important factor in Parliament's decision to mitigate slavery in 1823 and finally to emancipate the enslaved in the 1830s.[77]

Popular antislavery politics in the Age of Reason were less a rational pursuit than a national exorcism, a campaign to rid the British Empire of a great evil. Antislavery rhetoric and activism emerged as an important part of the British vision for the colonial moral order in the late eighteenth

and early nineteenth centuries. At its center was an evangelical understanding of death and redemption, couched in the rhetoric of moral sentiment.[78] Reacting to deep demographic changes and political-economic
tensions in Britain, mortuary politics in antislavery discourse projected
idealized resolutions of domestic crises onto the British West Indies. The
image of West Indian slaveholders as depraved killers satisfied a widespread
yearning, especially on the part of evangelicals, to find the evil at the root
of contemporary social strains. Yet as long as systematic murder was seen
largely as the result of moral failure, antislavery polemics were vulnerable
to at least one of the counterarguments by merchants and planters: that
the moral condition of black men and women was the source of their
failure to propagate.

Evangelical antislavery activists relied on a religious understanding of
population trends. As a result, they often believed that planters had only
to attend to the moral instruction of enslaved blacks in order to see their
numbers grow naturally. In 1806 Wilberforce assured skeptics that the
slaveholder need only ensure "that the negroes are well fed, regard paid to
their health, their habits, to their domestic comforts, and, above all, to
their moral improvement; and he will soon find them rapidly to increase
in numbers." In this respect, many evangelical abolitionists agreed with
planters that the slaves' "morally degraded condition," their savagery, was
partly to blame for rampant mortality among them. Abolitionists advocated the reformation of slaves' moral state as a means to achieve demographic increase. Much of their effort to "ameliorate" slaves' condition in
the 1820s focused on winning freedom for evangelicals to proselytize in the
colonies. Once protection had been guaranteed evangelist missionaries to
the colonies, many respectable reformers were content to see slavery continue in a milder, because more pious, form. But though this solution may
have soothed the conscience of evangelicals in Britain, overseas missionaries
actually had to confront the somewhat different spiritual convictions and
freedom struggles among the enslaved. The result of such encounters
would propel antislavery rhetoric and action well beyond British reformers'
more limited vision of moral reform.[79]

Holy Ghosts and Eternal Salvation

TO REDEEM THE SOUL of the British Empire, it was necessary to save the souls of its heathen inhabitants. If Britons were to avert a divine calamity, they would have to bring imperial subjects, including the enslaved in America, to God. Fearing that the souls of so-called heathens would face hell, eternal oblivion, or "spiritual death," evangelical Protestants in the second half of the eighteenth century entered into a worldwide competition to save souls. The matter was urgent, for the terrors of hell weighed heavily on the minds of evangelists, and they knew that heathens were damned unless they could be converted, "plucked from the burnings, and rescued from heathenish and savage darkness." Not to desire their salvation was considered "inhuman," even "devilish."[1]

Late in the year 1824 the Baptist missionary William Knibb embarked for Jamaica aboard the merchant ship *Ocean*, to assume the mission of his deceased brother Thomas. Violent weather in the English Channel delayed his passage for two months and forced Knibb, barely twenty-one years old, to reflect upon his own mortality. Death was often on William Knibb's mind as he lay in his berth. He was well aware that Jamaica was among the most dangerous places to which an evangelist could go, "the grave of the Europeans," a colony where no insurance society would underwrite a policy on any man's life, on any terms. Thomas had died after just fifteen months on the island, before he reached the age of twenty-five. "But if such a short period is allotted to me," William wrote to his relatives at Kettering, "my prayer is that I may be able to do the work of an Evangelist and be faithful to death, that thus I may receive the final and eternal benediction of well done, good, and faithful servants." Rejoicing at the thought of Thomas's role in the symbolic death and spiritual rebirth represented by baptism, William clearly hoped that his own endeavor would equal his exalted impression of his brother's. Thomas was doing the good work of John the Baptist, seen as the prototype of the missionary, who associated total immersion in water and the subsequent laying on of hands with "passing from death unto life."[2]

If Thomas's early success gave William cause for optimism, he grew more pessimistic once he began to learn something about slave society for himself. One morning during his voyage Knibb discussed slavery with a fellow passenger, a Jamaican planter. The planter related aspects of life in Jamaica that Knibb found intolerably wicked. The slaveholder claimed never to punish any slaves but women, "as they cannot be brought into subjection without it." He alleged that he personally knew overseers who employed an old woman "to bring them all the young females when they arrive at maturity for the purpose of debauchery and crime." Knibb was outraged to hear that masters commonly had sex with female slaves "for the purpose of *increasing their stock!!!*" The planter himself lived in adultery and had been doing so since he was seventeen years old. And though he was "employed in purchasing the bodies and in a certain sense the souls of his unhappy fellow-creatures," the planter, Knibb was astounded to hear, expected to go to heaven on account of his good deeds. "He is an odious picture," Knibb remarked in his journal, "of the brutalizing and immoral tendency of this execrable system."[3]

Knibb's initial experience of the state of religion in Jamaica confirmed his view of the deleterious effects of slavery on the condition of the human soul. In one of his first letters from the colony to his Bristol friend Samuel Nichols, Knibb was almost despairing: "I have now reached the land of sin, disease, and death, where Satan reigns with awful power, and carries multitudes captive at his will. Here religion is scoffed at, and those who profess it ridiculed and insulted. The Sabbath is violated, and a desire seems to manifest itself, by many of the inhabitants, to blot the Creator out of the universe he has formed." It is true that when Knibb arrived in Jamaica, the devout were few and scattered. Most planters paid little heed or financial support to the local clergy, and the Christianity practiced among blacks was thoroughly unfamiliar to the Englishman. He found cause for hope, however: Knibb had arrived in a colony whose enslaved population was undergoing widespread Christianization.[4]

Death and Salvation

Until the late eighteenth century, Christianity's influence among the enslaved was severely limited. The Anglican Church in Jamaica had no bishop until 1824, and it confronted a chronic shortage of clergy. Local concern for the welfare of the church was weak, and neither the vestries nor the legislature provided adequate financial support. The church could barely muster the resources to minister to the free white population, so it made few attempts to convert slaves or serve their religious needs. Evangelical missions, with a greater sense of purpose and the help of fortuitous circumstances, made slow and halting progress but ultimately achieved considerable success in bringing Christianity to the majority of the Jamaican population by the middle of the nineteenth century.[5]

The Grim Reaper cultivated a distinctive form of Christianity in Jamaica, more like the African forms of worship and fellowship that white missionaries hoped to dislodge. Like everyone else on the island, missionaries rarely survived long. Consequently, there were never enough of them among the overwhelmingly black population to inculcate unadulterated versions of Christian beliefs and ceremonies. And because until the end of the transatlantic slave trade Africans migrated to the island in steady numbers as replacements for the exhausted, black people could always find familiar alternatives to European cultural practices. White missionaries could only plant the seeds of interest in their religion; if it were to capture the imaginations of the enslaved, it would have to resonate with their deepest concerns. As a result, more than anything else, death and slavery determined the development of Jamaican Christianity.

The progress of Christianity on the island depended to a large degree on the course of theological struggles surrounding the representation of the afterlife and ceremonies of interment. The Protestant doctrine of the separation of body and soul—according to which souls were consigned immediately after death to heaven, hell, or oblivion—ran counter to widespread popular belief in the continuing presence on earth of the spirits of the dead. Despite their differing views on the institution of slavery, planters and missionaries shared a sense of superiority vis-à-vis the enslaved, agreed on their savagery, and desired that their burial ceremonies be reformed. Understanding funerals as contested arenas where people enacted their views on the afterlife, evangelical missionaries worked to change them and thereby reform black relations with the dead. Their efforts eventually had a significant impact on black religion and mortuary practice.

Nevertheless, Christianity did not simply supplant African-derived spirituality in Jamaica. The religious transformations encompassed basic continuities. Enslaved blacks underwent genuine conversions, but because they interpreted missionary teachings through their own experience, they adapted Christianity to their primary interest in the relation of death and spirit to the political tensions of slavery. In this way, struggles over the representation of the hereafter were at the same time contests over the moral worlds within Jamaican slavery. Most of the new Christians among the slaves did not abandon their belief in the persistence of earthly ghosts and spirits. Rather, they now tried to harness the specters of Jesus Christ and the Holy Ghost to their struggles against the indignities of enslavement. Equality in the afterlife, a central tenet of Christian teaching, inspired social egalitarianism among people who continued to believe in the imbrication of the spiritual and temporal worlds. Christianity offered an idiom of protest shared with allies in the United Kingdom, thus helping the enslaved argue that slavery was incompatible with righteous Christian imperial rule, even though the missionaries themselves were more circumspect about stating it. Yet for both missionaries and slaves the power of religion in this world revolved around ideas about death.

Protestant missionaries shared some fundamental approaches to the dead and the afterlife. They shared a belief in the separation of body and soul at death. Evangelicals also assumed that the souls of those who remained outside the influence of their spiritual teaching were doomed to extinction—or worse, eternal torture in hell—after the passing of the body. But Moravians, Methodists, and to a lesser extent Baptists all shared an abiding faith in the redeeming power of the death of Christ. Believing above all else that the path to eternal life had been opened by Christ's willingness to sacrifice himself for mankind, Protestant missionaries were obsessed with death and its meaning.[6]

Baptists like Thomas and William Knibb, arriving after the official establishment of the Baptist mission to Jamaica in 1814, emphasized the possibility of spiritual rebirth from the living death brought about by sin, a regeneration that could be achieved by ritual cleansing. When William Knibb thought of his brother's mission, he imagined him in the river, baptizing people who "seemed lost as though no man cared for their souls." Having been told of "Jesus the friend of sinners," the enslaved now had an opportunity to repent, "washed in his blood, and regenerated by his Spirit," metaphorically "*BURIED* (not sprinkled!!) with him in Baptism, that they may rise to newness of life."[7]

Other Protestants surpassed the Baptists in their preoccupation with death. The Moravians, who opened the first Protestant missions in Jamaica in 1754, made a fetish of Christ's crucified body. Nickolas Ludwig von Zinzendorf, the Austrian nobleman who emerged as the spiritual leader of the Moravian Unitas Fratrum in the eighteenth century, believed that because Christ had atoned for human sin, people had a duty to repay the suffering and dying Jesus with love and adoration. Among the brethren, this belief manifested itself in speech and song as a preoccupation with Christ's wounds, blood, and corpse, which "came to be revered as mystical entities deserving man's adoration in and of themselves," and not only as symbolic expressions of Christ's sacrifice. "Blest Flock in th' Cross's Atmosphere," went a verse of one Moravian hymn, "you smell of Jesu's Grave, / The Vapours of his Corpse so dear / Are the Perfume you have. / Its scent is penetrant and sweet; / When you kiss each other and greet, / This Scent discovers that you were / To Jesu's Body near." Such imagery was a prominent feature of Moravian proselytizing. "We will preach nothing but Jesus the Crucified," they maintained at midcentury. "We will look for nothing else in the Bible but the Lamb and His Wounds, and again Wounds, and Blood and Blood."[8]

In Jamaica, they avidly pursued this course. Once, stricken with a serious fever, Brother Zecharias Caries called the "baptized Negroes" to his bed. "I spoke to all of them of the suffering Saviour," he reported to his diary, "of going to be with him, and of seeing the wounds in his hands, and feet, and side." When they were feeling healthy, Moravians would preach for "upwards of two hours, the account of our Saviour's last words, his sufferings, and death." Such recitals formed the core of Moravian conversion efforts. One Moravian missionary admitted as much when he told a parliamentary committee in 1791 that "the plain Testimony concerning the Death and Passion of Christ the Son of God, together with its Cause and happy Consequences, delivered by a missionary touched with an experimental Sense of it, is the surest Way of enlightening the benighted minds of the heathen in order to lead them afterwards Step by Step into all Truth."⁹

The Methodists followed the Moravians, establishing a permanent mission in Jamaica in the 1791, but they emphasized the importance of the death of individual sinners over the event of Christ's death. All humankind was vile and doomed, Methodists agreed, but was loved by Christ nonetheless. In order to return the Savior's love, sinners must die and be reborn— "Die to Live, as He died that they might live." Eternal life would be the reward for a loving death. Methodists taught people to keep their thoughts on the afterlife, to remind themselves constantly that they were working toward a future state of eternal reward, "to look with tranquility upon the tomb, and to consider death only as a friendly messenger." Because death was the happy occasion when one passed from this life into eternity, Methodists often viewed the event as an opportunity to make sure that the last words spoken were a testimonial to faith in Christ: the deathbed scene was the conclusive evidence of a person's piety. The way of dying was testimony to the Christian way of living. Accounts of death experiences became a common feature of Methodist literature, read aloud at society meetings all over the world.¹⁰

In reports from Kingston, Rev. William Fish provided careful descriptions of all Methodists who passed away there and of their last days and their demeanor at the moment of death. In 1804, for example, he commented on the death of Elizabeth Poynter, an elderly black woman. "I am informed her last days were her best," related Fish. "She grew more fervent than ever; and enjoyed a great increase of the love of God," until the moment "when she cheerfully resigned her soul to Him who had bought it with His own blood." Elizabeth Poynter had been a devout and practicing Christian and her salvation was not in doubt, but even practicing sinners could be saved in their final hour, and the Methodists took special notice of expressions of faith from them. Expression by the dying of faith in Christ provided Methodists with the clearest proof of an individual's candidacy for eternal life. Without that proof they remained anxious over the fate of the person's soul. Fish described the case of an elderly black woman who had been sick for many years but regularly attended religious meetings. One night after an evening catechism, she died before a friend could be called to hear her last words. "Our hope of her is therefore founded on her conduct and experience in *life*, and not on her *dying* testimony," wrote Fish. He clearly would have felt greater certitude about her salvation if he had possessed an account of her last words.[11]

Methodists were most comforted when the aim of praising Jesus the Savior could sum up the meaning of an entire life. So they celebrated stories in which a person narrated in one final utterance the entire meaning of his or her existence through reference to Christ. In the published *Missionary Notices* devout Protestants of all sorts looked for deathbed anecdotes similar to the one concerning Mr. Allen, a young missionary sent to Jamaica from England in the 1820s. Just days after he arrived, Mr. Allen was seized with a fever and inflammation of the lungs and kidneys. "During his affliction he had severe struggles with the adversary of his soul," read the letter from his colleague, Mr. Young. As he lay dying, Mr. Allen wondered whether he had not angered God by failing in his mission to the heathens of Jamaica, but just before he passed away, he concluded, "The Lord hath not sent me to Jamaica to labour, but to praise him!" He implored his fellows to praise God with him, repeating again and again that Christ was with him. Finally, wrote Mr. Young, "he lifted his trembling hand, and waving it in token of victory, exclaimed, with emphasis, 'Praise! Praise! Praise!'—and then, sinking into the arms of death, left us to write, 'Blessed are the dead that die in the Lord.'" In the presence of more than fifteen hundred people, Mr. Allen's colleagues interred him in the Methodists' private burial ground, close by the tombs of five other missionaries recently fallen in the Jamaican "field of toil."[12]

The brevity of Mr. Allen's career, like that of Thomas Knibb's, underscored the most basic problem missionaries faced in Jamaica—and in the tropics in general: all had difficulty staying alive. All the missions to Jamaica suffered the high mortality rates that characterized life in tropical slave society. In his *History of the Moravians in Jamaica*, J. H. Buchner noted that of the sixty-four brethren and sisters who had been buried on the island between 1754 and 1854, only one had endured the rigors of mission work for as many as nineteen years. By contrast, six died within their first year and ten served only one year. The average term of service for those who died in Jamaica was less than five years. The Methodists fared no better. From the advent of the West India mission in the 1780s to the early 1820s not a single European missionary survived as long as twenty years in the field. The Wesleyan Methodist Missionary Society's official minutes tried to describe their plight lyrically: "By far the greater part were cut down 'like a flower:—as a flower, parched by the Sun's direct ray,' before it scarcely blooms." In the 1820s and 1830s, among missionaries of all denominations, terms of service averaged just three years. An aura of doom surrounded the missionaries' temporal endeavors; it was perhaps especially appropriate in Jamaica that they should focus most of their energies on preparing for the afterlife.[13]

Slavery and the Hereafter

As much as mortality retarded the progress of the missions, the entrenched institution of slavery shaped their development by setting limitations on the activities of evangelists and shaping the priorities of the enslaved. In the early eighteenth century, British churchmen were still loosely attached to the idea that only heathens should be enslaved. Slaveholders feared that christening slaves would "destroy the Property of them in their Masters and Mistresses, and the Right of selling them at Pleasure." By midcentury, however, no one was particularly worried about this difficulty; besides, other more important reasons kept Christianity from taking firm hold among the slaves. Their short life spans and the rapid importation of replacements from different parts of the African continent meant that the slave population continued to be divided by language and regional ethnicity. Church of England officials complained that they could not, without the benefit of a common tongue among the enslaved, effectively instruct them. This situation suited planters, however, "it being as impossible for Slaves that do not understand one another to carry on a plot against their Master, or the country in general, as it was for the Inhabitants of the primitive World to carry on the building of the Tower of Babel, after the confusion of languages happen'd amongst them." Security was always of paramount importance to the managers of slave society, and they often suspected that Christianity might provide a subversive, unifying language for slaves. In 1739 Governor Trelawney accused the rector of Saint Thomas-in-the-East of sedition for telling enslaved converts to keep the Sabbath holy: slaveholders interpreted the rector's exhortation as encouragement to slaves to defy their masters. Any intercession between a master and his slaves, no matter how piously intended, was unacceptable.[14]

Slaveholders, when they began to feel threatened by the emerging view in Britain that slaveholding and Christian virtue were incompatible, aggressively defended their way of life. Worried about the missionaries' connections to the antislavery movement in Britain and concerned about the "democratic manners" of evangelicals and their converts, slaveholders throughout the British Caribbean often saw mission work as a threat to the existing social order. Preaching to crowds that included slaves, missionaries often encountered hostility from whites, which made many of the evangelists feel "the spirit of Martyrdom." When the Haitian Revolution deepened their general insecurity, planters attempted a comprehensive crackdown. The Jamaican assembly, in passing legislation in 1802 that prohibited preaching by "ill-disposed, illiterate, or ignorant enthusiasts," sanctioned the widespread harassment of evangelists, especially those who were black. The imperial government voided the act, but in 1807 the assembly passed a new consolidated slave code, commonly called the persecution law, that banned all missions except for that of the Anglicans. Kingston went a step further, in making it illegal to sing psalms or hymns. Again, the metropolitan government in London intervened on behalf of the missionaries, ultimately guaranteeing their right to preach, in the "amelioration" legislation of 1823, yet the hounding continued in the consolidated slave act of 1826 and in the vigilantism of slaveholders.[15]

Mission work faced a severe cultural limitation, in addition to the obvious difficulty of survival in the tropics and persecution by slaveholders: the reluctance of Africans to accept the practicality or legitimacy of Christian rites. Among the most obvious considerations was that Sunday was the only day that slaves had to work in their gardens; resting on the Sabbath could lead to starvation. Also, the Methodists and Moravians found, just as the Anglicans had, that most slaves were not interested in their versions of Christianity. One reason was that the low status accorded to missionaries by powerful whites made their authority suspect in the eyes of slaves. Spiritual power was supposed to confer some mastery over the material world, but most of the missionaries were nearly destitute. Describing black people's attitude toward the poor Moravian craftsmen among them, the Anglican rector of Westmoreland observed: "Negroes in general make very shrewd remarks, and one observed to me 'that even the Overseer never goes to *hear* those people, or admits them to his table,—that they were never sent for as Clergymen to bury or baptize white people; that they never *heard* of my making shoes, binding books v.v.' and as they distinguish a mule by the name of A 'Horse-negroe,' so they call A Moravian Clergyman A 'Parson-Negroe'; and from his poverty generally hold him in contempt."[16]

The rector also commented on another aspect of the connection between material and spiritual power. He noted in 1788 that blacks generally thought of Christianity as another form of obeah. Obeah was practiced in part as a method of harnessing spiritual powers for material ends, and the practitioner required a fee for services rendered. Similarly, Anglicans customarily charged three dollars a head for baptizing slaves. But since planters generally refused to pay the fee, conscientious churchmen often baptized slaves for free. This practice had the effect of making Christianity appear valueless. As the rector put it: "They estimate the *strength* of the charms which they purchase from the Obea-man, by the *price* that he exacts; from whence they argue, that the *Christian Obea* (baptism) can be little worth, since obtained at no expence."[17]

The slaves' doubts about the social status of missionaries and the utility of their religious practices were fortified by skepticism about Christian eschatology. Most Protestant views of death and the afterlife had no resonance with those most commonly held by the enslaved. Even African Muslims in Jamaica, who shared the Christian belief in the God and heaven of the Bible, did not accept Christ as their principal savior. One leader of a Muslim community, Muhammad Kaba Saghanughu, who came from an important Islamic clerical family in West Africa, prepared a treatise in Arabic on prayer that implored his followers to think about death and "the matter of the tomb." His manuscript described the end of the world and the Day of Judgment, when only the prophet Muhammad could intercede on behalf of humankind. Few among the enslaved held even this much in common with the missionaries.[18] Thomas Coke realized that slaves had little inclination to believe in a worldview "which promised happiness in another life; but which professedly came from that God, who, though infinite both in justice and power, had so mysteriously withheld it from them in the present life." Moreover, why should slaves and poor blacks look beyond the grave to a future of rewards and punishments, Coke wondered, when the very existence of a Christian hereafter was so suspect? "Of miseries in a future state they could have little to fear, while estimating their present circumstances; and of felicities they could have but little to hope, when considering that they depended entirely upon the mercies of that God who had permitted their present condition."[19]

The missionaries emphasized the separation between this world and the next. Once the threshold was crossed, an individual soul had little or nothing more to do with temporal life. To Africans and their children, who considered that human spirits played an active role in daily affairs, such a partition between the living and the dead was implausible. As Coke understood, the idea of an afterlife occurring in a radically different and unfathomable place made little sense to the sons and daughters of Africa. Africans associated the afterlife with their ancestral lands. Creoles also seem to have refused to recognize a distinction between the material and spiritual worlds. One Anglican churchman knew a group of Jamaican-born slaves who supposedly believed the following: "After their Death, they shall serve their first Masters, or Mistresses, in the same Capacities, as they did in this; only with this Difference, that they shall be able to do any bodily Labour without being tired with it."[20] Even if the slaves were misleading their white interrogator, artfully pretending that they could not imagine a life outside slavery, the way they framed their representation of immortality indicates a settled belief in temporal and spatial continuity between life and afterlife.

When they did accept the basic idea of a future state of rewards and punishments, they generally understood that since suffering weighed so heavily upon them in this world, they could expect only happiness in the next. Whites, by contrast, must anticipate God's vengeance. "If you speak to them of future punishments," said a former plantation doctor in his testimony before the House of Commons in 1791, "they say—'Why should a poor Negro be punished; he does no wrong; and that fiery cauldrons, and such things, are reserved for the White people in the other world as a punishment for the oppression of Slaves.'"[21] Here, the enslaved clearly rejected the premise that each individual bears the burden for original, transcendental sin, believing instead that eternal judgments were determined by the temporal relations of social power.

With their own deities and cosmologies, Africans were, as one Christian observer put it, "accustomed to pagan rites." Of these, none were more important than the rites for the interment of the dead. The rector of Saint Catherine, John Venn, discovered as much when he offered to baptize a black man whom he found "sensible and well-inclined." The man refused to be christened because, according to the rector, then he "must go to no more Dances, nor have any of their antic Ceremonies about his Grave, of which these poor ignorant Creatures are fond to a surprising degree."[22] Venn probably should not have been surprised. Africans and their descendants drew vital communal sustenance and political power from their participation in funerals. In final rites of passage they established the categories of belonging and marks of distinction that organized social life. They also articulated moral principles. Common beliefs and rituals associated with death shaped the moral discourse that highlighted their common values, which often transcended and challenged the imperative of slavery. Whereas slaveholders preferred their slaves to be divided among themselves and, with few exceptions, degraded to the level of beasts, the enslaved used last rites to affirm their shared humanity and articulate their own principles of moral and social interaction. When social conflicts arose, slaves drew on the values expressed through relationships with the dead to challenge the domination and authority of masters. Gathering at night, beyond the gaze of their surveillants, slaves could consider their strength in numbers, recognize spiritual powers unavailable to the whites, and plan collective actions to improve their circumstances.

Many eighteenth-century Jamaican colonists recognized that black funerals posed a threat to their security. Though general laws had been passed in the late seventeenth century against large assemblies of slaves, the correlation between funeral "plays" and open revolts, like the connection between shamanism and political authority, emerged more clearly in the mid-eighteenth century. In particularly tense times, such as the 1760s, planters were reprimanded for permitting funerals on their estates. In that decade Edward Long concluded that slaves' funeral gatherings had "always been their rendezvous for hatching plots."[23]

By the early nineteenth century, the association between slave funerals and rebellions was firmly established in the minds of Jamaican lawmakers. In 1809 the Jamaican assembly examined evidence of a foiled conspiracy to revolt on New Year's Day. Witnesses came before a committee of the assembly to testify that the Society of Black Lads, a dancing club formed by Kingston slaves, had organized the plan around funeral ceremonies and had sealed pacts among themselves with grave-dirt oaths. Dr. Richard Chamberlain, a Kingston magistrate, told the committee that a few weeks before New Year's Day he had observed "symptoms with respect to the negroes' dresses and actions, similar to former conspiracies." On Sundays he noticed "the carrying of many coffins, with flags, but what were in the coffins I cannot say, with drums and boatswain's calls, accompanied with the Coromantee war-yell." The committee asked him if he had any reason to believe that anything other than corpses were carried in the coffins. "I always have been of opinion that they contrived to carry arms and ammunition in such coffins," Chamberlain answered. He had never dared to open and inspect the coffins. Instead, he based his supposition on the cryptic comments of the enslaved. He told the committee that he had often "heard the negroes say, 'something more in the coffins than dead bodies.'" What they had meant by "something more" was open to speculation, but whether the coffins contained material or spiritual weapons, the assemblymen were alert to the hazard that they represented.[24]

In 1816 an overseer in Saint Elizabeth parish discovered that Dick, an African man known also as the king of the Eboes, had attempted to organize a rebellion at the funeral of a child. According to Matthew Gregory Lewis, who described what he knew about the conspiracy in his diary, "above a thousand persons were engaged in the plot, three hundred of whom had been regularly sworn to assist in it," by "eating earth from graves." The overseer who detected the intrigue was a Frenchman from Saint-Domingue, who was understandably alert to potential disturbances among the enslaved. He had noticed the exceptionally large gathering of unfamiliar slaves for a child's funeral at Lyndhurst Penn, where the mourning father roasted a hog for the guests. The overseer "stole softly down to the feasting hut," wrote Lewis, "and listened behind a hedge to the conversation of the supposed mourners; when he heard the conspiracy detailed." At the high point of the funeral feast, the overseer heard Eboe Dick and a chorus of supporters rally for the insurrection with song:

> Oh me good friend, Mr. Wilberforce, make we free!
> God Almighty thank ye! God Almighty thank ye!
>   God Almighty, make we free!
> Buckra in this country no make we free:
> What Negro for to do? What Negro for to do?
> Take force by force! Take force by force!
>   CHORUS:
> To be sure! To be sure! To be sure!

The next morning the Frenchman revealed his discovery to the parish authorities, who arrested "the King of the Eboes" and one of his two co-captains. The plantocracy hanged the Eboe king within five days of his trial and had his head stuck on a pole at Lyndhurst. The captured co-captain, who was to be transported from the island, burned down his prison door and escaped briefly into the hills, before he was apprehended a week later, hiding in the hut of a "notorious Obeah-man" in the neighboring parish of Westmoreland.[25]

The Jamaican assembly responded to such threats by passing a revision and consolidation of existing slave law in 1816, including a measure explicitly prohibiting night burials. Ostensibly enacted "to prevent riots and nightly meetings" among the enslaved, and to stop slaves from disturbing the "public peace" and "endangering their healths," the regulation stipulated that "all negro burials shall in future take place in the day-time only, so that the same may be ended before sunset." Free persons permitting night funerals on plantations or other properties were to be fined; slaves attending such ceremonies were to be flogged.[26]

Christian missionaries had their own criticisms of slave funerals, and their own reasons for attempting to suppress or modify the ceremonies. Christianity's growing impact on Jamaican slave society at the turn of the century derived partly from an ability to engage with black views of the afterlife and the dead. Indeed, missionaries tried explicitly to change the slaves' moral outlook by transforming their relations with spirits and the afterlife and by changing their conduct at funerals. Anglican minister James Ramsay inspired many with his *Essay on the Treatment and Conversion of African Slaves in the British Sugar Colonies* (1784). "Religion has a two-fold purpose," Ramsay wrote: "man's ultimate fate as an individual, and his conduct as a member of society." Missionaries talked mostly as if it was conduct that determined one's ultimate fate, but just as often, they acted as though the conception of one's ultimate fate would determine conduct. For Christian lifestyles to take hold, it was necessary for missionaries to instill, in the words of the Methodist evangelist Thomas Coke, "adequate conceptions of rewards and punishments beyond the grave." Changing the attitude black people had toward death and the dead was a fundamental part of the missionary effort to make them good, "civilized" Christians, thereby ensuring their ultimate salvation.[27]

Discrepancies between "Negro" and "Christian" ways of understanding the afterlife underlay the struggles that played out around burial ceremonies. Christians of all stripes singled out black funerary rites for special condemnation, both for their disregard of biblical strictures and for their unfamiliarity. "Their practices at funerals were unnatural and revolting to a high degree," remarked Baptist missionary James Phillippo, expressing particular dismay at coffin divination and spiritual inquests. The Moravian historian J. H. Buchner excoriated the slaves, especially the Africans, for being "much attached to their heathenish religion, which is of the lowest kind . . . By far the greater part adhered to their heathenish practices, such as the sacrifice of fowls, and other offerings at the grave of departed friends."[28]

As white Christians eagerly acknowledged, such revulsion for and the urge to change black mortuary practices converged with slaveholders' concerns about security, however distasteful the institution of slavery may have been to many missionaries. In 1788 W. Stanford, the rector of Westmoreland parish, wrote a letter to Bishop Beilby Porteus in London explaining the urgent need to proselytize among the enslaved. Before Stanford had arrived in Jamaica in 1779, he had served as an army chaplain on the Mosquito Shore of British Honduras, where he had once enrolled a small company of Christian blacks to help to put down a slave revolt. In Honduras, as in Jamaica, the enslaved had organized rebellions based on authority derived from the sacred aura of the dead. They were "under the most powerful influence of Obea or witchcraft," Stanford told the bishop, the fear of which "prevented our best disposed Negroes being faithful in the instant of danger." Only the black Christians had proved reliable. "This affair pointed out to me the advantages that might be derived to Jamaica by a religious instruction of our Negroes," continued Stanford, which would help to suppress "those drunken nocturnal Funerals," where the enslaved planned and organized "intestine dangers" to the colony. Existing laws for the suppression of such meetings would inevitably be ineffective, Stanford maintained, as long as blacks favored autonomous cultural practices. Indeed, he thought that regulations banning large assemblies, drumming, and dancing among blacks rendered them more dangerous. "These very restrictions," asserted Stanford, "irritated and inflamed their minds, and at the same time furnished them with rebellious

Ideas, by contemplating their own strength in the multitudes that attended, for at many of those funerals I have seen above a thousand Negroes collected." Only a committed program of baptism and religious indoctrination would wean the enslaved from their subversive ceremonies for the dead.[29]

In an extended report on Jamaican slave religion in 1820, the Methodist district chairman John Shipman outlined just such a strategy for reforming black funerals. Shipman recognized that distinct relationships with the dead were among the most significant aspects of the cultural gulf separating "heathens" from Christians. He had discovered that many blacks who had already been converted to Christianity maintained notions and practices relating to the dead that did not derive from European Christianity. Shipman offered "their heathenish veneration for the dead," as the principal evidence of the need for a more effective program of Christian instruction. Black funeral processions, proceedings at graveside, annual visits and presents, and "prayers to the dead" all illustrated to Shipman the debased state of "Negro Religion." They might also have reminded him that communal bonds among the enslaved, extending to include the dead and reaching back to Africa, could function effectively in the absence of white tutelage.[30]

Shipman rejected the notion that the spirits of the dead maintained a presence in the material world or a relationship with the living. He was especially displeased with the account of an African woman who had lost her adolescent daughter. Every Christmas, he was told, this woman went to her daughter's grave "to mourn her death in the most feeling manner. She regularly makes a kind of sacrifice by killing a Fowl over the grave, and then brings it home, boils it, and rice, which she distributes to her fellow servants, but never tastes poultry herself." The connection between the graveside sacrifice and the sharing of a meal made no sense to Shipman. The kind of communion practiced by the old woman and her fellows offended Shipman's expectation that fellowship with the dead should be reserved for the celebration of Jesus Christ's death.[31] Indeed, for most Protestants, the afterlife was a matter of the exclusive relationship between the solitary sinner and the Son of God. Moral behavior in life was intended to prepare an individual for the final judgment. After that, one's spirit should have nothing more to do with society. For blacks, the spirit world remained intertwined with their own lives. The most significant difference was that blacks, rather than looking exclusively to the symbolic death of Christ to find a path to eternal salvation, looked to the spirits of dead friends and relatives to order their moral understanding of the temporal world.

To change that state of affairs, Shipman suggested a reordering of relations with the dead. He argued that missionaries should catechize slaves regarding death and immortality and manipulate burial rites, in order to transform belief and behavior. "It is well known," Shipman reminded his fellow missionaries, "that nothing operates so powerfully on the minds of negroes who understand the general principles of Christianity, as those important truths which relate to death and a future state." Blacks were to learn the truths about the future state through catechism. It was important that potential converts first understand that they were all, by virtue of the fall of Adam, "born in sin and guilt, and subject to pain and death." For slaves, redemption would require special attention to their duties as servants. The catechism contained several lines admonishing servants to obey happily and never speak ill of their masters, even behind their backs. Slaves were to be made to understand that their eternal future hinged on their willingness to remain subordinated. "To what place after death will wicked bad servants go?" asked the catechism, to which the slaves had to reply, "To hell; to be tormented forever." Then the lesson offered hope: "But where will good, obedient, faithful servants go after death?—To Heaven: to be happy with God forever."[32]

The catechism tried to render heaven and hell as explicitly as possible. Hell was a physical place, "a dark, bottomless pit, full of fire and brimstone," where one would spend eternity amid weeping and wailing and gnashing of teeth, as bodies lay burning in hellfire. Souls were to be perpetually tormented by their own emotions: pride, willfulness, malice, envy, grief, desire, fear, rage, and despair. Believers and good people, on the other hand, would assume their spiritual bodies in heaven, "a place of light and glory," where they would know and love God, and live in everlasting joy and happiness, suffering no want, pain, or sin. In short, the denizens of hell remained embodied and mortal, perpetually dying, while only those graced by God achieved immortal spirituality. By hammering home these two images of the afterlife, Shipman argued, evangelists would use fear and hope to entice slaves to feel "ashamed of their past errors," to "practice every virtue, and to experience that pleasing hope, through a conscious interest in Christ, which will disarm death of its sting, and render them happy in the joyful expectation of a glorious immortality."[33]

Shipman insisted that the repeated performance of Christian ceremonies to reinforce these principles would wipe out heathen funerary practices. Baptized blacks expected to have the biblical burial service read over them as part of their last rites. At countryside funerals the service was performed by anyone who could read, and in the towns by an acknowledged minister. Shipman noticed that at these funerals, despite some clamor and drinking, people seldom played drums, danced, or offered libations to the dead. The observation was cause for optimism: a change in burial practice must soon lead to a change in belief. When mourners repeatedly heard a funeral service reflecting what Shipman described as "our views on this subject," presumably, they were encouraged to converse and reflect on death in a less inappropriate manner. "There can be no doubt," Shipman declared, "that in time their superstitious notions respecting a future state will die away, and they led to form opinions of a future existence consonant to Scripture," powerfully stimulating them to "holiness of life."[34]

By itself, however, baptism was not enough to change behavior. It did so only in connection with black people's attachment to respectable burials. So while hoping that a change in practices would lead to a change in beliefs, Shipman also urged missionaries to use Christian burial services to reward proper conduct. Those who had engaged in unacceptable activities should "at death be disgraced, by being denied a Christian burial," he urged, repeating a suggestion made by James Ramsay in 1784. Adultery and obeah were the most egregious offenses. Even the bewitched, who had fallen under a curse and had "given themselves up for death through a heathenish, and superstitious belief that they have been obiahed by another, let them not have the privileges of a Christian burial; because such notions are not only heathenish but destructive to themselves, hurtful to their owners, and subversive to every Christian principle and practice." Recognizing that blacks placed enormous importance upon giving and having proper burials, no matter what beliefs underpinned the funeral itself, Shipman proposed that "any ceremony omitted on such occasions which contributes to make the funeral less pompous and respectable would have a great effect on the living." Changes in slaves' mortuary practices, thought Shipman, would mean changes in the symbolic representation of their moral order and alterations in the everyday politics of slave society. What a powerful weapon of indoctrination the Christian funeral could be when reserved for the worthy![35]

Conversion and Continuity

The circumstances were far more favorable to the efforts of Shipman and his fellow missionaries in 1820 than they had been for his predecessors in the eighteenth century. By the time Shipman took up his post as Methodist district chairman in Jamaica, sweeping changes in the social, demographic, and political climate of the West Indies had made a forceful impact on black relations with the dead and had helped create a more auspicious climate for the spread of Christianity. A few aims were actually shared by planters and evangelists—and slaveholders made some accommodations in response to pressure from London that facilitated the missionaries' success. At a deeper level, the social and demographic changes wrought by the Haitian Revolution and the abolition of the transatlantic slave trade, along with the continuing initiative of black people themselves, provided the impetus for significant transformations in black religion.

By the second decade of the nineteenth century, evangelists had learned some hard lessons from their persecution by slaveholders. White missionaries came to Jamaica with explicit orders not to get entangled in the politics of the "slavery question" and to avoid antagonizing the planters in any way. Regardless of the missionaries' attempts at appeasement, planters and the colonial assembly were vigilant about restraining missionaries' efforts, curtailing their autonomy whenever trouble arose, and routinely harassing their disciples. Colonial slaveholders continued to think of the missionaries as "designing demagogues, who, under the mask of extraordinary sanctity," meant to "disseminate the most poisonous political opinions." As Hope Waddell remembered it, "the religious instruction of the slaves, and their admission to church privileges, were fiercely resisted by the dominant portion of the community." Even though the British government, negotiating Britain's own Protestant revival, disallowed the most repressive legislation against the evangelists, they were subject to frequent harassment.[36]

Missionaries made every effort, short of abandoning their missions, to appease planters. Thomas Knibb had explained to his brother William that baptisms in Jamaica were administered early in the morning, so that slaves would not be late for work and slaveholders would have no reason to "scorch" the evangelists. John Shipman boasted that his report "Religion among the Negroes" contained nothing "either *for* or *against* slavery, but being solely confined to the subject of the moral improvement of the slaves." Content to give Caesar his due, Shipman sought to maintain a sharp distinction between the material and the spiritual, the eternal and the temporal. "I consider eternal things of infinitely greater importance than any thing earthly," he wrote, "so it has been my constant rule, to leave civil and political questions, for the discussion, and decision of Legislators and Politicians." Concerning the struggles of the enslaved, Shipman aimed to act according to Saint Paul's admonition, "to know nothing among those to whom I have spoken the word of life, but Christ, and him Crucified." This he affirmed despite his assertion of the worldly advantages that might accrue to planters once the hopes of their slaves were set on the Christian afterlife and their desire for heaven had made them more faithfully obedient (Figure 6.1).[37]

To some extent, the planters, who always feared developments they could not control, had to tolerate the missionaries. Smarting from sharp criticisms coming from Great Britain, and occasionally convinced by the argument that Christianity could be used as an implement of social control, many masters softened their resistance to the evangelists. Most planters still considered it dangerous to encourage slaves to submit to a higher authority than themselves, but if they were to convince outside authorities that they were responsible subjects of a Christian empire, they could not chase Christ's messengers off the island.[38] Slaveholders remained skeptical about whether coaxing slaves into better behavior with promises of heaven would make them more compliant. Nevertheless, they did agree that for reasons of security funerary rites of African origin should be monitored and modified. Yet even as increasing numbers of planters showed leniency toward white evangelists, developments in the Atlantic world allowed the enslaved to take the initiative in spreading Christianity on terms they could accept.

The Haitian Revolution had a powerful influence on the spread of Christianity in Jamaica. When enslaved Africans set fire to the northern plains of Saint-Domingue in 1791, they initiated a demographic transformation that had important religious consequences in nearby Jamaica. As the revolution engulfed their plantations, French slaveholders fled to

VISIT OF A MISSIONARY AND WIFE TO A PLANTATION VILLAGE.

Figure 6.1. *Visit of a Missionary and Wife to a Plantation Village,* engraved illustration, in James M. Phillippo, *Jamaica: Its Past and Present State* (London, 1843), facing 372. A missionary and his wife are shown as visiting dignitaries to a village of plantation workers. Though the image was published after the emancipation, Phillippo began his mission in Jamaica in 1823, and so the work probably reflects his experiences among the enslaved as well as the newly emancipated. Courtesy of Harvard College Library.

accessible slave societies, Jamaica among them, with as many of their slaves as they could still control. Many took advantage of the turmoil and escaped by traveling the short distance to Jamaica in small canoes. Despite the attempts of Jamaican officials to monitor and control the influx of black people from Saint-Domingue, thousands of "French negroes" arrived in Jamaica and began to interact with other slaves in towns and plantations. Many of these new slaves were already Christian. In Saint-Domingue, enslaved men and women worshipped and proselytized with the Jesuits—often forming separate congregations with an autonomous leadership—until the suppression of that order in the 1760s. After that, many slaves worked independently as catechists and spiritual counselors, employing approaches that combined Christian doctrine and practice with pre-Christian spiritual customs. Two decades before the Haitian Revolution, Edward Long, reviewing Christianity among slaves in French colonies, assumed it to be completely superficial. "I have seen many of them provided with store of crosses, relicks, and consecrated amulets," he wrote, "to which they paid the most sincere veneration, though wholly uninformed of any thing more than the efficacy of these baubles, the necessity of adoring the Blessed Virgin and a few chosen saints, the power of their priest to absolve sins, and the damnable state of all heretics." Contrary to Long's dismissive interpretation, black Catholics were true believers who had intermingled their traditional belief in the worldly presence of the dead and the power of spiritual medicine with a vision of Christ as a symbol of decentralized and democratized authority.[39]

While many such Christians came to Jamaica from Saint-Domingue during the revolution, even more came directly from Africa. Almost as soon as the Haitian Revolution erupted, French slave-trading operations in West-Central Africa utterly collapsed. British slavers rushed in to take advantage of the opportunity. During the revolution, Jamaican plantations drew about sixty thousand slaves from the Angolan trade, about a quarter of all the enslaved Africans who arrived between 1791 and 1805. Many of those who arrived from Saint-Domingue and West-Central Africa came from communities that had had long exposure to Christianity and maintained notions of the afterlife that joined Christian cosmology with traditional beliefs and practices. Christianity had been adopted as the state religion in Kongo in 1491, and thereafter the state maintained relations with the European Catholic Church. But elements of Christian doctrine and practice spread through West-Central Africa over several centuries as a result of lay Christians acting as interpreters and catechists to the Kongolese peasantry. From the earliest conversions, Africans adapted the motifs, symbols, and revelations of Christianity to fit their own needs, customs, and cosmological precepts. The symbolism of the Christian cross, for example, converged with more ancient perceptions of the cross as a symbolic meeting place of spirits, and the crucifix became, like other spiritually significant material objects, a sacred medicinal object. Similarly, the catechismal literature of the seventeenth century referred to the church as *nzo a nkisi*, which can be translated as "holy grave." Thus the church itself was associated with the burial site, the most important material focal point of relations between the living and the dead. Priests in Kongo even referred to themselves as *nganga*, the word used locally for spirit mediums.[40]

It is not clear precisely how such enslaved Catholics shared their religious beliefs and practices with other enslaved men and women in Jamaica. But in Saint-Domingue, as elsewhere in the Americas, enslaved Catholics served as the key interpreters of missionary doctrine to other slaves, and there are hints that the recently arrived "French Negroes" had some religious influence. One slave, Jupiter, was tried for obeah in Saint Ann parish in 1794 but was acquitted for lack of evidence. Five years later, after the importation of untold numbers of French-speaking slaves from Saint-Domingue and amid news of the disastrous British expedition to put down the revolution there, Jupiter appeared in court again. Again he stood accused of being an obeah man, of pretending to "have communication with the Devil and other Evil Spirits." This time, however, he went by the name of *mon ami*. It is difficult to draw any strong conclusions from this bit of information, but it hints at the influence French-speaking blacks may have had on those shamans who sought authority among the enslaved in Jamaica. It is likely that the Catholic newcomers from Saint-Domingue and West-Central Africa encouraged further reconciliation and amalgamation of traditional African and Christian beliefs and practices among the Jamaican slave population.[41]

The demographic transformation wrought by the end of the transatlantic slave trade complemented the changes initiated by the Haitian Revolution. After 1808 the proportion of Africans in the Jamaican slave population continued to shrink, from about 45 percent in 1807 to only 25 percent by 1832. High numbers of these surviving Africans were undoubtedly people from West-Central Africa, who made up more than a quarter of all those imported between 1792 and 1807.[42] So even while Creoles, who had no religious experience in Africa and were therefore more open to Christian teachings, came to predominate among the slave population, many of the remaining Africans could be expected to have had exposure to some form of Christian cosmology and ritual even before they arrived in Jamaica. Such demographic "creolization" precipitated a creolization of the spirit world.

Eighteenth- and nineteenth-century contemporaries often noted that unlike Africans, who believed they would return home after death, Creoles never anticipated a return to Africa. However, both Africans and Creoles believed that human souls remained attached to their birthplace. As the percentage of Africans in the enslaved population declined, more and more spirits stopped departing for the African ancestral lands, and Jamaica became overrun by restless and potentially dangerous specters. The enslaved population turned increasingly to novel sources of supernatural power to manage the situation. The spirits of the dead, or duppies, could be either benign or malevolent, and in time Christianity came to be the best protection against malicious ghosts. In the 1820s one enslaved Jamaican told another that he no longer believed in duppies, "that Duppy was all lies; that he was gone to the *Debbil*, who had tied a big chain round about him a thousand years long, and cursed him into a pit, and that he must not come out till Jerusalem should tumble down, and be built up again new." Clearly, the supernatural power of Christianity could be invoked against compelling metaphysical threats. By the end of the nineteenth century Jamaicans commonly understood that if a "duppy come at you and you call the name of 'God' it will not go away, but no sooner 'Jesus Christ' is called than it vanishes."[43]

Concern about the earthly presence of spirits made the Baptists' emphasis on the immanent and energizing Holy Spirit all the more attractive to the descendants of Africans, who took the lead in advancing Christianity among their enslaved fellows. In the mid-eighteenth century, itinerant preachers in Great Britain and the American colonies had flouted the institutional structures of the Church of England by speaking directly to large popular crowds in a movement that historians know as the Great Awakening. In passionate rhetoric, ministers admonished people to form personal and direct relationships with Jesus and with God, relatively unmediated by church authority. Enslaved blacks were often in the crowds that heard such messages. One of them was George Liele, born a slave in Savannah, Georgia, who experienced a vision of his own death and damnation at a Baptist meeting. Assuming the revelation to be a warning from God, he called upon the Lord to accept him as a dedicated servant. Liele had the good fortune to be owned by Henry Sharp, a deeply religious master, who freed Liele to travel and preach among the other slaves, but after Sharp was killed in the American Revolution, the family disputed Liele's claim to freedom and he fled to Jamaica, to settle in Kingston. There Liele began preaching again in 1784 and quickly built a sizable, predominantly enslaved congregation, for which he opened a Baptist chapel in 1793. Less than a decade later, Thomas Nicholas Swigle, one of Liele's free black converts, established a second Kingston church with about five hundred members. Liele also baptized Moses Baker, who later established a congregation in the parish of Saint James and eventually amassed a following of about three thousand slaves and free blacks on plantations in western Jamaica. Out of these early congregations emerged a network of black itinerant preachers, the Native Baptists, who won widespread conversions among the enslaved.[44]

Baptists emphasized spiritual rebirth over the constant hectoring about daily behavior and ritual practice that Methodists favored. More important, the prominence of the Holy Spirit in Baptist conversions facilitated dramatic progress in the spread of Christianity. In Jamaica, as in all the Atlantic territories controlled by Protestants, Christianity premised on individual access to the power of the Holy Spirit meant that many African and African-American converts could, as historian John Thornton has speculated, "practice a new form of spirit mediumship and thus accept a set of revelations that was acceptably Christian and yet conformed to their concepts of religious truth." Accentuating the ecstatic and experiential dimensions of Christianity, Baptist forms of worship among black people allowed extensive continuity between pre- and postconversion belief and practice.[45]

Black Baptists continued to understand that the spirits of the dead operated powerfully in the material world. The new Christians believed this upon conversion and continued to believe it as they spread the gospel. Blacks were moved emotionally by Christ and the Holy Spirit in a manner not wholly inconsistent with spirit mediumship. Thomas Burchell, a Baptist missionary in Montego Bay, described the intense passions generated by consideration of Christ among the newly baptized in his diary. "Whilst we contemplated the dying Redeemer, and partook of the memorial of his love," he noted, "we sat in wondering amazement, now weeping, now rejoicing." William Knibb was "surprised at the avidity" manifested by the "poor, oppressed, benighted and despised sons of Africa" when they received a sermon. "If the preacher feels affected," Knibb learned, "they are frequently melted to tears, and a sobbing is heard through the whole of the chapel." Many in his congregation seemed to believe that Knibb was a reincarnation of his late brother Thomas, or at least that Thomas's spirit accompanied William's ministry. "Ah, sweet Massa, him just like him broder," they would say, "him voice, him face . . . me hope Massa do well." Knibb preached at the funeral of one his brother's former students, who, his mother was convinced, had died of fright because he thought William was Thomas's ghost—an indication that younger generations retained their progenitors' readiness to see the spirits of the dead at work in the world.[46]

The Native Baptists, who had limited contact with white missionaries, most clearly evinced such continuities of both belief and practice. White Christians reviled the disciples of George Liele, Moses Baker, and the other early Baptists for their retention of African religious characteristics, much as Edward Long had deprecated black Catholics. Most troubling for them was the blacks' tendency to favor personal contacts with the Spirit over authorized interpretations of written text, an inclination that earned them the appellation "Spirit Baptists," as described in detail in the memoirs of Scottish missionary Hope Waddell: "The grand doctrine of these people was the Spirit's teaching. It gave life. The written word was a dead letter." These Baptists received revelations in "dreams and visions of the night," called "the work" of the Spirit, which guided the spiritual rebirth of converts and formed the subject of weekly class meetings with religious leaders. As Christ was led into the wilderness, these Baptists believed, his disciples must mimic his search and his journey. "To the bush, the pastures, or the cane fields, those people resorted at night, when preparing for baptism, and were ordered to lie down, each apart, without speaking, but keeping eye and ear open to observe what way the Spirit would come to them." Like Waddell, most whites considered the Spirit Baptists to be practicing a senseless and debased form of Christianity and spared few opportunities to criticize them for what they called "the nonsense into which they torture the texts of scripture, and scraps of the church service." Indeed, they considered the leaders of the Native Baptist sects to be little more than "Christianized obias."[47]

Black Jamaicans adapted Christianity to their social concerns, just as they adapted it to older spiritual beliefs. Frequently, enslaved convicts invoked Christianity in common conflicts with other slaves. Believing that being baptized, or becoming Christian, meant absolution for all past sins, many blacks turned to Christianity to relieve themselves of debts. Once, an old man complained to his master that a newly christened neighbor had refused to pay an outstanding debt of one doubloon. When the old man tried to collect his due, the Christian claimed ignorance of the debt, and he told his creditor that he had "lent the doubloon to Quamina, but he was not Quamina now; he was a new man, born again, and called Timothy, and was not bound to pay the dead man, Quamina's, debt." When the plantation master ruled against Quamina-cum-Timothy, he began to grumble that Christianity was "no worth." The elderly man, for his part, complained that the spread of Christianity had reduced the influence of the old spiritual talismans. "Formerly," he said, "people minded the puntees, hung up in trees and grounds as charms to keep off thieves," but now, "since there was so much preachy-preachy, the lazy fellows did nothing but thief."[48]

Many people, thinking that perhaps the missionaries wielded a superior species of magic, hoped Christianity would protect them from obeah. Yet at times they would turn to obeah practitioners to resolve problems that Christianity could not. John Shipman complained of black Christians who "continue[d] strongly attached to *Obiah*, attributing to second causes, or to what is worse, to infernal agency, what belongs to the Judge of all the earth." Some of the baptized had as much confidence in the power of obeah as they had ever had, and they continued to consult and respect the authority of shamans, especially to seek spiritual cure and to resolve Jamaica's persistent problems with haunting.[49]

This is not to say that Christianity had no impact on black religion, especially on mortuary practice. In response to legal pressure and missionary preaching, black burial rituals became less clamorous and elaborate. As early as 1818, the Kingston magistrate William Savage observed that the enslaved were now more likely to behave with "decency in the interment of the dead, which was formerly conducted in a very noisy manner." Black Christians who wished to have their loved ones buried in denominational graveyards observed strict standards of conduct handed down by the white missionaries, though many Africans, Christian and otherwise, carried on much as they had before, simply by disaggregating various elements of their burial ceremonies: they interred the body in the daytime, under supervision, then gathered together illegally at night to make sacrifices and to drink and dance with their shipmates and countrymen.[50] Under the pressure of proselytizing and demographic change, African national categories of belonging articulated during funerals slowly yielded to those of religious denominations, and the piety of Christian practice came to define group inclusion as much as regional origin or social status did. Yet funerals still set certain communal boundaries and remained a vital forum for the expression of social values, and ritual specialists among the enslaved still drew authority from their privileged understanding of the threshold between life on earth and the afterlife.

Preachers shaped perceptions of the hereafter and guided last rites, believed to be among the most basic of ethical obligations. Religious figures, as they presided over funerals, brought images of the afterlife into an emotional forum for publicizing worthy ideals and principles of human conduct and made death and the dead the focal point of moral distinctions. Black preachers defined good and evil in terms that slaves found compelling—and slaves recognized evil in the social relations of slavery. When Ebenezer, a Native Baptist traveling with Cynric Williams in 1823, preached to an assembly of two hundred to three hundred slaves on the Herenhausen plantation, he spoke of the afterlife in ways that recalled Shipman's catechism but that explicitly linked the terrors of hell to the horrors of slavery.

> Brothers . . . You think that when death comes, trouble comes no more—Ha! You will not be dead six minutes before the devil will catch you, put you in the bilboes, and set twenty thousand drivers on you. They have no cattle-whip, but they will poke you with fire stick till your teeth grind to the roots. Death will come no more.—You may be hungry till your entrails twist to pieces, they will give you no plantains—nothing but lead, and that only as hot as h—ll, it will burn a hole in your belly.—Your tongue will roast with fever,—they will give you no water—there is not a drop there—only boiling brimstone, nothing else to drink, till flames come through your nose. You think to run away!—you will never see the day—your foot will roast in the red hot bilboes for twenty thousand years.[51]

Hunger, fever, and sadistic overseers—hell appeared a lot like Jamaican slavery. Such tortures were agonizingly familiar to plantation slaves. They could only have been distressed to imagine that their plight could intensify and continue forever. Few of them would have been surprised to learn that the Devil's chosen henchmen were plantation drivers. And by implication, the sermon cast the planter in the role of the archfiend. Once listeners had identified drivers and planters as evil incarnate, they could proceed to a moral condemnation of the whole social hierarchy upon which slavery rested. Shortly before delivering his sermon, Ebenezer had taken the opportunity to speak at a funeral. Then he had ended his short oration on equality in death with a simple declaration: "Brethren, all Christians, white and black man, all one colour—Sambo and mulatto—no man bigger than another."[52]

The intersection of ideas about death and the dead with persistent social struggle produced Christian slaves who were restless in ways the missionaries had not anticipated. Enslaved Christians, maintaining their belief in the earthly presence of the spirits of the dead, and looking now to the Holy Spirit to restrain harmful ghosts, also found that Christianity could be used to secure status in slave society. What is more, they discovered that it could be used against the whites, and even against slavery itself. Christianity provided a framework for a moral critique of slavery in a language that metropolitan elites were obliged to regard. From what they could learn of developments in Great Britain, they knew that evangelical Christians were at the forefront of movements for political reform, and they could see for themselves that colonial slaveholders felt increasing pressure from demands for religious toleration. Christianity seemed in this context to provide a winning argument for improvement in conditions for the enslaved. The missionaries' association with the antislavery cause in Britain made Christianity more relevant to the enslaved people's habitual efforts to limit the power of their masters. It gave them a sense that in their struggles to attain dignity, concessions from the system, and ultimately freedom, they were allied with authorities greater than the local plantocracy.[53]

As much as they worried about obeah men, slaveholders ended up fearing the influence of black preachers, whose sermons could be a source of insurrectionary moral authority. Dr. Stewart West, a magistrate in the parish of Saint Thomas-in-the-East, admitted as much in 1818, when he complained that black Baptists were "overrunning the country, preaching nonsense and sedition in their nocturnal meetings." There was a black preacher on every estate in his neighborhood, West worried, "before it was known to the white people." Whites in the parish eventually discovered that these preachers advocated human equality on earth as in heaven, even as they preached on other topics "of the most dangerous tendency." Dr. West endorsed the wisdom of the 1816 law that prohibited "the practice of ignorant, superstitious, or designing slaves" of preaching without permission. Because slaves and whites ostensibly had Christianity in common, enslaved Christians often took the lead in proclaiming their concerns to authorities. Responding to a parliamentary inquiry into the effect of religious training on the enslaved population, one lawyer highlighted the role of Christians in representing slave grievances. "Whenever a party runs away from any Estate to the Governor, or to a Magistrate, to make complaint of their Master, or overseer, as is occasionally the case," he wrote, "upon strict investigation the Christians are commonly found to be the Ringleaders." As enslaved Christians took the lead in representing grievances to authorities, they also stoked the political ambitions of their fellows in bondage, drawing on their renewed ways of finding meaning in death, the afterlife, and the work of the dead.[54]

Still, white missionaries clung tenaciously to the idea that their ultimate aim was to redeem souls, not to end slavery. Under extremely perilous conditions, that intention gave them hope and satisfaction. Most would have agreed enthusiastically with the sentiments of the Methodist preacher J. Walters, who evaluated his effort "to promote the immortal welfare of my fellow man" from his sickbed at the end of 1831. He praised the Lord for several times pulling him "from the verge of the tomb" and salvaging his labors from the "gloom of death," which had resulted in the modest success of his mission. "In the past year," he rejoiced, "I have witnessed death bed scenes of persons of all colours in whom the triumph of religion has appeared conspicuously. I have read the funeral service over at least 30 or 40 whose disembodied spirits had reached the climes of unmingled bliss where the weary are at rest." While the missionaries gloried in saving benighted souls, many enslaved blacks celebrated Christianity because they thought it would bring justice to Jamaica. Even as Brother Walters lay dying, appraising his efforts, Christian slaves in the western parishes of the island were staging the largest slave revolt ever to take place in a British colony. Hope Waddell, in his own account of mission work in Jamaica, recognized that the enslaved continued to form their own ideas about the connections between Christianity, death, and the moral order of island life. When white masters succumbed to Jamaica's endemic morbidity, enslaved believers saw the power of Christianity at work against the slaveholders. " 'Buckra die hard this time,' said the negroes; 'since gospel come, buckra die hard!' "[55]

CHAPTER SEVEN

⬦

Gardens of Remembrance

MONUMENTS TO THE DEAD commemorated slavery even as it ended. In the 1830s, with the West Indian economy in decline and political pressure to emancipate the slaves increasing, people in Jamaica registered the struggle over slavery through their public memorials to departed friends, family members, and advocates. Slaveholders celebrated their dead fellows by praising their magnanimity and civic virtue, while the enslaved consecrated and defended their burial grounds. Tombs and memorials worked, as place-names did, "to impose a permanent memory" on the Jamaican landscape, which would shape future struggles to establish the political truth about slavery. Was it a civilizing institution that made it possible to extend English dominion abroad? Or did it represent the very reverse of English liberty and justice—a great historic evil? Had it left a scarred and haunted terrain, where survivors negotiated countless social, psychological, and spiritual hazards? Was slave society, by contrast, a cradle of redemption for black heathens brought at last to Christianity or the starting place for martyred rebels forging the path to freedom? Such questions could never be definitively answered, but they did frame a war of representation that recruited the dead for public service. Monuments and burial grounds, as enduring memorials to the dead, justified claims to territory and provided a focus for meaningful accounts of common history, by attaching sacred significance to noteworthy locations.[1]

Remembrance, as an attempt to found some continuity in the midst of flux, rupture, and loss, became a strategy for both black and white

Jamaicans: immortality might be achievable through symbols, in the enduring form of the physical landmark. By mobilizing individual and collective memories, the living honored the deeds of ancestors, while simultaneously legitimating past and future group struggles. The dead helped people identify personally with political positions taken during events past, thereby informing present agendas and political claims. Monuments to the dead were, as they still are, surrogates—not only for individuals but for groups of people as well, along with their values, desires, and exertions. The paradox is that "eternal remembrance" is sustained in temporal conflicts over particular places. Monuments and burial grounds attached communal memories to struggles over places, making partisan interpretations of events into a politics of death, in which nothing less than the right to belong in Jamaica was at stake.[2]

⊰⊱

On the night of 27 December 1831 a roaring fire at the Kensington estate, high above Montego Bay, signaled the start of the largest slave rebellion ever to threaten a British colony. In the weeks and months that followed, the western parishes of Jamaica were convulsed by what the Methodist missionary Henry Bleby later called "the death struggles of slavery." Black men and women, already convinced that their liberation was at hand, refused to work, burned cane fields and factories, and defended themselves with firearms and cutlasses when attacked. The action was organized largely by Sam Sharpe, a Baptist preacher and enslaved domestic worker in Montego Bay, along with a dedicated cadre of Native Baptists, many of whom held important positions in plantation hierarchies. Thousands stayed in rebellion for as long as two months, earning the revolt the enduring appellation of the Baptist War, as they wreaked havoc in the already debt-ridden sugar parishes of Saint James, Hanover, Westmoreland, Manchester, and Saint Elizabeth. According to the Jamaican assembly's summary report released in March 1832, 207 properties in these parishes, and another 19 elsewhere, had suffered some degree of damage. In all, the assembly estimated that the island had sustained over £1.15 million sterling in losses, mostly due to arson, looting, destroyed crops, and lost labor. The figure included the cost of those killed in the suppression of the revolt and those executed in the aftermath, though not the £175,000 spent on military operations.[3]

The repression was swift and bloody. Though the enslaved rebels had killed only 14 whites, about 200 slaves died in the fighting and at least 340 more were executed by the state after cursory trials. The bodies of the slain were left strewn on the roads or were tossed ignominiously into mass graves. Writing twenty years later, Henry Bleby described the carnage in Montego Bay. "At first shooting was the favourite mode of execution," he remembered, "but when the novelty of this had ceased the gallows was put in requisition." The condemned were hanged three or four at a time on a gibbet erected in the public square. "The bodies remained stiffening in the breeze," a fixture at the center of town for several weeks. "Other victims would then be brought out and suspended in their place, and cut down in their turn to make room for more; the whole heap of bodies remaining just as they fell until the workhouse Negroes came and took them away, to cast them into a pit dug for the purpose, a little distance out of the town." Around the town of Lucea, in Hanover parish, the authorities sent convicted slaves to their home plantations to die. In a letter to his Presbyterian brethren dated 8 May 1832, one witness described how the men were packed into ox carts, "each prisoner pinioned, with a rope on his neck and a white cap on his head . . . In this way they were carried up, under a strong guard, into the midst of the burned properties, distances of twelve to thirty miles, and the sentence was carried into effect on the estates." Under martial law, some of those convicted by courts-martial were decapitated, and their heads adorned poles in the towns and countryside. Others were sentenced to military-style floggings varying from fifty to five hundred lashes. When civil rule resumed on 5 February 1832, the repression continued. Sixty-five percent of those convicted in civil trials were condemned to death; almost no one was acquitted. Conceivably, sentiments similar to the last announcement of rebel leader Sam Sharpe sustained many of the condemned until the end: "I would rather die upon yonder gallows, than live in slavery."[4]

The plantocracy's vengeance also extended to the missionaries. Even before the end of martial law, planters and their supporters in the parish of Saint Ann formed the Colonial Church Union, which aimed to expel "sectarian" missionaries from Jamaica and organized mobs to harass anyone thought to be too friendly to the interests of the enslaved. The union quickly drew support from the majority of whites in the western parishes. Within days they had destroyed Baptist and Methodist chapels in the towns of Montego Bay and Falmouth. Mob violence spread out from there to engulf small towns throughout the island, where furious whites wrecked and torched Methodist and Baptist churches and molested nonconforming missionaries. An angry white mob tarred and feathered Henry Bleby. The Baptists William Knibb, Francis Gardner, and Thomas Burchell were arrested and arraigned before the assizes, perhaps luckily, for they might have been killed by the mobs had they not been incarcerated. "Should I escape," William Knibb wrote to his mother from the Montego Bay jail, "I shall return to England, as I am not safe from assassination in this part of the world." Knibb left for England on 26 April 1832. Thomas Burchell of Montego Bay was also driven from the island, despite having been cleared by the court of assizes of any responsibility for the rebellion.[5]

The Baptist War and the paroxysms of violence that followed it convinced powerful people in Great Britain that colonial slavery was doomed. Lord Goderich, Colonial Office secretary at the time of the rebellion, understood that "now that an indigenous race of men has grown up, speaking our own language and instructed in our religion, all the more harsh rights of the owner, and the blind submission of the slave, will inevitably at some period, more or less remote, come to an end." Blacks had become "unfit for slavery." Just as important, the lurid accounts of the white reaction related in public forums by Knibb and other missionaries when they returned to Britain demonstrated that Jamaican slaveholders were no exemplars of British civilization. With a revised understanding of imperial interests, the Colonial Office began seriously considering proposals for immediate emancipation. In this way, the last and the largest slave rebellion in Jamaica hastened the passage of the act of 20 August 1833, which decreed the formal abolition of chattel slavery throughout the British West Indies beginning 1 August 1834. As a concession to planters, the law stipulated that most freed people would still be required to work without pay for their former owners as "apprentices" for another six years, until August 1840, but a concerted abolitionist campaign and the resistance of black people to the new system of bondage forced an early end to apprenticeship. British Caribbean slavery finally passed away on 1 August 1838.[6]

In the midst of these momentous events, a politics of death, remembrance, and territory both reflected and animated the prevailing conflicts between masters and slaves, and between slaveholders and their white opponents. As slavery ended, the dead were invoked to commemorate particular interpretations of the history of the institution and to provide symbolic positions from which to fight future battles between former slaves and former masters, imperial subjects and foreign peoples, and pious Christians and their persecutors. Claims to freedom, claims to mastery, and claims on the civic life of Jamaica all emanated from memorials to the dead.

Revered in Rest

Reflecting the plantocracy's close cultural ties to the mother country, monuments and memorials to the dead among whites in Jamaica generally followed British precedent in their placement, literary conventions, and architectural style. In the old and densely populated Saint Andrew Parish Church cemetery, for example, the burial patterns, iconography, and memorial inscriptions broadly reflected changes in the response to death that resembled those in Great Britain over the seventeenth, eighteenth, and early nineteenth centuries. A seventeenth-century memorial style characterized by simplicity, stoicism, and practical depictions of physical death yielded, by the mid-eighteenth century, to a style that featured lavish neoclassical decoration, open sentimentality, and effusive encomiums of the character and achievements of the deceased. (Memorials for evangelicals, who preferred simple Christian motifs and sentiments and who criticized opulent styles of commemoration, were the exception.)[7]

Monumental inscriptions, much like the obituaries that appeared in late eighteenth- and early nineteenth-century newspapers, commonly highlighted the unique talents or civic accomplishments of the deceased. When John Waugh died of a "putrid fever" in 1794, the *Royal Gazette* carried an account of his passing and a "short sketch" of his character. As eulogies generally do, the entry highlighted the aspects of his life deemed worthy of commemoration and thus recommended for emulation. The memorial commended Waugh for his "temperance" and "beneficence," as well as his penchant for "reading the best authors" and perusing "the newest periodical publications." His passing was "greatly lamented by an extensive circle of friends and acquaintances." Upon his burial on his

Melrose estate, his friends were said to have shed "many a briny tear" in "mournful tribute to his memory." Like such obituaries, monumental inscriptions might mention the cause of death—a fever, an accident, or, in rare cases, a murder. Yet the more important purpose was to idealize the lives of dead by singling out aspects of character and personal history that could represent larger communities of memory and then promote the values of these communities in perpetuity, by usefully attaching them to a consecrated piece of ground. To this end, the greatest slaveholders favored monuments revolving around conquest, power, and friendship, masculine "virtues" integral to their social standing. By inscribing these in chapels, churchyards, and family mausoleums, the elite could hope to be revered in memory, to conjoin their attempt at immortality with the fate of their territory.[8]

William Beckford, who died in England in 1770, was among the wealthiest and most celebrated of the absentee planters. He is memorialized by a statue erected at Guildhall and paid for by the city of London. Beckford stands, in resplendent attire, the very image of the conquering patriarch, surrounded by symbols of church and state; a woman is seated beside him, and his foot rests on the back of a fallen slave. In the heart of London, the Beckford thus immortalized continues to this day to proclaim the political power of the eighteenth-century planter class and its central place in the British Empire.[9] This was how most among the resident plantocracy would have liked to be remembered, as valued agents of imperial power.

Residents of Jamaica generally imported their funerary monuments from Britain, and so they tended to be smaller and more allegorical, featuring "mourning figures, cherubs, cornucopias, urns and draperies," rather than the majestic portraiture so popular in English sculpture. Though they rarely approached the grandeur of their British counterparts, commemorative monuments in Jamaica attempted to evoke similar meanings. In the last decades of the eighteenth century the public erected monuments to popular governors. When Governor Basil Keith died in 1777, Jamaica's House of Assembly resolved to erect a marble monument in the Spanish Town parish church, so that he would "ever live in the remembrance of a people, to whose happiness he so much contributed"; Keith had acted decisively to suppress a slave rebellion in 1776. Ultimately costing nearly a thousand pounds by the time it was installed in 1780, the

life-sized winged cherub, hovering with a laurel wreath above an orna-
mented funerary urn, honored Keith's "zeal and unwearied assiduity"
during his brief three-year governorship.[10]

Still more impressive was the monument to William Beckford's nephew
Thomas, Earl of Effingham, and his wife Catherine, who died within
weeks of each other in 1791. Effingham governed Jamaica for only two
years before he died, but his passing was marked by elaborate ceremony.
His state funeral was magnificent, costing nearly eight thousand pounds
in Jamaican currency. For the monument, the assembly contracted John
Bacon of the Royal Academy, among the most celebrated English sculptors
of his time and the architect of the public memorial to Admiral Rodney's
victory over the French at the Battle of the Saints. Effingham's monument
is eighteen feet high and six feet wide, a dark gray panel framing a gray
and white obelisk, all in mottled marble. Near the apex are symbols of the
governor's office—mace and sword, scales, and a purse. At the base rests
an urn carved with classical motifs and Effingham's coat of arms. A female
figure, representing Jamaica, hugs the urn, as a cherub holding an olive
branch rests on a cornucopia spilling over with tropical fruit. On the
pedestal is an epitaph attributed to Bryan Edwards. The inscription
recounts Catherine's death at sea and the "melancholy return" of her
remains, and also romanticizes Effingham's death as a marital reunion.
"He—the fond and indulgent husband, She—the cheerful and obedient
wife—In their deaths they were not divided." The memorial was erected,
according to the inscription, "to perpetuate the remembrance of so illus-
trious a pattern of conjugal affection." But it also purposes to "manifest
the public sense of the many public and private virtues" of the respected
governor, which included, according to the assembly, his "firm and independent conduct" and his "mild and equitable administration." Effingham
had served in a time a great anxiety, when the plantocracy was suffering
the insults of the abolition campaign and, more dangerously, the threat
from the nearby Haitian Revolution. The governor earned the enthusiastic
gratitude of the slaveholders when he sent armaments and military stores
to the planters in French Saint-Domingue, thereby proving, even as the
slave trade came under attack back in England, that the interests and solidarity of slaveholders transcended national rivalry.[11]

Monuments to public officials were less common than physical tributes
to the dead representatives of power in the private sphere. In choosing a

burial ground, individuals and families chose to make a permanent identification with a particular place. The religiously devout often preferred to
take their last repose in church crypts (if they could afford the cost) or
churchyards. Most planters, however, especially those in the countryside,
chose to consecrate their own estates with their remains. Touring Jamaica
in 1689, Sir Hans Sloane noted, "Planters are very often buried in their
Gardens, and have a small Monument erected over them," adding, in a
gibe aimed at popular beliefs, "Yet I never heard of any of them who
walk'd after their deaths for being buried out of Consecrated ground."
William Lewis, the grandfather of Matthew Gregory Lewis, had his body
sent from England to Jamaica in 1774, so that he could be buried next to
his wife, Jane, in the family mausoleum at the Cornwall estate in Westmoreland parish. In 1816 Matthew Lewis, who observed that his ancestors
had "always had a taste for being well lodged after their decease," was effusive about the beauty of his family's mausoleum, situated in the heart of
a bountiful orange grove: "If I could be contented to live in Jamaica, I am
still more certain, that it is the only agreeable place for me to die in; for
I have got a family mausoleum, which looks for all the world like the the-
atrical representation of the 'tomb of all the Capulets.'" A statue of Time,
with scythe and hourglass, looked down on the entire structure. Lewis
admired its decorative exterior, festooned "with sculptured stones—Arms,
angels, epitaphs, and bones." Inside the mausoleum was a tomb of white
marble raised up on an ebony platform. Inspired, Lewis considered following his grandfather's example—"For I never yet saw a place where one
could lie down more comfortably to listen for the last trumpet."[12]

Lesser white plantation personnel were also laid to rest in garden burial
grounds. Even though only the wealthier whites could afford to erect
monuments and mausoleums, doing so remained an aspiration for others,
as attested by the semifictional *Marly* in 1828. The title character "did not
forget his ancestors" when he achieved success, but built a mausoleum in
the garden of his Happy Fortune estate over the grave of his grandfather,
"with suitable inscriptions, in commemoration of his merits, and of the
melancholy fate of those who gave him birth." Unwilling to be counted
among the infamous "rich-let heirs, that let their fathers lie without a
monument," Marly felt compelled to erect a "lasting memorial of his gratitude for the exertions of the first of the Marlys, which had been the means
of placing his rank among the highest in the land." As Marly's monument

suggests, epitaphs tied meaningful language to significant places. Inscriptions commonly named family members; those influenced by eighteenth-century sentimentalism and Romanticism did so in affecting terms. They also sometimes proclaimed the deceased's religious affiliation and hopes for the afterlife, though the inscriptions for women referred to heaven and God more often than did those for men.[13]

In a few cases, such as that of the merchant Thomas Hibbert, inscriptions explicitly championed secular materialism. Hibbert, among the most successful eighteenth-century slave traders at Kingston, died unmarried in 1780. Though in his will he expressed a desire to be interred in the garden of his Kingston house, he was ultimately buried in a vault at his Agualta Vale estate in the parish of Saint Mary. On a hilltop southwest of the plantation great house a funerary urn bearing the family coat of arms, boasting that Thomas Hibbert had resided on the island "with little interruption almost 46 years," defiantly flouts the authority of organized religion over the meaning of death:

> This lonely tomb can boast no church's care,
> No solemn sprinkling and no prelate's prayer,
> But rites more powerful sanctify the dust
> Where rest rever'd, the ashes of the just;
> Pray'rs from the poor, that sooner reach the sky,
> And holier drops that fall from friendship's eye.

Hibbert's monument claims the right to determine the bounds of virtue, in maintaining that despite his lying outside the sanctity of churchyard, the slaver had been a just and benevolent man, as well as a good friend. These qualities, rather than fealty to religious doctrine, had earned him the right to perpetuation of his memory.[14]

Members of Hibbert's family, who erected the monument, preferred that he be remembered for his public character more than for his religious piety. In this they were not alone. Indeed, in the 1820s Hibbert's monument came to represent the ideal memorial to slaveholders when it appeared in a painting by the artist and architect James Hakewill. Hakewill had won fame in London for paintings depicting Roman ruins in Italy and for his illustrations of the great homes of the Windsor gentry. When Jamaican planters hired him to portray their plantations, they

Figure 7.1. *Monument of the late Thomas Hibbert, Esq., at Agualta Vale, St. Mary's,* by James Hakewill, in his *Picturesque Tour of the Island of Jamaica, from Drawings Made in the Years 1820 and 1821* (London, 1825). By permission of Houghton Library, Harvard College Library (SA 2638.20*F).

hoped to associate themselves with the grandeur of Hakewill's earlier subjects, just at the time British colonial slavery was falling into economic and political decline. Perhaps they suspected that soon it would all be gone, and their descendants would be left with only these grandiose tributes. Hakewill's depictions show the plantations as their owners liked to see them, magnificent and productive places where contented slaves worked dutifully to help implant British civilization. Among the idyllic views of plantation scenery is the painting of Thomas Hibbert's monument, perched high above the fertile river valley below. Towering against the sky, the urn dominates the mountains in the background (Figure 7.1). The Hibbert coat of arms faces the viewer, only partially obscured by the high fence around the pedestal. It would be hard to make a stronger claim to permanent tenure on the land.[15]

Emphasizing the monument's commanding position in the island land-scape, Hakewill's painting broadcast the Hibbert family's claim to viewers throughout the empire, but it also advertised the Jamaican plantocracy's more general assertions of legitimacy. Undoubtedly aware of attacks on the morality of West Indian slaveholding, Hakewill painted a scene testi-fying to the serenity of slavery. Occupying the center, instead of the mon-ument itself, are a white gentleman in top hat and coattails, two dogs frolicking on the grass, a saddled horse, and a black attendant, surely enslaved. The relationship between the master and the slave anchors the social meaning of the monument. The master, directing the slave's atten-tion to the monument, compels him to note the prominence of the dead slaveholder, while the intimacy of the figures in the image allows a viewer to believe that the black man might respect or even appreciate the dom-inance of such men. For a monument, this conveyed an unusually direct statement about the institution of slavery. Though faithful servants had appeared in British portraiture since at least the seventeenth century and figured in many eighteenth-century military scenes, mortuary monu-ments rarely remarked on the politics of slavery or relations with slaves, whether friendly or hostile, until the demise of the institution was immi-nent. Drawing on an old convention, Hakewill's depiction of a master tutoring his vassal on the greatness of dead slaveholders carried a new meaning in the 1820s. It registered a shift in practices of remembrance from the confident expressions of power and civic virtue displayed by eighteenth-century monuments to a kind of recalcitrant nationalism, which had to protest slaveholders' public worth.[16]

Such posthumous declarations reached something of a crescendo with the Baptist War and emancipation. In the western parishes of the island, no fewer than five monumental inscriptions referred directly to the Baptist War, naming the rebels as savage murderers and the defenders of slavery as models of virtue. John Pearce's tomb in Hanover noted his widow's grief and promised vengeance to the insurgents: "John Pearce, most barbarously murdered 30 Dec. 1831 by the slaves on the adjoining estate, leaving his dis-consolate widow to deplore his untimely end. Who so sheddeth mans blood by man shall his blood be shed." The officers and men of the Sixth Battalion Company, which defended the plantocracy during the rebellion, similarly memorialized their fallen comrade, light infantry private Obed Bell Chambers. The monument inscription, which observes that Chambers "fell to an Ambush of Rebellious Slaves near this spot" on 3 January 1832 and "was cruelly butchered," urges viewers to remember that he "died a Soldier and an honest man." One monument even held the insurgents responsible for the deaths of several infants. On the Carlton estate in Saint James, a family erected a memorial to "ANNA, JEMIMA, and JESSIE, three infant daughters of Robert and Anna Cron; the two former d. on the eve of Christmas 1831, being the period when the fatal rebellion of that date broke out in this island; the last d. two days afterwards."[17]

As much as some memorials cited the rebels for cruelty, butchery, and barbarism, a few monuments, including the rare ones dedicated by planters to slaves, represented slaves as devoted supporters, and slavery as a benign institution. The memorial to William Walker at Lucea parish church in Hanover set paternalist fantasies in stone.

> Wm. CARR WALKER Esq., of Bamboo estate in this parish, b. 11 Jan. 1778, d. 16 May 1832, whose mortal remains were interred at Bamboo. This monument is erected by his afflicted wife. He was an affectionate husband, kind brother, sincere friend and universally beloved master by his peasantry, who protected his property during the rebellion of 1831, while all around were in flames.

Not far from Lucea, a Hanover gravestone similarly heralded the fidelity of Robert, head driver on the Tyrall estate, "who was shot by the rebels defending his master's property, 8 Jan. 1832."[18]

Such commemorations of slave revolt were fairly new. No extant memorial inscription refers to Tacky's Revolt in 1760, though more than sixty whites were killed. By contrast, only fourteen whites died at the hands of the Baptist War insurgents. Indeed, for almost the entire duration of British slave society in Jamaica, from 1655 to the eve of the 1831–1832 revolt, only two monument inscriptions connected with slave rebellion have been recorded. One of them was for Martha of Saint Catherine's parish, the wife of Edmon Ducke, "she being Most Barbarously Murthered by Some of their own Negro Slaves" in 1678, and the other, erected at Cross Path (now Banbury Crossroads) in Westmoreland parish, touted the civic accomplishment of John Guthrie, colonel of the parish militia, who fought with more success than his predecessors during the protracted Maroon Wars of the 1730s.[19] Perhaps slaveholders were reluctant to commemorate great moments in the history of slave resistance for fear of inspiring future generations of would-be rebels. If memorializing the dead as either victims of slave rebellions or defenders of slavery was rare throughout the turbulent history of British slavery in Jamaica, then it is unclear why, to repudiate insurrection and vindicate slave society, whites suddenly felt the impulse to enlist the assistance of the dead in the wake of Jamaican slavery's final great revolt.

The most likely possibility is that when acceptance of antislavery activism in the United Kingdom put West Indian slaveholders outside the pale of acceptable British social norms, the monuments of the slaveholders registered their disaffection. Slaveholders and their supporters were enraged in the era of the Baptist War to find themselves on the wrong side of British history. As the successful campaign to abolish the slave trade reemerged in the 1820s in the form of influential campaigns first to alleviate slavery and then to emancipate the slaves, many white West Indians reacted with fierce resentment, inflammatory speeches, and threats of secession from Great Britain.[20] White protest merely convinced many enslaved men and women that powerful forces in Great Britain were on their side, and emboldened them to strike for their liberation. In turn, the revolt ratified slaveholders' sense of betrayal by the colonial power. Slaveholding whites finally stood face to face with the specter of a world turned upside-down and, recognizing their loss of influence in the British Empire, many reacted with bitter territorialism. Even as they were being written out of the British national narrative, the planters used their monuments to claim a place for their preferred version of local social history.

In the immediate aftermath of the rebellion, before they set about commemorating their own dead, they attempted to deny commemorations by their enemies. Militias and state executioners intentionally prevented proper burial of convicted rebels. "They were consigned with every incident of indignity to a felon's grave," recalled Thomas Burchell in his memoirs, "or left to moulder where they perished by the hand of violence: 'Their ashes flew—No marble tells us whither; with their names, No bard embalms and sanctifies his song.'" Slaveholders and their supporters also reacted against memorials for missionaries, whom they considered the local representatives of metropolitan antislavery. White mobs persecuted nonconformist missionaries by destroying their chapels and defiling their burial monuments. The cenotaph to the memory of evangelist James Mann "was torn down," wrote Burchell, "and dashed to pieces by men who arrogate to themselves the almost exclusive possession of intelligence and good breeding, but who showed themselves capable of trampling with equal recklessness on the rights of the living and the relics of the dead."[21] These frenzied desecrations were purposeful. They engaged the critics of slavery by attacking their capacity to mark the landscape of memory. This tactic was not reserved for slaveholders. The enslaved also joined death, remembrance, and place in a struggle to ensure that their own claims would endure—and they were not entirely unsuccessful.

A Coffin for Slavery

The Baptist War represented a departure from eighteenth-century slave rebellions. Rather than staging a revolt to escape enslavement, while leaving the slave system intact, and rather than representing a struggle to achieve complete autonomy, the Baptist War evinced Creole aspirations to an integrated Jamaican society, where blacks might live as free farmers, in dignified relations with whites. In essence, the war illuminated the birth of an inchoate nationalism. Claims to territory, manifested in proprietary, familial, and emotional attachments to land, formed a significant part of those aspirations. Struggles over memorials to the dead and over burial grounds were, in turn, important elements in those claims and a critical dimension of the politics of the enslaved.[22]

A charged conflict over the memorial to a fallen leader distinguished one of the revolt's hardest-fought battles. As fire began to engulf the sugar estates of Saint James parish on 28 December 1831, the Western Interior Militia under the command of Colonel James Gringon retreated from Shettlewood barracks to the Old Montpelier plantation, three kilometers closer to Montego Bay. They were pursued by bands of slaves who had risen up, led by the rebel "Black Regiment," 150 men under the command of the popularly appointed Colonel Johnson, who had been a slave only the day before. Just as the rebels prepared to destroy Old Montpelier's sugar works on the evening of 29 December, the Saint James militia regiment arrived to reinforce Grignon's troops. Though less than a quarter of the black rebels held firearms, they engaged the militia and suffered heavy casualties, including the death of Colonel Johnson. But the next morning Grignon panicked and ordered another retreat. "With such ignoble haste was the retreat conducted," remembered Henry Bleby, "that the Colonel did not stop to inter the only one of his own men who had been killed in the action of the preceding night." Both the dead militiaman and the body of Colonel Johnson lay unburied, as the insurgents took the estate and set its buildings ablaze; then, "taking the corpse of the white man out of the coffin which had been hastily prepared for it, they threw it into the flames, and, putting the body of the black leader Johnson in its place, buried it with the usual ceremonies."23

Bleby neglected to mention just what the usual ceremonies were. Since the majority of those involved in the rebellion were Native Baptists, the service probably involved some recitation of scriptural wisdom, a reminder of the sacrifice of Jesus Christ, and an assurance of Johnson's place in God's kingdom. The desecration of the white body and the confiscation of the coffin were even more significant. Coffins were themselves memorials. Protecting the enduring integrity of the body, they were simple monuments to the dignity of the dead. By swapping the cadavers, the rebels consciously and explicitly inverted the symbolic order that placed white above black. Yet their action also signaled an attachment to burial practices adopted from whites. Far from being universally accessible in early nineteenth-century Jamaica, coffins were a status symbol that marked the place of the deceased in the social hierarchy. In fact, coffin burials had also become an index of adaptation to Jamaican Creole society, where whites and blacks defined dignity in increasingly similar terms, while maintaining their social antagonism.24

Coffins traveled to the Caribbean with whites, having come into general usage in Europe only in the seventeenth century. Archaeological records suggest that Africans and their descendants in the Caribbean began to use coffins over the course of the eighteenth century, as slaves were integrated into plantation hierarchies or as they converted to Christianity and came to expect equality in the afterlife. On the Gold Coast, it appears that Africans did not use coffins until the mid-nineteenth century. Caribbean slaves were interred in coffins much earlier. Evidence from a large plantation cemetery in Barbados indicates that masters reserved coffins as a reward for highly valued slaves. The limited archaeological data from Jamaica show a mixed pattern. Sometime between 1670 and 1760, three enslaved young adult males (aged twenty-one to twenty-five at death) were buried in coffins at the Seville plantation in Saint Ann parish. Because their interment occurred before evangelization became widespread in

Jamaica, their conversion to Christianity is an unlikely explanation for the presence of the caskets. Moreover, all three were buried with their heads facing east, in contrast to the prevailing contemporary Christian custom of west-facing burials, and two of the three were interred with grave goods, including a knife and two new clay tobacco pipes. More likely, the young men were native to Jamaica, and whoever buried them was still heavily influenced by West African burial customs and cosmologies, yet alert to the social value of European material symbols.[25]

In Jamaica, as in other slave societies in the Americas, coffin burials became ever more common, and eventually universal. By the 1820s, if the proslavery writer Alexander Barclay is to be believed, when slaves died who had been especially "valuable and faithful servants," masters generally gave "immediate directions" to the plantation's carpenters to make a coffin, while the family of the deceased provided "the shroud and furniture." More than simply indicating the transformation of African cultural practices, the increasing use of coffins suggests that the enslaved used them to claim status in Jamaican society. As the actions of the Baptist rebels at Old Montpelier made abundantly clear, coffins were as much political symbols as cultural artifacts. A coffin burial showed respect for the dead and signified honor among the living, who created communities of memory from such gestures of esteem. When those Baptist rebels took care to bury their Colonel Johnson, they demanded such respect and claimed places for themselves by seizing a permanent place for Johnson at the site of his heroic death.[26]

Just as coffins indicated something about the social position or aspirations of slaves, the spatial arrangements for interment connoted social claims on territory. Near towns, and on some plantations, special burial grounds were set aside for slaves, but on most countryside plantations the family determined the place of interment. Many blacks were accustomed to burying their kin beneath their houses or in their yards. In his *Manners and Customs in the West India Islands* (1790), J. B. Moreton mentioned that enslaved families in Jamaica buried their deceased kin inside their houses, sometimes under their beds. John Baillie, the resident owner of the Roehampton estate in Saint James parish from 1788 to 1826, also noticed that Africans buried their dead in their own houses. The practice was associated most strongly with people from West Africa. Ludewig Ferdinand Rømer, who worked on the Gold Coast for the

Danish West India and Guinea Company in the 1740s, wrote that Africans normally buried the deceased "in the house where the person has lived, but no one, except for the closest friends, knows the exact place."[27]

When the dead were not interred beneath or inside the house, they were commonly buried in the small gardens nearby. Matthew Lewis insisted in 1816 that black people always buried the dead in their own gardens. "Adjoining to the house is usually a small spot of ground, laid out into a sort of garden and shaded by various fruit-trees," noted John Stewart in 1823. "Here the family deposit their dead, to whose memory they invariably, if they can afford it, erect a rude tomb." Alexander Barclay described slave tombs that were "built commonly of brick, and neatly white-washed." The white-washing was dutifully repeated every Christmas, observed Barclay, "and formerly it was on these occasions customary to kill a white cock, and sprinkle his blood over the graves of the family."[28] In 1825 Reverend Henry Beame even claimed to have desecrated a black mausoleum: "I once saw on one of those tombs a raised niche. On taking away a marble slab from before it, I found two small figures or images rudely sculptured, and on asking the man what this meant, he replied, that the one reminded him of his wife, and the other of his child. I wished to take them away, but the agitation of the man at once proved that they were connected with superstitious feelings."[29]

The figurines that Breame wanted to seize were common in black burial grounds of the period. In one graveyard near Spanish Town, according to James Phillippo, "there was scarcely a grave that did not exhibit from two to four rudely carved images." These embodied another continuity with African mortuary practice. Europeans in West Africa often remarked upon similar little monuments—male and female figures, generally made of terra-cotta, often painted and adorned—that represented either the deceased or the notable persons who had attended him or her in life. Yet whereas in Africa these effigies commonly indicated the presence of a dead king or great man, in Jamaica they seem to have been more ordinary memorials for the benefit of friends, families, and communities. Most important, they highlighted the reverence in which the enslaved held burial *places*, which demarcated both social and spiritual space.[30]

Edward Long speculated in 1774 about slaves' emotional attachment to burial grounds. "It cannot be imagined," he hypothesized, "but that they have a powerful attachment to the spot where they were born; to the place which holds the remains of their deceased friends and kindred." By the early nineteenth century it was clear that he had been essentially correct. In 1807 John Blackburn, a planting attorney and thirty-five-year resident of Jamaica who had managed thirty sugar estates, offered the following testimony before a government committee: "Every [slave] house has a garden round it, of a quarter or half acre or more; they are attached to the spot, and they are attached to the graves of their forefathers." Henry John Hinchcliffe, a judge of the Jamaican Vice-Admiralty Court, asserted in 1833 that a family's burial plot was "one of the Means of identifying their Residence, and it goes to their Relations."[31]

Tombs and burial plots marked out more than claims to real estate. Such sites also mapped the spiritual terrain, helping the enslaved to navigate a treacherously haunted landscape. Matthew Lewis, with his gothic author's sensibility, wondered about the spiritual dimension of burial grounds in 1816. Understanding that his slaves were "very much afraid of ghosts (whom they call the *duppy*)," Lewis questioned why they would have their dead buried in their own gardens. "But I understand their argument to be, that they need only fear the duppies of their enemies, but have nothing to apprehend from those after death, who loved them in their lifetime." Lewis also learned that the enslaved paid careful attention to the spiritual history of different tracts of land. An African man on his plantation had recently been stricken with fits and seizures, and Lewis suspected that he had eaten a poisonous plant from a nearby grove. That explanation earned no credibility with the enslaved, who assured him, "one and all, that nothing could possibly have induced him to eat an herb or fruit from that grove, as it had been used as a burying ground for " 'the white people.' " They proposed an alternative theory: "They had no sort of doubt," wrote Lewis, "that in passing through the burying-ground he had been struck down by the duppy of a white person not long deceased, whom he had formerly offended, and that these repeated fainting fits were the consequence of that ghostly blow." Whatever the actual cause of the man's fits, it was obvious to Lewis's slaves that the afflicted African had failed to learn his way around.[32]

Once people acquired an attachment to a particular place and an understanding of its sociospiritual landscape, they were loath to move to unfamiliar territory. Planters found that when they tried to move "negro villages," they could meet fierce resistance. William Shand, a prolific estate owner and planting attorney in the early nineteenth century, ran into trouble when he tried to resettle a village that was situated on a riverbank that often flooded. "They strongly objected, but did not give any Reason for this." Though "houses were prepared for them, equally good as those they had left," the enslaved were still set against the relocation. Shand and his brother went down to the village "to distribute clothing, and in order to prevail on them to remove," but once they had given out the clothes, as many as three hundred people attacked the Shands with brickbats and stones. Shand was adamant, and he eventually got his way. Another planter, John Baillie, had to give up on a similar effort. He told a committee of the House of Lords that he had once had insurmountable difficulties when he attempted to relocate some of his slaves to new lands. "They have been so reluctant," he testified, "that after purchasing a property of 1,000 acres of land and 137 negroes, they expressed themselves so unwilling to remove that I gave up the purchase and abandoned the removal."[33]

Enslaved families were reluctant to leave property that they considered their own, houses and gardens they had tended, and burial grounds that allowed an increasingly native population to feel an ancestral connection to the land. Just as important, slaves also hesitated to encroach on new and perhaps spiritually perilous grounds where the unfamiliar dead, unplacated by ritual and ceremony, might be unwilling to countenance alien settlements. The concern was immediate. Following the end of the transatlantic slave trade in 1807, when planters fell deeper into debt and began to break up estates and sell off movable assets, enslaved men and women suffered frequent displacements, entailing separations from families, living and dead, and removal to foreign landscapes. In 1834, the magistrate R. R. Madden visited an abandoned plantation in the parish of Saint Mary where the resting places of the dead demarcated safe and unsafe territory. His guide, a local black man, told him that the estate was overrun with ghosts and necromancers: "'It was no good to walk about such a place, buckras all dead, niggers all dead too, no one live there but duppies and obeah men.'" There was danger in this place where none but wizards tended the memory of the deceased. It was better to stay in territory rendered familiar by the cultivation of communal remembrance.[34]

One month before the final emancipation of 1 August 1838 Jamaica's governor, Sir Lionel Smith, issued a proclamation to the soon-to-be freed slaves on their new rights and duties. It recognized their desire to "remain on those properties on which you have been born, and where your parents are buried" but warned them not to suppose that their houses, gardens, and provision grounds were their own property. Governor Smith knew that the dead marked the land as surely as legal deeds and titles, but he may not have anticipated the degree to which practices pertaining to death and commemoration would also mark the passage from slavery to freedom.[35]

⋇

When emancipation finally came, it was greeted by celebrations all over the island. In Falmouth, where the recently returned William Knibb had his congregation, slavery was given a funeral—not as a sign of respect or to mark a sacred spot, but as a countermemorial, a way of fixing fear and hatred upon an unloved thing and tying it to the ground. In a paradoxical inversion of customary ceremonies of respect, as the enslaved claimed their freedom, they used the rites of death, which had been the focal point of so many struggles within slavery, to commemorate its end and determine its future meaning.

An hour before midnight on the last night of July 1838, the final evening of enslavement, more than two thousand black men, women, and children gathered at the Baptist chapel to sing a funeral dirge:

> The death-blow is struck—see the monster is dying,
> He cannot survive till the dawn streaks the sky;
> *In one single hour,* he will prostrate be lying,
> Come, shout o'er the grave where so soon he will lie.

When the clock struck midnight, William Knibb shouted to the emotional throng, "The monster is dead! The negro is free!" and begged three cheers for the queen of England. The crowd erupted in cheers, its exultation rattling the windows of the chapel with what Knibb called a "strange yet sacred joy." At dawn, a multitude assembled around a coffin containing a chain, handcuffs, an iron collar, and other "hateful ensigns of usurped command." The names of two proslavery newspapers were painted on the sides. The coffin's memorial plate bore the inscription,

"Colonial Slavery died July 31st, 1838, aged 276 years," and also "Sir Hawkins," the pioneering sixteenth-century British slave trader. The crowd sang, "Now slavery we lay thy vile form in the dust; / And buried forever, there let it remain; / And rotted, and covered with infamy's rust, / Be every man-whip, and fetter, and chain!" They buried the sarcophagus and planted a young coconut tree at its head, which acted simultaneously as a symbolic tree of liberty and a prison for slavery's spirit.[36]

Two days later, a group of more than five hundred children held a similar rite at the chapel on Salter's Hill. As they prepared for the "burial of slavery," they produced and then condemned its symbols—the whip, the chain, and the shackles—in demanding that the whip be cut up, the chain broken, and the shackles destroyed. When this was done, the children let out a cheer. Then, when the question arose, "What was to be done with the remains of slavery?" they answered in unison, "Bury them, bury them." Yet there was disagreement about where the remains should be interred. Some hesitated to bury slavery near the chapel, out of concern that they might desecrate sanctified ground. However, others won the argument by contending that "Salter's Hill would be the most appropriate place, as its grave could be watched, so as to prevent its rising again." It was a wise consideration, based, one might say, on a prescient understanding that the dead would give meaning to future struggles over land, labor, and civic rights, that the ghost of slavery would continue to haunt black people, and that watching over slavery's memorial was a vital and abiding duty.[37]

In Restless Memoriam

The meaning of places is never fixed, even those sacred places which hold the memories of the dead. Significance shifts restlessly with time, as populations move, monuments accumulate, and new memories are layered upon the old. Despite people's best efforts to claim a permanent meaning for a chosen location, their markers merely enter into future battles over the commemoration of historical events and the future of the social order. This was especially the case with Jamaican slave society, where the dead were active participants in successive generations of conflict.

In the last decades of British West Indian slavery, slaves and slaveholders competed for possession of Jamaica. The primary weapons they employed in this contest were the same as they had always been—firearms, whips, cutlasses, as well as law, religion, and racial ideology. Nearly as important, however, were landmarks for the dead, which turned disputed frontiers into domestic provinces of communal belonging, gardens for the remembrance of privileges, rights, and sacred duties. This was a significant facet of what historians and anthropologists often call creolization, the development of local institutions, customs, and worldviews peculiar to West Indian society. Increasingly, Creole slaveholders and Creole slaves staked their claim to Jamaican territory and history with monuments, coffins, memorial inscriptions, and spiritual cartography.

Staking a claim to places of memory was not the same thing as controlling them. Competing interests and the play of power shaped the meaning of location, just as they did the meaning of death. The dead and their monuments carried multiple legacies. Consider the fate of Simon Taylor's Prospect Pen, where he lived for much of the last three decades of his life, where he buried his brother Sir John Taylor, and where he himself was initially buried, according to his wishes. Taylor would have wanted Prospect Pen to serve as a lasting landmark for his family, but his desire to claim it as sacred family soil clashed with his instincts as a shrewd and ruthless property owner. When he died in 1813, Taylor's remains were taken to the pen and interred next to his brother's in the central courtyard of the mansion. Yet in his will he had directed that Prospect Pen be sold, and his executor John Shand saw no way of both selling the property and protecting the graves "from profanation." "Under these circumstances," Shand wrote to the heir, "I submit to you the propriety of taking up the bodies of Sir John and Mr. Taylor and removing them either to the churchyard of Saint Andrew or Saint Thomas-in-the-East where the principal family Estates are situated where a proper tomb and vault might be erected with such a monument as you shall think proper." Taylor's nephew agreed, moving his father and uncle to Taylor's Lyssons estate, where he raised a monument to both men in 1814. Sir John Taylor was remembered for being "amiable in his manners, steady in his attachments, and exemplary in the practice of social and domestic duties," while Simon Taylor was praised as "a loyal subject, a firm friend and honest man," who had "faithfully and ably fitted the highest offices of civil and military duty" in Jamaica.[38]

Simon Taylor was born, lived, and died in a society organized to satisfy his desires, the quintessential Creole. During his lifetime no one had a more secure claim to historic significance in Jamaica. But his legacy now is not as he would have wished it. Today, none care to remember the personal qualities memorialized on his tomb. Taylor is recalled now only as one of the greatest of slaveholders, who elevated property above humanity, and whose restless claim to a lasting legacy is everywhere contested by the descendants of the enslaved. Taylor's first resting place, Prospect Pen, renamed Vale Royal, became in 2006 the official residence of Jamaica's first black woman prime minister, Portia Simpson Miller. It was easy to imagine Simon Taylor turning in his grave, kicking at the top of his lead coffin in an attempt to burst back into the world and set things right.[39]

The monuments to Simon Taylor's social enemies would have a better claim on the future. Through the end of chattel slavery and apprenticeship in 1838, the rebel leader Sam Sharpe lay in an unmarked grave. In the 1840s, William Knibb and a group of fellow Baptists exhumed Sharpe's body and reburied him in a newly rebuilt Montego Bay chapel. When Knibb died in 1845 at just forty-two years of age, freed men and women returned the favor by erecting a monumental pillar in the churchyard of the Knibb Memorial Baptist Chapel in the town of Falmouth. "This Monument was erected by the Emancipated slaves," the inscription reads, "to whose enfranchisement and elevation his indefatigable exertions so largely contributed, by his fellow labourers who admired and loved him, and deeply deplore his early removal, and by friends of various creeds and parties." The memorial expressed esteem for Knibb as "A Man, a Philanthropist, and a Christian Minister," praised universally by people of faith, "and who being dead yet speaketh." Of course, Knibb was not speaking for himself; he was made to speak for his fellows. By allying himself with Sam Sharpe, Knibb had earned a place in popular memory that Simon Taylor, for all his power and property, would never have. The cenotaph was more than a tribute to Knibb. It embodied memories of the struggle against slavery, engaging the dead to evoke a polemical history of Jamaica that could validate ongoing efforts to liberate the descendants of the enslaved.[40]

⊰⊱

The end of slavery was by no means the end of its story. The hopeful years immediately after emancipation were followed by the reassertion of merchant and planter dominance. The social antagonisms established in slavery governed the tensions that shaped a very tenuous freedom. While newly freed workers claimed houses and grounds for peasant farming, the masters' offspring continued to use the power of property against them. The legacy of slavery persisted through the nineteenth and twentieth centuries' reign of white supremacy. What came after emancipation was the memory of what had gone before. The "days of slavery" came to signify the origin of a new battle in the eternal conflict between the weak and the powerful, a war in which the dead were not indifferent. Jamaica's occupants all recognized, in various ways, that the landscape was haunted, visited by the spirits of heroes, villains, and victims of the past, who would continue to intervene in unfolding developments. Remembrance of the dead made an ineffable history intimate, accessible, and inspirational, in turning a usable past into a useful one, which could motivate consequential action in future struggles. And because these struggles never end, the dead rarely rest in peace.

EPILOGUE

⁓❧⁓

Regeneration

THE GRIM REAPER, death personified as a living entity, is often portrayed brandishing a scythe or sickle, an agricultural tool used to reap a harvest of the dead. In this vision of death, the scythe signifies the cutting off of temporal existence and the removal of the dead from life's flourishing field. But in order to understand the world of Atlantic slavery, it is helpful to envision the reaper as a gardener as well as a harvester. In Jamaican slave society and its transatlantic hinterlands, at least, death tended and nurtured the activities of the living, cultivating their understanding of the world and their struggle to shape it. In this reaper's garden, death helped to constitute life, and the dead were an undeniable presence.

Was the reaper's garden peculiar to Jamaica? Were its features exceptional phenomena in a unique place? The story of death and power in the Jamaican world of Atlantic slavery is admittedly bizarre, even monstrous. Its telling follows few straight chronologies and requires a bundle of interpretive approaches, encompassing analyses of the supernatural and the physical, the diplomatic and the violent, the artistic and the brutally mechanical. The resulting narrative may be unfamiliar, but it is central to the greater history of America and to the way in which that history is told.

Jamaica *was* unique in many ways. Its central role in the fortunes of British imperial slavery, its particular mix of peoples and their cultural inheritance and innovations, and its distinguishing events all gave the island a singular history. Nevertheless, Jamaica shared many characteristics with societies elsewhere in the world of Atlantic slavery. From North

America to Brazil, in different ways, death cultivated the principal features of social and political existence: short life cycles, rapid accumulation of wealth, the intensity of efforts to reconstitute social belonging, and the efficacy of symbolic identification with the dead.

Variations in migration patterns, governing institutions, labor regimes, and political developments made other histories of slavery, death, and power distinctive. Demographic catastrophe struck wherever sugar plantations or mining were at the base of commercial enterprise. In nearby Saint-Domingue, which surpassed Jamaica in economic profitability, the conditions of life were parallel. On the sugar estates of Bahia and Pernambuco in the northeast of Brazil, death rates were even higher than in Jamaica, and birth rates lower. The dead piled up around Brazil's gold mines at Minas Gerais too, and in the silver mines of Spanish New Granada, Peru, and Mexico. Only where the enslaved toiled in less rigorous labor regimes, growing coffee, tobacco, or cotton, could their numbers increase without overseas recruitment. Wherever mortality exceeded fertility, the slave trade sustained the development of the Americas and brought a shifting assortment of African workers, with their ideas about death and their strategies for managing relations with the dead. The trade fed each region differently. Brazil, for example, drew a greater percentage of its population from West-Central Africa and fewer people from the Bight of Biafra or the Gold Coast. The transatlantic trade was never as important in North America, where predominantly self-reproducing Creole populations emerged beginning in the mid-eighteenth century and the descendants of Europeans were nearly everywhere in the majority (the sugar-growing region in the lower Mississippi River valley and the rice swamps of the Carolina lowcountry being exceptions).[1]

Differences in demographic patterns complemented institutional differences in slave societies. Where the Catholic Church was an established presence, state officials took an even deeper interest in death rites and the way they defined the intersection of spiritual and civic order. In the nominally Catholic societies, those who deviated from church dogma concerning the sacraments could be punished as heretics, and the pressure to conform brought African and European cosmologies and practices together under the umbrella of the Church. In at least one well-documented case in Brazil, there was a great rebellion over an 1836 law that banned traditional church burials and mandated the creation of a new cemetery on the outskirts of the city of Salvador. Wherever Africans and their descendants maintained their own fragile institutions under slavery, they interpreted it in the light of ideas about relations between the living and dead, to organize their lives within the institution or plot their resistance against it, most famously in the *Vodou* ceremonies that bolstered the morale of the Haitian revolutionaries. Even in the northern reaches of the North American mainland, where black bodies were barred from white burial grounds, graveyards and burial societies emerged as the first African-American institutions—to such an extent, in fact, that by the early eighteenth century, officials felt compelled to ban night funerals. As the North American example suggests, occasions for mortuary politics did not depend on the mortality rate. Even where demographic conditions were least destructive, the meaning people made of death and the dead formed a crucial part of their political lives.[2]

Indeed, this was not a politics limited to life in the world of slavery. The heirs of slavery in the United States continued to create alliances and antagonisms from the carnage of the Civil War and the Jim Crow lynching pogroms that produced the "strange fruit" immortalized by Abel Meeropol and Billie Holiday. Victims of racial terror haunted and animated the civil rights movement. Similarly, urban America's drug wars and the HIV-AIDS crisis of late twentieth and early twenty-first centuries have generated new, highly political categories of belonging that inspire action—one thinks immediately of the street gang affiliations cemented by bonds of death, commemoration, and honor, or of same-sex marriage, emerging from communities ravaged by fatal disease. As the dead circulate with accelerating speed and near-boundless reach in today's electronic media, who can tell what kinds of social formations, political movements, and practices of remembrance will result from the global AIDS pandemic and the twenty-first century wars of terror, in which mass killing, martyrdom, and the rhetoric of perpetual hostility dominate the cultural landscape?[3]

The question can arise only because relations between the living and the dead are an important part of the historical process well beyond Jamaican slave society. They have perhaps featured to some degree in all of human history. The case of Jamaica, then, merely throws more general processes into sharp relief. It is common for people to organize their social lives to preserve some continuity between life and death; to claim authority by associating with and invoking the dead; to allow perceptions of the afterworld to guide worldly activity; and to stake out territory by erecting commemorative landmarks. Though the way people do these things may vary, the same kinds of questions can be asked about other times and places: How have people made sense of death culturally and use of the dead politically? What has been the consequence of mortuary politics?

⚜

What might reading politics through the social and cultural history of death mean for our general understanding of history—the way we think, write, and read about the past? To begin with, the history of death, power, and slavery in British colonial Jamaica suggests a new perspective on the history of the present. It is customary to narrate the history of America alongside conventional accounts of modernity, which chronicle the retreat of the sacred and the spiritual when confronted by the advance of reason and science, the expansion of freedom, and the extension of material progress. Although such histories represent some broad trends, progressive narratives do little to explain popular politics within and beyond the world of slavery, where it is evident that the spiritual and supernatural inspired purposeful action. The emphasis on secularization accounts better for certain types of elite discourse than for the actual trajectory of social and political change in world history. "Modern" ways of thinking about the dead, whether expressed in the building of cemeteries apart from population centers or in the declining authority of established religion, did not mean that the dead had been banished from the concerns of the living, only that the dead would enter the social struggle in new ways. The immaterial continued to shape the material; the sacred and secular remained intertwined. The world of Jamaican slavery, where the dead were active players in the most significant political disputes, at the very heart of Britain's imperial enterprise, serves as a reminder that the modern world was still an enchanted one.[4]

For several reasons, Jamaica's place in the history of Anglo-America is rarely given due consideration. First, narratives of historical progress customarily focus on what Europeans and their descendants have done. Following conventions derived from nineteenth-century white supremacy, territories with predominantly nonwhite populations have remained segregated from mainstream accounts of economic, political, and social evolution. Modernity, as indicated by capitalist accumulation, the experience of dislocation, and a self-conscious sense of the novelty of one's predicament, is rarely claimed for acquisitive slaveholders and their heterogeneous armies of laborers, drawn from far-off worlds to work in protoindustrial agriculture. Second, national historiography, which anachronistically reduces imperial and colonial history to the prehistory of the nation-state, conventionally excludes the British Caribbean from histories of North America. Because Jamaica, along with the other Caribbean colonies, failed to join the American Revolution, its history, as crucial as it was to the implantation of the British in America, has been consigned to that of the "Third World" or the "non-West," a mélange of poor, postcolonial states on the margins of official memory. Finally, Jamaica's history is inconvenient. Because "progress" generally signifies a positive good, the violent rule of great slaveholders does not fit comfortably into chronicles of political development. The popular perception (which appears in some professional histories too) that the rise of Anglo-America represents the advance of liberty, justice, and civil rights requires that the prevailing story of the British colonies overlook or explain away slavery's ghastly brutality. Tales about the heroic struggle of liberal principles in a tyrannical world have seemed more credible as a result of this exclusion. Where economic success coincided with the extension of representative government, slavery could be seen as a "peculiar institution," and its existence as an anomaly, a paradox.[5]

To read Jamaican slavery as representative of early America, rather than as anomalous, is unsettling, but also illuminating. The shift in perspective yields insights into the ways in which people have negotiated the catastrophic effects of a successful imperial economy, into unlikely patterns of identification, into affiliations and collective struggles that enlist the intangible to accomplish worldly ends, and into the claims the dead make on the living or that the living make for the dead. Just as people have invested the dead with their own desires for the future, we make meaning of the past to chart our way forward from the present. "We understand that history never repeats itself," wrote the historian Emilia Viotti da Costa, "but we transform historical events into metaphors and see universality in uniqueness." Such metaphors guide our knowledge of imminent predicaments, but only when we can perceive precedent in the past.[6]

What could we possibly have in common with the British colonial America I have described? One might see similarities between the brutal, deadly, and profitable world of Jamaican slavery, on the one hand, and, on the other, twenty-first-century America's gross material inequalities, burgeoning prison populations, and the seemingly constant warfare that provides billions to profiteers and steady work for morticians. Today's world of accelerating ruin and reconstruction might seem an inheritance from an earlier time. From that point of view it might be easier to recognize the story of death and power in the world of slavery as a specter that troubles the present. Jamaica's story would be just one dark episode in the larger history of what the writer Colin Dayan has memorably called the gothic Americas, a vast territory "filled not only with spirits of the dead seeking rest and recognition but with other corporeal spirits who recall the terrors of slavery," as well as the "monstrous, institutionalized magic" involved in turning humans into commodities.[7]

If people looked to the past to find the roots of contemporary forms of inequality, domination, and terror, rather than the origins of freedom, rights, and universal prosperity, they might see early colonial Jamaica as home to the people who made the New World what it became. Simon Taylor might be seen as a founding father, Thomas Thistlewood, a model colonist, and those who fought against them, heroes to be celebrated and emulated. If circumstances should ever make such a reading inevitable, this dark vision of British America certainly would seem an undeniable precedent, and the reaper's garden a haunting metaphor for popular politics in an age of catastrophe. And perhaps this image embodies a useful parable too, for stories of political experience that teach us how people in the most catastrophic circumstances have struggled to make their world anew could one day teach us how to do the same.

⊯

"The dead have no rights," believed the great political philosopher and slaveholder Thomas Jefferson. "Our Creator made the world for the use of the living and not of the dead." One generation could not "foreclose or burden its use to another." For Jefferson, the dead represented tradition and stasis, their claims on the living an encumbrance. He was only partly correct. As an Enlightenment revolutionary, he both assumed and advocated the possibility of a radical disjuncture separating past, present, and future, and at the same time he slighted the impulse to look to the dead for guidance. True, any dominion the dead might possess is granted by the living. Yet human beings cannot help situating themselves in time, by uniting in imagined communities that include the dead as well as the unborn. Especially in the midst of crisis, flux, and chaos, people "anxiously conjure up the spirits of the past to their service," in order to navigate through a turbulent present. In such periods, the dead are used less as an anchor than as a rudder, offering the weight of precedent not merely to sustain a "cult of continuity," as some would have it, but to animate a politics of regeneration for a fluid world. None of the practices that make up political history are givens: belonging must be articulated, authority constituted, inheritance disputed, communal morality acknowledged, territory claimed, and memory revised. In these activities, the dead not only provide a focus for continuity—they are the inspiration for change. In the struggle to shape the future the dead do not necessarily have the last word, but they always have a voice. Perhaps the most valuable fruit to be obtained from the *Reaper's Garden*, then, is a simple truth. For those who know that tomorrow is not promised, yesterday is not past.[8]

❦

African Immigration to Jamaica,
1741–1807

The following two illustrations show the volume and
regional distribution of the transatlantic slave trade
to Jamaica from 1741 to 1807. The data have been
drawn from David Eltis, Stephen D. Behrendt,
David Richardson, and Herbert S. Klein, eds., *The
Trans-Atlantic Slave Trade: A Database on CD-ROM*
(Cambridge, U.K., 1999).

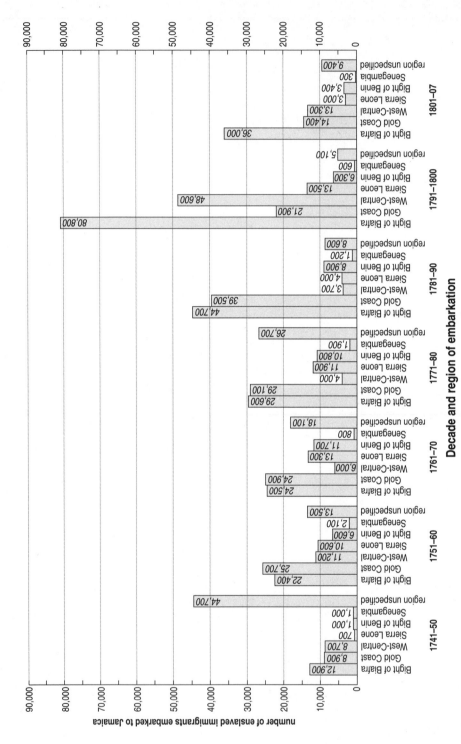

Figure A.1. The Transatlantic Slave Trade to Jamaica, 1741–1807: African Regional Distributions

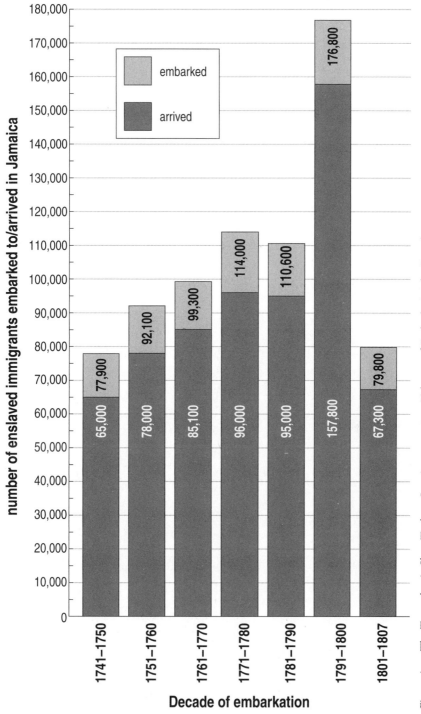

Figure A.2. The Transatlantic Slave Trade to Jamaica, 1741–1807: Volumes of Embarkation by Decade

Abbreviations in Notes

Add. MSS	Additional Manuscripts
ADM	Admiralty Series
BMS	Baptist Missionary Society Archives, Regent's Park College, University of Oxford, Oxford
BT	Board of Trade Series
C	Chancery Series
CO	Colonial Office Series
FBN	Fiche Box Number
ICS	Institute for Commonwealth Studies, London
PRO	Public Record Office, Kew, London
T	Treasury Series
Vanneck Papers	Vanneck Papers, Cambridge University Library, Cambridge
WI	West Indies
WMMS	Wesleyan Methodist Missionary Society Archives, School of Oriental and African Studies, London

Notes

Prologue

1. Robert Renny, *A History of Jamaica* (London, 1807), 241.

2. Trevor Burnard, "European Migration to Jamaica, 1655–1780," *William and Mary Quarterly* 53, no. 4 (October 1996): 779, 776. These were survival rates for people who served as resident factors for the Royal African Company between 1684 and 1732. See K. G. Davies, "The Living and the Dead: White Mortality in West Africa, 1684–1732," in Stanley L. Engerman and Eugene D. Genovese, eds., *Race and Slavery in the Western Hemisphere: Quantitative Studies* (Princeton, N.J., 1975), 83–98.

3. F. G. Cassidy and R. B. Le Page, eds., *Dictionary of Jamaican English*, 2nd ed. (Kingston, 2002), 18; Richard Allsopp, ed., *Dictionary of Caribbean English Usage* (Oxford, U.K., 1996), 61; *Oxford English Dictionary Online*, 2nd ed. (Oxford, U.K., 2007); Michael Craton, *Testing the Chains: Resistance to Slavery in the British West Indies* (Ithaca, N.Y., 1982), 336–337; "An Act for the Better Order and Government of Slaves," article 24, 1696, *Acts of Assembly Passed in the Island of Jamaica from 1681 to 1737, inclusive* (London, 1738). When members of the Assembly of Jamaica clarified the law in 1744, they explained: "It was the true intent and meaning of the said recited act that the words 'crime of encompassing and imagining the death of any white person, by any slave or slaves,' should be deemed and adjudged a crime of as high nature as the crime of murder, and should be punished as such." *Journals of the Assembly of Jamaica*, entry of 20 December 1744, 3:673.

4. W. Bruce Willis, *The Adinkra Dictionary: A Visual Primer on the Language of Adinkra* (Washington, D.C., 1998), 162–163; J. F. Ade Ajayi, "On the Politics of Being Mortal," *Transition*, issue 59 (1993): 32–44.

5. Katherine Verdery, *The Political Lives of Dead Bodies: Reburial and Postso-cialist Change* (New York, 1999), 23; Peter Brown, *The Cult of the Saints: Its Rise and Function in Latin Christianity* (Chicago, 1981), esp. 25–26.

6. Verdery, *The Political Lives of Dead Bodies,* 31; Philippe Ariès, *The Hour of Our Death,* trans. Helen Weaver (Oxford, 1991 [1981]); David Cressy, *Birth, Marriage, and Death: Ritual, Religion, and the Life-Cycle in Tudor and Stuart England* (Oxford, 1997), 475; Bruce Gordon and Peter Marshall, "Introduction: Placing the Dead in Late Medieval and Early Modern Europe," in Bruce Gordon and Peter Marshall, eds., *The Place of the Dead: Death and Remembrance in Late Medieval and Early Modern Europe* (Cambridge, U.K., 2000), 15. For a somewhat different approach to the politics of mortality, see Achille Mbembe, "Necropolitics," *Public Culture* 15, no. 1 (Winter 2003): 11–40.

7. Renny, *History of Jamaica,* 193; Francisco Guerra, "The Influence of Disease on Race, Logistics, and Colonization in the Antilles," *Journal of Tropical Medicine and Hygiene* 69 (1966): 23–35; Philip D. Curtin, "Epidemiology and the Slave Trade," *Political Science Quarterly* 83, no. 2 (New York, 1968): 190–216; Alfred W. Crosby, *The Columbian Exchange: Biological and Cultural Consequences of 1492* (Westport, Conn., 1972); B. W. Higman, *Slave Populations of the British Caribbean* (Baltimore, Md., 1984); Kenneth Kiple, ed., *The African Exchange: Toward a Biological History of Black People,* (Durham, N.C., 1987); Richard Sheridan, *Doctors and Slaves: A Medical and Demographic History of Slavery in the British West Indies, 1680–1834,* (Cambridge, U.K., 1985); Robert Jay Lifton, *The Broken Connection: On Death and the Continuity of Life* (New York, 1979). For a particularly impressive study of the impact of death on everyday life in Brazil, a former slave society, see Nancy Scheper-Hughes, *Death without Weeping: The Violence of Everyday Life in Brazil* (Berkeley, Calif., 1992).

8. Sidney W. Mintz and Richard Price, *The Birth of African-American Culture: An Anthropological Perspective* (Boston, 1992 [1976]); Richard Price, "The Miracle of Creolization: A Retrospective," *New West Indian Guide* 75, nos. 1 and 2 (2001): 35–64; Michel-Rolph Trouillot, "Culture on the Edges: Creolization in the Plantation Context," *Plantation Society in the Americas* 1, no. 1 (Spring 1998): 8–28; Stephan Palmié, "Is There a Model in the Muddle? 'Creolization' in African Americanist History and Anthropology," in Charles Stewart, ed., *Creolization: History, Ethnography, Theory* (London, 2007), 178–200.

9. For historians' approaches to cultural transformation in slavery, see especially Kamau Brathwaite, *The Development of Creole Society in Jamaica, 1770–1820* (Oxford, 1971); Ira Berlin, *Many Thousands Gone: The First Two*

Centuries of Slavery in North America (Cambridge, Mass., 1998); Philip D. Morgan, *Slave Counterpoint: Black Culture in the Eighteenth-Century Chesapeake and Lowcountry* (Chapel Hill, N.C., 1998); John Thornton, *Africa and Africans in the Making of the Atlantic World, 1400–1800,* 2nd ed. (Cambridge, U.K., 1998); Michael Gomez, *Exchanging Our Country Marks: The Transformation of African Identities in the Colonial and Antebellum South* (Chapel Hill, N.C., 1998); Paul E. Lovejoy, ed., *Identity in the Shadow of Slavery* (London, 2000); Gwendolyn Midlo Hall, *Slavery and African Ethnicities in the Americas* (Chapel Hill, N.C., 2005). For a compelling critique of the way the concept of identity has constrained histories of politics, see Frederick Cooper, *Colonialism in Question: Theory, Knowledge, History* (Berkeley, Calif., 2005), 59–91. On cultural borrowing and appropriation, see Stephan Palmié, *Wizards and Scientists: Explorations in Afro-Cuban Modernity and Tradition* (Durham, N.C., 2003), esp. 137–139; and Joseph Roach, *Cities of the Dead: Circum-Atlantic Performance* (New York, 1996).

10. Patrick Browne, *The Civil and Natural History of Jamaica* (London, 1789 [1756]), v, 9; Specifically, I employ what historian David Armitage has termed a *cis*-Atlantic approach. See David Armitage, "Three Concepts of Atlantic History," in David Armitage and Michael J. Braddick, *The British Atlantic World, 1500–1800* (New York, 2002), 11–27.

11. James C. Scott, *Domination and the Arts of Resistance: Hidden Transcripts* (New Haven, Conn., 1990), xii.

12. Grey Gundaker, "Creolization, Complexity, and Time," *Historical Archaeology* 34, no. 3 (2000): 124; Lee Drummond, "The Cultural Continuum: A Theory of Intersystems," *Man* 15, no. 2 (June 1980): 352–374; Philip D. Morgan, "The Cultural Implications of the Atlantic Slave Trade: African Regional Origins, American Destinations, and New World Developments," *Slavery and Abolition* 18, no. 1 (April 1997): 122–145.

1. *Worlds of Wealth and Death*

1. Charles Leslie, *A True and Exact Account of Jamaica* (Edinburgh, 1740), 50–51.

2. Richard S. Dunn, *Sugar and Slaves: The Rise of the Planter Class in the English West Indies, 1624–1713* (New York, 1972), 19–21.

3. Philip D. Curtin, *The Rise and Fall of the Plantation Complex: Essays in Atlantic History* (Cambridge, U.K., 1990), 23–27; Dunn, *Sugar and Slaves,* 46–83.

4. Dunn, *Sugar and Slaves,* 20; Kenneth Morgan, *Slavery, Atlantic Trade, and the British Economy, 1660–1800* (Cambridge, U.K., 2000), 18–24.

5. Dunn, *Sugar and Slaves,* 149–223; Richard Sheridan, *Sugar and Slavery: An Economic History of the British West Indies, 1623–1775* (Baltimore, Md., 1973), 208–233; "State of Jamaica in the Year 1739 at the Time of Pacification of the Maroon Blacks," Long Papers, Papers on the Statistics of Jamaica, British Library, Add. Ms. 12435; Trevor Burnard, "A Failed Settler Society: Marriage and Demographic Failure in Early Jamaica," *Journal of Social History* 28, no. 1 (Fall 1994): 64; Jack P. Greene, *Pursuits of Happiness: The Social Development of Early Modern British Colonies and the Formation of American Culture* (Chapel Hill, N.C., 1988), 159–160; Trevor Burnard, "E Pluribus Plures: African Ethnicities in Seventeenth and Eighteenth Century Jamaica," *Jamaican Historical Review* 21 (2001): 10; Return of the Number of White Inhabitants, Free People of Colour, and Slaves in the Island of Jamaica, November 1788, PRO, CO 137 / 87, f. 173. The population figure for 1838 is estimated from the census of 1841. See George W. Roberts, *The Population of Jamaica* (Cambridge, U.K., 1957), 330.

6. These figures are drawn from T. G. Burnard, "'Prodigious Riches': The Wealth of Jamaica before the American Revolution," *Economic History Review* 54, no. 3 (2001): 506–524.

7. Andrew Jackson O'Shaughnessy, *An Empire Divided: The American Revolution and the British Caribbean* (Philadelphia, 2000), 3–33; O'Shaughnessy, "The Formation of a Commercial Lobby: The West India Interest, British Colonial Policy and the American Revolution," *Historical Journal* 40, no. 1 (March 1997): 71–95.

8. Leslie quoted in Burnard, "'Prodigious Riches,'" 506; Edwards quoted in O'Shaughnessy, *An Empire Divided,* 3.

9. Burnard, "E Pluribus Plures," 777; Trevor Burnard, "European Migration to Jamaica," *William and Mary Quarterly* 53, no. 4 (October 1996), 9–10; Roberts, *The Population of Jamaica,* 32–33; Burnard, *Mastery, Tyranny, and Desire: Thomas Thistlewood and His Slaves in the Anglo-Jamaican World* (Chapel Hill, N.C., 2004), 16–17.

10. David W. Galenson, *White Servitude in Colonial America: An Economic Analysis* (Cambridge, U.K., 1981), 84–85; Burnard, "European Migration to Jamaica," 778, 782–783; N. A. M. Rodger, *The Wooden World: An Anatomy of the Georgian Navy* (London, 1988), 104.

11. *Johnny New-come in the Island of Jamaica* (William Holland, Oxford St., 1800), Institute of Jamaica, P / 132 D.VI; Roger Norman Buckley, *The British Army in the West Indies: Society and the Military in the Revolu-*

tionary Age (Gainesville, Fla., 1998), 37–38, 179–184; Buckley, "The Frontier in the Jamaican Caricatures of Abraham James," *Yale University Library Gazette* 58, nos. 3–4 (April 1984): 152–162.

12. Bernard Bailyn, *Voyagers to the West: A Passage in the Peopling of America on the Eve of the Revolution* (New York, 1986), 220–221, 224, 215, 238.

13. M. Dorothy George, *London Life in the 18th Century* (New York, 1925), 21–61; John Landers, *Death and the Metropolis: Studies in the Demographic History of London, 1670–1830* (Cambridge, U.K., 1993), 86–88.

14. Bailyn, *Voyagers to the West*, 238; Alan L. Karras, *Sojourners in the Sun: Scottish Migrants in Jamaica and the Chesapeake, 1740–1800* (Ithaca, N.Y., 1992), 14–15; T. C. Smout, N. C. Landsman, and T. M. Devine, "Scottish Migration in the Seventeenth and Eighteenth Centuries," in Nicholas Canny, ed., *Europeans on the Move: Studies on European Migration, 1500–1800* (Oxford, 1994), 76–112.

15. *Marly; or, a Planter's Life in Jamaica* (Glasgow, 1828), 5; Jack Jingle, quoted in B. W. Higman, *Slave Population and Economy in Jamaica, 1800–1934* (Kingston, 1995 [1976]), 129.

16. Douglas Hall, "Absentee Proprietorship in the British West Indies, to about 1850," *Jamaican Historical Review* 4 (1964): 15–35; Lowell J. Ragatz, "Absentee Landlordism in the British Caribbean, 1750–1833," *Agricultural History* 5 (1931): 7–24; Gad Heuman, "The Social Structure of Slave Societies in the Caribbean," in Franklin W. Knight, ed., *General History of the Caribbean,* vol. 3, *The Slave Societies of the Caribbean* (London, 1997): 153–154.

17. R. B. Sheridan, "Simon Taylor, Sugar Tycoon of Jamaica, 1740–1813," *Agricultural History* 45 (1971): 285–296; quotation, 286; Betty Wood, ed., "The Letters of Simon Taylor of Jamaica to Chaloner Arcedeckne, 1765–1775," in Betty Wood and Martin Lynn, eds., *Travel, Trade and Power in the Atlantic, 1765–1884* (Cambridge, U.K., 2002), 1–155.

18. Heuman, "The Social Structure of Slave Societies," 154; Edward Brathwaite, *The Development of Creole Society in Jamaica, 1770–1820* (Oxford, 1971), 135–150; Burnard, *Mastery, Tyranny, and Desire,* 19–22, 41–45, 66; quotation in *Marly,* 7; Christer Petley, "Slavery, Emancipation and the Creole World View of Jamaican Colonists, 1800–1834," *Slavery and Abolition* 26, no. 1 (April 2005): 93–114.

19. Burnard, *Mastery, Tyranny, and Desire,* 40; Philip D. Morgan, "Slaves and Livestock in Eighteenth-Century Jamaica: Vineyard Pen, 1750–1751," *William and Mary Quarterly* 52, no. 1 (January 1995): 47–76; Morgan, "Three Planters and Their Slaves: Perspectives on Slavery in Virginia, South Carolina, and Jamaica, 1750–1790," in Winthrop D. Jordan and Sheila L.

Skemp, eds., *Race and Family in the Colonial South* (Jackson, Miss., 1987), 68–78; Douglas Hall, *In Miserable Slavery: Thomas Thistlewood in Jamaica, 1750–1786* (Kingston, 1999 [1989]).

20. Burnard, *Mastery, Tyranny, and Desire,* 19; Daniel Defoe quoted in Peter Earle, *The World of Defoe* (New York, 1977), 131; Barbara Solow, "Slavery and Colonization," in Solow, ed., *Slavery and the Rise of the Atlantic System* (Cambridge, U.K., 1991), 21–42.

21. Richard B. Sheridan, *Doctors and Slaves: A Medical and Demographic History of Slavery in the British West Indies, 1680–1834* (Cambridge, U.K., 1985), 196. Slaves born on the island could generally expect to live longer than African migrants.

22. David Richardson, "The British Empire and the Atlantic Slave Trade, 1660–1807," *Oxford History of the British Empire,* vol. 3, *The Eighteenth Century* (New York, 1998), 440–464.

23. Ibid., 442; Richard Sheridan, "The Slave Trade to Jamaica, 1702–1808," in Barry W. Higman, ed., *Trade, Government and Society in Caribbean History, 1700–1920* (Kingston, 1983), 2; Colin Palmer, *Human Cargoes: The British Slave Trade to Spanish America, 1700–1739* (Urbana, Ill., 1981); David Eltis, Stephen D. Behrendt, David Richardson, and Herbert S. Klein, *The Trans-Atlantic Slave Trade: A Database on CD-ROM* (Cambridge, U.K., 1999).

24. David Richardson, "Through a Looking Glass: Olaudah Equiano and African Experiences of the British Atlantic Slave Trade," in Philip D. Morgan and Sean Hawkins, eds., *Black Experience and the Empire* (Oxford, 2004), 69.

25. Paul E. Lovejoy and David Richardson, "Trust, Pawnship, and Atlantic History: The Institutional Foundations of the Old Calabar Slave Trade," *American Historical Review* 104, no. 2 (April 1999): 333–355.

26. Philip D. Curtin, *The Atlantic Slave Trade: A Census* (Madison, Wisc., 1969), 22; Philip D. Morgan, "The Cultural Implications of the Atlantic Slave Trade: African Regional Origins, American Destinations and New World Developments," *Slavery and Abolition* 18, no. 1 (April 1997): 135. For Africans, these ethnic designations had more specific meanings. See Gwendolyn Midlo Hall, *Slavery and African Ethnicities in the Americas: Restoring the Links* (Chapel Hill, N.C., 2005).

27. This point is tellingly made in Stephanie Smallwood, "Commodified Freedom: Interrogating the Limits of Anti-Slavery Ideology in the Early Republic," *Journal of the Early Republic* 24 (Summer 2004): 292; Barbara L. Solow, "The Transatlantic Slave Trade: A New Census," *William and Mary Quarterly* 58, no. 1 (January 2001): 9–16.

28. See, for example, Herbert S. Klein and Stanley L. Engerman, "Long-Term Trends in African Mortality in the Transatlantic Slave Trade," in *Routes to Slavery: Direction, Ethnicity, and Mortality in the Transatlantic Slave Trade,* special issue, *Slavery and Abolition* 18, no. 1 (April 1997): 36–48.

29. For a summary of fifteen important autobiographical accounts, see Jerome S. Handler, "Survivors of the Middle Passage: Life Histories of Enslaved Africans in British America," *Slavery and Abolition* 23, no. 1 (April 2002): 25–56.

30. Igor Kopytoff and Suzanne Miers, "African 'Slavery' as an Institution of Marginality," in Kopytoff and Miers, eds., *Slavery in Africa: Historical and Anthropological Perspectives* (Madison, Wisc., 1977), 3–81; Paul E. Lovejoy, *Transformations in Slavery: A History of Slavery in Africa,* 2nd ed. (Cambridge, U.K., 2000), 112–139; Jane I. Guyer and Samuel M. Eno Belinga, "Wealth in People as Wealth in Knowledge: Accumulation and Composition in Equatorial Africa," *Journal of African History* 36, no. 1 (1995): 91–120; quotation from Robin Law, "Introduction," in *The British Atlantic Slave Trade,* vol. 1, *The Operation of the Slave Trade in Africa,* ed. Robin Law (London, 2003), quotations, xli–xlii, xlvii–xlix.

31. Richardson, "Through a Looking Glass," 64; C. G. A. Oldendorp, *A Caribbean Mission,* ed. Johann Jakob Bossard, trans. Arnold R. Highfield and Vladimir Barac (Ann Arbor, Mich., 1987 [1770]), 208; P. E. H. Hair, "The Enslavement of Koelle's Informants," *Journal of African History* 6, no. 2 (1965): 193–203.

32. As historian Joseph C. Miller has powerfully demonstrated for West-Central Africa, individuals were "kidnapped, sold, resold, and captured again in the course of repeatedly disrupted lifetimes." See Joseph C. Miller, *Way of Death: Merchant Capitalism and the Angolan Slave Trade, 1730–1830* (Madison, Wisc., 1988), 225. For a sensitive examination of "serial displacement" in the Bight of Biafra, see Alexander X. Byrd, "Captives and Voyagers: Black Migrants across the Eighteenth-Century World of Olaudah Equiano" (Ph.D. diss., Duke University, 2001), 37–49; Jerome S. Handler, "Life Histories of Enslaved Africans in Barbados," *Slavery and Abolition* 19, no. 1 (April 1998): 129–141; quotation, 132–133; Alexander Falconbridge, *An Account of the Slave Trade on the Coast of Africa* (London, 1788), 12; David Northrup, *Trade without Rulers: Pre-Colonial Economic Development in South-Eastern Nigeria* (Oxford, 1978), 105–107.

33. Quotation from Igor Kopytoff, "The Cultural Biography of Things: Commoditization as a Process," in Arjun Appadurai, ed., *The Social Life of Things: Commodities in Cultural Perspective* (Cambridge, U.K., 1986),

65; Orlando Patterson, *Slavery and Social Death: A Comparative Study* (Cambridge, Mass., 1982), 35–76; Walter Johnson, *Soul by Soul: Life inside the Antebellum Slave Market* (Cambridge, Mass., 1999), 19–44.

34. Olaudah Equiano, *The Interesting Narrative and Other Writings,* ed. Vincent Carretta (New York, 1995 [1789]), 47–54; Vincent Carretta, *Equiano the African: Biography of a Self-Made Man* (Athens, Ohio, 2005), 17–30; Vincent Carretta has raised reasonable doubts about Equiano's birthplace and the veracity of his account of enslavement in Africa. Nevertheless, whether it represented his personal experience or a composite of life histories, gleaned from other formerly enslaved Africans with whom he shared his London milieu, Equiano was accountable for the truth of collective experiences. Therefore, his account of Africa remains a reliable memorial of the enslavement process. See also Alexander X. Byrd, "Eboe, Country, Nation, and Gustavus Vassa's Interesting Narrative," *William and Mary Quarterly* 63, no. 1 (January 2006): 123–148.

35. Law, "Introduction," in *The British Atlantic Slave Trade,* 1:xliv.

36. Northrup, *Trade without Rulers,* 83, 153; Equiano, *The Interesting Narrative,* 54.

37. Patrick Manning, *Slavery and African Life, Occidental, Oriental, and African Slave Trades* (Cambridge, U.K., 1990), 58; Falconbridge, *An Account of the Slave Trade,* 19; Thomas Fowell Buxton, *The African Slave Trade and Its Remedy* (London, 1840), 117; Boniface Obichere, "Slavery and the Slave Trade in Niger Delta Cross River Basin," in Serge Daget, ed., *De la traite à l'esclavage* (Nantes, 1988), 2:48.

38. Falconbridge, *An Account of the Slave Trade,* 51–52; Hugh Crow, *Memoirs of the Late Captain Hugh Crow* (London, 1830), 36–37; "James Jones to Lord Hawkesbury," 26 July 1788, in Elizabeth Donnan, ed., *Documents Illustrative of the History of the Slave Trade to America* (New York, 1965), 2:590.

39. For a historical treatment of Atlantic African military campaigns, see John K. Thornton, *Warfare in Atlantic Africa, 1500–1800* (London, 1999); Lovejoy, *Transformations in Slavery,* 68–70; John Thornton, *Africa and Africans in the Making of the Atlantic World, 1400–1800,* 2nd ed. (Cambridge, U.K., 1998), 116–125; W. A. Richards, "The Import of Firearms into West Africa in the Eighteenth Century," *Journal of African History* 21 (1980): 45–46; Ray Kea, "Firearms and Warfare on the Gold and Slave Coasts from the Sixteenth to the Nineteenth Centuries," *Journal of African History* 12, no. 2 (1971): 185–213; Phyllis Martin, "The Trade of Loango in the Seventeenth and Eighteenth Centuries," in Richard Gray and David Birmingham, eds., *Pre-Colonial African Trade: Essays on Trade in Central and Eastern Africa before 1900* (London, 1970), 153.

40. Kwame Yeboa Daaku, *Trade and Politics on the Gold Coast, 1600–1720* (Oxford, 1970), 180; "W. de la Palma to Ass. of X, 5 September 1705," in A. Van Dantzig, ed., *The Dutch and the Guinea Coast, 1674–1742: A Collection of Documents at the Hague* (Accra, 1978), 112; "Short Memoir to Demonstrate That the Slave Trade Is Inseparable of the Free Trade" in Van Dantzig, *The Dutch and the Guinea Coast,* 240–244; J. D. Fage, *A History of West Africa: An Introductory Survey* (Aldershot, U.K., 1992 [1955]), 107–110; J. K. Fynn, *Asante and Its Neighbours, 1700–1807* (London, 1971), 57–83.

41. Manning, *Slavery and African Life,* 65–66; Adams quotation in John Adams, *Remarks on the Country Extending from Cape Palmas to the River Congo* (London, 1966 [1823]), 45. For descriptions of the coastal trading garrisons, see A. W. Lawrence, *Trade Castles and Forts of West Africa* (Stanford, Calif., 1964); Colin Palmer, *Human Cargoes: The British Slave Trade to Spanish America, 1700–1739* (Urbana, Ill., 1981), 42–44.

42. Robin Law, "Slave-Raiders and Middlemen, Monopolists and Free-Traders: The Supply of Slaves for the Atlantic Trade in Dahomey, c. 1715–1850," *Journal of African History* 30 (1989): 45–68; Law, *The Slave Coast of West Africa, 1550–1750: The Impact of the Atlantic Slave Trade on an African Society* (Oxford, 1991); Mahdi Adamu, "The Delivery of Slaves from the Central Sudan to the Bight of Benin in the Eighteenth and Nineteenth Centuries," in Henry A. Gemery and Jan S. Hogendorn, eds., *The Uncommon Market: Essays in the Economic History of the Atlantic Slave Trade* (New York, 1979), 172–178; Lovejoy, *Transformations in Slavery,* 59, 80; Michael A. Gomez, *Exchanging Our Country Marks: The Transformation of African Identities in the Colonial and Antebellum South* (Chapel Hill, N.C., 1998), 64–65, 91; John Matthews, *A Voyage to the River Sierra-Leone* (London, 1788), reprinted in Kenneth Morgan et al., eds., *The British Atlantic Slave Trade,* 1:189, 209–210.

43. See Miller, *Way of Death,* 442, 381, 151, 385, 389, 391, 399, 176, 201–203; see also Miller, "The Numbers, Origins, and Destinations of Slaves in the Eighteenth-Century Angolan Slave Trade," in Joseph E. Inikori and Stanley L. Engerman, eds., *The Atlantic Slave Trade: Effects on Economies, Societies, and Peoples in Africa, the Americas, and Europe* (Durham, N.C., 1992), 77–115; and Miller, "Central Africa during the Era of the Slave Trade, c. 1490s–1850s," in Linda M. Heywood, ed., *Central Africans and Cultural Transformations in the American Diaspora* (Cambridge, U.K., 2002), 56. See also Martin, "The Trade of Loango," 153.

44. Equiano, *The Interesting Narrative,* 55.

45. William Bosman, *A New and Accurate Description of the Coast of Guinea, Divided into the Gold, the Slave, and the Ivory Coasts* (London, 1967 [1704]), 365; John Newton, "Thoughts upon the African Slave Trade," in

Bernard Martin and Mark Spurrell, eds., *The Journal of a Slave Trader* (London, 1962), 103; Miller, *Way of Death,* 5; Robert Harms, *The Diligent: A Voyage through the Worlds of the Slave Trade* (New York, 2002), 299; Elisabeth Isichei, *Voices of the Poor in Africa* (Rochester, N.Y., 2002), 29, 30, 35, 39–41.

46. Incidences of ritual cannibalism occurred in West Africa as part of the practice of medicinal magic, especially to enhance military prowess or supernatural power. The Imbangala of West-Central Africa, ruthless warriors and inveterate slave traders, were known to practice ritual cannibalism in the seventeenth century. See Robin Law, "Human Sacrifice in Pre-Colonial West Africa," *African Affairs* 84, no. 334 (January 1985), 58; and John Thornton, "Religious and Ceremonial Life in the Kongo and Mbundu Areas," in Heywood, *Central Africans,* 82–83.

47. Hugh Crow, *Memoirs of the Captain Crow* (London, 1830), 33; Ashy quoted in Handler, "Life Histories of Enslaved Africans in Barbados," 134; Law, "Human Sacrifice," 57–58, 73.

48. Law, "Human Sacrifice," 67–68, 70; diary of Antera Duke, 6 November 1786, in Daryll Forde, ed., *Efik Traders of Old Calabar* (London, 1956), 50, 52. For clarity's sake, I have used the modern English transcription by A. W. Wilkie and D. Simmons; ibid., 19 December 1786, 52; Eltis, Behrendt, Richardson, and Klein, *The Trans-Atlantic Slave Trade;* Sheila Lambert, ed., *House of Commons Sessional Papers of the Eighteenth Century* (Wil-mington, Del., 1975) (hereafter *HCSP*), 69:276.

49. Robert W. Harms, *River of Wealth, River of Sorrow: The Central Zaire Basin in the Era of the Slave and Ivory Trade, 1500–1891* (New Haven, Conn., 1981), 197, 210; John Thornton, "Cannibals, Witches, and Slave Traders in the Atlantic World," *William and Mary Quarterly* 60, no. 2 (April 2003): 273–294.

50. Olifert Dapper, quoted in Isichei, *Voices of the Poor in Africa,* 53; Stephan Palmié, *Wizards and Scientists: Explorations in Afro-Cuban Modernity and Tradition* (Durham, N.C., 2002), 176–181; Rosalind Shaw, "The Production of Witchcraft/Witchcraft as Production: Memory, Modernity, and the Slave Trade in Sierra Leone," *American Ethnologist* 24, no. 4 (1997): 861–868; James H. Sweet, *Recreating Africa: Culture, Kinship, and Religion in the African-Portuguese World, 1441–1770* (Chapel Hill, N.C., 2003), 162–163; John M. Janzen, *Lemba, 1650–1930: A Drum of Affliction in Africa and the New World* (New York, 1982).

51. Miller, *Way of Death,* 4–5; Wyatt MacGaffey, "The West in Congolese Experience," in Philip D. Curtin, ed., *Africa and the West: Intellectual Responses to European Culture* (Madison, Wisc., 1972), 54–57. The legend

of the cowries maintained that the shells came from the waters just off the coast—they actually originated in the Indian Ocean—where they fed on the corpses of slaves dumped there. According to oral testimonies, "the bodies, or sometimes dismembered limbs, when pulled ashore were covered with attached cowries." Jan Hogendorn and Marion Johnson, *The Shell Money of the Slave Trade* (Cambridge, U.K., 1986), 156.

52. Committee instructions to Richard Miles, 14 November 1781, PRO, BT 6/6, f. 128; As an example of "death duties," in 1793 Captain Samuel Gamble paid "the King a duty of 15 Barrs and 3/4 for every Whiteman that died in the River" at Rio Nuñez, Sierra Leone. Bruce L. Mouser, *A Slaving Voyage to Africa and Jamaica: The Log of the Sandawn, 1793–1794* (Bloomington, Ind., 2002), 56, 82, 90; Jerome Bernard Weaves to Committee of Merchants, 30 January 1782, PRO, T 70/33, f. 10; extracts of letter from Cape Coast Castle relating to Mr. Hope, 8 March 1738, PRO, T 70/4, 122–123; Richard Miles to Company of Merchants, 6, 12, and 22 June 1782, PRO, T 70/33, f. 20; Mouser, *A Slaving Voyage,* 80.

53. Thornton, *Africa and Africans,* 251–253.

54. Equiano, *The Interesting Narrative,* 55. For a perceptive discussion of death among enslaved Africans from the Gold Coast see Stephanie E. Smallwood, *Saltwater Slavery: A Middle Passage from Africa to American Diaspora* (Cambridge, Mass., 2007), 135–152.

55. Lambert, *HCSP,* 69:276; Richardson, "Through a Looking Glass," 72.

56. Mouser, *A Slaving Voyage,* 98; Equiano, *The Interesting Narrative,* 58; James Field Stanfield, *Observations on a Guinea Voyage, in a Series of Letters Addressed to the Rev. Thomas Clarkson* (London: James Phillips, 1788), reprinted in John Oldfield, ed., *The British Transatlantic Slave Trade* (London, 2003), 3:124.

57. Attempts by abolitionists at the time and by modern scholars to quantify and explain slave mortality have a long history. See especially Buxton, *The African Slave Trade and Its Remedy,* chap. 2; Curtin, *The Atlantic Slave Trade,* 279–286; Miller, *Way of Death;* Stephen Behrendt, "The Annual Volume and Regional Distribution of the British Slave Trade, 1780–1807," *Journal of African History* 38 (1997): 187–211; and Herbert S. Klein and Stanley L. Engerman, "Long-Term Trends in African Mortality," 36–48. For the period 1780–1799 Behrendt puts the mortality rate for British ships much lower, between 0.8 and 5.1 percent. Behrendt, "The Annual Volume and Regional Distribution," 193; Richardson, "Through a Looking Glass," 73; For general discussions of mortality during the middle passage, see James Walvin, *Black Ivory: A History of British Slavery* (Washington, D.C., 1994), 38–58; Herbert S. Klein, *The*

Middle Passage: Comparative Studies in the Atlantic Slave Trade (Princeton, N.J., 1978); and Smallwood, *Saltwater Slavery,* 122–152.

58. Testimony of Alexander Falconbridge in Lambert, *HCSP,* 72:303. The shipmate relationship was fundamental to social organization among the enslaved in widely scattered areas of the Americas. See Sidney Mintz and Richard Price, *The Birth of African-American Culture: An Anthropological Perspective* (Boston, 1992), 43–44.

59. Thomas Walker to James Rogers, 20 February 1792, PRO, C 107/14; John Kennedy to James Rogers, 22 March 1792, PRO, C 107/6; David Richardson, ed., *Bristol, Africa, and the Eighteenth-Century Slave Trade to America,* vol. 4, *The Final Years, 1770–1807* (Bristol, 1996), 176; John Kennedy to James Rogers, 3 May 1792, PRO, C 107/6. On the practice of selling "refuse slaves" for discounted rates in an earlier period, see Smallwood, *Saltwater Slavery,* 176–177.

60. Kenneth Morgan, "James Rogers and the Bristol Slave Trade," *Historical Research* 76, no. 92 (May 2003): 199; John Cunningham to James Rogers, 20 April 1792, PRO, C 107/6.

61. Sales of One hundred and Twenty-nine Slaves imported in the Barque *Ruby,* Montego Bay, 11 April 1792, PRO, C 107/13. The mortality list was drawn up in compliance with the 1788 Dolben Act regulating the slave trade. See Montego Bay Customs House to James Rogers, Mortality List of Ship *Ruby,* 2 May 1792, PRO, C 107/6; Eltis, Behrendt, Richardson, and Klein, *The Trans-Atlantic Slave Trade.*

62. Equiano, *The Interesting Narrative,* 58.

63. Testimony of Alexander Falconbridge, Lambert, *HCSP,* 72:303.

64. Trevor Burnard and Kenneth Morgan, "The Dynamics of the Slave Market and Slave Purchasing Patterns in Jamaica, 1655–1788," *William and Mary Quarterly,* 3rd series, 58, no. 1 (January 2001): 205–228; Sales of One hundred and Twenty-nine Slaves imported in the Barque *Ruby,* Montego Bay, 11 April 1792, PRO, C 107/13; John Taylor to Simon Taylor, 6 January 1790, Taylor Family Papers, Institute for Commonwealth Studies, Taylor XIV, A, 51; Richardson, *Bristol, Africa,* 4:156.

65. Deaths from smallpox did decline over the course of the eighteenth century. Though plantation doctors in Jamaica began to inoculate slaves for smallpox as early as the 1760s, the Jamaican assembly approved establishment of a public vaccine only in 1813. See Sheridan, *Doctors and Slaves,* 254–267; Major Gen. Robert Hunter, Governor, to Lords of Trade and Plantation, 4 July 1732, cited in David L. Chandler, *Health and Slavery in Colonial Colombia* (New York, 1981 [1972]), 49–50; Edward Long, quoted in Sheridan, *Doctors and Slaves,* 254; Simon Taylor to Chaloner

Arcedeckne, 21 July 1787, Vanneck Papers, 3A/1787/12; Simon Taylor to Chaloner Arcedeckne, 26 January 1788, ibid., 3A/1788/1.

66. Burnard and Morgan, "The Dynamics of the Slave Market," 205–228.

67. Leslie, *A New and Exact Account of Jamaica,* 238; Mr. Stanley's 1791 testimony before Parliament, quoted in Buxton, *The African Slave Trade and Its Remedy,* 195; testimony of William Fitzmaurice, 9 March 1791, in Lambert, *HCSP,* 82:232; Thomas Thistlewood quoted in Douglas Hall, *In Miserable Slavery: Thomas Thistlewood in Jamaica, 1750–86* (Kingston, 1999 [1989]), 299; Burnard, *Mastery, Tyranny, and Desire,* 56.

68. See for example, Simon Taylor's comments on seasoning new arrivals in "The Letters of Simon Taylor," in Wood and Lynn, *Travel, Trade and Power,* 58, 87; Michael Mullin, *Africa in America: Slave Acculturation and Resistance in the American South and the British Caribbean, 1736–1831* (Urbana, Ill., 1992), 130–131.

69. Higman, *Slave Population and Economy in Jamaica,* 121–123.

70. Higman estimates that in 1832, no more than 50 percent of slaves were settled on sugar estates and another 6.4 percent worked on jobbing gangs that primarily serviced sugar plantations. Using the Jamaica poll tax roll for 1768, Richard Sheridan concludes that at least 84 percent of slaves were "involved either directly or indirectly in the sugar industry" by 1773. Though Higman suspects that the higher percentage is exaggerated, part of the discrepancy can be attributed to the expansion of the coffee industry in the late eighteenth and early nineteenth centuries. Even in Saint Andrew, which included Kingston, sugar planters owned nearly 50 percent of the slaves in the parish, according to the Saint Andrew Census of 1753. Ibid., 9–17; Richard Sheridan, "The Wealth of Jamaica in the Eighteenth Century," *Economic History Review* 18 (1965): 292–311; and David B. Ryden, "'One of the fertilist pleasentest Spotts': An Analysis of the Slave Economy in Jamaica's St. Andrew Parish, 1753," *Slavery and Abolition* 21, no. 1 (April 2000): 32–55; Robert Dirks, *The Black Saturnalia: Conflict and Its Ritual Expression on British West Indian Slave Plantations* (Gainesville, Fla., 1987), 19.

71. Richard S. Dunn, "'Dreadful Idlers' in the Cane Fields: The Slave Labor Pattern on a Jamaican Sugar Estate, 1762–1831," in Barbara L. Solow and Stanley L. Engerman, eds., *British Capitalism and Caribbean Slavery: The Legacy of Eric Williams* (Cambridge, U.K., 1987), 163–190. Much of the time that women spent disabled—noted down as "invalids" in the records—was during the late stages of pregnancy. Also see Dunn, "Sugar Production and Slave Women in Jamaica," in Ira Berlin and Philip D. Morgan, eds., *Cultivation and Culture: Labor and the Shaping of Slave*

Life in the Americas (Charlottesville, Va., 1993), 49–72; and "The Story of Two Jamaica Slaves: Sarah Affir and Robert McAlpine of Mesopotamia Estate," in Roderick A. McDonald, ed., *West Indies Accounts: Essays on the History of the British Caribbean and the Atlantic Economy* (Kingston, 1996), 188–210.

72. Dirks, *The Black Saturnalia,* 22; *Marly,* 164–165; Simon Taylor to Chaloner Arcedeckne, 23 July 1770, Vanneck Papers, 3A / 1770 / 9.

73. Simon Taylor to Chaloner Arcedeckne, 26 November 1781, ibid., 3A / 1781 / 27; Simon Taylor to Chaloner Arcedeckne, 30 January 1782, ibid., 3A / 1782 / 2; Benjamin McMahon, *Jamaica Plantership* (London, 1839), 58.

74. Dirks, *The Black Saturnalia,* 67–68, 77, and see also 56–96; Sheridan, *Doctors and Slaves,* 207–219; Kenneth F. Kiple and Virginia H. Kiple, "Deficiency Diseases in the Caribbean," *Journal of Interdisciplinary History* 11, no. 2 (1980): 197–215.

75. Higman, *Slave Population and Economy,* 123; Dunn, "'Dreadful Idlers,'" 178–179.

76. Sheridan, *Doctors and Slaves,* 200; William Sells, *Remarks on the Condition of the Slaves in the Island of Jamaica* (Shannon, U.K., 1972 [1823]), 18; Orlando Patterson, *Sociology of Slavery: An Analysis of the Origins, Development, and Structure of Negro Slave Society in Jamaica* (London, 1967), 101; Matthew Gregory Lewis, Esq., M.P., *Journal of a West India Proprietor, Kept during a Residence in the Island of Jamaica* (London, 1834), 97; Betty Wood and T. R. Clayton, "Slave Birth, Death and Disease on Golden Grove Plantation, Jamaica, 1765–1810," *Slavery and Abolition* 6, no. 2 (September 1985), 109; Sells, *Remarks on the Condition of the Slaves,* 18.

77. Lewis, *Journal of a West India Proprietor,* 97; Hall, *In Miserable Slavery,* 184–185.

78. Wood and Clayton, "Slave Birth, Death and Disease on Golden Grove Plantation," 108, 116; Dunn, "'Dreadful Idlers,'" 165; Journal of Radnor Plantation, 1822–1826, Institute of Jamaica, MS 180, 242–243; Michael Craton and Garry Greenland, *Searching for the Invisible Man: Slaves and Plantation Life in Jamaica* (Cambridge, Mass., 1978), 97; Michael Craton and James Walvin, *A Jamaican Plantation: The History of Worthy Park, 1670–1970* (Toronto, 1970), 130. For the 1739–1787 decrease of 2.4 percent see Patterson, *Sociology of Slavery,* 97; for the 1817–1832 decrease of 2.8 percent, see Higman, *Slave Population and Economy in Jamaica,* 101–102.

79. Richard B. Sheridan, "The Crisis of Slave Subsistence in the British West Indies during and after the American Revolution," *William and Mary Quarterly* 33, no. 4 (October 1976): 615–641; Sheridan, *Doctors and Slaves,* 158–162; William Beckford, *Remarks upon the Situation of the Negroes in*

Jamaica (London, 1788), 115–116; Simon Taylor to Chaloner Arcedeckne, 13 August 1786, Vanneck Papers, 3A/1786/15.

80. Simon Taylor to Chaloner Arcedeckne, 27 January 1769, Vanneck Papers, 3A/1769/2; B. W. Higman, *Slave Populations of the British Caribbean, 1807–1834* (Kingston, 1995 [1984]), 77.

81. Dunn, *Sugar and Slaves,* 334. Dunn's insight has been amplified by the careful research of Trevor Burnard, "A Failed Settler Society." First Nugent quotation from Philip Wright, ed., *Lady Nugent's Journal of Her Residence in Jamaica from 1801 to 1805* (Kingston, 2002), 18; Theodore Foulks, *Eighteen Months in Jamaica; with Recollections of the Late Rebellion* (London, 1833), 68–69; second Nugent quotation from Wright, *Lady Nugent's Journal,* 184.

82. Wright, *Lady Nugent's Journal,* 65. William Dodd, *Reflections on Death* (London, 1796 [1763]), 5.

83. I borrow the term "space of death" from the anthropologist Michael Taussig, *Shamanism, Colonialism, and the Wild Man: A Study in Terror and Healing* (Chicago, 1987). Joseph Roach's explication of anthropological approaches to funerary practice is useful here: "In Arnold van Gennep's seminal formulation of death as a rite of passage, the binary distinction that creates two categories, dead and alive, simultaneously creates in its interstices a threefold process of living, dying, and being dead. The middle state (dying, or more expressively, "passing") is the less stable stage of transition between more clearly defined conditions: it is called the 'liminal' (literally, 'threshold') stage, and it tends to generate the most intense experiences of ritual expectancy, activity, and meaning." See Joseph Roach, *Cities of the Dead: Circum-Atlantic Performance* (New York, 1996), 37.

2. Last Rites and First Principles

1. *Johnny New-come in the Island of Jamaica,* printed by William Holland, Oxford St., London, 1800, Institute of Jamaica, P/132 D.VI. The panel refers to the story of the three living and the three dead, popularized in England during the fourteenth century, in which three hunters meet three dead men, who tell them, "What you are, we were, and what we are, you will be." On memento mori icons, see Peter C. Jupp and Clare Gittings, *Death in England: An Illustrated History* (New Brunswick, N.J., 2000), 93–94, 151–152; James A. Hijaya, "American Gravestones and Attitudes toward Death: A Brief History," *Proceedings of the American Philosophical Society* 127, no. 5 (14 October 1983): 343–346.

2. Peter Brown, *The Cult of the Saints: Its Rise and Function in Latin Christianity* (Chicago, 1981), 24; Thomas W. Laqueur, "Bodies, Death, and Pauper Funerals," *Representations* 1, no. 1 (February 1983): 109–131.

3. Trevor Burnard, "A Failed Settler Society: Marriage and Demographic Failure in Early Jamaica," *Journal of Social History* 28, no. 1 (Fall 1994): 63.

4. For a fascinating example of the political power of a funeral oration, see the speech purportedly given in early eighteenth-century Guadeloupe at the burial of an enslaved man killed by his master for taking a loaf of bread. *A Letter from a Merchant at Jamaica to a Member of Parliament in London, Touching the African Trade; To which is added, a Speech made by a Black of Guadaloupe at the Funeral of a Fellow-Negro* (London, 1709).

5. William Beckford, *A Descriptive Account of the Island of Jamaica* (London, 1790), 2:388; Alexander Barclay, *A Practical View of the Present State of Slavery in the West Indies* (London, 1826), 135–136.

6. Barclay, *A Practical View,* 135–136. For a comparison to nineteenth-century Brazil see João José Reis, *Death Is a Festival: Funeral Rites and Rebellion in Nineteenth-Century Brazil* (Chapel Hill, N.C., 2003 [1991]), esp. 66–152.

7. Olaudah Equiano, *The Interesting Narrative and Other Writings,* ed. Vincent Carretta (New York, 1995 [1789]), 172; John Thornton, *Africa and Africans in the Making of the Atlantic World, 1400–1800,* 2nd ed. (Cambridge, U.K., 1998), 183–205; John Thornton, "The Coromantees: An African Cultural Group in Colonial North America and the Caribbean," *Journal of Caribbean History* 32, nos. 1 and 2 (1998): 161–178; Alexander X. Byrd, "Eboe, Country, Nation, and Gustavus Vassa's Interesting Narrative," *William and Mary Quarterly* 63, no. 1 (January 2006): 123–148; Douglas B. Chambers, "Ethnicity in the Diaspora: The Slave Trade and the Creation of African 'Nations' in the Americas," *Slavery and Abolition* 22, no. 3 (December 2001): 25–39. For a sophisticated interpretation of this process, see Joseph Roach, *Cities of the Dead: Circum-Atlantic Performance* (New York, 1996), esp. 59–63.

8. Edna Greene Medford, ed., *The New York African Burial Ground: History Final Report* (Washington, D.C., 2004), 175–179; Thornton, "The Coromantees," 168–169; Chambers, "Ethnicity in the Diaspora," 26–28; Michael Mullin, *Africa in America: Slave Acculturation and Resistance in the American South and the British Caribbean, 1736–1831* (Urbana, Ill., 1992), 62–74; Stephan Palmié, "Ethnogenetic Processes and Cultural Transfer in Afro-American Slave Populations," in Wolfgang Binder, ed., *Slavery in the Americas* (Würzburg, Germany, 1993), 337–363.

9. Melville J. Herskovits, *Trinidad Village* (New York, 1947), 300. See also Herskovits, *The Myth of the Negro Past* (Boston, 1990 [1941]), 201–206; R. Frey and Betty Wood, *Come Shouting to Zion: African American Protestantism in the American South and British Caribbean to 1830* (Chapel Hill, N.C., 1998), 22–26, 51–56. For a comparison with North America, see David R. Roediger, "And Die in Dixie: Funerals, Death, and Heaven in the Slave Community, 1700–1865," *Massachusetts Review* 22, no. 1 (Spring 1981): 163–183.

10. Richard Price, "Commentary on Monica Schuler, 'Afro-American Slave Culture," in Michael Craton, ed., *Roots and Branches: Current Directions in Slave Studies* (Toronto, 1979), 148.

11. Thornton, *Africa and Africans,* 235–246; Thornton, "Religious and Ceremonial Life in the Kongo and Mbundu Areas, 1500–1700," in Linda M. Heywood, ed., *Central Africans and Cultural Transformation in the American Diaspora* (Cambridge, U.K., 2002), 72–90; Thornton, "The Coromantees," 166–168; C. G. A. Oldendorp, *History of the Mission of the Evangelical Brethren on the Caribbean Islands of St. Thomas, St. Croix, and St. John,* ed. Johann Jakob Bossard, trans. Arnold R. Highfield and Vladimir Barac (Ann Arbor, Mich., 1987 [1770]), 198–199; Herskovits, *The Myth of the Negro Past,* 206; Trevor Burnard, *Mastery, Tyranny, and Desire: Thomas Thistlewood and His Slaves in the Anglo-Jamaican World* (Chapel Hill, N.C., 2004), 4; F. G. Cassidy and R. B. Le Page, eds., *Dictionary of Jamaican English,* 2nd ed. (Kingston, 2002), 164–165. For an example from the Gold Coast, see Thomas Thompson, *An Account of Two Missionary Voyages* (London, 1937 [1758]), 44–47. See also John S. Mbiti, *Introduction to African Religion,* 2nd ed. (London, 1991), 116–130; Mary Turner, "Religious Beliefs," in Franklin W. Knight, ed., *General History of the Caribbean,* vol. 3, *The Slave Societies of the Caribbean* (London, 1997), 287–321; Thornton, *Africa and Africans,* 235–271; Philip D. Curtin, *Two Jamaicas: The Role of Ideas in a Tropical Colony, 1830–1865* (Cambridge, Mass., 1955); Frey and Wood, *Come Shouting to Zion,* 30, 22–26, 51–54.

12. Charles Leslie, *A New and Exact Account of Jamaica* (Edinburgh, 1740), 325; Edward Long, *History of Jamaica* (London, 1970 [1774]), 2:421; Mathew Gregory Lewis, *Journal of a West India Proprietor Kept during a Residence in the Island of Jamaica* (London, 1834), 97–98; Stewart, *A View of the Present State of the Island,* 275–276; Barclay, *A Practical View,* 135; James M. Phillippo, *Jamaica: Its Past and Present State* (London, 1843), 244–245.

13. Leslie, *A New and Exact Account of Jamaica*, 325.

14. Phillippo, *Jamaica*, 244–245.

15. Oldendorp, *History of the Mission*, 183–184; Roger Bastide also traces the practice from French and Dutch Guiana to "Fanti-Ashanti culture," in Roger Bastide, *African Civilisations in the New World*, trans. by Peter Green (London, 1971), 58. Father Giovanni Antonio Cavazzi described the interrogation of a corpse at a burial ceremony in West-Central Africa. See James H. Sweet, *Recreating Africa: Culture, Kinship, and Religion in the African-Portuguese World, 1441–1770* (Chapel Hill, N.C., 2003), 176–179; John Matthews, *A Voyage to the River Sierra-Leone* (London, 1788), reprinted in Kenneth Morgan, Robin Law, John Oldfield, and David Ryden, eds., *The British Atlantic Slave Trade*, vol. 1, *The Operation of the Slave Trade in Africa*, ed. Robin Law (London, 2003), 163–167; Equiano, *The Interesting Narrative*, 42–43.

16. Victor Turner applied the term "communitas," a sense of comity considered by participants in a ritual as "a timeless condition, an eternal now, as 'a moment in and out of time,' or as a state to which the structural view of time is not applicable." Victor Turner, *Dramas, Fields, and Metaphors: Symbolic Action in Human Society* (Ithaca, N.Y., 1974), 238.

17. Stewart, *A View of the Present State of the Island*, 275.

18. Thornton, "The Coromantees," 168–170; W. J. Gardner, *A History of Jamaica from Its Discovery by Christopher Columbus to the Year 1872* (London, 1971 [1873]), 385–386; diary of Thomas Thistlewood, 5 June 1767, cited in Douglass Hall, *In Miserable Slavery: Thomas Thistlewood in Jamaica, 1750–1786* (London, 1989), 145; Leslie, *A New and Exact Account of Jamaica*, 326.

19. Diary of Thomas Thistlewood, 21 March 1758, quoted in Hall, *In Miserable Slavery*, 83, 145.

20. Long, *The History of Jamaica*, 2:421; Barclay, *A Practical View*, 132–133. I am grateful to Ingrid Monson, Quincy Jones Professor of Music at Harvard University, for sharing her interpretation of Barclay's musical notation.

21. Leslie, *A New and Exact Account of Jamaica*, 325–326; Beckford, *A Descriptive Account*, 390. For a penetrating account of seventeenth-century African music in Jamaica, see Richard Cullen Rath, "African Music in Seventeenth Century Jamaica: Cultural Transit and Transition," *William and Mary Quarterly*, 3rd series, 50, no. 4 (October 1993): 700–726. For a comparison with antebellum North America, see Shane White and Graham White, *The Sounds of Slavery: Discovering African American History through Songs, Sermons, and Speech* (Boston, 2005), 11–19, 162–164.

22. W. Stanford to Bishop Porteus, 22 July 1788, Fulham Papers, Lambeth Palace Library, vol. 18, f. 66; diary of Thomas Thistlewood, 7 August 1767, quoted in Hall, *In Miserable Slavery,* 145; Mullin, *Africa in America,* 64; Beckford, *A Descriptive Account,* 388; Leslie, *A New and Exact Account of Jamaica,* 325; Long, *History of Jamaica,* 2:421. For a comparison with twentieth-century Africa, see J. H. Kwabena Nketia, *Funeral Dirges of the Akan People* (London, 1955).

23. Burnard, *Mastery, Tyranny, and Desire,* 4; James Stewart, *A View of the Present State of the Island of Jamaica* (Edinburgh, 1823), 270, 274–276; Leslie, *A New and Exact Account of Jamaica,* 326.

24. Dirks, *The Black Saturnalia,* 148; Leslie, *A New and Exact Account of Jamaica,* 325; Phillippo, *Jamaica,* 246; Edwards, *History of the British Colonies,* 4:66–67.

25. Thornton, "The Coromantees," 169; Long, *History of Jamaica,* 2:416; Edwards, *History of the British Colonies,* 4:77.

26. Burnard, *Mastery, Tyranny, and Desire,* 128.

27. Long, *History of Jamaica,* 2:421–422; David Hackett Fischer, *Albion's Seed: Four British Folkways in America* (New York, 1989), 700, 702.

28. Lewis, *Journal of a West India Proprietor,* 98; Stewart, *A View of the Present State of the Island,* 276.

29. On the relation between compensation claims and slave resistance in another British Caribbean slave society, see David Barry Gaspar, "'To Bring Their Offending Slaves to Justice': Compensation and Slave Resistance in Antigua, 1669–1763," *Caribbean Quarterly* 30, nos. 3–4 (1984): 45–59. See also the explanation of a nineteenth-century apologist for Jamaican slavery in Barclay, *A Practical View,* 205–207; Saint Thomas-in-the-Vale Vestry Minutes, 16 April 1791, Jamaica Archives, Local Government, 2/1, 56.

30. Kingston Vestry Minutes, 8 July 1745, Jamaica Archives, Local Government, 2/6, 27; *Journals of the Assembly of Jamaica* (St. Jago de la Vega, Kingston, 1663–1826), vols. 4, 15; Diana Paton, "Punishment, Crime, and the Bodies of Slaves in Eighteenth-Century Jamaica," *Journal of Social History* 34, no. 4 (2001): 935; *Journals of the Assembly of Jamaica,* 4:491, 493, 502; Leslie, *A New and Exact Account of Jamaica,* 232.

31. See Burnard, *Mastery, Tyranny, and Desire,* 21; Christer Petley, "Slavery, Emancipation and the Creole Worldview of Jamaican Colonists, 1800–1834," *Slavery and Abolition* 26, no. 1 (April 2005): 98–100.

32. "An Act for Settling the Proceedings and Fees of the Coroners of This Island," 19 December 1770, *The Laws of Jamaica: Comprehending all the*

Acts in Force, passed between the First Year of the Reign of King George the Third, and the Thirty-Second Year of the Reign of George the Third (St. Jago de la Vega, Jamaica, 1792–1799), 2:97–98; Michael MacDonald, "The Secularization of Suicide in England, 1660–1800," *Past and Present,* no. 111 (May 1986): 50–100; and R. F. Hunnisett, "The Importance of Eighteenth-Century Coroners' Bills," in E. W. Ives and A. H. Manchester, eds., *Law, Litigants and the Legal Profession* (London, 1983), 126–139; "An Act for Regulating Fees," 1711, *The Laws of Jamaica,* 1:106.

33. *Journals of the Assembly of Jamaica,* entry of 4 November 1758, 5:95; ibid., 6:304, 306, 314, 329; vol. 7:34, 42, 99, 104, 123, 127, 274, 338, 340, 348, 407, 424, 436, 550, 562, 631, 641; ibid., 8:302, 212, 317, 353, 451, 474; ibid., 10:529, 556; "An Act for Settling the Proceedings and Fees of the Coroners of This Island," *The Laws of Jamaica,* 2:97–98.

34. "Extract from the Supplement to the Cornwall Chronicle," 29 December 1787, Fulham Papers, vol. 18, ff. 12–14; For inquest rates, see, for example, Saint Thomas-in-the-Vale Vestry Minutes, 1792–1795, Jamaica Archives, Local Government, 2/1, 1. The principle of differentiating the value of state services performed upon bodies was established in the 1711 Act for Regulating Fees, which stipulated that provost-marshals be paid five pounds for the execution of white persons and one pound for the execution of slaves. *The Laws of Jamaica,* 1:104–105. The principle was upheld in the lesser rate paid to parish rectors to perform burials for free people of color. See Saint Ann Vestry Minutes, 28 May 1796, Jamaica Archives, Local Government, 2/9, 161. The Assembly of Jamaica raised the fees for coroners islandwide to five pounds in 1801, following another petition from several coroners for the county of Cornwall. See *Journals of the Assembly of Jamaica,* 10:529, 556; John Lunan, ed., *An Abstract of the Laws of Jamaica Relating to Slaves* (St. Jago de la Vega, Jamaica, 1819), 145–147.

35. Benjamin McMahon, *Jamaica Plantership* (London, 1839), 24–26.

36. Ibid.

37. Alfred Spencer, ed., *Memoirs of William Hickey* (London, 1918), 2:19–20. The expectant undertaker became a stock figure in white folklore, on down to the twentieth century: "The author's maternal grandfather," writes J. W. Fortesque, "served as a subaltern at Jamaica in the first years of the nineteenth century, and used to tell a story that when he landed he saw a mysterious individual with a long wand, who looked at him up and down with extreme attention and seemed particularly interested in his height and build. He discovered that this was an undertaker, who was resolved not to be taken unawares, for burial of course must follow death

very speedily in the tropics." J. W. Fortesque, *History of the British Army,* vol. II, *1815–1838* (London, 1923), 38n.

38. *Journals of the Assembly of Jamaica,* 4:202, 241, 263, 265–266; Kingston Vestry Minutes, 16 March 1747, Jamaica Archives, Local Government, 2/6, 100.

39. "Act for Marriages, Christenings, Churchings & Burialls," 1662, PRO, CO 139/1, f. 51; Peter Mardsen, *An Account of the Island of Jamaica; with Reflections on the Treatment, Occupation, and Provisions of the Slaves* (Newcastle, 1788), 41; According to John Stewart, who spent the first two decades of the nineteenth century in Jamaica, the fixed stipend accounted for less than a quarter of a rector's income. Stewart maintained that rectors could collect between fifteen hundred and three thousand pounds annually in fees for baptisms, marriages, and funerals. All values listed are in Jamaican currency unless otherwise noted. John Stewart, *A View of the Past and Present State of the Island of Jamaica* (Edinburgh, 1823), 149–150; R. A. Minter, *Episcopacy without Episcopate: The Church of England in Jamaica before 1824* (Worcester, U.K., 1990), 119–121.

40. "State of the Church in Jamaica," Fulham Papers, Lambeth Palace Library, vol. 18, ff. 45–52; Kingston Vestry Minutes, 12 January 1747, Jamaica Archives, Local Government, 2/6, 94, and 22 January 1746, 2/6, 55, 96.

41. Saint Ann Parish Vestry Minutes, 28 May 1796, Jamaica Archives, Local Government, 2/9, 161; Kingston Vestry Minutes, 24 March 1746, Jamaica Archives, Local Government, 2/6, 57; *Royal Gazette,* 8–15 May 1813, postscript to the *Royal Gazette,* vol. 35, no. 20, 1813, PRO, CO 141/2, 24.

42. Long, *History of Jamaica,* 2:238–239.

43. John Barton to Lord Bishop Porteus of London, 21 May 1796, Fulham Papers, Lambeth Palace Library, vol. 18, ff. 78–81.

44. Ibid.

45. "State of the Church in Jamaica," ibid., ff. 51, 151–152; *Marly; or, a Planter's Life in Jamaica* (Glasgow, 1828), 205.

46. Kingston Vestry Minutes, 19 July 1745, Jamaica Archives, Local Government, 2/6, 28; David Cressy, *Birth, Marriage, and Death: Ritual, Religion, and the Life Cycle in Tudor and Stuart England* (Oxford, 1997), 425; *Journals of the Assembly of Jamaica,* 8:555; *Journals of the Assembly of Jamaica,* 9:24–25, 29, 32, 58; Saint Ann Vestry Minutes, 16 May 1795, Jamaica Archives, Local Government, 2/9, 143; Westmoreland Vestry Minutes, 20 January 1817, Jamaica Archives, Local Government 2/7, 13.

47. See, for example, the description of the 1820 funeral for Henry Grattan in the *Jamaica Courant,* Saturday, 26 August 1820, 15, no. 205; Sir Hans Sloane, *A Voyage to the Islands Madera, Barbados, Nieves, S. Christophers and Jamaica* (London, 1707), xlviii.

48. Funeral bill of Thomas Hall, 10 November 1772, Barnett-Hall Collection, Mandeville Special Collections Library, University of California, San Diego, MSS 220, box 3, folder 40.

49. Hall, *In Miserable Slavery,* 257; Vere Langford Oliver, ed., *Caribbeana, being Miscellaneous Papers Relating to the History, Topography, and Antiquities of the British West Indies* (London, 1916), 4:95; Philip Wright, ed., *Monumental Inscriptions of Jamaica* (London, 1966), 18, 176–177.

50. Diary of Thomas Thistlewood, 17 June 1778, quoted in Hall, *In Miserable Slavery,* 256–257; Cressy, *Birth, Marriage and Death,* 435–438.

3. *Expectations of the Dead*

1. Raymond T. Smith, *Kinship and Class in the West Indies: A Genealogical Study of Jamaica and Guyana* (Chicago, 1988); B. W. Higman, "The Slave Family Household in the British West Indies, 1800–1834," *Journal of Interdisciplinary History* 6, no. 2 (Fall 1975): 261–287; Orlando Patterson, "Persistence, Continuity, and Change in the Jamaican Working-Class Family," *Journal of Family History* 7, no. 2 (Summer 1982): 135–161.

2. *Johnny New-come in the Island of Jamaica,* published by William Holland, Oxford St., 1800, Institute of Jamaica, P/132 D.VI.

3. Trevor Burnard, "Female Continuity and Female Independence in Jamaica, 1665–1734," *Continuity and Change* 7, no. 2 (1992): 181–198; Burnard, *Creole Gentlemen: The Maryland Elite, 1691–1776* (New York, 2002), 139–166; Jonathan E. Crowley, "The Importance of Kinship: Testamentary Evidence from South Carolina," *Journal of Interdisciplinary History* 16, no. 4 (Spring 1986): 559–577; Carole Shammas, "English Inheritance Law and Its Transfer to the Colonies," *American Journal of Legal History* 31, no. 2 (April 1987): 145–163; Lee J. Alston and Morton Owen Schapiro, "Inheritance Laws across Colonies: Causes and Consequences," *Journal of Economic History* 44, no. 2 (June 1984): 277–287; Holly Brewer, "Entailing Aristocracy in Colonial Virginia: 'Ancient Feudal Restraints' and Revolutionary Reform," *William and Mary Quarterly* 54, no. 2 (April 1997): 307–346. For an examination of the way in which enslaved women's reproductive labor figured in testators' expectations in seventeenth-century Barbados and South Carolina, see Jennifer L. Morgan, *Laboring Women: Reproduction and Gender in New World Slavery* (Philadelphia, 2004), 69–106.

4. Trevor Burnard, "Inheritance and Independence: Women's Status in Early Colonial Jamaica," *William and Mary Quarterly,* 3rd series, 48 (1991): 97; Edward Long, cited in R. A. Minter, *Episcopacy without Episcopate: The*

Church of England in Jamaica before 1824 (Worcester, U.K., 1990), 126–127; *Journals of the Assembly of Jamaica,* 10:63–64.

5. R. B. Sheridan, "Simon Taylor, Sugar Tycoon of Jamaica, 1740–1813," *Agricultural History* 45 (1971): 288; Simon Taylor to Chaloner Arcedeckne, 25 January 1773, in Betty Wood, ed., "The Letters of Simon Taylor of Jamaica to Chaloner Arcedeckne, 1765–1775," in Betty Wood and Martin Lynn, eds., *Travel, Trade and Power in the Atlantic, 1765–1884* (Cambridge, U.K., 2002), 111–112; B. W. Higman, *Plantation Jamaica, 1750–1850: Capital and Control in a Colonial Economy* (Kingston, 2005), 173–176.

6. Simon Taylor to Sir John Taylor, 27 January 1783, Taylor Family Papers, ICS, I/A/27.

7. Ibid.

8. Ibid.; Simon Taylor to Robert Taylor, 18 June 1804, ibid., ICS, I/F/56.

9. Philip Wright, ed., *Lady Nugent's Journal of Her Residence in Jamaica from 1801 to 1805* (Kingston, 2002), 68.

10. Ibid., 65; Simon Taylor to Chaloner Arcedeckne, Kingston, 1 June 1786, Vanneck-Arcedeckne Papers, 3A/1786/10. For a penetrating analysis of the correspondence between Simon Taylor and Sir Simon Richard Brisset Taylor, see Sarah M. S. Pearsall, "'After All These Revolutions': Epistolary Identities in an Atlantic World, 1760–1815" (Ph.D. diss., Harvard University, 2001), 182–209; quotations from Simon Taylor, 186 and 188–189.

11. Simon Taylor to Robert Taylor, 14 January 1806, Taylor Family Papers, ICS, I/G/40; Simon Taylor to Robert Taylor, 23 December, 1811, ibid., I/J/49; Pearsall, "After All These Revolutions,'" 205; John Shand to Sir Simon Richard Brissett Taylor, 25 November 1812, ibid., VI/C/8; John Shand to Sir Simon Richard Brissett Taylor, 21 April 1813, ibid., VI/C/9; Sir Simon Richard Brissett Taylor to Andrew Bogle, 7 July 1813, ibid., VI/C/11; Pearsall, "After All These Revolutions,'" 205, 208–209. Will of Simon Taylor, proved 1813, Island Record Office, Spanish Town, Jamaica.

12. *Journals of the Assembly of Jamaica,* 6:303.

13. Mary Ricketts to William Henry Ricketts, Esq., 23 June 1757, Correspondence of the Families of Ricketts and Jervis, vol. 1: Letters Relating to Jamaica, 1757–1799, British Library Add. MS 30001, f. 6. For an interesting discussion of Mary Ricketts's dislike of Jamaica see Pearsall, "After All These Revolutions,'" 301–306.

14. Edward Long, *History of Jamaica* (London, 1970 [1774]), 2:286; Trevor Burnard, "'A Matron in Rank, A Prostitute in Manners': The Manning Divorce of 1741 and Class, Gender, Race and the Law in Eighteenth-Century Jamaica," in Verene A. Shepherd, ed., *Working Slavery, Pricing*

Freedom: Perspectives from the Caribbean, Africa, and the African Diaspora (New York, 2002), 133–151; Hilary McD. Beckles, "White Women and Slavery in the Caribbean," *History Workshop Journal* 36 (Autumn 1993): 66–82. For Phillips's story, see Clinton V. Black, *Tales of Old Jamaica* (London, 1966), 89–99; and Kathleen Wilson, *The Island Race: English-ness, Empire and Gender in the Eighteenth Century* (New York, 2003), 129–168.

15. Burnard, "Inheritance and Independence," 97, 104, 106; Burnard, "Female Continuity and Female Independence," 181–198; *Journals of the Assembly of Jamaica,* 6:589.

16. *Journals of the Assembly of Jamaica,* 6:303, 307, 312, 314, 329; W. H. Ricketts to Polly, 18 December, 1770, British Library, Add. MS 30001, f. 44.

17. S. Jervis to Mrs. Ricketts [n.d., c. 1790s], British Library, Add. MS 30001, ff. 85–86; George Ricketts to Mrs. Ricketts, 30 October, 1798, British Library Add. MS 30001, f. 80; George Ricketts to Mrs. Ricketts, Will of Anne Ricketts enclosed, 1799, British Library Add. MS 30001, ff. 80–81.

18. Trevor Burnard, *Creole Gentlemen,* 140; Crowley, "The Importance of Kinship," 568; Burnard, "Inheritance and Independence," 101.

19. Simon Taylor to Chaloner Arcedeckne, 25 January 1773, in Wood, "Letters of Simon Taylor," 110–111. See also Higman, *Plantation Jamaica,* 175–176.

20. Charles Kelsall to Simon Taylor, 25 June 1777, Vanneck-Arcedeckne Papers, 3G/2; Frances Harris, Simon Taylor, and John Kelly to Charles Kelsall, 26 June 1777, ibid.; The Narration of Charles Kelsall, 27 June 1777, ibid; Simon Taylor to Chaloner Arcedeckne, 8 April 1781, Vanneck-Arcedeckne Papers, 3A/1781/4.

21. *The Laws of Jamaica,* vol. 1, *Comprehending all the Acts in Force, passed between the Thirty-Second Year of the Reign of King Charles the Second, and the Thirty-third Year of the Reign of George the Third* (St. Jago de la Vega, Jamaica, 1792), 278–280. The inventories required by the law have provided historians with valuable records of eighteenth-century Jamaican wealth and estate management. See especially Richard Pares, *Merchants and Planters* (Cambridge, U.K., 1960); R. B. Sheridan, "The Wealth of Jamaica in the Eighteenth Century," *Economic History Review,* series 2, 18 (1965): 292–311; and B. W. Higman, *Slave Population and Economy in Jamaica, 1807–1834* (Kingston, 1995 [1976]); *Journals of the Assembly of Jamaica,* 4:443, 446; and *The Laws of Jamaica,* vol. 2, *Comprehending all the Acts in Force, passed between the First Year of the Reign of King George the Third and the Thirty-Second Year of the Reign of George the Third* (St. Jago de la Vega, 1792–1799), 184–185.

22. Benjamin McMahon, *Jamaica Plantership* (London, 1839), 224; *Marly, or, a Planter's Life in Jamaica* (Glasgow, 1828), 205–207.

23. McMahon, *Jamaica Plantership*, 222–231.

24. "Testimony of Hercules Ross, Esq.," 16 March 1791, in Sheila Lambert, ed., *HCSP,* 2:257; Long, *History of Jamaica,* 1:399.

25. Long, *History of Jamaica,* 1:499–502; *Journals of the Assembly of Jamaica,* 6:551, 620; *The Laws of Jamaica,* 2:185.

26. Long, *History of Jamaica,* 1:502; Lowell Joseph Ragatz, *The Fall of the Planter Class in the British Caribbean, 1763–1833* (New York, 1963 [1928]), 9; Gilbert Mathison, Esq., *Notices Respecting Jamaica in 1808, 1809, 1810* (London, 1811), 15; "Return of the Provost Marshal General of Jamaica, of the Number of Slaves Sold under Execution for Debt, 1808–1827" (no. 524), 1828, *British Parliamentary Papers* (Shannon, 1968), 26:26–29. Not until the end of 1826 did the assembly pass a law to prevent separation of families by writ and seizure. See "An Act to Alter and Amend to the Slave Laws of this Island," 22 December 1826, clause 5, *The Laws of Jamaica, Passed in the Seventh Year of the Reign of King George the Fourth* (Kingston, 1827), 198.

27. See Orlando Patterson, *Sociology of Slavery: An Analysis of the Origins, Development and Structure of Negro Slave Society in Jamaica* (London, 1967), 90–92; Barbara Bush, *Slave Women in Caribbean Society, 1650–1838* (Bloomington, Ind., 1990), 31–32.

28. Bush, *Slave Women in Caribbean Society,* 110–119; Hilary McD. Beckles, *Centering Women: Gender Discourses in Caribbean Slave Society* (Princeton, N.J., 1999), 22–37; Trevor Burnard, "The Sexual Life of an Eighteenth-Century Jamaican Slave Overseer," in Merril D. Smith, ed., *Sex and Sexuality in Early America* (New York, 1998), 163–189.

29. Douglas Hall, ed., *In Miserable Slavery: Thomas Thistlewood in Jamaica, 1750–1786* (Kingston, 1999 [1989]), 313–314; Trevor Burnard, *Mastery, Tyranny, and Desire: Thomas Thistlewood and His Slaves in the Anglo-Jamaican World* (Chapel Hill, N.C., 2004), 228–240; Trevor Burnard, "'Do Thou in Gentle Phibba Smile': Scenes from an Interracial Marriage, Jamaica, 1754–1786," in Darlene Clark Hine and David Barry Gaspar, eds., *Beyond Bondage: Free Women of Color in the Americas* (Urbana, Ill., 2004), 82–105; Beckles, *Centering Women,* 38–58.

30. Patterson, *Sociology of Slavery,* 90–91; John Lunan, ed., *An Abstract of the Laws of Jamaica Relating to Slaves* (St. Jago de la Vega, Jamaica, 1819), 120–121; Minutes of Evidence taken before the Select Committee of the House of Lords appointed to inquire into the Laws and Usages of the several West India Colonies in relation to the Slave Population, &c. &c. &c., House of Lords Record Office, London, session of 1832, 970–971; *The Laws of Jamaica, Passed in the Fifty-Seventh Year of the Reign of King George the Third* (Jamaica, 1817), 510.

31. Some slaveholders did free their children. Thomas Thistlewood arranged to free John, the son he had by Phibba, at two years of age. Burnard, *Mastery, Tyranny, and Desire,* 235; Richard S. Dunn, "The Demographic Structure of American Slavery: Jamaica versus Virginia," unpublished paper presented to the Boston Area Early America Seminar, 11 May 2006, 17n29; John Scott to Thomas Hall, 13 May 1768, Barnett-Hall Collection, Mandeville Special Collections Library, University of California, San Diego, MSS 220, box 2, folder 9.

32. Simon Taylor to Chaloner Arcedeckne, 3 December 1771, in Wood, *Letters of Simon Taylor,* 107–108.

33. Timothy Penny to Chaloner Arcedeckne, enclosing the will of Jacob Gutteres, 6 February 1783, Vanneck-Arcedeckne Papers, 3A / 1783 / 4.

34. Matthew Gregory Lewis, Esq., M.P., *Journal of a West India Proprietor, Kept during a Residence in the Island of Jamaica* (London, 1834), 76, 399–403.

35. Extracts from Messrs. Forsyth & Co. to Messrs. Pitcairn & Amos, Kingston, 9 July 1832 and 10 October 1832, Chiswick Plantation Papers, Jamaica, vol. 2: 1832–1835, Bodleian Library, Rhodes House, Oxford, MSS. W. Indies, 18, ff. 37, 43.

36. Edward Brathwaite, *The Development of Creole Society in Jamaica, 1770–1820* (Oxford, 1971), 168; Higman, *Slave Population and Economy,* 176, 178; Long, *History of Jamaica,* 1:327–328.

37. *Journals of the Assembly of Jamaica,* 5:310–312, 315–316, 322, 372, 376–377; Long, *History of Jamaica,* 1:323–327.

38. Long, *History of Jamaica,* 1:327; *Journals of the Assembly of Jamaica,* 8:586, 592.

39. Gad J. Heuman, *Between Black and White: Race, Politics, and the Free Coloreds in Jamaica, 1792–1865* (Westport, Conn., 1981), 7, 23–32; Douglas Hall, "Jamaica," in David W. Cohen and Jack P. Greene, eds., *Neither Slave Nor Free: The Freedmen of African Descent in the Slave Societies of the New World* (Baltimore, Md., 1972), 193–213; Brathwaite, *The Development of Creole Society,* 172.

40. Higman, *Slave Population and Economy,* 142; Benjamin McMahon, *Jamaica Plantership,* 226; Sheila Duncker, "The Free Colored and the Fight for Civil Rights in Jamaica, 1800–1830" (M.A. thesis, University of London, 1960), cited in Brathwaite, *The Development of Creole Society,* 174.

41. Roderick A. McDonald, *The Economy and Material Culture of Slaves: Goods and Chattels on the Sugar Plantations of Jamaica and Louisiana* (Baton Rouge, La., 1993), 16–49; Ira Berlin and Philip D. Morgan, eds., "Introduction: The Slaves' Economy—Independent Production by Slaves in the Americas," *Slavery and Abolition* 12 (1991): 1–27; Sidney W. Mintz,

"The Origins of the Jamaican Market System," in *Caribbean Transformations* (New York, 1974), 180–213; Sidney W. Mintz and Douglas Hall, "The Origins of the Jamaican Marketing System," *Yale University Publications in Anthropology,* no. 57 (1960): 1–26.

42. McDonald, *Economy and Material Culture,* 31–32, 49; Long, *History of Jamaica,* 2:410–411; Patterson, *Sociology of Slavery,* 229.

43. Simon Taylor to David Reid, 10 March 1801, Taylor Papers, ICS, I / D / 53; David Barry Gaspar, "Working the System: Antigua Slaves and Their Struggle to Live," *Slavery and Abolition* 13, no. 3 (December 1992): 131–155.

44. Minutes of Evidence taken before . . . the House of Lords, session of 1832, 156–157; Bryan Edwards, *The History, Civil and Commercial, of the British Colonies in the West Indies* (London, 1793), 2:133; Cynric R. Williams, *A Tour through the Island of Jamaica, from the Western to the Eastern End, in the Year 1823* (London, 1826), 17–18; For comparisons to the U.S. South, see Dylan Penningroth, "Slavery, Freedom, and Social Claims to Property among African Americans in Liberty County, Georgia, 1850–1880," *Journal of American History* 84, no. 2 (September 1997): 405–435; and Penningroth, *The Claims of Kinfolk: African American Property and Community in the Nineteenth-Century South* (Chapel Hill, N.C., 2003), 89–91.

45. Born in London in 1796, De la Beche lived briefly on his family estate in Jamaica as a young child and visited again for one year in 1823–24, when he prepared his notes on Jamaican slavery. T. Sharpe and P. J. McCartney, *The Papers of H. T. De la Beche (1796–1855) in the National Museum of Wales* (Cardiff, 1998), 7–10; H. T. De la Beche, *Notes on the Present Condition of the Negroes in Jamaica* (London, 1825), 48–49, 62–63.

46. On British ideas for reform, see Christopher L. Brown, "From Slaves to Subjects: Envisioning an Empire without Slavery, 1772–1834," in Philip D. Morgan and Sean Hawkins, eds., *Black Experience and the Empire* (New York, 2004), 111–140.

47. De la Beche, *Notes on the Present Condition of the Negroes,* 49.

48. Thistlewood, as quoted in Hall, *In Miserable Slavery,* 83.

49. Jean Besson, "The Creolization of African-American Slave Kinship in Jamaican Free Village and Maroon Communities," in Stephan Palmié, ed., *Slave Cultures and the Cultures of Slavery* (Knoxville, 1995), 190; Williams, *A Tour through the Island of Jamaica,* 18.

50. Long, *History of Jamaica,* 2:410; William Beckford, *A Descriptive Account of the Island of Jamaica* (London, 1790), 2:323–324; Besson, "The Creolization of African-American Slave Kinship," 193–194; Hector McNeill, *Observations on the Treatment of the Negroes in the Island of Jamaica,*

including some account of their Temper and Character (London, 1788), 9; Minutes of Evidence taken before . . . the House of Lords, 156.

51. Williams, *A Tour through the Island of Jamaica,* 103; Lewis, *Journal of a West India Proprietor,* 390.

52. Lewis, *Journal of a West India Proprietor,* 349.

53. Long, *History of Jamaica,* 2:410; Sidney W. Mintz and Richard Price, *The Birth of African-American Culture: An Anthropological Perspective* (Boston, 1992 [1976]), 66; John Thornton, *Africa and Africans in the Making of the Atlantic World, 1400–1800,* 2nd ed. (Cambridge, U.K., 1998 [1992]), 74–79; Michael Mullin, *Africa in America: Slave Acculturation and Resistance in the American South and the British Caribbean, 1736–1831* (Urbana, Ill., 1992), 160; Long, *History of Jamaica,* 2:411; William Beckford, *Remarks upon the Situation of the Negroes in Jamaica* (London, 1788), 53; Lewis, *Journal of a West India Proprietor,* 61. For a perspective on slavery and landed inheritance in the late nineteenth-century Gold Coast, see Penningroth, *The Claims of Kinfolk,* 20–21; for a comparison with property and inheritance among a twentieth-century African population, see Jack Goody, *Death, Property, and the Ancestors: A Study of Mortuary Customs among the LoDagaa of West Africa* (Stanford, Calif., 1962), esp. 273–357.

54. Minutes of Evidence taken before . . . the House of Lords, 338; McDonald, *Economy and Material Culture of Slaves,* 110; Besson, "The Creolization of African-American Slave Kinship," 194.

55. Simon Taylor to Chaloner Arcedeckne, 7 October 1769, in Wood, "Letters of Simon Taylor," 84; Simon Taylor to Chaloner Arcedeckne, 16 January 1783, Vanneck manuscripts, Cambridge University Library, bundle 2/11; Beckford, *A Descriptive Account,* 323; Mintz, "The Origins of the Jamaican Market System," 209. For the most thorough treatment of the issue of family land in Jamaica, see Jean Besson, *Martha Brae's Two Histories: European Expansion and Caribbean Culture-Building in Jamaica* (Chapel Hill, N.C., 2002).

56. Edmund Burke, *Select Works of Edmund Burke, Miscellaneous Writings* (Indianapolis, 1999 [1874]), 4:153–170; Christopher Leslie Brown, *Moral Capital: Foundations of British Abolitionism* (Chapel Hill, N.C., 2006), 228–240.

57. Edwards, *History of the British Colonies* (London, 1793), 2:133.

58. The defense of slaves' property rights against the incursions of other slaves and against the instability brought by revolts could at times encourage a conservative approach to struggle against slavery. See Burnard, *Mastery, Tyranny, and Desire,* 173–174; Long, *History of Jamaica,* 2:410; McNeill, *Observations on the Treatment of the Negroes,* 9.

59. Williams, *A Tour through the Island of Jamaica*, 102–103; Minutes of Evidence taken before . . . the House of Lords, 157.

60. Williams, *A Tour through the Island of Jamaica*, 18.

61. *The Laws of Jamaica, Passed in [1826]*, 201; "An Act for the Government of Slaves," 19 February 1831, clause 15, *The Laws of Jamaica, Passed in the First Year of the Reign of King William the Fourth* (Kingston, 1831), 47; *Journals of the Assembly of Jamaica*, 14:667, 717–718; Minutes of Evidence taken before . . . the House of Lords, 974; To examine a similar struggle over land described outside the context of metropolitan scrutiny, see the correspondence between John Shand and George Watson Taylor about attempts to move some families from their grounds during an outbreak of whooping cough. George Watson Taylor to John Shand, 7 December 1815, Taylor Papers, ICS, VIII / A / 6; John Shand to George Watson Taylor, 7 October 1815, ibid., VIII / B / 3; George Watson Taylor to John Shand, 7 December 1815, ibid., VIII / B / 6; John Shand to George Watson Taylor, 30 December 1815, ibid., VIII / B / 6.

62. Minutes of Evidence taken before . . . the House of Lords, 574, 787.

63. Lewis, *Journal of a West India Proprietor*, 405–406.

64. Orlando Patterson, *Slavery and Social Death: A Comparative Study* (Cambridge, Mass., 1982), 5–6, emphasis mine. For two recent examples of important scholarship on slavery that incorporates Patterson's thesis, see Saidiya V. Hartman, *Scenes of Subjection: Terror, Slavery, and Self-Making in Nineteenth-Century America* (New York, 1997), 94, 231n; Burnard, *Mastery, Tyranny, and Desire*, 195. The "social death" thesis has been circulated widely outside the historiography of slavery and now operates as a general description of slavery's most fundamental impact on black subjectivity. See, for example, Sharon Patricia Holland, *Raising the Dead: Readings of Death and Black Subjectivity* (Durham, N.C., 2000).

4. *Icons, Shamans, and Martyrs*

1. Hugh Crow, *Memoirs of the Late Captain Hugh Crow* (London, 1830), 118; David Eltis, Stephen D. Behrendt, David Richardson, and Herbert S. Klein, *The Trans-Atlantic Slave Trade: A Database on CD-ROM* (Cambridge, U.K., 1999).

2. My use of the term "necromancy" is inspired by, but differs somewhat from, that of the historian Walter Johnson, who uses it to describe the "magic of the [slave] market," which "could steal a person and inhabit their body with the soul of another—the forcible incorporation of a slave with the spirit of the slaveholder's fantasy." See Johnson, *Soul by Soul:*

Life inside the Antebellum Slave Market (Cambridge, Mass., 1999), 117–118, 134.

3. Bryan Edwards, *The History, Civil and Commercial, of the British Colonies in the West Indies* (London, 1801), 3:36; Katherine Verdery, *The Political Lives of Dead Bodies: Reburial and Postsocialist Change* (New York, 1999), 27–28.

4. I have borrowed the term "government magic" from Fela Anikulapo ("he who carries death in his pouch") Kuti, "Unknown Soldier," *Coffin for Head of State* (Lagos, 1981); Michael Taussig, *Colonialism, Shamanism, and the Wild Man: A Study in Terror and Healing* (Chicago, 1987), 374. For a provocative take on such practices, see Achille Mbembe, "Necropolitics," *Public Culture* 15, no. 1 (2003): 11–40.

5. Testimony of Henry Coor, 16 February 1791, in Sheila Lambert, ed., *HCSP,* 82:74; testimony of Dr. Harrison, 12 February 1791, ibid., 50; testimony of William Fitzmaurice, 9 March 1791, ibid., 82:230–231.

6. Testimony of Mr. Thomas Clappeson, 8 March 1791, ibid., 82:213; William D. Piersen, "White Cannibals, Black Martyrs: Fear, Depression, and Religious Faith as Causes of Suicide among New Slaves," *Journal of Negro History* 62, no. 2 (April 1977): 151, 154–155; Michael Gomez, *Exchanging Our Country Marks: The Transformation of African Identities in the Colonial and Antebellum South* (Chapel Hill, N.C., 1998), 114–134; Philip D. Morgan, *Slave Counterpoint: Black Culture in the Eighteenth-Century Chesapeake & Lowcountry* (Chapel Hill, N.C., 1998), 641–642; testimony of Mr. Mark Cook, 5 March 1791, in Lambert, *HCSP,* 82:197; testimony of Lt. Baker Davidson, 25 February 1791, ibid., 82:185.

7. Richard Ligon, *A True and Exact History of the Island of Barbadoes, 1647–1650* (London, 1976 [1657]), 17.

8. C. G. A. Oldendorp, *History of the Mission of the Evangelical Brethren on the Caribbean Islands of St. Thomas, St. Croix, and St. John,* ed. Johann Jakob Bossard, trans. Arnold R. Highfield and Vladimir Barac (Ann Arbor, 1987 [1770]), 246; Moreau de St. Méry, cited in Piersen, "White Cannibals, Black Martyrs," 154; Also see Joan Dayan, *Haiti, History, and the Gods* (Berkeley, Calif., 1995), 247–248; Gwendolyn Midlo Hall, *Social Control in Slave Plantation Societies: A Comparison of St. Domingue and Cuba* (Baton Rouge, La., 1971), 21.

9. Anonymous planter, cited in Orlando Patterson, *Sociology of Slavery: An Analysis of the Origins, Development and Structure of Negro Slave Society in Jamaica* (Rutherford, N.J., 1969 [1967]), 196; John Venn to Bishop Sherlock, 15 June 1751, Fulham Papers, vol. 8, 1740–undated, f. 47, Lambeth Palace Library, London; John Stewart, *A View of the Past and Present State*

of the Island of Jamaica, with Remarks on the Moral and Physical Condition of the Slaves, and on the Abolition of Slavery in the Colonies (Edinburgh, 1823), 281.

10. Fear of mutilation after death terrorized London commoners as much as, or more than, than the gallows itself. See Peter Linebaugh, *The London Hanged: Crime and Civil Society in the Eighteenth Century* (London, 2003 [1991]), and "The Tyburn Riots against the Surgeons," in Douglass Hay, Peter Linebaugh, John G. Rule, E. P. Thompson, and Cal Winslow, eds., *Albion's Fatal Tree: Crime and Society in Eighteenth-Century England* (New York, 1975); Frank McLynn, *Crime and Punishment in Eighteenth-Century England* (New York, 1989), 229; and Piersen, "White Cannibals, Black Martyrs," 154–155. See also Robin Law, "'My Head Belongs to the King': On the Political and Ritual Significance of Decapitation in Pre-Colonial Dahomey," *Journal of African History* 30 (1989): 399–416; "Letters of Philip Quaque," in Philip D. Curtin, ed., *Africa Remembered: Narratives by West Africans from the Era of the Slave Trade* (Madison, Wisc., 1967), 128–129; and the diary of Antera Duke, a slave-trading chief in the Bight of Biafra during the eighteenth century, in Daryll C. Forde, ed., *Efik Traders of Old Calabar* (New York, 1956).

11. For the impact of punishment as spectacle on slave "self-making" in antebellum North American slavery, see Saidiya V. Hartman, *Scenes of Subjection: Terror, Slavery, and Self-Making in Nineteenth-Century America* (New York, 1997); Sir Hans Sloane, *A Voyage to the Islands Madera, Barbados, Nieves, S. Christophers and Jamaica* (London, 1707), 1:lvii; diary of Thomas Thistlewood, 18 May 1750, quoted in Michael Craton, *Testing the Chains: Resistance to Slavery in the British West Indies* (Ithaca, N.Y., 1982), 39; and diary of Thomas Thistlewood, 9 October 1752, quoted in Douglas Hall, *In Miserable Slavery: Thomas Thistlewood in Jamaica, 1750– 1786* (London, 1989), 30.

12. Philip Wright, ed., *Lady Nugent's Journal of Her Residence in Jamaica from 1801 to 1805* (Kingston, 2002 [1966]), 165; Matthew Gregory Lewis, *Journal of a West India Proprietor Kept during a Residence in the Island of Jamaica* (London, 1834), 181–183; Verdery, *The Political Lives of Dead Bodies*, 27; Returns of Slave Trials, Saint Elizabeth, 16 March 1816, PRO, CO 137/147, f. 55.

13. Folke Strom, *On the Sacral Origins of the Germanic Death Penalties* (Lund, Sweden, 1942); Michel Foucault, *Discipline and Punish: The Birth of the Prison,* trans. Alan Sheridan (New York, 1979 [1977]), 32–69; Graeme Newman, *The Punishment Response* (Philadelphia, 1978), 27–51; Pieter Spierenburg, *The Spectacle of Suffering* (New York, 1984), 57; Leon

Radzinowicz, *A History of English Criminal Law and Its Administration from 1750,* vol. 1, *The Movement for Reform, 1750–1833* (New York, 1948), 213–214.

14. Douglass Hay, "Property, Authority and the Criminal Law," in Hay, Linebaugh, Rule, Thomson, and Winslow, *Albion's Fatal Tree,* 27–29, 40–49; Radzinowicz, *A History of English Criminal Law,* 178–181; V. A. C. Gatrell, *The Hanging Tree: Execution and the English People, 1770–1868* (New York, 1994), 80; Spierenburg, *The Spectacle of Suffering,* 57.

15. Gatrell, *The Hanging Tree,* 83; Hay, "Property, Authority and the Criminal Law," 63.

16. David Eltis, *The Rise of African Slavery in the Americas* (Cambridge, U.K., 2000); Edward Long, cited in David Barry Gaspar, "With a Rod of Iron: Barbados Slave Laws as a Model for Jamaica, South Carolina, and Antigua, 1661–1697," in *Crossing Boundaries: Comparative History of Black People in Diaspora* (Bloomington, 2001 [1999]), 346; Gaspar, "'Rigid and Inclement': Origins of the Jamaica Slave Laws of the Seventeenth Century," in Christopher L. Tomlins and Bruce H. Mann, eds., *The Many Legalities of Early America* (Chapel Hill, N.C., 2001), 78–96. For the classic analysis of Caribbean slave law, see Elsa V. Goveia, "The West Indian Slave Laws of the Eighteenth Century," in Hilary Beckles and Verene Shepherd, eds., *Caribbean Slave Society and Economy* (New York, 1991), 346–362.

17. Edward Long, quoted in Gaspar, "Rigid and Inclement," 95.

18. Diana Paton, "Punishment, Crime, and the Bodies of Slaves in Eighteenth-Century Jamaica," *Journal of Social History* 34, no. 4 (2001): 923–954; quotations, 923, 927, 950n; Saint Thomas-in-the-Vale Vestry Minutes, 1789–1802, Jamaica Archives, Local Government 2/1, 1; William Beckford, *Remarks upon the Situation of the Negroes in Jamaica* (London, 1788), 93.

19. Paton, "Punishment, Crime, and the Bodies of Slaves," 931, 939–940.

20. Diary of Thistlewood, 10 October 1766 and 20 August 1774, as quoted in Hall, *In Miserable Slavery,* 142, 235; Testimony of Capt. Thomas Lloyd, 25 February 1791, in Lambert, *HCSP,* 82:147.

21. Saint Thomas-in-the-Vale Vestry Minutes, 1789–1802, Jamaica Archives, Local Government 2/1, 1, 168; Roger Norman Buckley, *The British Army in the West Indies: Society and the Military in the Revolutionary Age* (Gainesville, Fla., 1998), 203–247.

22. "Petition from the Carpenter's Mountains," 14 May 1731, *Journals of the Assembly of Jamaica,* 3:8. Thomas Murray to WMMS, Montego Bay, 3 April 1832, WMMS, West Indies General Correspondence, box 131, FBN 9, no. 446.

23. Paton, "Punishment, Crime, and the Bodies of Slaves," 940, 942.

24. Thomas Thompson, *An Account of Two Missionary Voyages* (London, 1937 [1758]), 44–45; John K. Thornton, "Religious and Ceremonial Life in the Kongo and Mbundu Areas, 1500–1700," in Linda M. Heywood, ed., *Central Africans and Cultural Transformation in the American Diaspora* (Cambridge, U.K., 2002), 80–81; Robert Farris Thompson and Joseph Cornet, *The Four Moments of the Sun: Kongo Art in Two Worlds* (Washington, D.C., 1981), 37; Lewis, *Journal of a West India Proprietor,* 98–99.

25. Nicholas Beasley, "'Death is more busy in this Place': Mortuary Ritual in the British Plantation Colonies, 1640–1780," International Seminar on the History of the Atlantic World, Harvard University, August 2006, p. 17; Lewis, *Journal of a West India Proprietor,* 182.

26. John Newton, *The Journal of a Slave Trader, 1750–1754, with Newton's Thoughts upon the African Slave Trade,* ed. Bernard Martin and Mark Spurrell (London, 1962), 55–56; Thomas Walduck, as quoted in Jerome S. Handler, "Slave Medicine and Obeah in Barbados, circa 1650 to 1834," *New West Indian Guide* 74, nos. 1 and 2 (2000): 59.

27. Diary of Thomas Thistlewood, 25 April 1753, 6 January 1754, quoted in Hall, *In Miserable Slavery,* 56, 61.

28. For insightful discussions of African and American spiritual warfare in slavery, see James H. Sweet, *Recreating Africa: Culture, Kinship, and Religion in the African-Portuguese World, 1441–1770* (Chapel Hill, N.C., 2004); Stephan Palmié, *Wizards and Scientists: Explorations in Afro-Cuban Modernity and Tradition* (Durham, N.C., 2002), 176–181; Wyatt MacGaffey, *Religion and Society in Central Africa* (Chicago, 1986), esp. 156–164. For an introduction to witchcraft as social sanction in Africa, see Ralph A. Austen, "The Moral Economy of Witchcraft: An Essay in Comparative History," in Jean Comaroff and John Comaroff, eds., *Modernity and Its Malcontents: Ritual and Power in Postcolonial Africa* (Chicago, 1993), 89–110.

29. The term probably originated among Ibo-speaking peoples transported from the Bight of Biafra. There, the closest semantic and phonological analogue of "obeah," *dbia,* refers to an "adept," or "master" of knowledge and wisdom. Thus, the anglophone Caribbean term "obeah man" probably similarly designated a "master of knowledge and wisdom" in the sacred arts." See Jerome S. Handler and Kenneth M. Bilby, "Obeah: Healing and Protection in West Indian Slave Life," *Journal of Caribbean History* 38, no. 2 (2004): 153–183; and Handler and Bilby, "On the Early Use and Origin of the Term 'Obeah' in Barbados and the Anglophone Caribbean," *Slavery and Abolition* 22, no. 2 (August 2001): 87–100. See also Douglas Chambers, "'My Own Nation': Igbo Exiles in the Diaspora,"

Slavery and Abolition 18, no. 1 (1997): 72–97; Lambert, *HCSP,* 69:216–217; and R. R. Madden, *A Twelvemonth's Residence in the West Indies* (Philadelphia, 1835), 2:69. The materials used in obeah are reminiscent of those Robert Faris Thompson mentions in his description of the Kongo *minkisi* in West-Central Africa. Believers held that *minkisi* worked through "two basic classes of medicine within the charm, *spirit-embedding medicine* (earths, often from a grave site, for cemetery earth is considered at one with the spirit of the dead), and *spirit-admonishing objects* (seeds, claws, miniature knives, stones, crystals, and so forth." See Thompson and Cornet, *The Four Moments of the Sun,* 37. On *minkisi* and their role in manifesting sacred authority in African and American contexts, see also MacGaffey, *Religion and Society in Central Africa*; and Palmié, *Wizards and Scientists,* 159–200.

30. Robert Dirks, *The Black Saturnalia: Conflict and Its Ritual Expression on British West Indian Slave Plantations* (Gainesville, Fla., 1987), 152–153; St. Ann Slave Court, 1787–1814, 3 March 1794 and 5 May 1799, Institute of Jamaica, MS 273; Alexander Barclay, *A Practical View of the Present State of Slavery in the West Indies* (London, 1826), 190–191.

31. Long, *History of Jamaica,* 2:416–417; diary of Thomas Thistlewood, 22 March 1769 and 16 April 1769, cited in Hall, *In Miserable Slavery,* 217; Monica Schuler, "Myalism and the African Religious Tradition in Jamaica," in Margaret E. Crahan and Franklin W. Knight, eds., *Africa and the Caribbean: The Legacies of a Link* (Baltimore, Md., 1979), 65–79; Mervyn Alleyne, *Africa: Roots of Jamaican Culture* (Chicago, 1996), 76–103; Joseph M. Murphy, *Working the Spirit: Ceremonies of the African Diaspora* (Boston, 1994), 114–121; Joseph J. Williams, *Voodoos and Obeahs: Phases of West India Witchcraft* (New York, 1932), 142–208; Edward Kamau Brathwaite, *The Folk Culture of the Slaves in Jamaica* (London, 1981), 11–16.

32. See especially Mindie Lazarus-Black, *Legitimate Acts and Illegal Encounters: Law and Society in Antigua and Barbados* (Washington, D.C., 1994); and Schuler, "Myalism and the African Religious Tradition." Myal was often used to counter the power of obeah, especially in the nineteenth century, and both were generally focused inward, directed more often at malefactors among the enslaved than between masters and slaves. However, as Burton has suggested, "it may be that Obeah and Myalism confront each other less as absolute opposites than as private and public manifestations of the same magicospiritual power. As power and counterpower neither is inherently political, but given the appropriate context, both can be redirected from the 'enemy within' to the common 'enemy

without.'" Richard D. E. Burton, *Afro-Creole: Power, Opposition, and Play in the Caribbean* (Ithaca, N.Y., 1997), 101; Long, *History of Jamaica*, 2:416; Edward Long, quoted in *The Proceedings of the Governor and Assembly of Jamaica, in regard to the Maroon Negroes* (London, 1796), xxvii.

33. For contemporaneous accounts of the war and its aftermath, see Long, *History of Jamaica*, 2:447–472; quotation, 462; and Edwards, *History of the West Indies*, 2:75–79; see also Michael Craton, *Testing the Chains: Resistance to Slavery in the British West Indies* (Ithaca, N.Y., 1982), 125–139; Richard Hart, *Slaves Who Abolished Slavery: Blacks in Rebellion* (Kingston, 2002 [1985]), 130–156; and Monica Schuler, "Akan Slave Rebellions in the British Caribbean," in Beckles and Shepherd, *Caribbean Slave Society and Economy*, 373–386.

34. Long, *History of Jamaica*, 2:457; Edwards, *History of the British West Indies*, 2:270–271; Hall, *In Miserable Slavery*, 107.

35. On grave dirt and oath taking among Africans and their descendants, see Charles Leslie, *A New and Exact Account of Jamaica* (Edinburgh, 1740), 324; Long, *History of Jamaica*, 2:422–423; Kenneth Bilby, "Swearing by the Past, Swearing to the Future: Sacred Oaths, Alliances, and Treaties among the Guianese and Jamaican Maroons," *Ethnohistory* 44, no. 4 (Fall 1997): 655–689; Lambert, *HCSP*, 69:219, contains perhaps history's first reference to the use of electricity for purposes of torture. "Copies of the Several Acts for the Regulation of Slaves, Passed in the West India Islands," in Lambert, *HCSP*, 67:111; Vincent Brown, "Spiritual Terror and Sacred Authority: The Power of the Supernatural in Jamaican Slave Society," in Edward E. Baptist and Stephanie Camp, eds., *New Studies in the History of American Slavery* (Athens, Ga., 2006), 194–196; diary of Thomas Thistlewood, 22 July 1768, cited in Hall, *In Miserable Slavery*, 161.

36. Helen Tunnicliff Caterall, ed., *Judicial Cases concerning American Slavery and the Negro*, vol. 5, *Cases from the Courts of States North of the Ohio and West of the Mississippi Rivers, Canada, and Jamaica* (Washington D.C., 1937), 356. The 1823 law is quoted in "First Report of the Commissioners of Enquiry into the Administration of Criminal and Civil Justice in the West Indies, dated 29th June 1827," in *Irish University Press Series of British Parliamentary Papers: Colonies, West Indies* (Shannon, 1968), 3:381.

37. Srinivas Aravamudan, "Introduction" to William Earle, *Obi; Or, The History of Three-Fingered Jack*, ed. Aravamudan (Toronto, 2005), 7–51; "The Examination of a Negro named Frank, Belonging to Orange Vale, in the Parish of Saint George, Taken before William Bullock Esquire, one of the Magistrates for the Parish of Saint Catherine," 8 March 1807, PRO, CO

137/ 118, ff. 115–118; John Shipman, "Thoughts upon the Present State of Religion among the Negroes of Jamaica," 1820, WMMS Archive Special Series, Biographical, West Indies, box 588, FBN 2, nos. 27–31, 12–13.

38. Verdery, *The Political Lives of Dead Bodies,* 37.

39. Bryan Edwards, "Stanzas, Occasioned by the Death of Alico, an African Slave, Condemned for Rebellion in Jamaica, 1760," *Poems Written Chiefly in the West Indies* (Kingston, 1792), 38; James G. Basker, *Amazing Grace: An Anthology of Poems about Slavery, 1660–1810* (New Haven, Conn., 2002), 131–132.

40. *Pennsylvania Gazette,* 24 July 1760; ibid., 9 June 1763.

41. *Gentleman's Magazine and Historical Chronicle* 30 (April 1760): 179–181; ibid., June 1760, 294; ibid., July 1760, 307–308; ibid., August 1760, 393; ibid., 31 (July 1761), 321; ibid., August 1761, 377.

42. Christopher L. Brown, "From Slaves to Subjects: Envisioning Empire without Slavery, 1772–1834," in Philip D. Morgan and Sean Hawkins, eds., *Black Experience and the Empire* (Oxford, 2004), 116–120; Linda Colley, *Britons: Forging the Nation, 1707–1837* (New Haven, Conn., 1992), 25–28; Brad S. Gregory, *Salvation at Stake: Christian Martyrdom in Early Modern Europe* (Cambridge, Mass., 1999).

43. Thomas Day and John Bicknell, *The Dying Negro, A Poetical Epistle,* reprinted in Debbie Lee, ed., *Slavery, Abolition, and Emancipation: Writings in the British Romantic Period* (London, 1999), 4:13.

44. Edwards, "Stanzas Occasioned by the Death of Alico," 37–39; Basker, *Amazing Grace,* 131–132; James G. Basker, "'The Next Insurrection': Johnson, Race, and Rebellion," *Age of Johnson: A Scholarly Annual* 11 (2000): 37–51.

45. Simon Taylor to Chaloner Arcedeckne, 9 December 1765, in Betty Wood, ed., "The Letters of Simon Taylor," 29–30; Simon Taylor to Robert Taylor, 24 October 1807, ICS, Taylor Papers, I/I/44; Simon Taylor to George Hibbert, 31 October 1807, ICS, ibid., I/I/43. For comparison's sake, see James Sidbury, *Ploughshares into Swords: Race, Rebellion, and Identity in Gabriel's Virginia, 1730–1810* (Cambridge, U.K., 1997), esp. 256–276; and Richard Price, *First-Time: The Historical Vision of an African American People* (Chicago, 2002 [1983]).

5. *The Soul of the British Empire*

1. David Eltis, Stephen D. Behrendt, David Richardson, and Herbert S. Klein, *The Trans-Atlantic Slave Trade: A Database on CD-ROM* (Cambridge, U.K., 1999); Jerome Bernard Weaves to Committee of the Com-

pany of Merchants Trading to Africa, 27 July 1781, PRO, T 70/33; Robert Stubbs to Committee of the Company of Merchants Trading to Africa, 30 January 1781, PRO, BT 6/6. The narrative of the voyage of the *Zong* is drawn from the following sources: Ian Baucom, *Specters of the Atlantic: Finance Capital, Slavery, and the Philosophy of History* (Durham, N.C., 2005), 10, 14–15, 129–130, 195–202; Robert Weisbord, "The Case of the Slave-Ship *Zong*, 1783," *History Today* 19, no. 8 (August 1969): 561–567; Granville Sharp, "An Account of the Murder of One Hundred and thirty-two Negro Slaves on Board the Ship Zong, or Zung, with some Remarks on the Arguments of an eminent Lawyer in Defence of that inhuman Transaction, enclosed in the Letter of the 2d July, 1783 to the Lords of the Admiralty," in Granville Sharp, *Memoirs of Granville Sharp, Esq., Composed from His Own Manuscripts and Other Authentic Documents in the Possession of His Family and of the African Institution by Prince Hoare* (London, 1828), appendix 8, xxvi–xxxiii; and Henry Roscoe, *Reports of Cases Argued and Determined in the Court of King's Bench, 1782–1785* (London, 1831), 232–235.

2. Sharp, "An Account of the Murder," xxvii.

3. John Weskett, *A Complete Digest of the Theory, Laws, and Practice of Insurance* (London, 1781), as cited in Baucom, *Specters of the Atlantic,* 107, 137–138.

4. Certainly, Collingwood was not the only captain in the trade to do what he did. A decade before the *Zong* massacre, the Moravian missionary C. G. A. Oldendorp remarked upon certain occasions when "the captain [was] faced with the painful necessity of sacrificing a part of his slaves in order to keep the rest of them alive on the scanty provisions that remain." Oldendorp, *A Caribbean Mission,* ed. Johann Jakob Bossard (Ann Arbor, Mich., 1987), 216.

5. Supplement to the *Royal Gazette,* 28 December 1781, 818.

6. For the most compelling recent explanation of the origins of the British antislavery movement, see Christopher Leslie Brown, *Moral Capital: Foundations of British Abolitionism* (Chapel Hill, N.C., 2006). See also Seymour Drescher, *The Mighty Experiment: Free Labor versus Slavery in British Emancipation* (New York, 2002); David Brion Davis, *Inhuman Bondage: The Rise and Fall of Slavery in the New World* (New York, 2006), 231–249; and Adam Hochschild, *Bury the Chains: Prophets and Rebels in the Fight to Free an Empire's Slaves* (Boston, 2005).

7. Ralph Houlbrooke, "The Age of Decency: 1660–1760," in Peter C. Jupp and Clare Gittings, eds., *Death in England: An Illustrated History* (New Brunswick, N.J., 2000), 174.

8. Rev. John Brown, *An Estimate of the Manners and Principles of the Times* (London, 1757), quoted in D. V. Glass, *Numbering the People: The Eighteenth-Century Population Controversy and the Development of Census and Vital Statistics in Britain* (London, 1973), 26; Glass, *Numbering the People*, 17–21.

9. See Philip C. Almond, *Heaven and Hell in Enlightenment England* (Cambridge, U.K., 1994), 68–69, 110; David Cressy, *Birth, Marriage, and Death: Religion, Ritual, and the Life-Cycle in Tudor and Stuart England* (Oxford, 1997), 379–420; William Sherlock, quoted in Houlbrooke, "The Age of Decency," 178.

10. Julie Rugg, "From Reason to Regulation: 1760–1850," in Jupp and Gittings, *Death in England,* 204; Roy Porter, "Death and the Doctors," in Ralph Houlbrooke, ed., *Death, Ritual, and Bereavement* (New York, 1989), 84–86.

11. D. W. Bebbington, *Evangelicalism in Modern Britain: A History from the 1730s to the 1980s* (London, 1988), 20–74; John Walsh, "'Methodism' and the Origins of English-Speaking Evangelicalism," in Mark A. Noll, David W. Bebbington, and George A. Rawlyk, eds., *Evangelicalism: Comparative Studies of Popular Protestantism in North America, the British Isles, and Beyond, 1700–1900* (New York, 1994), 19–34.

12. See Roger Anstey, *The Atlantic Slave Trade and British Abolition, 1760–1810* (London, 1975), 157–183, 198.

13. John Foxe, *Foxe's Book of Martyrs: A History of the Lives, Sufferings, and Triumphant Death of the Early Christian and the Protestant Martyrs,* ed. William Byron Forbush (Peabody, Mass., 2004); Linda Colley, *Britons: Forging the Nation, 1707–1837* (New Haven, Conn., 1992), 25–28; quotation, 27.

14. Robert N. Essick and Morton D. Paley, *Robert Blair's The Grave, Illustrated by William Blake* (London, 1982), 3; Stephen Cornford, ed., *Edward Young: Night Thoughts* (Cambridge, U.K., 1989), 134; Houlbrooke, "The Age of Decency," 179; William Dodd, *Reflections on Death* (London, 1796 (1763)), 6.

15. Essick and Paley, *Robert Blair's The Grave,* 9–10; Cornford, *Edward Young: Night Thoughts,* 8; Houlbrooke, "The Age of Decency," 179.

16. Edmund Burke, *A Philosophical Enquiry into the Origin of Our Ideas of the Sublime and Beautiful and other Pre-Revolutionary Writings,* ed. David Womersley (New York, 1998 [1757]), 91; Adam Smith, *Theory of Moral Sentiments,* ed. Knud Haakonssen (Cambridge, U.K., 2002 [1759]), 16, 82–83; Baucom, *Specters of the Atlantic,* 242–264; Cornford, *Edward Young: Night Thoughts,* 17.

17. Thomas W. Laqueur, "Bodies, Details, and the Humanitarian Narrative," in Lynn Hunt, ed., *The New Cultural History* (Berkeley, Calif., 1989), 177;

Markman Ellis, *The Politics of Sensibility: Race, Gender and Commerce in the Sentimental Novel* (Cambridge, U.K., 1996); Adam Lively, *Masks: Blackness, Race, and the Imagination* (Oxford, 2000), 83; Debbie Lee, *Slavery and the Romantic Imagination* (Philadelphia, 2002), 23–43; E. J. Clery, *The Rise of Supernatural Fiction, 1762–1800* (Cambridge, U.K., 1995); Steven Bruhm, *Gothic Bodies: The Politics of Pain in Romantic Fiction* (Philadelphia, 1994), 23.

18. Robin Blackburn, *The Overthrow of Colonial Slavery, 1776–1848* (London, 1988), 59–60.

19. Edward Young, "Night II," verses 127, 120–123," in Cornford, *Edward Young: Night Thoughts,* 54.

20. O. F. Christie, ed., *The Diary of the Rev.d William Jones, 1777–1821* (London, 1929), 51; Bryan Edwards, *Poems Written Chiefly in the West Indies* (Kingston, 1792), 46–47; James G. Basker, *Amazing Grace: An Anthology of Poems about Slavery, 1660–1810* (New Haven, Conn., 2002), 131–136.

21. John Wesley, *Thoughts upon Slavery* (London, 1774), 46–53; Sharp, *Memoirs of Granville Sharp,* 352.

22. Anstey, *The Atlantic Slave Trade,* 244; David Brion Davis, *The Problem of Slavery in the Age of Revolution, 1770–1823* (New York, 1999 [1975]), 470–500. On the Somerset case, see Steven Wise, *Though the Heavens May Fall: The Landmark Trial That Led to the End of Human Slavery* (Cambridge, Mass., 2005).

23. Granville Sharp, "Just Limitation of Slavery in the Laws of God, Compared with the Unbounded Claims of the African Traders and British American Slaveholders," in Sharp, *Tracts on Slavery* (Westport, Conn., 1969 [1776]), 18, 20–21, 67; Sharp, "An Essay on Slavery, Proving from Scripture Its Inconsistency with Humanity and Religion," in Sharp, *Tracts on Slavery,* 28; Philip Doddridge, quoted in Anstey, *The Atlantic Slave Trade,* 165.

24. Sharp, "Just Limitation of Slavery"; quotation, 36 (emphasis in original); see also 33, 50.

25. Roscoe, *Reports of Cases Argued,* 232; Weisbord, "The Case of the Slave-Ship *Zong,*" 563.

26. John Lee, quoted in Roscoe, *Reports of Cases Argued,* 233 (emphasis in original); Lord Mansfield, quoted in Weisbord, "The Case of the Slave-Ship *Zong,*" 564; Roscoe, *Reports of Cases Argued,* 234; Baucom, *Specters of the Atlantic,* 169.

27. Sharp, *Memoirs of Granville Sharp,* 362–363, xxxii–xxxiii; Baucom, *Specters of the Atlantic,* 8, 135.

28. Sharp, *Memoirs of Granville Sharp*, 362, xxxiii.

29. Baucom, *Specters of the Atlantic*, 123–128; Weisbord, "The Case of the Slave-Ship *Zong*," 566; Baucom, *Specters of the Atlantic*, 3.

30. Sharp, *Memoirs of Granville Sharp*, 361.

31. Ibid., 363; "Dr. Hinchcliff to Granville Sharp," 31 August 1783, and "Dr. Porteus to Granville Sharp" [n.d.], in Sharp, *Memoirs of Granville Sharp*, 367–368.

32. Davis, *The Problem of Slavery in the Age of Revolution*, 406.

33. James Ramsay, *An Essay on the Treatment and Conversion of African Slaves in British Sugar Colonies* (London, 1784), 35; Folarin Shyllon, *James Ramsay: The Unknown Abolitionist* (Edinburgh, 1977); Quobna Ottobah Cugoano, *Thoughts and Sentiments on the Evil of Slavery and Other Writings*, ed. Vincent Carretta (New York, 1999), 85; John Newton, *Thoughts upon the African Slave Trade* (London, 1788), reprinted in Bernard Martin and Mark Spurrell, eds., *The Journal of a Slave Trader (John Newton), 1750–1754, with Newton's Thought upon the African Slave Trade* (London, 1962), 105; Ellen Gibson Wilson, *Thomas Clarkson: A Biography* (London, 1989).

34. See also Davis, *The Problem of Slavery in the Age of Revolution*, 406; Thomas Clarkson, *An Essay on the Slavery and Commerce of the Human Species, Particularly the African*, 2nd ed. (London, 1788), xiii, 98–99.

35. Clarkson, *An Essay on Slavery and Commerce*, 114, 103.

36. Ibid., 103–104; Thomas Clarkson, quoted in Alan Bewell, *Romanticism and Colonial Disease* (Baltimore, Md., 1999), 102–103.

37. Clarkson, *An Essay on Slavery and Commerce*, 164–165, 112.

38. Ibid., 165–166; Cugoano, *Thoughts and Sentiments*, 84–85; Olaudah Equiano, *The Interesting Narrative and Other Writings*, ed. Vincent Carretta (New York, 1995), 58.

39. Anstey, *The Atlantic Slave Trade*, 249, 264–265.

40. Lively, *Masks*, 58–59; Lee, *Slavery and the Romantic Imagination*, 25–26.

41. Anstey, *The Atlantic Slave Trade*, 159; Equiano, *The Interesting Narrative*, 50, 56, 62, 203, xix–xx.

42. Blackburn, *The Overthrow of Colonial Slavery*, 440–441, 139; Anstey, *The Atlantic Slave Trade*, 265–266; J. R. Oldfield, *Popular Politics and British Anti-Slavery: The Mobilisation of Public Opinion against the Slave Trade, 1787–1807* (London, 1998), 115.

43. Helen Thomas, *Romanticism and Slave Narratives: Transatlantic Testimonies* (Cambridge, U.K., 2000), 35–36; Ernest Marshall Howse, *The Saints in Politics: The Clapham Sect and the Growth of Freedom* (London, 1953), 10–64; Granville Sharp, quoted in Anstey, *The Atlantic Slave Trade*, 256.

44. On John Newton's career as a slave trader turned evangelical abolitionist, see D. Bruce Hindmarsh, *John Newton and the English Evangelical Tradition between the Conversions of Wesley and Wilberforce* (Oxford, 1996); Reginald Coupland, *Wilberforce, a Narrative* (Oxford, 1923), 37–38; Anstey, *The Atlantic Slave Trade,* 250–251.

45. Anstey, *The Atlantic Slave Trade,* 267; "Debate on Mr. Wilberforce's Motion for the Abolition of the Slave Trade," *The Parliamentary History of England, from the Earliest Period to the Year 1803,* vol. 29, *1791–92* (New York, 1966), cols. 250–359.

46. Simon Taylor to Chaloner Arcedeckne, 7 April 1788, 1 May 1788, 29 May 1788, 30 August 1788, and 6 November 1788, Vanneck Papers, 3A/1788/3, 3A/1788/8, 3A/1788/10, 3A/1788/21, and 3A/1788/26, respectively, Cambridge University Library.

47. Edward Long, *The History of Jamaica, or General Survey of the Antient and Modern State of that Island,* (London, 1970 [1774]), 2:267, 270–271; William Beckford, *Remarks upon the Situation of the Negroes in Jamaica* (London, 1788), 5, 49; Hector McNeill, *Observations on the Treatment of the Negroes in the Island of Jamaica, including Some Account of Their Temper and Character* (London, 1788), 4–5.

48. Edward Long, quoted in Michael Craton, James Walvin, and David Wright, eds., *Slavery, Abolition, and Emancipation: Black Slaves and the British Empire* (London, 1975), 105; Beckford, *Remarks upon . . . the Negroes,* 73–74 (emphasis in original); Long, *History of Jamaica,* 2:499–502; McNeill, *Observations on the Treatment of the Negroes,* 37–39.

49. Long, *History of Jamaica,* 2:398–399, 498.

50. Ibid.; also 435–436, 378, 396.

51. Beckford, *Remarks upon . . . the Negroes,* 79, 82; James Pinnock, Barrister of Jamaica, Brief Diary, 1758–1794, 22 October 1781, British Library, Add. MS 33316, 10; William Wright, M.D., to Chaloner Arcedeckne, 1 March 1788, Vanneck Papers, 3G/3, i–ii.

52. "First Report of the Committee of the House of Assembly of the Island of Jamaica," 16 October 1788, in Sheila Lambert, ed., *HCSP,* 69:266.

53. Simon Taylor to Chaloner Arcedeckne, 7 April 1788, Vanneck Papers, 3A/1788/3; "Second Report of the Committee of the House of Assembly of the Island of Jamaica," 12 November 1788, in Lambert, *HCSP,* 69:267–272; quotation, 268.

54. *An Abstract of the Evidence Delivered before a Select Committee of the House of Commons in the Years 1790 and 1791; on the part of the petitioners for the Abolition of the Slave Trade, second edition* (London, 1791).

55. *Abstract of the Evidence,* v; Lambert, *HCSP,* 82:68 (emphasis in original), 71.

56. Testimony of Dr. Jackson, 14 February, 1791, ibid., 56.

57. Testimony of Captain Robert Cross, 15–16 February 1791, ibid., 68.

58. Testimony of Henry Coor, 16 February 1791, ibid., 71.

59. Ibid.

60. Ibid.; *Abstract of the Evidence,* 111; Rugg, "From Reason to Regulation," 212–213; Lee, *Slavery and the Romantic Imagination,* 30–31.

61. Testimony of William Fitzmaurice, 9 March 1791, in Lambert, *HCSP,* 82:220; Testimony of William Fitzmaurice, 10 March 1791, ibid., 226, 232, 223.

62. Testimony of William Fitzmaurice, 10 March 1791, ibid., 225–226; Testimony of Dr. Harrison, 12 February 1791, ibid., 46; Cugoano, *Thoughts and Sentiments,* 76; "Testimony of Capt. Thomas Lloyd," 25 February 1791, in Lambert, *HCSP,* 82:147.

63. Testimony of Hercules Ross, 17 March 1791, in Lambert, *HCSP,* 82:259; *Abstract of the Evidence,* 44–45, 141.

64. Blackburn, *The Overthrow of Colonial Slavery,* 146.

65. Anstey, *The Atlantic Slave Trade,* 269; James W. LoGerfo, "Sir William Dolben and 'The Case of Humanity': The Passage of the Slave Trade Regulation Act of 1788," *Eighteenth-Century Studies* 6, no. 4 (Summer 1973): 431–451; Herbert S. Klein and Stanley L. Engerman, "Slave Mortality on British Ships, 1791–1797," in Roger Anstey and P. E. H. Hair, eds., *Liverpool, the African Slave Trade, and Abolition: Essays to Illustrate Current Knowledge and Research* (Liverpool, 1976), 113–125; Weisbord, "The Case of the Slave-Ship *Zong,*" 567; Anstey, *The Atlantic Slave Trade,* 277–278.

66. Lively, *Masks,* 61, 68–69; Lee, *Slavery and the Romantic Imagination,* 28, 40–41.

67. Cornford, *Edward Young: Night Thoughts,* 13.

68. Richard Price and Sally Price, eds., *Stedman's Surinam: Life in an Eighteenth-Century Slave Society* (Baltimore, Md., 1992); Anne Rubenstein and Camilla Townsend, "Revolted Negroes and the Devilish Principle: William Blake and Conflicting Visions of Boni's Wars in Surinam, 1772–1796," in Jackie DiSalvo, G. A. Rosso, and Christopher Z. Hobson, eds., *Blake, Politics, and History* (New York, 1998), 273–298; memento mori images were often used by artists to signify the universality and inevitability of death. See Nigel Llewellyn, *The Art of Death: Visual Culture in the English Death Ritual, c. 1500–1800* (London, 1991), 9–14; and David V. Erdman, *Blake, Prophet against Empire: A Poet's Interpretation of the History of His Own Times* (Princeton, N.J., 1969 [1954]), 228.

69. Essick and Paley, *Robert Blair's The Grave,* 11–12, 18.

70. Oldfield, *Popular Politics and British Anti-Slavery,* 172–179. See also Marcus Wood, *Blind Memory: Visual Representations of Slavery in England and America, 1780–1865* (New York: Routledge, 2000).

71. For the history of the *Brookes* image, see Cheryl Finley, "Committed to Memory: The Slave Ship Icon in the Black Atlantic" (Ph.D. diss., Yale University, 2002); Oldfield, *Popular Politics and British Anti-Slavery,* 51, 56, 99, 163–66.

72. Oldfield, *Popular Politics and British Anti-Slavery,* 165.

73. Thomas Clarkson, *The History of the Rise, Progress, and Accomplishment of the Abolition of the African Slave Trade by the British Parliament* (London, 1808), 2:111; Cheryl Finley, "Committed to Memory: The Slave-Ship Icon in the Black-Atlantic Imagination," *Chicago Art Journal* 9 (1999): 12; Ian Baucom, "Specters of the Atlantic," *South Atlantic Quarterly* 100, no. 1 (Winter 2001): 64. See Wilberforce's reference to the *Zong* case as proof of a general practice of making Africans "walk the plank," British House of Commons, *Substance of the Debates on a Resolution for Abolishing the Slave Trade* (London, 1968 [1806]), 56–57.

74. David Beck Ryden, "Does Decline Make Sense? The West Indian Economy and the Abolition of the British Slave Trade," *Journal of Interdisciplinary History* 31, no. 3 (Winter 2001): 347–374; Blackburn, *The Overthrow of Colonial Slavery,* 315.

75. James Stephen, *Reasons for Establishing a Registry of Slaves in the British Colonies: Being a Report of a Committee of the African Institution* (London, 1815), 13–14; A West Indian, *Notes in Defence of the Colonies: On the Increase and Decrease of the Slave Population of the British West Indies* (Jamaica, 1826); Jamaican assembly, quoted in B. W. Higman, "Slavery and the Development of Demographic Theory in the Age of the Industrial Revolution," in James Walvin, ed., *Slavery and British Society, 1776–1846* (Baton Rouge, La., 1982), 183; Blackburn, *The Overthrow of Colonial Slavery,* 323; B. W. Higman, *Slave Population and Economy in Jamaica, 1807–1834* (Kingston, 1995 [1976]), 99–138.

76. For slaveholders' explanations of population decrease, see Alexander Barclay, *A Practical View of the Present State of Slavery in the West Indies . . . Containing More Particularly an Account of the Actual Condition of the Negroes in Jamaica* (London, 1826), 336–346; *Marly; or, A Planter's Life in Jamaica* (Glasgow, 1828), 98–103; Matthew Gregory Lewis, *Journal of a West India Proprietor, kept during a Residence in the Island of Jamaica* (London, 1834), 388.

77. Higman, "Slavery and the Development of Demographic Theory," 181, 184, 182. For the most thorough analysis of the influence of popular

politics on antislavery legislation, see Seymour Drescher, *Capitalism and Antislavery: British Mobilization in Comparative Perspective* (New York, 1987) and Drescher, "Whose Abolition? Popular Pressure and the Ending of the British Slave Trade," *Past and Present,* no. 143 (May 1994): 136–166.

78. Michael Gamer, *Romanticism and the Gothic: Genre, Reception, and Canon Formation* (Cambridge, U.K., 2000).

79. British House of Commons, *Substance of the Debates,* 38; Thomas Cooper, *Facts Illustrative of the Condition of the Negro Slaves in Jamaica* (London, 1824), 9–10; Mary Turner, *Slaves and Missionaries: The Disintegration of Jamaican Slave Society, 1787–1834* (Kingston, 1998 [1982]), 102–108.

6. Holy Ghosts and Eternal Salvation

1. Thomas Coke, *History of the West Indies, Containing the Natural, Civil, and Ecclesiastical History of Each Island* (Liverpool, 1808), 1:10; John Shipman, "Thoughts upon the Present State of Religion among the Negroes of Jamaica," WMMS Archive Special Series, Biographical, West Indies, box 588, FBN 2, nos. 27–31, 71–72.

2. Philip Wright, *Knibb "the Notorious" Slaves' Missionary, 1803–1845* (London, 1973), 11–12; Rev. Hope Masterton Waddell, *Twenty-nine Years in the West Indies and Central Africa: A Review of Missionary Work and Adventure, 1829–1858,* 2nd ed. (London, 1970 [1863]), 22–23; copy of Mr. Knibb's Journal of His First Voyage to Jamaica, January–February 1824, William Knibb letters, BMS, WI / 3.

3. Copy of Mr. Knibb's journal, 28 January 1824, BMS, WI / 3.

4. Knibb to Samuel Nichols, Kingston, March 1825, William Knibb letters, BMS, WI / 3; to compare similar developments in North America, see Sylvia R. Frey and Betty Wood, *Come Shouting to Zion: African-American Protestantism in the American South and British Caribbean to 1830* (Chapel Hill, N.C., 1998); Mechal Sobel, *Trabelin' On: The Slave Journey to an Afro-Baptist Faith* (Princeton, N.J., 1988); and Albert J. Raboteau, *Slave Religion: The "Invisible Institution" in the Antebellum South* (New York, 1978).

5. R. A. Minter, *Episcopacy without Episcopate: The Church of England in Jamaica before 1824* (Worcester, U.K., 1990), 289–291, 150–151.

6. Brian Stanley, *The Bible and the Flag: Protestant Missions and British Imperialism in the Nineteenth and Twentieth Centuries* (Leicester, 1990), 59.

7. William Knibb to Thomas Knibb, Bristol, 6 May 1823, William Knibb letters, BMS, WI / 3. Knibb is here referring to Romans 6:3–4: "Do you

not know that all of us who have been baptized into Christ Jesus were baptized into his death? There we have been buried with him by baptism into death, so that, just as Christ was raised from the dead by the glory of the Father, so we too might walk in newness of life." *Holy Bible: New Revised Standard Version* (New York, 1989), 162.

8. Gillian Lindt Gollin, *Moravians in Two Worlds: A Study of Changing Communities* (New York, 1967), 13. On the Moravian mission in the Caribbean, see Richard S. Dunn, *Moravian Missionaries at Work in a Jamaican Slave Community, 1754–1835* (Minneapolis, 1994); and John F. Sensbach, *Rebecca's Revival: Creating Black Christianity in the Atlantic World* (Cambridge, Mass., 2005); Zinzendorf's *Hymns Composed for the Use of the Brethren,* quoted in Richard Price, *Alabi's World* (Baltimore, Md., 1990), 57, 59.

9. Quoted in J. H. Buchner, *The Moravians in Jamaica: History of the Mission of the United Brethren's Church to the Negroes in the Island of Jamaica, from the Year 1754 to 1854* (London, 1854), 29, 53; "A Short Account of the Endeavours of the Episcopal Church, known by the Name of Unitas Fratrum, or United Brethren, for promoting true Christianity amongst the Heathen, particularly amongst the Negroes in the West India Islands," in Sheila Lambert, ed., *HCSP,* 69:469.

10. Arnold Rattenbury, "Methodism and Tatterdemalions," in Eileen Yeo and Stephen Yeo, eds., *Popular Culture and Class Conflict, 1590–1914: Explorations in the History of Labour and Leisure* (Atlantic Highlands, N.J., 1981), 32; Coke, *History of the West Indies,* 1:27. One of the earliest devotional texts mentioned in John Wesley's Oxford diary was Jeremy Taylor's *Holy Living and Holy Dying.* Richard P. Heitzenrater, *Wesley and the People Called Methodists* (Nashville, Tenn., 1995), 128; For an analysis of deathbed scenes in colonial North America, see Erik R. Seeman, "Reading Indians' Deathbed Scenes: Ethnohistorical and Representational Approaches," *Journal of American History* 88, no. 1 (June 2001): 17–47.

11. Rev. William Fish to Benson, Kingston, 26 April 1804; Fish to Benson, Kingston, 26 April 1804; Fish to Benson, 11 May 1804 (emphasis in original)—all in WMMS, West Indies General Correspondence, box 111, FBN 1, nos. 2, 4.

12. "Letter of Mr. Young, Kingston, 19 April 1824," in *Missionary Notices, relating principally to the Foreign Missions,* no. 103, July 1824, vol. 4, *1823–1825* (London, 1825), 298.

13. Buchner, *The Moravians in Jamaica,* 14–15; 1822 minutes of the WMMS, WMMS synod minutes, 1822–1838, box 148, FBN 1, no. 1; Catherine

Hall, *Civilising Subjects: Metropole and Colony in the English Imagination,
1830–1867* (Chicago, 2002), 96.

14. G. Dusquesne to Newman, May 15 1728, Fulham Papers, vol. 17, Bermuda
and Jamaica, 1661–1739, Lambeth Palace Library, ff. 250, 252; de Bonneval
to Gibson, 24 November 1739, Fulham Papers, 17:287–289.

15. John A. Vickers, ed., *The Journals of Dr. Thomas Coke* (Nashville, Tenn.,
2005), 148–149; Mary Turner, *Slaves and Missionaries: The Disintegration
of Jamaican Slave Society, 1787–1834* (Kingston, 1998 (1982)], 1–37; Emilia
Viotti da Costa, *Crowns of Glory, Tears of Blood: The Demerara Slave
Rebellion of 1823* (New York, 1994), 11–12, 303n; Frey and Wood, *Come
Shouting to Zion,* 136–137; Hall, *Civilising Subjects,* 98–106.

16. W. Stanford to Bishop Porteus, Westmoreland, 22 July 1788, Fulham
Papers, Lambeth Palace Library, vol. 18, Jamaica, 1740–undated, f. 67.

17. W. Stanford to Bishop Porteus, Westmoreland, 22 July 1788, ff. 66–67.
The rector of Westmoreland, W. Stanford, had ostensibly baptized eight
hundred slaves for free and was arguing with an acute sense of his lost
revenue. It is certainly possible that his assertion of a direct correlation
between price and spiritual value says more about his own assumptions
than about those of the slaves.

18. Yaccine Daddi Addoun and Paul Lovejoy, "The Arabic Manuscript of
Muhammad Kaba Saghanughu of Jamaica, c. 1823," Studies in the History of the African Diaspora—Documents (SHADD), available online at
www.yorku.ca/nhp/shadd/kaba/index.asp; Yaccine Daddi Addoun and
Paul Lovejoy, "Muhammad Kaba Saghanughu and the Muslim Community of Jamaica," in Lovejoy, ed., *Slavery on the Frontiers of Islam*
(Princeton, N.J., 2004), 199–218; Michael A. Gomez, *Black Crescent: The
Experience and Legacy of African Muslims in the Americas* (Cambridge,
U.K., 2005), 50–56.

19. Coke, *History of the West Indies,* 1:31.

20. G. Dusquesne to Newman, 15 May 1728, Fulham Papers, Lambeth Palace
Library, vol. 17, Bermuda and Jamaica, 1661–1739, f. 253.

21. Testimony of Dr. Jackson, M.D., of Stockton upon Tees, Monday, 14
February 1791, in Lambert, *HCSP,* 82:57. One is tempted to read in this
comment an early articulation of liberation theology. Perhaps, if he was
African, whoever made this comment to Dr. Jackson had heard black
religious figures condemn the whites even before he arrived in Jamaica.
An itinerant African holy man toured the Gold Coast in the 1740s
warning people not to emulate the Europeans. "You shall not follow the
example of the Blankes [Whites], since, although they have God's pure
word before them, as you (the Blacks) do not, they are damned after

death because of their evil ways." Quoted in Ludewig Ferdinand Rømer, *A Reliable Account of the Coast of Guinea (1760)*, trans. and ed. Selena Axelrod Winsnes (Oxford, 2000), 85–86.

22. Dusquesne to Newman, 15 May 1728, Fulham Papers, 17:250; John Venn to Bishop Sherlock, 15 June 1751, ibid., vol. 18, Jamaica, 1740–undated, f. 47.

23. Diary of Thomas Thistlewood, 5 May 1764, quoted in Douglas Hall, *In Miserable Slavery: Thomas Thistlewood in Jamaica, 1750–86* (Kingston, 1999 [1989]), 133. Long spoke especially of the Coromantees from the Gold Coast. Edward Long, *History of Jamaica, or General Survey of the Antient and Modern State of That Island* (London, 1970 [1774]), 2:475; Michael Mullin, *Africa in America: Slave Acculturation and Resistance in the American South and the British Caribbean, 1736–1831* (Urbana, Ill., 1992), 62–74.

24. *Journals of the Assembly of Jamaica*, 12:127–128, 133–134.

25. Matthew Gregory Lewis, *Journal of a West India Proprietor* (London, 1834), 224–225, 227–228, 234–236.

26. John Lunan, *An Abstract of the Laws of Jamaica Relating to Slaves, from 33 Charles II [1681] to 59 George III inclusive [1818]* (St. Jago de la Vega, 1819), 118–119.

27. James Ramsay, *An Essay on the Treatment and Conversion of African Slaves in the British Sugar Colonies* (London, 1784), 151; Coke, *A History of the West Indies*, 1:30. Coke founded the Wesleyan Methodist mission in the West Indies.

28. James M. Phillippo, *Jamaica: Its Past and Present State* (London, 1843), 244; Hall, *Civilising Subjects*, 187–188; Buchner, *The Moravians in Jamaica*, 30.

29. W. Stanford to Bishop Porteus, 22 July 1788, Fulham Papers, 18:66.

30. Shipman, "Thoughts upon the Present State of Religion," 4–8.

31. Ibid., 6–7.

32. Ibid., iii, 5–7, 11. Shipman derived his catechism for slaves from John Wesley's *Instructions for Children*, adding special sections on obedience to masters and an enhanced lesson on the eternal consequences of moral deviance. See Turner, *Slaves and Missionaries*, 72.

33. Shipman, "Thoughts upon the Present State of Religion," 14, 15, 48.

34. Ibid., 24, 18.

35. Ibid., 18–19, 23. In 1784 James Ramsay had suggested that "a burying ground should be set apart for the decent interment of the dead, and it should be allotted out according to their families. It would have an excellent effect on them, if only tractable, well-disposed persons were buried with their families, and every worthless fellow buried in a place apart." Ramsay, *An Essay on the Treatment and Conversion of African Slaves*, 184.

36. Mary Turner, "The Colonial State, Religion and the Control of Labour: Jamaica, 1760–1834," in Bridget Brereton and Kevin A. Yelvington, eds., *The Colonial Caribbean in Transition: Essays on Postemancipation Social and Cultural History* (Gainesville, Fla., 1999), 34–35, 38–39; Turner, *Slaves and Missionaries,* 132–144; Gilbert Mathison, *A Short Review of the Reports of the African Institution, and of the Controversy with Dr. Thorpe, with Some Reasons against the Registry of the Slaves in the British Colonies* (London, 1816), 11; Waddell, *Twenty-nine Years in the West Indies,* 17.

37. Thomas Knibb to William Knibb, Kingston, 11 February 1823, William Knibb letters, BMS, WI / 3; Shipman, "Thoughts upon the Present State of Religion," ix–x; Matthew 22:21, *Holy Bible: New Revised Standard Version* (New York, 1989).

38. Turner, *Slaves and Missionaries,* 10.

39. Edward Kamau Brathwaite, *The Development of Creole Society in Jamaica, 1770–1820* (London, 1971), 88–89; *Journals of the Assembly of Jamaica,* entry of 6 February 1800, 10:453–454; Julius S. Scott, III, "The Common Wind: Currents of Afro-American Communication in the Era of the Haitian Revolution" (Ph.D. diss., Duke University, 1986), 213–219; Sue Peabody, "'A Dangerous Zeal': Catholic Missions to Slaves in the French Antilles, 1635–1800," *French Historical Studies* 25, no. 1 (Winter 2002): 53–90; Long, *The History of Jamaica,* 2:430; John Thornton, "'I Am the Subject of the King of Congo': African Political Ideology and the Haitian Revolution," *Journal of World History* 4, no. 2 (Fall 1993): 181–214.

40. David Eltis, Stephen D. Behrendt, David Richardson, and Herbert S. Klein, eds., *The Trans-Atlantic Slave Trade: A Database on CD-ROM* (Cambridge, U.K., 1999). On Christianity in West-Central Africa, see John Thornton, "On the Trail of Voodoo: African Christianity in Africa and the Americas," *Americas* 44, no. 3 (1988): 261–278; Thornton, "The Development of an African Catholic Church in the Kingdom of Kongo, 1491–1750," *Journal of African History* 25, no. 2 (1984): 147–167; Robert Farris Thompson, *The Four Moments of the Sun* (New Haven, Conn., 1981), 45. *Nkisi* is the Kikongo term used for a material object that houses spiritual forces. Objects that carried the adjective "holy" in European terminology could usually be considered *minkisi* in Kikongo. See Thornton, "The Development of an African Catholic Church," 155, 157; and Thornton, "On the Trail of Voodoo," 266–267.

41. Peabody, "'A Dangerous Zeal,'" 53–90; Thornton, "On the Trail of Voodoo," 261–278; Saint Ann Slave Court, 1787–1814, 3 March 1794 and 5 May 1799, Institute of Jamaica, MS 273.

42. B. W. Higman, *Slave Population and Economy in Jamaica, 1807–1834* (Kingston, 1995 [1976]), 75–76.

43. Lewis, *Journal of a West India Proprietor,* 100; Dusquesne to Newman, 15 May 1728, Fulham Papers, 17:253; For similar developments in North America, see Sobel, *Trabelin' On,* 48; Cynric Williams, *A Tour through the Island of Jamaica in the Year 1823* (London, 1826), 87; "Folklore of the Negroes of Jamaica," in *Folk-Lore: A Quarterly Review of Myth, Tradition, Institution, and Custom* 15 (London, 1904): 90.

44. On the Great Awakening, see especially Jon Butler, *Awash in a Sea of Faith: Christianizing the American People* (Cambridge, Mass., 1990); John W. Pulis, "Bridging Troubled Waters: Moses Baker, George Liele, and the African American Diaspora to Jamaica," in Pulis, ed., *Moving On: Black Loyalists in the Afro-Atlantic World* (New York, 1999), 191, 203; Turner, *Slaves and Missionaries,* 11; and Frey and Wood, *Come Shouting to Zion,* 131–132.

45. John Thornton, *Africa and Africans in the Making of the Atlantic World, 1400–1800* (Cambridge, U.K., 1998 [1992]), 271; Frey and Wood, *Come Shouting to Zion.*

46. W. F. Burchell, *Memoir of Thomas Burchell, Twenty-two Years a Missionary in Jamaica, by his Brother William Fitz-er Burchell* (London, 1849), 62; Knibb to Samuel Nichols, Kingston, March 1825, William Knibb letters, BMS, WI / 3.

47. Waddell, *Twenty-nine Years in the West Indies,* 26; Williams, *A Tour through the Island of Jamaica,* vi; Mary Turner, "Religious Beliefs," in Franklin W. Knight, ed., *General History of the Caribbean,* vol. 3, *The Slave Societies of the Caribbean* (London, 1997), 317.

48. Testimony of Sir Michael Clare, M.D., Minutes of Evidence taken before the Select Committee of the House of Lords appointed to inquire into the Laws and Usages of the several West India Colonies in relation to the Slave Population, &c. &c. &c., House of Lords Record Office, London, 280; Williams, *A Tour through the Island of Jamaica,* 18–19.

49. Thomas Cooper, *Facts Illustrative of the Condition of the Negro Slaves in Jamaica* (London, 1824), 15; Lewis, *Journal of a West India Proprietor,* 374; Shipman, "Thoughts upon the Present State of Religion," 38; Saint Ann Slave Court, 1787–1814, Institute of Jamaica, MS 273, f. 163.

50. William Savage to Joseph Butterworth and Thomas Thompson, M.P.'s, Kingston, 18 March 1818, WMMS Archive, Biographical, Special Series, West Indies, 1818, box 588, 97; testimony of Rev. Henry Beame, 1825, *British Sessional Papers, Commons, Accounts and Papers* (London, 1826).

51. Williams, *A Tour through the Island of Jamaica,* 108–113.

52. Ibid., 106; Frey and Wood, *Come Shouting to Zion,* 173–174.

53. For a slightly different interpretation, see Turner, "The Colonial State," 36.

54. Dr. Stewart West, magistrate for Bath, Saint Thomas in the East, 15 March 1818, WMMS Archive, Biographical, Special Series, West Indies, 1818, box 588, 107–108; Lunan, *An Abstract of the Laws of Jamaica Relating to Slaves,* 123–124; Richard Dick to Joseph Butterworth and Thomas Thompson, 8 May 1818, WMMS Archive, Biographical, Special Series, West Indies, 1818, box 588, 102.

55. J. Walters to WMMS, Port Antonio, 28 December 1831, WMMS Archive, box 130, FBN 9, no. 437; Waddell, *Twenty-nine Years in the West Indies,* 21.

7. Gardens of Remembrance

1. Kirk Savage, "The Politics of Memory: Black Emancipation and the Civil War Monument," in John R. Gilles, ed., *Commemorations: The Politics of National Identity* (Princeton, N.J., 1994), 143; Catherine Hall, *Civilising Subjects: Metropole and Colony in the English Imagination, 1830–1867* (Chicago, 2002), 107–115; Laurence Brown, "Monuments to Freedom, Monuments to Nation: The Politics of Emancipation and Remembrance in the Eastern Caribbean," *Slavery and Abolition* 23, no. 3 (December 2002): 93–116.

2. Natalie Zemon Davis and Randolph Starn, "Introduction: Memory and Counter-Memory," *Representations,* no. 26 (Spring 1989): 1–6; Pierre Nora, "Between Memory and History: Les Lieux de Mémoire," *Representations,* no. 26 (Spring 1989): 7–24; John R. Gilles, "Memory and Identity: The History of a Relationship," in Gilles, *Commemorations,* 3–24; Savage, "The Politics of Memory: Black Emancipation and the Civil War Monument," 127–149.

3. Henry Bleby, *The Death Struggles of Slavery: Being a Narrative of Facts and Incidents, which Occurred in a British Colony, during the Two Years Immediately Preceding Negro Emancipation,* 3rd ed. (Coconut Grove, Fla., 1972 [1853]). See also Richard Hart, *Slaves Who Abolished Slavery: Blacks in Rebellion* (Kingston, 2002 [1985]), 244–324; Mary Turner, *Slaves and Missionaries: The Disintegration of Jamaican Slave Society, 1787–1834* (Kingston, 1998 [1982]), 148–173; Abigail Bakan, *Ideology and Class Conflict in Jamaica: The Politics of Rebellion* (Montreal, 1990); Michael Craton, *Testing the Chains: Resistance to Slavery in the British West Indies* (Ithaca, N.Y., 1982), 291–321; Kamau Brathwaite, "Caliban, Ariel, and Unprospero in the Conflict of Creolization: A Study of the Slave Revolt

in Jamaica in 1831–32," in Vera Rubin and Arthur Tuden, eds., *Comparative Perspectives on Slavery in the New World Plantation Societies* (New York, 1977); and Mary Reckford, "The Jamaican Slave Rebellion of 1831," *Past and Present* 40 (July 1968): 108–125.

4. Hope Masterton Waddell, *Twenty-nine Years in the West Indies and Central Africa: A Review of Missionary Work and Adventure, 1829–1858,* 2nd ed. (London, 1970 [1863]), 65–66; Craton, *Testing the Chains,* 313–321; Henry Bleby quoted on 313, Sam Sharpe quoted on 321.

5. William Knibb quoted in Philip Wright, *Knibb "the Notorious" Slaves' Missionary, 1803–1845* (London, 1973), 111; Waddell, *Twenty-nine Years in the West Indies,* 76; Turner, *Slaves and Missionaries,* 166–170.

6. Lord Goderich quoted in Thomas C. Holt, *The Problem of Freedom: Race, Labor, and Politics in Jamaica and Britain, 1832–1938* (Baltimore, Md., 1992), 19–21. On the reverberations of the Baptist War in Great Britain, see, for example, William Knibb, *Facts and Documents Connected with the Late Insurrection in Jamaica, and the Violations of Civil and Religious Liberty Arising out of It* (London, 1832). See also Hall, *Civilising Subjects,* 107–115; James Williams, *A Narrative of Events, since the First of August, 1834, by James Williams, an Apprenticed Labourer in Jamaica,* ed. Diana Paton (Durham, N.C., 2001).

7. See Elizabeth Pigou, "Western Responses to Death in a Jamaican Context," *Jamaica Journal* 20, no. 2 (May–July 1987): 12–16; Betty Bailey, "Tombstones in the Jewish Cemetery and What They Tell," *Jamaica Journal* 20, no. 2 (May–July 1987): 17–22; Frederick Burgess, *English Churchyard Memorials* (London, 1963).

8. "A Short Sketch of the Character of the late John Waugh, Esq.," *Jamaica Royal Gazette, Supplement to the Royal Gazette,* 29 November 1794, PRO, CO 141/1, 568.

9. Andrew Jackson O'Shaughnessy, *An Empire Divided: The American Revolution and the British Caribbean* (Philadelphia, 2000), 16.

10. *Journals of the Assembly of Jamaica,* entry of 23 October 1777, 7:5, 11, 13–14; Craton, *Testing the Chains,* 172–179; Leslie Lewis, "English Commemorative Sculpture in Jamaica," *Jamaican Historical Review* 9 (1972): 52–56.

11. Lewis, "English Commemorative Sculpture," 57–59; Frank Cundall, *Historic Jamaica* (London, 1915), 95–98.

12. Sir Hans Sloane, *A Voyage to the Islands Madera, Barbados, Nieves, S. Christophers and Jamaica* (London, 1707), xlviii; Hall, *In Miserable Slavery,* 233; Matthew Gregory Lewis, Esq. M.P., *Journal of a West India Proprietor, Kept during a Residence in the Island of Jamaica* (London, 1834), 102, 161.

13. *Marly; or, a Planter's Life in Jamaica* (Glasgow, 1828), 362–363; Pigou, "Western Responses to Death," 13.

14. Cundall, *Historic Jamaica,* 179–180, 265; Vere Langford Oliver, ed., *Caribbeana* (London, 1916), 4:193, 200; Philip Wright, ed., *Monumental Inscriptions of Jamaica* (London, 1966), 281.

15. James Hakewill, *A Series of Views of the Neighborhood of Windsor, including the Seats of the Nobility and Gentry* (London, 1820); Hakewill, *A Picturesque Tour of Italy, from Drawings Made in 1816–1817* (London, 1820); *Monument to the Late Thomas Hibbert, Esq.,* in Hakewill, *A Picturesque Tour of the Island of Jamaica, from Drawings Made in the Years 1820 and 1821* (London, 1825).

16. *Monument to the Late Thomas Hibbert, Esq.*

17. Wright, *Monumental Inscriptions,* 217, 203, 235.

18. Ibid., 204–205, 218.

19. Ibid., 121, 191.

20. Turner, *Slaves and Missionaries,* 150.

21. W. F. Burchell, ed., *Memoir of Thomas Burchell, Twenty-two Years a Missionary in Jamaica* (London, 1849), 228–229, 203.

22. Craton, *Testing the Chains,* 241–253; Turner, *Slaves and Missionaries,* 148–173; Holt, *The Problem of Freedom,* 15–16; Richard D. E. Burton, *Afro-Creole: Power, Opposition, and Play in the Caribbean* (Ithaca, N.Y., 1997), 83–89.

23. Turner, *Slaves and Missionaries,* 157; Bleby, *Death Struggles of Slavery,* 11.

24. The pioneer archaeological and ethnohistorical study of West Indian slave burial practices is Jerome S. Handler and Frederick Lange, *Plantation Slavery in Barbados: An Archaeological and Historical Investigation* (Cambridge, Mass., 1978), 171–215.

25. Christopher R. DeCorse, "Culture Contact, Continuity, and Change on the Gold Coast, AD 1400–1900," *African Archaeological Review* 10 (1992): 183–184; Handler and Lange, *Plantation Slavery in Barbados,* 191–192; Douglas V. Armstrong, "Archaeology and Ethnohistory of the Caribbean Plantation," in Theresa Singleton, ed., *"I, too, am America": Archaeological Studies of African-American Life* (Charlottesville, Va., 1999), 180–181; Ross W. Jamieson, "Material Culture and Social Death: African-American Burial Practices," *Historical Archaeology* 29, no. 4 (1995): 52–53; Jerome S. Handler, "An African-Type Healer/Diviner and His Grave Goods: A Burial from a Plantation Slave Cemetery in Barbados, West Indies," *International Journal of Historical Archaeology* 1, no. 2 (1997): 111.

26. Jamieson, "Material Culture and Social Death," 53. See also David R. Watters, "Mortuary Patterns at the Harney Site Slave Cemetery, Mon-

serrat, in Caribbean Perspective," *Historical Archaeology* 28, no. 3 (1994): 56–73, esp. 63–64; João José Reis, *Death Is a Festival: Funeral Rites and Rebellion in Nineteenth-Century Brazil* (Chapel Hill, N.C., 2003 [1991]), 132–135; Alexander Barclay, *A Practical View of the Present State of Slavery in the West Indies . . . Containing More Particularly an Account of the Actual Condition of the Negroes in Jamaica* (London, 1826), 164; Eugene D. Genovese, *Roll, Jordan, Roll: The World the Slaves Made* (New York, 1974 [1972]), 202.

27. Barclay, *A Practical View*, 166; Moreton quoted in Roderick A. McDonald, *The Economy and Material Culture of Slaves: Goods and Chattels on the Sugar Plantations of Jamaica and Louisiana* (Baton Rouge, La., 1993), 110; Minutes of Evidence taken before the Select Committee of the House of Lords appointed to inquire into the Laws and Usages of the several West India Colonies in relation to the Slave Population, &c. &c. &c., House of Lords Record Office, London, 59; Ludewig Ferdinand Rømer, *A Reliable Account of the Coast of Guinea (1760)*, trans. and ed. Selena Axelrod Winsnes (Oxford, 2000), 185. Rømer's observations have been corroborated by the excavations conducted by DeCorse; see Christopher DeCorse, "Culture Contact, Continuity, and Change," 183–184.

28. Douglas V. Armstrong, "Archaeology and Ethnohistory," 181. For evidence of household burials in Brazil, see Reis, *Death Is a Festival,* 341n58; Lewis, *Journal of a West India Proprietor,* 97; John Stewart, *A View of the Past and Present State of the Island of Jamaica; with Remarks on the Moral and Physical Condition of the Slaves and on the Abolition of Slavery in the Colonies* (Edinburgh, 1823), 267; Barclay, *A Practical View,* 166.

29. Quoted in Michael Craton, James Walvin, David Wright, eds., *Slavery, Abolition, and Emancipation: Black Slaves and the British Empire* (London, 1975), 141–142.

30. James M. Phillippo, *Jamaica: Its Past and Present State* (London, 1843), 283; Christopher R. DeCorse, *An Archaeology of Elmina: Africans and Europeans on the Gold Coast, 1400–1900* (Washington, D.C., 2001), 189–191, 250n; McDonald, *The Economy and Material Culture of Slaves,* 110.

31. Edward Long, *The History of Jamaica* (London, 1970 [1774]), 1:399; Blackburn quoted in McDonald, *The Economy and Material Culture of Slaves,* 110; Minutes of Evidence taken before . . . the House of Lords, 338.

32. Lewis, *Journal of a West India Proprietor,* 98–99.

33. Minutes of Evidence taken before . . . the House of Lords, 196, 161–162.

34. R. R. Madden, *Twelve Months' Residence in the West Indies, during the Transition from Slavery to Apprenticeship* (Philadelphia, 1835), 1:161.

35. Quoted in Rev. F. A. Cox, *History of the Baptist Missionary Society, from 1792–1842* (London, 1842), 245–246.

36. Ibid., 250–252; Hall, *Civilising Subjects,* 117–118.

37. Cox, *History of the Baptist Missionary Society,* 248.

38. John Shand to Simon Richard Brissett Taylor, 21 April 1813, ICS/VI/C/9; Wright, *Monumental Inscriptions,* 299.

39. B. W. Higman, *Jamaica Surveyed: Plantation Maps and Plans of the Eighteenth and Nineteenth Centuries* (Kingston, 1988), 228–230; Cundall, *Historic Jamaica,* 250–251. Following recent practice, Miller did not live in Vale Royal, though it was still used for diplomatic state functions, ceremonies, and entertaining.

40. Wright, *Knibb "the Notorious,"* 128; Wright, *Monumental Inscriptions,* 252–253.

Epilogue

1. Laurent Dubois, *Avengers of the New World: The Story of the Haitian Revolution* (Cambridge, Mass., 2004), 8–35; Joseph C. Miller, *Way of Death: Merchant Capitalism and the Angolan Slave Trade, 1730–1830* (Madison, Wisc., 1988), 437–442, 537–538; Stuart B. Schwartz, *Sugar Plantations in the Formation of Brazilian Society: Bahia, 1550–1835* (Cambridge, U.K., 1985), 338–378; Philip D. Morgan, *Slave Counterpoint: Black Culture in the Eighteenth-Century Chesapeake and Lowcountry* (Chapel Hill, N.C., 1998), 79–101; Ira Berlin, *Many Thousands Gone: The First Two Centuries of Slavery in North America* (Cambridge, Mass., 1998); David Eltis, Stephen D. Behrendt, David Richardson, and Herbert S. Klein, eds., *The Trans-Atlantic Slave Trade: A Database on CD-ROM* (Cambridge, U.K., 1999).

2. Colin A. Palmer, *Slaves of the White God: Blacks in Mexico, 1570–1650* (Cambridge, Mass., 1976); Herman L. Bennett, *Africans in Colonial Mexico: Absolutism, Christianity, and Afro-Creole Consciousness, 1570–1640* (Bloomington, Ind., 2003); James H. Sweet, *Recreating Africa: Culture, Kinship, and Religion in the African-Portuguese World, 1441–1770* (Chapel Hill, N.C., 2003); Joan Dayan, *Haiti, History, and the Gods* (Berkeley, Calif., 1995); João José Reis, *Death Is a Festival: Funeral Rites and Rebellion in Nineteenth-Century Brazil* (Chapel Hill, N.C., 2003); Dubois, *Avengers of the New World,* 99–102; Berlin, *Many Thousands Gone,* 62.

3. Drew Gilpin Faust, *This Republic of Suffering: Death and the American Civil War* (New York, 2008); Karla F. C. Holloway, *Passed On: African American Mourning Stories, a Memorial* (Durham, 2002); Kath Weston, *Families We Choose: Lesbians, Gays, Kinship* (New York, 1991).

4. Paul Gilroy, *Black Atlantic: Modernity and Double Consciousness* (Cambridge, Mass., 1993); Michael Saler, "Modernity and Enchantment: A Historiographic Review," *American Historical Review* III, no. 3 (June 2006): 692–716.

5. Michel-Rolph Trouillot, *Global Transformations: Anthropology and the Modern World* (New York, 2003), 29–46; Frederick Cooper, *Colonialism in Question: Theory, Knowledge, History* (Berkeley, Calif., 2005), 113–149; Prasenjit Duara, *Rescuing History from the Nation: Questioning Narratives of Modern China* (Chicago, 1995), 3–50; for corrections, see Orlando Patterson, *Slavery and Social Death: A Comparative Study* (Cambridge, Mass., 1982), vii–xi; David Brion Davis, *Inhuman Bondage: The Rise and Fall of Slavery in the New World* (New York, 2006), 77–102.

6. Emilia Viotti Da Costa, *Crowns of Glory, Tears of Blood: The Demerara Slave Rebellion of 1823* (New York, 1994), xix.

7. Dayan, *Haiti, History and the Gods*, 187–267; quotation, 264.

8. Jefferson quoted in David Lowenthal, *The Past Is a Foreign Country* (Cambridge, U.K., 1985), 108; Stephan Palmié, *Wizards and Scientists: Explorations in Afro-Cuban Modernity and Tradition* (Durham, N.C., 2002), 3; Karl Marx, "The Eighteenth Brumaire of Louis Bonaparte," in Robert C. Tucker, ed., *The Marx-Engels Reader*, 2nd ed. (New York, 1978), quotation, 595; Robert Pogue Harrison, *The Dominion of the Dead* (Chicago, 2003), ix–xii; Pierre Nora, "Between Memory and History: Les Lieux de Mémoire," *Representations*, no. 26 (Spring 1989), 7–24; quotation, 16; David William Cohen, *The Combing of History* (Chicago, 1994), 78–111.

Index

Abolitionism. *See* Antislavery movement; Emancipation

Absentee planters, 16, 21, 22, 110, 115, 236

Abstract of the Evidence, An, 184–190

Africa, 7, 182, 246; benefits of slave trade, 29; burial customs, 64, 245, 246–247; ceremonial music, 71; funerals, 91, 187; mortality rates of seized slaves, 33–34; mortuary practice in, 247; political organizations, 28; scale of slavery in, 30; veneration for ancestors in, 120. *See also specific regions*

Afterlife, 5, 8, 11, 59, 118, 128, 206, 228, 258; African visions of, 135; ancestral lands and, 211; association with whites, 41; black understanding of, 131, 215; enjoyed by rebels, 155; equality in, 204, 245; images of heaven and hell, 164, 203, 214, 217–218, 220, 228; impact on obedience of slaves, 220; Protestant view of, 210; religious considerations of, 137, 165; slavery and, 208–219; slave views of, 210–211; superstitions regarding, 218. *See also* Eternity

Alienation, 31, 32, 38, 43, 45, 49. *See also* Social death

American Revolution, 156, 224, 259

American War of Independence, 17, 19

Ancestors, 42–43, 64, 65, 69, 73, 94, 122; annual visit to graves of, 73, 216; communal bonds of slaves to, 216; evocation of, during funerals, 62; isolation from, 127; reunion with, after death, 132–133; veneration of slaves for, 77, 120–123. *See also* Relations of living to the dead

Ancestral lands, 249; association with the afterlife, 211; longing of slaves to return to, 132–133, 134–135, 152, 187, 223–224

Anglican Church, 83, 203

Antislavery movement, 12, 79, 122–123, 128, 152, 154–155; and anger at triumph of greed over human life, 162; fear of damnation and, 157; literature of, 154–155; memorials to the dead and, 243–244; missionaries and, 209, 229, 230; moral dimensions of, 157, 164, 169–170, 174, 177, 185, 198–200; mortuary politics and, 200; petition campaigns, 178–179, 183, 189; political dimensions of, 157, 160, 162; portrayal of suffering, 116; relations of living to the dead and, 157; religious dimensions, 170, 173–174; rhetoric and activism, 199–200; slave